THE PRINT OF MY
REMEMBRANCE

AUGUSTUS THOMAS.

THE PRINT OF MY REMEMBRANCE

BY

AUGUSTUS THOMAS

MEMBER OF THE AMERICAN ACADEMY OF ARTS AND LETTERS

ILLUSTRATED WITH PHOTOGRAPHS AND NUMEROUS
DRAWINGS BY THE AUTHOR

CHARLES SCRIBNER'S SONS

NEW YORK · LONDON

1922

TO BRANDER MATTHEWS

DEAR BRANDER,

The publishers are doing all they possibly can to make a success of this book—they call it a book—and they have asked me for a dedication.

After the manner of mid-Victorian poets, I could have made the dedication mysteriously to "Dear B—— M——," but I used to know a girl of those initials; my wife also knew her. Her name was Mary Brannigan. But nobody of intelligence is going to be deceived by a mere transposition of initials, so I thought I might win as much as I stood to lose by coming right out with it and saying Brander Matthews.

I learned in the railroad yard that separate cars thrown in on the same track could subsequently be coupled up, then hitched to something with power enough to push or pull them out as a freight train; perhaps with hopeful attention to the English market I should say, "goods train." Nobody knows better than yourself the difference between push and pull, and having both you might be willing, I thought, to assist a fellow who has neither, especially as my cars when they are not empty contain stuff that is perishable.

Then I had another idea. There is a story of General Custer at the head of a marching column on our American plains one day in the middle seventies. He suddenly threw up his hand after the manner of Western commanders, gave a signal, and moved sharply "column right" over a rod or so, then resumed direction. Every pair of troopers reaching the first angle peered eagerly forward to see what had deflected the march. In the dried brush was the nest of a meadow-lark. The bird was frightened and had flown, but the nest had four eggs in it.

At the head of the marching column of reviewers your gesture has all the authority that Custer's had with those troopers, and you have the same sympathetic apprehension of possibilities. Many readers will immediately infer the low and defenseless character of my hopes and incubations when I simply say Dear Brander.

And some critics are as gentle as cavalrymen.

Affectionately yours,
AUGUSTUS THOMAS.

NEW ROCHELLE, N. Y.

CONTENTS

ILLUSTRATIONS

THE PRINT OF MY REMEMBRANCE

I

A CHILD'S IMPRESSIONS OF CIVIL WAR DAYS

In the month of January, 1857, Abraham Lincoln was practising law in Springfield, Illinois. At Guernsey, Victor Hugo, in exile, was preparing the last volume of "Les Misérables," and was writing Shakespeare, the greatest of his single volumes. Germany was alarmed over the success of the French in Lombardy, and Bavaria was preparing for war. The Queen of England, then in the twentieth year of her reign, was planning to establish the Order of the Victoria Cross, and was having bronze medals cast from Russian cannon recently captured at Sebastopol. In the United States, President Franklin Pierce was getting ready to retire in March, and James Buchanan, his successor, was preparing his inaugural address.

Ralph Waldo Emerson, then in his fifty-third year, was lecturing in Philadelphia, New York, Ohio, and Illinois, and John Brown, of Ossawatomie, Kansas, was making speeches in Eastern States, and stimulating the committees who were financially helping the people of Kansas to resist the raids of the Missouri Border Ruffians. U. S. Grant was living with his wife's folks on a farm near St. Louis, much distressed by fever and ague, and occasionally driving a load of cordwood to the city. The Supreme Court at Washington was considering for the second time the question of the liberty of the negro slave, Dred Scott. Mr. Lincoln, at Springfield, was anxiously awaiting their decision before expressing himself as he subsequently did in such immortal fashion.

On the eighth day of that month, in that year, I was born in a little house in what was then the outskirts of St. Louis, Missouri.

Of this important concurrent event none of the great personages above referred to knew anything at first hand, which must not fairly imply neglect on their part, because all of my own impressions of them were subsequently and slowly formed on hearsay and report. I mention these great personages principally to fix in the reader's mind some conditions and the time. But they are mentioned, also, because most of them began soon afterward to take place and shape—somewhat distorted shape, perhaps—in my first permanent memories.

Buchanan took office under the handicap of our family disapproval, because responding to certain preelection pledges he permitted the recall from Falmouth, England, of my maternal grandmother's second husband, who had been sent there as United States consul by Franklin Pierce; and, without generalizing too hastily, I may say that a similar lack of judgment, according to my people, characterized nearly the whole of Buchanan's administration. Grandmother was there with this second husband. I don't know how the wife of a consul at Falmouth could do it, but in some way grandmother, while in England, arranged a presentation to the Queen, so that with us in North St. Louis, Victoria was a household word.

I was two years old when John Brown was hanged, and, of course, understood nothing of it. Victor Hugo, in his exile for liberty, with his great sympathy for the oppressed in every land, was eloquent in his appeal to the American public to save itself from this moral stain and from a crime "odious as the first sad fratricide." He cried: "Let America be aware that more terrible than Cain slaying Abel would be Washington killing Spartacus."

By the time I was four and able in childish fashion to carry a tune the land was alive with the music of brass bands. Of course, the spirit of John Brown was the important element, but for many years after that time I was not so acutely conscious of anything else as that "John Brown's body lies a-mouldering in the ground." If we recall the persistence of George Cohan's "Over There," during the two years of the war just passed, we will have some fractional measurement of the hold that tune of the sixties took upon the Northern heart.

Concerning Grant, I had something to say in 1900. Because this something was spoken under excitement and with a distinctness of recollection twenty years clearer than my present impressions, I will print it here, notwithstanding its forensic taint: "To me Grant is not a personage. He is an epoch. There is a morning filled with the music of martial bands and the color of waving banners. I am just tall enough to reach the door-latch with my mother's help. A booted trooper at the door asks for Captain Thomas, while in the gutter stand two champing steeds with saddles of black and brass, deep as the baby's cradle. I see my father ride through the city park, and note with wonderment my mother's tears. The sound of 'Grant—Grant—Grant' is through it all like some infiltrating and saturating echo—that

meaningless sound of 'Grant,' which seems to have some
trouble with another called 'Fort Donelson.' There are
shouts and salvos, and mingling with the cheers there is
the derisive song:

> " 'It was on the tenth of May,
>   Captain Kelly was away,
>   The Hessians surrounded Camp Jackson.'

"Years afterward I learned that the Hessians were
the loyal Germans of St. Louis, who under Francis P.
Blair marched to her defence.

"Another happening of that Homeric day is a fair
where my mother holds me high in the crowd that I may
see a child impersonating the old woman who lived in a
shoe, and had so many children she didn't know what
to do. That little girl with the cap and spectacles is
Nellie Grant, selling her dolls to buy clothes for soldiers;
and now there drifts into my ideas vaguely the conception that this echo, this shibboleth, this Grant is a man,
a father, not nearly so kind and low-voiced as my own
father, not so tender, nor so full of laughter, nor so long
away from home as my father, but still a father, tangible
and human, and maybe good to that little girl at whom
the men and women wave their handkerchiefs.

"Then there is the illumination, when the night is
come. The candles stuck in potatoes behind the tri-
color tissue-paper in the windows; and the tar barrels
are crackling in the street. Suddenly all is dark. I am
frightened by an undefined menace. The young mother,
in her night-robe, is kneeling with me at the open window, one blanket above us both, the sky filled with the
twinkle of the summer stars, and the air heavy with the
weedy smell from the bottom-lands of Illinois. Yet it is

IMOGENE GARRETTSON THOMAS, MOTHER OF AUGUSTUS THOMAS,
AT EIGHTEEN YEARS OF AGE.

From a daguerreotype taken in 1851.

none of these, but rather a tump-tump-tump-like pulse, a rhythm that my mother whispers is the tramp of soldiers.

"It was the heartbeat of a startled nation. I can recall it now, with all the mystery and magic of the potent and unseen, and it is moving to some ghostlike place called Island Number 10 or Vicksburg, and Grant is there in whispers.

"That is my Grant, a member of that Apocrypha of the nursery to which belong the Bluebeards and the Giant Killers.

"I saw him once, in the winter of 1870, at Washington, when the Senate and House had gathered in the Hall of Representatives, at the funeral of General George H. Thomas. The imperial Blaine was in the chair, and in a semicircle of seats in front of his desk were the cabinet and a short, high-shouldered, round-headed man with whiskers. Grant! I felt the same shock that a little girl of to-day, full of 'Alice in Wonderland,' would feel if she were shown Lewis Carroll and told, 'That is your story.' "

Before the war my father was associated with Mr. W. N. Wells, among others, in the formation of the Republican Party in the St. Louis district. They were in occasional correspondence with Mr. Lincoln at Springfield, not yet the great emancipator, but just a clever debater who was attracting attention in the West. One of those original letters, addressed to Mr. Wells, not to my father, is between two panes of glass in a frame and a folder in my library. It does not add much to the volume of Lincoln's product, but as it has been in print only in connection with my play, "The Copperhead," this extract may have for many a genuine interest:

All dallying with Douglas by Republicans, who are such at heart, is at the very least, time and labor lost; and all such, who so dally with him, will yet bite their lips in vexation for their own folly. His policy which rigorously excludes all idea of there being any *wrong* in slavery, does lead inevitably to the denationalization of the Constitution; and all who deprecate that consummation and yet are seduced into his support, do but cut their own throats. True, Douglas *has* opposed the administration on one measure, and yet *may* on some other; but while he upholds the Dred Scott decision, declares that he cares not whether slavery be voted down or voted up; that it is simply a question of dollars and cents, and that the Almighty has drawn a line on one side of which labor *must* be performed by slaves, to support him or Buchanan is simply to reach the same goal by only slightly different roads.

Very respectfully,

A. LINCOLN.

I remember vividly incidents of the presidential campaign, when I was three years old, that preceded Lincoln's first election. Father and the family were black Republicans, but in my private heart I was stoutly for Bell and Everett of the so-called Union Party. Their torchlight processions were the most picturesque, and at intervals in their lines animated men rang hand-bells, with now and then a larger one on a wagon. There may have been older spectators and auditors as deeply impressed.

I remember the neighborhood rejoicing over the election and, very soon thereafter, everybody and the soldiers singing, "We are coming, Father Abraham, a hundred thousand strong." St. Louis, except for the Germans, was predominantly a Southern city; the divided feeling ran high; neighborhood animosities were intense. There was a builder named McCormick on the other side of our street who had threatened to kill my father. The opportunity apparently never safely offered, but that and other hatred lasted. For example, the war had been over ten years when on a local election day McCormick, who was a powerful fellow, came behind a buggy in which I sat with my father and endeavored to overturn it by lifting the rear axle. I was big enough to engage in the contest that followed, but the police prevented a decision.

These Civil War events and childish impressions from them have no historic value, but they are the stuff that focused and perhaps formed my tendencies; the stuff that influenced my mature associations and endeavors, and became the background and much of the material of my professional work. When I compare these early influences to determine which of them was the most potent in fixing whatever may be persistent in my course, I think I must give predominance to the influence of the grandmother already mentioned. She was so unswerving in her intentions toward me, so positive in her assumptions, so constant that I remember her influence not only as personal and intimate but also as oracular and imperative. I have written her into three different plays quite intentionally, and perhaps into forty others by some indirection. I think, therefore, that a fuller statement of grandmother is pertinent.

Her father's name was Wilson, her mother's name was Walker—both names recently crowded from the advertisements, but they had spirited associations even in my childhood. William Walker, who led his filibusters into Nicaragua, was grandmother's cousin, and she was proud of him. Her only brother was killed on that expedition. Grandmother's first husband was Daniel Garrettson, a boat-builder of Cincinnati. He was lost in a river accident while my mother was still a little girl.

The second husband was an actor turned editor when Pierce gave him the consulship at Falmouth. After Buchanan's inauguration this second husband made his home in Washington City, while grandmother lived in St. Louis to be near us and as far as possible from him. I remember his monthly remittances, which were regular and not large, but beautiful. They came during the early war period in newly printed paper shinplasters, in sheets measuring each about eighteen by twenty-four inches; each sheet having one hundred pieces of fractional currency and each piece with a value of three, five, ten, or twenty-five cents, according to the respective denomination of the sheet.

When I grew big enough not to make the sport too expensive I was permitted to cut these sheets into their component units. Any one who has ever cut a coupon from a Liberty Bond that didn't belong to him can estimate my thrills over these small, crisp steel engravings of historic Americans serving as scenery for federal promises to pay on demand. A percentage of these remittances each month went into the war relief of the time. Recruits from Illinois and Iowa passed grandmother's door and cheered it. The flag with its thirty-four stars hung from her window, and whenever a marching detachment swung into view a table draped with bunting in her little dooryard was quickly equipped with refreshments. Some of the fellows needed them. For any chap especially distressed a reviving nip could be unostentatiously produced. At that time whiskey, which had cost eighteen cents a gallon when Lincoln kept store in Sangamon County, had risen to thirty-five cents a gallon. You can't stop the profiteers. Between times grandmother did volunteer work on uniforms.

On the mantel-shelf of the study in which I am writing in New Rochelle is a black wooden crucifix about sixteen inches high supported by a base. The brass figure of the Saviour is apparently a copy of Donatello. This was always a prominent object in grandmother's parlor. Archbishop Purcell, of Cincinnati, returning from a visit to Rome, had brought it to her when she was first married, with the blessing of Pius IX. Grandmother was then a Catholic, but some act or failure to act, some utterance or some silence by some Missouri churchman upon the question of secession sent grandmother over to the M. E. Church North.

In Simpson Chapel, Union sentiments were vocal and extemporaneous, and there grandmother inhaled and exhaled an atmosphere of militant loyalty. Twice every Sunday and at least one night of the week she went there to meeting. With father at the front, I was the only male creature in our two households, and though mother thought a boy of six or seven shouldn't be up so late, I loved to act as the old lady's escort. The streets of North St. Louis at night were not lighted at that period; the chapel was four blocks away and the natives were not friendly. But grandmother had a square lantern such as Dogberry carries, with three sides of tin, perforated like a horseradish grater, and a fourth side of glass. It held a candle and swung by a tin ring larger than a muffin mold. With that candle lighted and the right wing of her Valley Forge circular thrown over her left shoulder, the handsome old lady, then about fifty, used to go forth with me. In that fashion I began to save the nation as vaguely then as we all of us still continue—a few steps in the dark, each holding to some fallible hand in which we have great faith.

At that time our home was still in my birthplace, the end house of a dozen called Bates' Row on Tenth Street; brick buildings of almost toy dimensions, having three rooms and a lean-to kitchen each, and little dooryards back and front. Grandmother occupied the house next to us with her widowed sister and a pretty niece named Alice Witham. As a youngster I thought she was the Sweet Alice discussed in the lyrical appeal to Ben Bolt, and I had Ben cast in the person of a sturdy soldier who called irregularly until a black-bordered envelope with crossed flags on it explained his absence. I remember Alice still disconsolate as a handsome youth, also living in the same row and not quite old enough for the war— except as drummer-boy, which he was for a while—sang under her window. The police then tolerated that nocturnal custom. This singer was J. K. Emmett, about sixteen years old at that time. Grandmother forgave him when he sang, as everybody did, but at other times he was on her bad books. His sister Eliza had a contralto voice as fine as Jo's tenor. Eliza sang at Simpson Chapel, and Jo, who came to take her home now and then, preferred to practise jig steps on the board walk in front rather than wait inside, where vociferously mine and grandmother's and the little congregation's "days were passing swiftly by." Eliza Emmett Wycoff became one of the notable singers of the city. With Jo Emmett, Our Fritz, the women of two continents fell in love, and true to precedent forgave completely his many missteps.

Grandmother's opinion was the most decisive in our family. I had no way of knowing it wasn't so in the na-

SARAH WILSON GARRETTSON, MR. THOMAS'S GRANDMOTHER,
IN HER FIFTIES.

tion. Her impatience with McClellan and Grant and
even Lincoln seemed to have an effect. At any rate,
things happened when she got mad enough. She permanently affected my early admirations. After a soldier, an orator was the finest type. She had heard Webster in the Senate and Andrew Jackson elsewhere, and
gauged my early diction by those standards. As I review it mentally, I think there may have been a little of
the theatre about her, but it was good theatre; a sense
of the effective, nothing of the insincere. In her prophecy
I joined her strangely assorted gallery of the great, and
always found her hope and her belief associating me with
Jackson and Webster, Lincoln, Edwin Forrest, Charlotte Cushman and Archbishop Purcell. It was a good
deal to ask of a lad of seven, but I took a run at it.

My father, as a bachelor aged nineteen, had gone to
the Mexican War via Leavenworth on the historic Doni-
phan Expedition and during the subsequent experience
was an aide-de-camp on General Taylor's staff. He
sustained there an injury that disqualified him somewhat
from extended service when he raised a company of
volunteers for the Civil War, and therefore as soon as
the immediate menace to Missouri was past he resigned
from the army, and was elected to the Missouri Legislature. When Farragut ran the blockade at the mouth
of the Mississippi and took New Orleans there was a
demand for entertainment by the Northern troops who
occupied the city similar to the demand that came from
the American Expeditionary Forces recently in France.

Father thereupon resigned his seat in the legislature,
and together with Ben de Bar, one of the foremost comic
actors of America, the only great *Falstaff* I ever saw,
and a manager named Tom Davey—who subsequently

married one of the Maddern sisters and became the father of Minnie Maddern, now Mrs. Harrison Grey Fiske— reopened the St. Charles Theatre in New Orleans. This was in the fall of 1863. The party took with them the Revel family, dancers and acrobats, and among others a comedian named George Chapman.

Although New Orleans had fallen a year before, the Mississippi for much of its length below St. Louis was sporadically commanded by Confederate guns, so that this little theatrical company had to run their blockades on a steamboat protected by piled-up cotton-bales. There was a long, successful season at the theatre, which those lessees closed at the end of March in 1865. I distinctly remember my father's return, bringing with him a large cage holding two mocking-birds, which had to have boiled eggs, and also carrying several bunches of bananas protected by pink mosquito-netting. A third item in his baggage was a box of photographs of theatrical celebrities who had been visiting stars at the theatre. Among these were some pictures of the talented and eccentric Adah Isaacs Menken. According to my mother, these photographs did not warrant my father's estimate of Adah's beauty. I remember the pictures too imperfectly at this date to umpire the difference of opinion.

Another attractive photograph was that of a young woman in a pancake hat, a short smart basque and a wide expanse of crinoline. She was the gifted Mathilda Heron, mother of Bijou Heron, now Mrs. Henry Miller, and grandmother of Gilbert Miller, who has recently been announced as the manager to succeed the late Alf Hayman in charge of the Empire Theatre, New York.

There were a half dozen photographs of a singularly handsome man, each of them inscribed "To my dear

Tom"—my father's friends called him intimately by his last name in preference to the given one of Elihu—and signed John Wilkes Booth. Although my father was ten years Booth's senior, he and Booth had been rather boon companions in New Orleans, and coming from the same theatre, wearing the same kind of mustachios and the clubbed hair of the period, were so alike that each was sometimes mistaken for the other.

Father had not been back long enough at our St. Louis home to lose the guestlike novelty of his presence, when on the morning of April fifteenth, something having gone wrong the day before with the family baking, I was sent from the breakfast-table to the corner grocery for an extra loaf of bread. The weather was unusually warm for that season, even in St. Louis. Saturday was a school holiday. I was barefoot in the first kid freedom of the year, and snail-like on this errand I travelled the short block over the unpaved road, which was ankle-deep with its cool bed of dust.

At the grocery I was unable to get attention in the group that had gathered there and was increasing. As soon as I learned the cause of the excitement I ran home, burst into the little dining-room with a repetition of the cry "Lincoln's been shot!"

I can see the family at that table now, each in his or her proper place, as definite as if the occurrence were to-day. My mother and father, my elder sister and a younger one, a baby brother, my grandmother, and a hired girl. It was the democratic custom in that section and time for the hired girl to serve the food in bulk and then sit with the family at the table. My father, refusing to accept my message, rushed to the street. I see the terror on my mother's face and the tragic intensity of grandmother. I am pressed with questions. I remember my inadequate replies, and then my father coming back, his face grown strangely older. As the women look at him he says, "Wilkes Booth——"

"Shot Lincoln?"

"Yes."

As the women get this confirmation my mother sobs with her head upon the table; grandmother, erect, is making short dramatic denunciations, of which I have forgotten all except their vehemence. Not only that day but an ensuing period of dislocation and excitement followed; a period recalled as interminable compared to the swift actions that the records show. During that crowded time every word of the reports in every paper was read aloud and discussed; every rumor too. The subject occupied the talk and filled all minds through every silence. The apprehension and arrest of conspirators; the pursuit and killing of Booth; the arrangements for the dead President's funeral; the trial of persons charged with complicity in his assassination; bitter division on the question of the guilt of Mrs. Surratt, and upon the right at all to hang a woman; suspicions that arose and were increased concerning Vice-President Johnson's possible knowledge of or blindness to the plot banished all unrelated topics. Letters came, neighbors ran in and out to carry or to match their news. Persons heretofore uncertain as to policies took a prompt stand in condemnation of the deed. Many Southern sympathizers honestly arranged themselves with the Northerners; some sullen ones closed their blinds and kept out of view. The excitement extended to the children; and picture papers were cut out, pasted into peep shows and reeled off in soap-boxes, back-lighted by bits of candles.

The death of Lincoln came with crushing force to every household in the North. To these ours was an exception only in the added poignancy given by our familiarity with the assassin's name and looks and my father's recollections of a recent playful companionship. Booth's photographs were brought out, discussed in horror and then put away and avoided. In the next year or two, through the willing agency of secesh playmates, I quietly gave these pictures to other parents who prized and kept them.

When Lincoln's funeral was held at Springfield there was a ceremony in St. Louis, with a stately representative catafalque set in the rotunda of the classical courthouse, where thousands with bowed head and reverent step passed to express openly their sorrow. I was in that line, and though no doubt truthfully informed at the time, for years I retained the belief that Lincoln's body had been under those flowers and flags. There must have been many who thought the same.

II

A PAGE BOY IN THE MISSOURI LEGISLATURE

Soon after that time my father was planning and surveying what was called the St. Louis and Glencoe Railroad. There was an onyx quarry at one end of it—the other end, I think. Grandmother called it a mare's-nest, which seems to be bad rating for a new railroad, and father suffered in the enterprise in other ways. He had to go to New York about bonds and money, and took me with him to Brooklyn, where his sisters lived. On that visit I learned that father himself had a maternal grandmother, who before her marriage had been a Miss La Farge. It required half a day to get from Brooklyn by ferry-boat to New York and by Broadway stage to her house in a thinly settled district near Central Park in the East Sixties. She spoke with a French accent—difficult for me to understand. The only topic on which we got earnestly together was the Civil War—grandmothers seemed to be unanimous on that—but she was a dark and very old lady and in no wise comparable to my grandmother. I felt sorry for father, but was careful never to say anything about her that hurt his feelings.

We went back to St. Louis. An older railroad man, the family said, named Colonel Tom McKissock, had euchered father out of the Glencoe Railroad, and in our historic apportionments McKissock joined Buchanan.

There was in those days a touch of economical management by my mother that will appeal to two classes of readers. The first it will impress with mild astonishment; and the second, millions in number, if the statement should reach them, it will strike familiarly. The flour for the baking came in coarse cotton sacks. These sacks when empty and with their seams ripped open washed up into serviceable domestic cloth. For the five children in our household in 1868 this cloth was available as nightgowns. Sometimes the brand of the flour stenciled into the bag was indelible. One dealer, dyeing for immortality, identified his product by a pardonable pun which had for my parents a third application, gratifying though not prophetic, as they watched me bundle into bed with The Flower of the Family blazoned on the southern exposure of my gabardine.

In similar ways and by like episodes my neighborhood horizon widened and took on state and national dimensions. Among father's optimistic friends was a man named Cavanaugh, with whiskers and blue eyes and a broad broken nose. Mr. Cavanaugh never put water in his whiskey, as General Frank P. Blair and father did while conversing at the Planter's House bar, but drank it with a nervous toss and considerable display of teeth under his wet mustache and then thoughtfully went "Ha" with a sandpaper exhaust.

Then and again, years and other years afterward, standing at the same bar, I tried to dramatize for my own mind's eye the story of General Frank P. Blair, smiling and unarmed, saying, oh, so confidentially, to another man he had never met before: "Are you Billy Ryder? Well, I'm told you say you will kill me on sight. My name is Frank P. Blair, Mr. Ryder."

"Right where we're standing," Cavanaugh explains, and Mr. Blair laughs it off and says something amusing about a bluff.

Billy Ryder was a political Monk Eastman. As a

boy and man I heard him make fiery speeches in Gaelic to his compatriots from the court-house steps, but I always remembered Mr. Cavanaugh's story to my father as I stood listening, nine years of age. Even at sixty-four I like it.

My father was a fine man with a great brain, and now that he is gone I would say nothing of him that could prejudice a reader against him, but he always treated me as an equal. I knew his friends man fashion. They were many and important, and such informing anecdotes as the one just related he always told me in order that I might rightly measure men. On all public questions there was always also grandmother, sometimes mistaken but never in doubt, and from the time I was eligible at six years of age until the time I was indigent at twelve, I had an almost uninterrupted attendance at regular sessions of the St. Louis grammar-schools, including at that period their compulsory study of German. When I finished I had a card publicly given me for my recitation of Marco Bozzaris. The scene is indelible. I had walked to the teacher's platform, as was then uniformly required, on tiptoe; we thought in order that our shoes should not squeak too much, but, as a matter of fact, to train us against falling arches. I see my teacher now, the bunch of lilacs on her desk and just behind her the Tropic of Capricorn. It had been there all winter, but never so plain as on that fragrant morning in the spring of 1868, with the girls in white and ribbons, and through the open windows trees and grass and cowbells, and beyond the sky-line of a great round world turning upon its own axis once in every twenty-four hours, except in February, which has twenty-nine. The safety of our republic rests upon our public schools.

During this early period we lived not always in the same house. Places were rented, and like many uneasy families of that time we occasionally removed. Amongst our plunder there were a few book-shelves well furnished and some other volumes with bindings too dilapidated to be shown. These cripples drifted to the garret, where I used to run across them on holidays. Three of these old books I studied with keen interest. One was Blair's "Rhetoric"; a second was Jefferson's "Manual on Parliamentary Law," which had evidently been useful to father at different times; a third was a small copy of Hardee's "Military Tactics."

About this time the remittances of new money from Washington City began to get irregular and now and then to lack a few sheets of the stipulated limit, but to be accompanied by peace-offerings of useless merchandise, stuff that the sender had probably got at little cost from a War Department that was reforming. In one shipment of that kind there came a pasteboard box containing a gross or more of officers' epaulets in gold and silver on different colored cloths, ready to be sewed on the shoulders of soldier coats. Nobody wanted these things apparently, not even grandmother, and they fell to me. Nothing would have been more acceptable except perhaps a consignment of Indian war bonnets. I distributed them among my comrades, and with the help of the Hardee "Tactics" organized two or three squads, fairly proficient in the manual, with wooden guns, but composed entirely of officers from brigadier-generals to captains. When manœuvring in the streets and encouraged by veterans at the corner grocery we must have looked like a miniature and migratory general staff.

This would be too trivial to record were it not for the

fact that it was at a time when two national conventions had made their nominations. With the entire country still wrought up and resentful over the assassination of Lincoln, the Republican Party took no chances on the character of its candidate, and General Ulysses S. Grant was the nominee. His Democratic opponent, Governor Horatio Seymour, of New York, had smirched his record a little by addressing an audience of draft rioters in New York in a pacificatory speech as "My friends."

To offset the doubts which that phrase inspired, the Democratic convention gave Seymour as his running mate that gallant Democrat of undoubted loyalty of whom I have already spoken, General Francis P. Blair. My father was so fond of Blair that, partisan as he was, it hurt him to oppose him in the local districts, but he vigorously did so. I was by this time taking a wider interest in politics and on higher grounds than those which I held in the Bell and Everett campaign. But still the theatrical features of the contest were the ones that interested me most.

In the torchlight processions the marching voters, besides their soldier caps and capes, wore little aprons, because their candidate, U. S. Grant, when a boy, had worked in his father's yards as a tanner. More than in any other district that I have ever observed, and more than in any other campaign, the juniors took an interest in this one, doubtless because of the contentious atmosphere in which they had all been raised. The men encouraged them and there were many marching clubs of boys. My organization of shoulder straps was active two or three nights in the week at the tail end of the tanners' procession.

It is probable that neither Seymour nor Blair, experienced politicians as they were, had much hope of election. At any rate, upon many occasions in which I saw him soon after the decision, I could discover nothing crestfallen about our Missouri member in particular, nor did he carry any animosity against the comrades who had remained loyal to the commander in chief rather than support their local favorite. Blair and my father were warm friends as ever, and Blair himself was influential in having me appointed a page in the Missouri legislature the following session, at which time I was eleven years old.

There were five page boys in the Missouri House of Representatives at that time. They were appointed by the clerk, and there was considerable political competition for the places. As the boys were paid ninety dollars a month, the appointments came under the head of patronage. There were plenty of competent lads in Jefferson City who would have been glad to get the work at twenty dollars a month, but under the spoils system the clerk endeavored to distribute the appointments through different sections of the State. The salary was fixed upon the knowledge that the boys would be under considerable expense away from their homes, and perhaps the committee on appropriations justified the amount also under the theory that the work was educational and to a boy the opportunity would be a kind of scholarship.

Any man who can remember working as a page boy in any legislative body will approve this theory. Every session was punctuated by points of order from the members and rulings by the chair, and perhaps because their attention to these contests was not so divided as that of the members, the boys were better average parliamentarians than 90 per cent of the legislators themselves. Besides the ninety dollars, each boy got one hundred three-cent postage stamps every month, a bunch of lead-pencils, a supply of quill pens such as a theatre property man still provides for *Richelieu*, and a pocket-knife to keep these pens in order. The same allotment was made to every official employee and to every member. In excess of this the members received a supply of black sand, for which a box sat on each desk. Most of the members preferred blotting-paper to the use of the sand boxes, but as blotting-paper was a novelty some of the old men shook sand on to their wet letters and then shook most of it back again into the perforated lignum-vitæ boxes. I remember the page boys laughing over an editorial comment of one of the St. Louis papers concerning the city's oldest representative then in the house, a certain erratic Doctor Smythe. The paragraph said:

Doctor Smythe writes his letters with a lead-pencil and uses the blotting-paper, which he says is much superior to the old sand.

Our duties as page boys were to carry a bill or a resolution from the member who introduced it to the desk of the clerk who was to read it aloud; to take messages from one member to another or to go to the other end of the building on some errand to the senate; or to one of the departments under the same roof. We were seldom sent outside of the capitol. We were not always busy and our leisure naturally fell when the members themselves were most engrossed; that is to say, when something of real interest was proceeding in the house. There were generally two sides to every question that came up, and it would be difficult to conceive of any method more instructive than that with which the boys

constantly were in contact. The measures were not always of equal importance; there were times of comedy
and even of horse-play. Under each desk at that time
there was a large individual cast-iron cuspidor with a
hinged cover of a Renaissance pattern. If a man by
accident slipped his toe under one of these heavy covers,
allowing the cover to fall back on the basin, it made a
noise as loud as a stove lid treated in the same way.
Sometimes when a member strictly within his rights was
speaking beyond the patience of his hearers these accidents occurred, and were repeated with increasing frequency, until the din reduced his oratory to pantomime.
There were more than one editorial protest throughout
the State against this system of cloture, and I remember
reading these protests as late as the middle eighties; but
I used the device as a comic episode in a play some
twenty years ago and was roundly denounced by a Missouri statesman for misrepresentation.

Another example of a kind of humorous relief was
furnished when a desk neighbor of the Doctor Smythe
above mentioned got from his optician duplicate pairs
of Smythe's spectacles. In the heat of a debate the old
doctor had a way of reading from some authority and
then, as he spoke to the question, pushing his glasses to
the top of his head. On the occasion in mind, as the
doctor finished one reading, the member slipped his second pair on the desk in front of him. The doctor spoke
a moment and, during his rest, again mechanically adjusted this second pair of glasses, read his second quotation and pushed the second pair of spectacles up to
the first. The effect and his own astonishment caused
an uproar and made a serious contribution ridiculous
and ineffective.

That winter of '68 in the Missouri legislature, of which John D. Orrick was speaker, is notable for three events: The Fifteenth Amendment, giving the vote to the negro, was adopted; Miss Phœbe Couzins, a pretty girl, then in her twenties, just graduated as a lawyer, addressed a joint session upon the question of female suffrage; and Carl Schurz, at the end of a spirited joint debate, was elected to the United States Senate.

Miss Couzins made a pretty picture as she finished her address to the legislators, and with a graceful wave of a white-gloved hand closed by saying, "Let it be flashed across the continent that Missouri leads the van, and the nation must follow."

In Broadway parlance of to-day that would be called hokum, but at that time every listener, to use another phrase, ate it up. Opinion on the policy was divided, but nobody doubted Missouri's ability to lead the van.

Phœbe Couzins, the first woman to hold a Federal executive appointment, served during President Arthur's administration as deputy for her father, who was United States marshal for the Missouri district, and upon Major Couzins' death the President appointed her to the office. She was an earnest suffrage advocate for years, and an ardent prohibitionist, but before her death in 1913 her accumulated experience, and it may be her wisdom, led her to oppose both measures.

Carl Schurz electrified his hearers. He then had been only sixteen years in America, during which time he had rallied his German-American fellow citizens to the support of abolition, had served with distinction through the Civil War, had acquired a perfect mastery of the English language, and as he said to his fiery little opponent in the debate, Senator C. D. Drake, who chal-

lenged him on some point, "had gained a very dangerous knowledge of the Constitution of the United States."

The Schurz-Drake debates were held at night, with
the members of the senate crowded into the larger house
and the lobby holding on its full benches more than one
distinguished man who thought the lightning might
strike him. I remember first seeing at that time the
romantic-looking David P. Dyer, the scholarly John F.
Benjamin, and ex-Senator John B. Henderson, who because of his vote in the United States Senate against the
impeachment of Andrew Johnson was no longer acceptable to his Missouri constituency as United States senator. Mr. Henderson was the author of the Thirteenth
Amendment, which in regular form made Lincoln's proclaimed emancipation part of the Constitution. At one
stage of the proceedings in these joint debates, in response to many calls for an expression, Henderson, instead of taking the speaker's rostrum as Drake and
Schurz had done, arose modestly from a chair well back
in the chamber, and beginning to speak in playful fashion
moved with much charm and persuasiveness to such
dangerous ground that the partisans of the more prominent candidates broke in upon his address.

The page boys' hours were about nine to four. We
liked to sit up late occasionally but not repeatedly, and
in front of the Wagner House, where I roomed with another boy, the local statesmen, when the weather permitted, had a convention fashion of holding group consultations on the sidewalk. My first active service as
a member of the Vigilantes grew out of that. Our organization was not extensive, containing, in fact, only
this other boy of about my own age, Robert H. Cornell,
now a prominent citizen of St. Louis, and myself.

To break up the sidewalk meetings Cornell suggested an effective method. We brought home with us from the capitol newspapers which soon accumulated in bulk, and when soaked in our water-pitcher and reduced to mash we compressed moderately into missiles of the size of a football. Our rooms were on the top floor of this five-story hotel. At what seemed the proper hour for a curfew Bob would lean from one window and I from another and at a concerted signal intrust these heavy and mushy bundles to that power described in the Newtonian law. Under favorable conditions one of them would cover an entire committee meeting. We had to judge the effect of our attack only by what we heard, as by the time these things had travelled their distance we were back in bed. It was a disgraceful and lawless procedure and we both deserved the house of correction at least, but now that I tell of it under the protection of the statute of limitations, and think of the frequent protests against the destruction of our national forests, I am not sure that any other equal amount of paper pulp has finally performed more useful service.

Another source of annoyance on these open-window nights was a card-room behind a saloon extending at right angles to the rear wall of the Wagner Hotel. We couldn't reach or appeal to these offenders with the literary matter that was so useful in front of the house, but the Wagner Hotel dining-room was separated from its supply department only by a wooden partition eight feet high. As Cornell was the lighter of us boys, I used to boost him over this partition when the help had retired, and from the inside, standing on one of the shelves, he would procure and pass back a hatful of raw eggs. At the rear of the hotel on every story, there was a Southern gallery or porch.

The one on our floor commanded the tables nearest the door of the card-room just mentioned.

Oliver Herford once answered a lady who asked him if he had any one unsatisfied ambition in life by saying that he had always wanted to throw a raw egg into an electric fan. I have never seen that done, but I am sure that whatever would be lost in mechanical regularity from that reaction is fully compensated by the human interest that can be elicited by two raw eggs suddenly exploded in a pinochle foursome. Let me say to any immature readers that this was very reprehensible conduct, and that on my part there has been complete reformation.

I cannot speak so hopefully of Cornell, because when I last saw him in 1917 he was trying to sell real estate.

The year before this one at Jefferson City parts of Kansas and a part of Missouri had been seriously overrun by a plague of grasshoppers. The United States Government had sent a distinguished entomologist by the name of Riley to study the conditions. I don't know what Mr. Riley was recommending to the legislature, but at the Wagner House dinner-table, where for a few days he had a seat next to mine, he advocated eating the grasshoppers. He used to bring to the table a paper-bag, holding about a quart of them, roasted and buttered. These he put on a platter and was just as unselfish with them as a dog is with fleas. Very few of his neighbors joined him in their consumption. I ate two or three and found that they tasted not unlike peanuts.

As I try now to recall the impelling motive of this courageous deed on my part I think it was a combination of curiosity, a wish to please Mr. Riley, a desire to report the occurrence at home, where it did make a sensation, and also my recollection of the Sunday-school verses which I used to recite about John the Baptist's liking for them. Perhaps it was the absence of wild honey at our table that accounts for my lack of sustained enthusiasm.

The old capitol building of which I write was destroyed by fire in February, 1911. It was of the dome-and-wings type, like the National Capitol, and stood a few hundred feet nearer to the river than its handsome successor, and on a bluff. The muddy Missouri rolled almost beneath, and wild woods and bushes were on the opposite bank, where we looked for Indians and sometimes saw them, but disappointingly reconciled and orderly. On our bank one day my father, who paid us a visit that session and from whom until his death I was always getting some new glimpse of a varied experience, pointed out to me, on the Missouri Pacific track below, the spot where in 1861 an engine and baggage-car had stopped after a record run from St. Louis to unload some fifty self-organized patriots who came with revolvers and clambered up the bank Indian fashion just as Governor Claiborne Jackson and a majority of the legislators, who were trying to pass an ordinance of secession over a filibuster of a loyal minority, took to their heels and Missouri stayed in the Union. Father was one of that carload.

My father introduced me to the Honorable Erastus Wells, then a congressman from a St. Louis district. Mr. Wells had some boys himself. One of them, Rolla Wells, when he grew up, became mayor of St. Louis.

If a man likes your dog heartily he probably owns one. A father of two boys is an easy acquaintance for some other's boy. I don't think I was especially forward, but

after two or three talks with Erastus Wells he had promised me to do what he could to get me a pageship at
Washington. He sicked me onto D. P. Dyer and John F.
Benjamin, who were also visiting Jefferson City, and told
them I was Tom's boy. As a result all of the nine con-
gressmen from Missouri signed my application for the
place.

III

MY INTRODUCTION TO WASHINGTON

A powerful publisher in Philadelphia, Pennsylvania, when he knew I planned to write these recollections, sent a word of caution to me by a friend. He didn't come himself. A rash or inexperienced or undiplomatic publisher, seeing a sign, "Angels Wanted," might have rushed in; but knowing that Napoleon even in his highest power sent M. de Narbonne to represent him at Vienna, this prudent printer, moving by indirection, said to his ambassador, "Tell Thomas to raise a mustache in his story as soon as possible." By which he meant, get through with his boyish memories briefly.

The Autocrat of the Breakfast-Table, one morning in 1858, said to his fellow boarders: "My hand trembles when I offer you this. Many times I have come bearing flowers such as my garden grew; but now I offer you this poor, brown, homely growth; you may cast it away as worthless. And yet—and yet it is something better than flowers; it is a *seed-capsule*. Many a gardener will cut you a bouquet of his choicest blossoms for small fee, but he does not love to let the seeds of his rarest varieties go out of his hands. You don't remember the rosy pudency of sensitive children. The first instinctive movement of the little creatures is to make a *cache*, and bury in it beliefs, doubts, dreams, hopes, and terrors. I am uncovering one of these *caches*."

Some day when my Philadelphia friend outgrows his timidity he and I will meet, and not chiding him openly for this threatened surrender to the material rush of his generation and his calling, I shall say: "Is your great paper, founded by a great, unhurried American philosopher, read principally in subways and on commutation trains or in simple households after nightfall, with mother and the children near the lamps? And what are the passwords to those family groups?" I shall show him those breakfast-table lines of Doctor Holmes and remind him also of some religionist who somewhere said to somebody in what must have been a mood and moment of great intimacy, "Give us the children before they are seven and you may preach what you will to the adults." Give us the sensitive and malleable retentive soul tissue when it is tender and impressionable and later try what intellectual veneer and overlay you like.

I shall remind him of weary little Dick Whittington day-dreaming on the wayside boulder and listening to the distant London bells; remind him of the German manikin Diogenes Teufelsdröckh in the sunset with his porringer on the coping of the orchard wall at Entepfuhl. I shall say: "Recall to your mind Sir John Millais' canvas, famous by the personal question of those enterprising soap-makers, showing the English boy on the cottage doorstep in rapt wonderment at his iridescent bubbles." I shall say: "Think of the face of Richter's Neapolitan Boy—of the unutterable poetry in the eyes of the winged youth between the supporting knees of Doré's grim-sculptured Fate; think of Eli's little kneeling Hebrew protégé listening to answer, 'Speak, Lord, for thy servant heareth.'" And I shall say: "Except for your inhibiting honk about a mustache I would have opened my heart to that subscribing brood around the family lamp. I would have given the high sign of

brotherhood to those boys and girls in the prairie states
who know the pungent blend of dew and tomato-vines,
and who understand better than the grown-ups the cry
of Kipling's Australian in that South African fight:

> "And through the crack and the stink of the cordite,
>   (Ah, Christ! My country again!)
> The smell of the wattle by Lichtenberg,
>   Riding in, in the rain!"

I would have told them how my dad, who hadn't wept
through two important wars, explained his wet eyes to
me when for the first time after thirty years he inhaled
the salty odor of low tide as we crossed the Hudson at
dusk in a ferry-boat. But you can't explain a subtle
thing like that to a man selling safety razors. He
wouldn't believe that a boy four blocks from the Mississippi River on a roped bed with no mosquito bar in a
gable attic could tell at midnight and just by the sound
of her long melancholy whistle whether an upriver packet
coming in was the *Belle of Alton* or the *Red Wing* or the
Keokuk.
But I wanted to tell those children about those float-
ing side-wheeled palaces and other finer ones from the
Southern river routes tied up to the levee so closely that
only their bows could nose in with their gangplanks—
the *Natchez*, the *Robert E. Lee*, the *Grand Republic* and
scores of others, all vanished now from that neglected
shore, and living only in melodrama and romance; in
such stories as Mark Twain's and George Cable's; in
the hearts of grandmothers who can show you daguerreo-
types of frills and flounces; and in the memories of tired
business men voodooed by efficiency and the income
tax. I wanted to tell them of my grandmother's story

that is good enough for a play about Colonel Jim Bowie, who got a big steel file from the engineer on the boiler deck and ground it into a knife with which he killed the other man in a duel on an island where the boat stopped to let them fight it out; a bigger knife than Buffalo Bill had in his duel when he killed that Indian chief, while both their fighting crowds looked on— A good friend of mine when I got to be a man. I hope I don't forget to speak of Buffalo Bill later.

In the early winter of 1870 I left St. Louis for Washington City, after getting a letter about it from Mr. Wells. I had a funny little sole-leather trunk of antiquated pattern, of which I was told to take good care, as it had held father's luggage when he went from Chicago by the Fox, Illinois and Rock rivers with a group of pioneers who founded Winona, Minnesota. At the O. & M. depot in East St. Louis father gave me into the care of General Blair and his friend, Mr. Cavanaugh, who were going on the same train. I am not sure of Mr. Cavanaugh's business or his exact relation to General Blair, but I have recently seen something like the relationship in that of Mr. Steve Reardon to Georgie Cohan: unswerving admiration and solicitude, coupled with a capacity to give comfort in times of threatened depression. Along with General Blair and Mr. Cavanaugh were two others whose names I forget, but who owned the poker chips and parted with them only temporarily. I can't remember General Blair as playing. He was early pointed out on the train by some who knew him, and many passengers introduced themselves, so that his trip was a reception for most of the way.

On our O. & M. and B. & O. trains there were no dining-cars, no automatic brakes, no system of heating except the stoves, one to each car. We stopped twenty minutes for breakfast, dinner, or supper, and with no uncertainty about dinner being the midday meal, and into the high-toned heater the porter fed anthracite coal, the first I had ever seen.

The engineer whistled one short sharp call for brakes, with staccato repetitions in moments of emergency, and then blew two reassuring toots for their release. Five blasts then, as now, sent back the brakeman with his red flag and track torpedoes when we made unscheduled stops, and four whistles called him in. There was no auditor on the train and the conductor unprotestingly took money where the tickets had not been provided.

The trim of our sleeper was of black walnut; the upper berths when closed had flat surfaces, angular corners instead of the slightly convex mahogany boards that now furnish them; and when open they were not held down with the wire cables that now anchor upper berths. That security was introduced in the late seventies, after an upper berth in an overturned private car had shut up and smothered its occupant, Mr. Taussig, the treasurer of the old Kansas City and Northern Railroad. In this old-style Pullman the rails for the curtains, stout horizontal bars, ran the full length of the car on each side, supported by uprights at each section. The water in the wash-rooms did not flow under pressure as now, but at each basin passengers worked a brass-and-ebony pump handle. Watches were to be set forward nearly an hour to adjust the difference between St. Louis and Washington City time. In our party there was uncertainty about this interval, and I recall the astonishment of the men when I calculated it for them mentally, as the dullest boy or girl in our Webster School class of

fifty would have done, and in order to do so knew, of
course, the meridians of the two cities in the problem.
I couldn't do it now without complete quiet, a large atlas,
and paper and pencil. Can any settled citizen do it, or
has any the needed items of information except perhaps
Mr. Edison?

At Washington our B. & O. train on that earlier B. &
O. Railroad was some hours late, and arrived in the collection of sheds that then did duty as a station a little
north of the Capitol somewhere near midnight. My
father had arranged for me to board with an army friend
and printer companion of his, Major Stone, popularly
known in St. Louis as Fighting Harry Stone because of
his gallant conduct at the battle of Wilson's Creek, when
General Nathaniel Lyon was killed. Harry Stone's wife,
who was a friend of my mother's, had been Alice Buck,
a celebrated soprano associate upon concert programmes
with Eliza Emmett, the talented sister of the famous
J. K. Emmett already mentioned. Mr. and Mrs. Stone
had three children. One of the daughters, Patti Stone,
became well known in light opera on Broadway in the
early nineties; a son, Blair, became a star acrobat.

In this winter of 1870 patriotism, rewarded by a job
in the public printer's, took Mr. Stone to Washington,
where he found for his family a house on F Street near
Fifteenth, in what is now the Shoreham Hotel district.
Before leaving St. Louis I had taken the precaution to
find a map of Washington City in the public-school
library and get a fair idea of the relative location of this
address. A December rain was falling as General Blair
and his group of politicians came from the station with
me. I saw the looks of amusement on the faces of his
friends as they considered the General and his embarrass-

ing protégé, and was quick to tell him I thought I could find my way if he would start me right as to the points of the compass. There was a little council between the men, and after further insistence on my part I was put alone into a bobtail car drawn by a mule and carrying a Slawson box for the passengers' fares, all reassuringly like our St. Louis horse-cars.

Upon my arrival at the house I was a long time waking the family, and was finally admitted by Fighting Harry himself. He sleepily showed me to the room that was to be mine and said good-night. I don't think at any time in my life since has there been an equal feeling of loneliness to what I then had as I put down my bag and took off my wet clothes in an unheated room. The house had only open grates, and there was no fire for this belated guest. As I stood on the sagging mattress to reach the gas-jet when I turned it out for the night I found that I was still a little seasick from the oscillating beauties of the Susquehanna Valley.

The next morning, one of those crisp sunshiny winter days that Washington can show in early December cheered me completely. Mrs. Stone I had known as a neighbor all my life. She gave me a hot breakfast passed from stove to table just as my own mother would have done it, and I set out for the Capitol in the best of spirits. I knew which was the House end if I could strike the familiar view shown on the two-dollar bill on which my father had indicated it. I soon found this, and the door-keeper, Mr. Buxton, was expecting my report for duty.

In that handsome Hall of Representatives, at ten o'clock on that morning, there were besides myself twenty other page boys. The layout of the place and its relation to the larger building conformed with the understudied impressions I had from the State capitol at Jefferson City, but on a scale of true magnificence for which I was unprepared. I think the Capitol at Washington is the only building I ever saw while a boy which after a lapse of years did not seem smaller on a second view. At that time it fully symbolized what I felt was the grandeur of the nation and the power of the Government with which I was officially connected.

When the House assembled at noon in its semicircle of dignified desks and chairs, with aisles converging at the tables of administration, I felt more at home than I had thought I should.

The statesmen of that day were the successful soldiers of the earlier part of the same decade. In that historic Congress of reconstruction there were more than a dozen faces with which I was already familiar by their portraits in the heavy album that stood on the little oval marble-topped table in its place of honor in grandmother's parlor. Among those whom I soon identified were Generals Banks, Logan, Butler, Schenck, Garfield, and Slocum. I do not name them alphabetically, but as I see them now in a mental picture of the chamber, reading from left to right as the modern group photograph instructs.

That night as I sat at supper with Fighting Harry Stone, the grand army comrade of these heroes I had left in the Capitol, and felt myself the son of another soldier and prompt fighting man off there in Missouri so undeniably of their company, too, I refrained from all mention of the close association, but in my heart I longed for a confidential and glowing hour with grandmother and her noble gallery.

All of these fellow page boys of mine were away from

their homes proper and many of them without supervision. It was a rule of the then superintendent that
each boy should take two baths a week in one of the several large bathrooms provided for the House. An adult
interpretation of Article VIII of the Constitutional
Amendments made things easier for the statesmen themselves. These bathrooms, of which there were four or
five, were built of marble, with a tub cut from a solid
block, the cavity of which must have been quite eight
feet long and proportionately wide. A boy of twelve or
thirteen could take a good swimming stroke in one of
them. In the winter these baths had a touch of regimen
about them. The tickets, two a week, were issued on
certain days at the doorkeeper's desk and had to be returned by the attendant in the bathroom as used, but
it wasn't always possible to make the lad to whom the
ticket was given take the bath it called for. And so as
the weather grew warmer—and it can grow warmer in
Washington—and as the asphalt began to run—and it
does—the boys with hotel tubs sold a government ticket
now and then to a comrade not so well fixed.

　This is the time for me to state a fact heretofore with-
held because its earlier telling would not have been an
economy of attention. Grandmother's second husband,
the Honorable Augustus Wallace Scharit, was the half-
brother of my father, born of an earlier marriage of
father's mother. A. W., as he was usually called by our
family, was about fourteen years father's senior, and
being at once his stepbrother and by marriage his step-
father-in-law, bore to my father a complicated relationship that made father's qualified support of A. W.'s wife
in the differences between that pair difficult for A. W.
to tolerate. These two half-brothers were not hostile,

but they had little correspondence. I had been in Washington only a fortnight when a letter from father withdrew all implied restraint and gave me A. W.'s address. My short note to him—I was his namesake—was answered by a call at the Capitol, and A. W., of whose distinguished bearing any boy could be proud, took me to his home and arranged for my stay there during the rest of my time in Washington.

In appearance A. W. strongly reminded me of Carl Schurz, minus the whiskers; the same alert, wiry figure; the same brow; the same full shock of hair; the same tragic directness of glance and an actor-orator's developed power in the mask. He lived apparently alone in his own house and took his meals at the table of an attractive widow whose house adjoined his in the one detached garden of some two hundred feet frontage next to Waugh Chapel, on North A Street, three blocks east of the Capitol. My meals were arranged for at this widow's, and as the widow had a son the prospect was agreeable. The experience did not disappoint the promise. This boy, then at the age of fourteen, was being trained for the stage. For some reason of her own his mother gave him the invented family name Palmoni.

A. W. took a deep interest in him, and while I was there generally had me share his theatrical lessons. A. W. was encouraging to me in his early questionnaires, and was especially amused with my giving grandmother's version of Charlotte Cushman's reading of the lines, "Infirm of purpose! Give me the daggers." At unexpected and genial moments he would sometimes even ask for its repetition. Until then I had not suspected that *Lady Macbeth* was anything of a comedy part.

In the rear of the acre garden was a stucco stable and

carriage-house some three years old, finished perhaps about the time that the paper money remittances began to be irregular. It had evidently never been used as a stable, but was what the contractors call broom clean. A. W. helped the boy and me rig it as a little playhouse. There was a box of army things in it which came in usefully and reminded me to tell A. W. of my having got the shipment of epaulets. He affected astonishment that grandmother had not wanted them—at least wanted a pair of them. Among this army stuff were two sabers that A. W. had cut off to a proportionate length and with which he taught this boy and me such broadsword exercises as would be useful in the theatre.

For that family playhouse I did my first dramatic writing. It must be truthfully told that it was largely in collaboration. Having seen two performances of Mr. Joseph Jefferson's "Rip Van Winkle" I made from memory a juvenile condensation of Mr. Boucicault's book. As author I cast myself for *Rip* and my boy friend played *Nick Vedder*.

Few dramatists begin with more distinguished even though unwitting collaborators than Dion Boucicault and Washington Irving. With the insistence of A. W., I also tackled Sir Walter Scott, and made a workable dialogue of the principal conflicts in "The Lady of the Lake" in which I played *Roderick Dhu*, and Palmoni played *Fitzjames*. A. W. himself rehearsed us in the quarrel between *Brutus* and *Cassius*.

At the widow's table, where he was A. W.'s guest, I met the senior E. L. Davenport. During that week I had seen Mr. Davenport play *Macbeth, Hamlet,* and *Sir Giles Overreach*.

I watched him closely, but neither as himself nor in

any of the three rôles named could I trace an identifying resemblance between Mr. Davenport and the handsome steel engraving of him in the part of *Benedick* that was in the 1855 edition of *Ballou's Pictorial*.

In that meeting Mr. Davenport said nothing that I remember about his son Edgar or his daughter Fannie. I had no way of foretelling that I should one day know and admire them both and be friendly with them, or that his younger son, Harry Davenport, probably not born at that time, would be a member in my company.

Among other theatrical friends who came there was the actor James Murdock, whose recitation of "Sheridan's Ride" made the popularity of those verses by Thomas Buchanan Read.

Another visitor at A. W.'s table, Margaret Meade, a distinguished spinster, aged perhaps fifty years, brought with her sometimes her two adopted daughters, who, however, retained the family names of their dead soldier fathers. One of these girls, two or three years my junior, was named Marie. I have forgotten the name of the other. Marie, not yet too old to slump on Miss Meade's lap and lean her blond head against her guardian's lace collar, had steady gray eyes, big as an Angora cat's. She almost made me forget the thirty-year-old Sunday-school teacher who had owned my heart since I was eight. Margaret Meade had two religions—Catholicism and her distinguished brother, General George Meade, of Gettysburg fame.

Margaret told us one day that while the Battle of Gettysburg was on, its uncertain tide in ebb and flow, she had gone to the White House and sent her card in to Abraham Lincoln. When admitted she asked the President if he had any word of the issue. He answered no.

She said: "Neither have I; but I'm George Meade's sister, and I thought you might like to know that whatever he undertakes he carries through."

It was small assurance, but there are crises in which even a word from a courageous heart is of help. Lincoln thanked her for her call and said it had been of comfort. My own anxiety about Marie lasted longer than the Battle of Gettysburg, and nobody helped any.

During all that season about twice a week A. W. took the other boy and me to the theatre, and was always particular when the curtain fell after an act to indicate what he thought had been excellent in the performance. At that time the street-cars from the National Theatre stopped at the west front of the Capitol. To reach home we had to circle its big hill on foot and walk three more blocks to the house. One jolly winter night, after a performance with a stiff north gale in our faces, A. W. took us boys both up this hill, one on each side, completely covered and protected under a great black broadcloth circular, with velvet collar and throat clasps of silver lion's heads linked together, a counterpart of the one that grandmother wore in St. Louis. Both were of English make.

IV

ADVENTURES OF A PAGE BOY IN CONGRESS

I was in A. W.'s home with the advantage of his instruction and the companionship of young Palmoni for a little over seven months, as the second session of the Forty-first Congress lasted well into July. Besides his interest in my education and his personal hospitality I am glad to record his help in other ways. At that period father's loss of time and other investments in the Glencoe enterprises, together with a general hard-luck story, all useful only in their bloc aspect, had made this work in Washington or some equal employment imperative on my part. In other words, the family needed the money. I was able to send home my entire salary every month. A. W. provided my clothes as they needed renewal, and a page boy's perquisites gave me a very liberal allowance for my personal needs. These perquisites, which at first I refused, were accepted later with a Western boy's real reluctance; reluctance not that the perquisites were at all unlawful in their character, but because of our independent training. Among all the barefoot boys with whom I played in St. Louis I cannot recall one to whom a stranger for any casual service could have given what is now called a tip. Not only would it have been refused, but the boy in declining it would have colored with indignation.

The boys reported for duty in the Hall of Representatives at nine in the morning. Two or three days in the week the work was there. It consisted in getting from the document room the House bills that had been ordered printed, sometimes four or five at a time, and adding them to the individual files, so that each member of the two hundred and twenty-six then there, as he came to the daily session, found under his desk the measures that would come up for consideration. On the busy days work was generally through in an hour, and on other days there was nothing to do, which gave us always two or three hours before the gavel fell at noon.

The official guides now in the Capitol had not then been appointed; the page boys took visitors to the points of interest in the great building, from dome to crypt. We showed them the Chamber of the Supreme Court, which in the early days had been the Senate Chamber, a comparatively little room, but the one in which Webster, Clay, Calhoun, and others had spoken their great orations. We showed them what had been in former days the House of Representatives, but now in 1870 used only as a Hall of Statuary. The crypt, several floors lower than the rotunda, designed by the architects as a tomb for George Washington, and in 1865 unsuccessfully urged as a vault for Lincoln, was a chill, unlighted place containing at that time only a stately platform and somber pall that five years before had held the casket of the murdered Lincoln when his body lay in state at the White House.

This pall was now a neglected object, tattered by the vandal mutilations of the relic-seekers.

A second source of revenue was autographs. Nearly every visitor had one or more favorite statesmen whose signatures he coveted. If for no other reason than that it was a favor to the boys, the members without exception were very glad to write their names, and perhaps publicity was valued even then. The only one who made any special fuss about his autograph was Mr. Clarkson N. Potter, of New York, who, being at the head of a large banking institution, had to be careful. His system was to write his name and then scratch a very positive cancellation of some kind on the back of it.

A third source of income, which probably still exists, was getting orders for printed speeches. A speaking member had the right to designate the boy who should circulate a subscription paper for his speech. An order blank was furnished and as an oratorical effort stirred the listening colleagues the boy in charge of it slipped from desk to desk gathering his orders, because many a brilliant effort once cold and in the Congressional Record was unmarketable. This list turned in to the printing company was good for three cents a hundred on all orders obtained. I have known a boy to make as high as one hundred dollars on some misleading effort; more than once I made ten or twelve myself, which was perhaps the average. The boys were able to estimate the value of a measure as it was introduced, and by knowing the chairman of the committee to which it would be referred to get far in advance the promise of the speeches that would be forthcoming. There was a kind of real political sagacity about it.

These visitors sometimes paid the pages to go on with a certain impromptu show. In order that the human faculty of speech should be acquired and grow Nature ordained that childhood should be imitative. And whether, as Max Müller claims, the words "go" and "va" were instituted by the hungry and complaining cow, the child speech follows imitatively the sounds of

the mother's voice.   Much of juvenile fun is mimicry
in all the wide range from polar bear to lady-come-to-
see.   Self-consciousness and chill criticism check this as
we gather years until few old human dogs can learn new
tricks; but the page boys were still responsive.

It was great fun, with only some score of other pages
as audience, for a boy in the otherwise empty House to
get into the place of a prominent member and spout
ridiculous fragments of that member's speech the day
before.   Often this example would organize all sections
of the chamber.   One boy would get Mr. Blaine's gavel
and smartly call for order, and the rest would scamper
each to the seat where he felt sure of making the greatest
hit.   One would mouth and mush like General Butler;
another would scold like Sunset Cox; a third, like Bingham, would wave the bloody shirt; and others would
yell points of order and questions of privilege, with quite
as much effect on legislation as any average night session.   I've seen and heard as recognizable and as scream-
ingly funny imitations of national legislators by those
boys of thirteen to fifteen years of age as ever Nat Goodwin, Elsie Janis, or Frank Fay gave of their selected celebrities.   Once started, we were so intent on our mock
session that visitors or early members sometimes caught
us at it.   I'm sure that I could now suggest any member
more vividly by imitation than I can by description.

My thoughts jump ahead in the years to the only imitation I ever heard attempted of Abraham Lincoln, and
because it is so related to my present subject in character and in time I hope I may be permitted to take it
from its deferred date of later accident.   The imitation
was very respectfully made at the request of a number
of men at a small dinner-party in 1914.   The host was

Mr. Charles R. Flint, the father of the trusts. Among the eight or ten guests were Mr. Charles Schwab, the Honorable Martin Littleton, Patrick Francis Murphy, Robert H. Davis, editor of *Munsey's*, and the late F. Hopkinson Smith, the distinguished novelist and artist, whom the country best remembers as author of "Colonel Carter of Cartersville." Senator Chauncey M. Depew was the *raconteur* for the moment.

As Secretary of State of New York in 1864 it had been Mr. Depew's duty to spend some months in Washington endeavoring to get the result of the soldier vote in the presidential election of that year. His duty as well as his inclination threw him into very frequent intercourse with President Lincoln. Mr. Depew had begun to tell the celebrated Longnecker story, which I do not think has been in print, but as it is part of the senator's repertoire belongs in his recollections and not these. It was then that one of the men present asked him as to Lincoln's manner. The senator answered that the voice was moderately pitched and pleasant, the speech very slow, having about it, as he indicated, somewhat of the Mark Twain drawl which is so generally the manner with men in whom humor predominates, and proceeding with his story for a few phrases gave what we thought a very characteristic suggestion of the Lincoln manner.

I had been reading in "Emerson's Journal," just published, the account of his visit to President Lincoln on the morning of January 31, 1862, in which he says: "The President impressed me more favorably than I had hoped; a frank, sincere, well-meaning man, with a lawyer's habit of mind; good, clear statement of his fact; correct enough; not vulgar, as described, but with a sort of boyish cheerfulness, or that kind of sincerity and jolly good meaning that our class meetings on commencement days show in telling our old stories over. When he has made his remark he looks up at you with great satisfaction, and shows all his white teeth, and laughs."

Mr. Depew's imitation, coupled with the swift description of the Lincoln manner by Mr. Emerson, has given me an impression of the great President that protects me against the occasional attempts to portray him lugubriously. If, actor fashion, guided by Senator Depew's suggestion, one tries to realize that description of Emerson's—the quick, boyish, upward glance, the flash of the white teeth, followed by a laugh, the pathetic legend of Lincoln crumbles. One cannot convey in print Mr. Depew's pleasant imitation, and few writers have Emerson's genius for description; but the acceptability of impressions so attempted encourages me to think that descriptions of manner, especially as the manner fixes itself in the mind of an impressionable and as yet unprejudiced boy, may not be unwelcome. May I fortify this belief by another example from Emerson, a description of Daniel Webster in the Senate, seeking for a word that does not come?

"He pauses, puts his hand to his brow—you would think then there was a mote in his eye. Still it comes not; then he puts his hands, American fashion, first into his breast under his waistcoat, deeper than I can—then to the bottom of his fobs, bends forward—then the word is bound to come; he throws back his head, and out it comes with a leap, and I promise you, it has its full effect on the Senate."

Mr. Webster could hardly have been more pausy than General Benjamin F. Butler of our Congress under similar conditions. General Butler's way to search for the proper word, which when found came with a marksman's precision to the bull's-eye, was to throw back his head until the undulating line from his nether lip to his collar button ran at the general angle of forty-five degrees; to drop his heavy eyelids for a curtained introspection; issue two or three inaudible poof-poofs as the mask wore the misleading effect of a broad grin, the mood of which was no more in the general's mind than playfulness was behind the permanent grimace of *l'Homme qui rit*, and then to blurt out his word with a rasping of the sibilants suggestive of artificial teeth. When indignant, as he often was, he spoke with this backward toss of the head and a pouting combination of flexible underlip and mustache that made difficult work for the stenographers.

My sponsor, Mr. Erastus Wells, had been shown a pencil drawing of General Blair that I had made on the train, and now in the House encouraged me in making caricatures of the members. There was no great demand or market for these productions until one day, knowing the calumnies against General Butler by the Southerners, who charged him with appropriating silver when he was in command of the army of occupation in the South, I made a profile drawing of the general sitting in the bowl of a large soupspoon with his feet extended along the handle. Some critic, writing of the general at that time, said that his head was like an egg laid sideways and so smooth that a phrenologist must pronounce it uniformly bad or monotonously good. That bald egg-shaped crown with its heavy fringe of clubbed hair was easy to draw. On the Democratic side of the House these caricatures were in demand, and on more than one occasion their cunning circulation took attention from Mr. Butler as he was speaking.

One of those afternoons the doorkeeper told me to

stay after school. The members departed until only
three or four were in the chamber finishing some belated
correspondence. Among these was General Butler at
his desk. The doorkeeper told me to follow him.

When he reached the desk he said, "General, this is
the boy who has been making those caricatures."

The general laid down his pen, looked up either at me
or the doorkeeper—he was very cross-eyed—and after
an intimidating pause, rose to his feet. I watched both
men. I won't pretend to interpret what passed between
them.

The silence was broken by General Butler saying,
"Go to the cloakroom and bring me my hat and cloak."

His cloak was a military cape, not so large as some I
knew; the hat was of the kind subsequently called the
Hancock because General Hancock wore it long after it
had been abandoned by others: a high, soft crown, with
a stiff, sharp, uncurved brim of felt. The gentleman
from Massachusetts took his hat, regarded me calmly
for a moment, blew his soft cheeks with a sudden puff,
as John Drew does when making a comedy point, and
then dropped the hat over my head with the brim resting on my shoulders. I can still revive the reeking bergamot with which it was redolent. My mother had used
bergamot on my curls, and grandmother's antimacassars
smelled of it. After a time of penance beneath this
snuffer, where I feared to move, I heard the general's
mushy voice:

"When you can fill that hat, young man, you make
caricatures of General Butler."

I was sent home for the day with a caution from the
doorkeeper instead of the dismissal I had earned. I have
always remembered this act of generosity to a fresh kid

who had been ignorantly circulating graphic repetitions
of a heinous slander against an earnest and able patriot.

General Butler was a man of laconic and significant
utterances. A speech of his, an example of these qualities, occurred in that session which was nation-wide in
its report and consequent enjoyment. At that distance
from the war many songs were sung with more or less
popularity, taking a comedy view of the soldier, songs
of the Captain Jinks order. Among these was an inane
doggerel called "Shoo, Fly," of which the jingling chorus
ran:

> "Shoo, fly, don't bother me,
> Shoo, fly, don't bother me,
> Shoo, fly, don't bother me,
> For I belong to Company G."

In one of the debates Mr. Butler had made some remark that enraged Mr. Samuel S. Cox, a member from
New York. Mr. Cox was known as Sunset Cox, because
of a description of a sunset written by him for the Ohio
statesman, and his initials lent themselves to the name.
He was a fiery, voluble little speaker, not more than five
feet three inches tall, who apparently tried to overcome
this defect of stature by a profusion of gesture. He had
besides, in speaking, a cradling motion of the head combining emphasis with menace, very like the personal
mannerism of our present talented State Senator J. J.
Walker.

Getting the chairman's recognition when General
Butler offended him, Mr. Cox broke into one of the most
vituperative and personal tirades ever heard in a parliamentary body. The House and the gallery were all
attention, and more than one member was endeavoring

to interrupt in the cause of decorum, but the general disposition was to let Mr. Butler answer. Cox took his seat amid a buzz of expectancy. General Butler looked over at him with that ambiguous gaze I have referred to, paused for a moment while the silence fell, and then half turning away as though the whole episode were closed, and with a wave of his left hand in dismissal of the little member from New York, he said: "I would reply to the gentleman as any newsboy on the street would answer him, 'Shoo, fly, don't bother me.'" Mr. Cox was on his feet in an instant, with a volleyed retort bitter and extended, but unheard by any except those nearest him as the House and the gallery rocked with laughter, and as the nation did the following day.

On strictly party measures the Democrats were incapable of any action other than to protect their record. The country paid more attention to the daily proceedings of Congress then than it seems to now, and on all important questions the votes were published. Democrats, unable to make a dent in the steam-roller progress of legislation and unwilling to listen to much of the debate upon a measure, frequently passed the time at draw poker.

General Robert C. Schenck, of Ohio, who codified the rules of this noble national game, was a member of that Congress, and his very presence was a constant reminder of the recreation. Just across from the Capitol, where the Business Building of the House now stands, was a small brick hotel, with restaurant and café, called the Casparis. The highest games of poker outside of Chamberlin's were conducted there. When a measure reached a vote of record—that is to say, reached a call of the ayes and nays—it was my standing instruction to drop whatever was in hand and in the language of the sprightlier symbolists do a Paul Revere to the Casparis House, and the adjacent committee rooms in the Capitol itself; to dash without ceremony into the rooms where the men were handling the chips and pasteboards and cry, "Calling the roll on the admission of Virginia," or whatever the measure happened to be. The players would then make the best time possible to their places in the House, where it was each member's privilege before the vote was announced to get the recognition of the chair and have his name, which in the case of his absence had been called twice by the clerk, again repeated and his answer registered. The roll call began with Adams, Allison, Ambler, and so on, and proceeded alphabetically. We could generally get our reserves into the House as the clerk was doing the Whitmans and Wilkinsons. The telegraph thereupon carried to his district this evidence of a member's vigilance which cost but slight interruption to the game.

On one of these Marathon round-ups I made my last call at the room of the Committee on Indian Affairs. This committee was not in session; but two or three members, including Mr. Cox, were sharing with some of the visiting Indians whose claims were before the committee a bottle of fire-water. Mr. Cox, who was just my own height, but protected from page-boy calls by as many whiskers as Secretary Hughes, did not need support; but he threw his arm around my neck, partly as a result of the entertainment they had been sharing and ostensibly to show to the petitioning chiefs that even a little boy was safe with him. The other arm he threw around the waist of Red Cloud himself, who on that formal visit was in buckskins, blanket and feathers,

and in that fashion we marched abreast, the gentleman
from New York in the middle, the big chief on his right,
and on his left the unsophisticated page boy from Missouri, down the multicolored corridor, past the statue
of Jefferson and past Emanuel Leutze's mural painting,
"Westward, Ho!" We would have so appeared upon the
floor if a doorkeeper in Grand Army uniform had not
helped Red Cloud and me to get away.

Night sessions were pretty hard on the boys. We had
come from school and home life, where thoughtful
mothers would shepherd us at bedtime, and the night
session, with its droning monotony of soporific drivel
intended only for print, would sometimes lag on until
two in the morning. There was little for the page boys
to do at such a time but sleep on the marble steps of the
Speaker's stand, so we took turns at night duty in squads
of seven. These sessions were always thinly attended.
Sometimes the attendance was so slack that it was impossible for a self-respecting orator to maintain the pretense that he was in any way persuading his colleagues.
It was then within his right, if joined by a definite number of others, to demand a call of the House. This call
was made by a sergeant-at-arms and his deputies, which
force was for the time increased by the use of the pages
present and on duty. Each was given a list of absent
members with their addresses, and while the night session took a short recess these process servers moved
throughout the city, hunting the delinquents.

On one of these calls my list contained the name of
General Butler. He had a residence then somewhere in
the neighborhood of the old Arlington. It was a snowy
night. Although his house was brilliantly illuminated,
I could make no impression with the front doorbell.

Electric bells were then unknown, and servants were summoned to the front door by the old knob-and-wire bell-pull. Failing at this device, I went to the side of the building. The house was on the corner, a protruding bay window some eight feet from the ground was protected by a stone balustrade. The Douglas Fairbanks scaling pictures had not at that time been run, but there were personal experiences in pantries and elsewhere that helped me to get to the top of this coping. Inside of the brilliantly lighted room stood General Butler at the head of a table surrounded by some fifteen or twenty members of Congress, many of whom I was surprised to see in such amiable relationship after their hostile attitude in the House. The food had disappeared. Coffee cups and crumpled napkins were on the cloth and a fine display of glassware. Servants who should have answered the doorbell were standing against the wall; all were evidently entertained.

It was a few minutes before my cold tapping on the window got attention above the words and laughter, and then like Poe's Raven I came in through the open window with my unwelcome message. One or two of the members got up as if to obey the call, but on the advice of General Butler they resumed their seats and I was sent back to report progress. At that time the rule of the House imposed a fine of ten dollars for a failure to respond to a call. The next day, among other gentlemen, our friends of the Butler dinner-table passed in front of the Speaker briefly to render their different excuses.

When it came to the turn of General Butler himself he smiled up at the presiding officer, and waving a new ten-dollar greenback said: "Mr. Speaker, there is my excuse."

The method has been progressive. To-day, from Washington to Reno, few excuses go better.

That Congress was overwhelmingly Republican. In those days of the spoils system I think that very few Democrats were upon the appointive list. Certainly among the pages not any besides myself was there at the request of a Democratic delegation. This fact humorously and mildly singled me out for as much attention from the Republican members as from any of the minority. One Republican, who was at times inclined to wait until I could run his special errand for him, was Mr. Ebon C. Ingersoll, of Illinois, familiarly known to his friends by his middle name, Clark, which is what his brother, Colonel Robert G. Ingersoll, called him.

Speaker Blaine was rather partial to Mr. Ingersoll as a chairman when the House resolved itself into a committee of the whole. As this temporary presiding officer it was his job to listen to the long talks often made only for purposes of publicity and requiring little activity on the part of the chairman. As the season advanced and the weather grew warmer Mr. Ingersoll more than once intrusted to me the delicate mission of going to the restaurant in the basement, kept at that time by a mulatto named Downing, and bringing back to him one of the tall mint juleps of which he was fond. One door to the Hall of Representatives is immediately to the right of the Speaker's desk. By reaching this through what was called the Speaker's lobby a boy could pass from the door up four or five marble steps to the Speaker, completely hidden from two-thirds of the House, and, if he moved quietly, almost unnoticed by the rest.

Following the chairman's careful instructions I used to wrap the glass of julep, its crown of green and its protruding straws in a folded newspaper and pass it to him below the level of the desk. Here was a shelf on which the chairman might lay a book of reference or a manuscript. It was sufficiently depressed from the top of the desk to admit our julep glass.

With the beverage once there, Mr. Ingersoll would make one or two disarming passes of his handkerchief across his face and then sit with his hand over his mustache as though listening to the flood of oratory while the handkerchief fell from his hand to the desk-top and masked the straws that he manipulated.

Clark Ingersoll had all the qualities that his brother attributed to him in that forever-memorable eulogy, and had besides a humor quite as keen as that of Colonel Bob himself. There was one stormy scene growing out of a clash between members, and with incidental unparliamentary language, which the magic of his humor transmuted. Some of the terms were so violent that seemingly disinterested members were asking for a rebuke from the chair.

Mr. Ingersoll evaded one or two demands, but when another member insisted upon his ruling upon the character of the remarks he answered, after a pause, "The chair decides that the language of the gentleman was certainly very"—then, after a moment's reflection with a search for the word, he added—"pungent."

This amiable characterization made everybody laugh, and out of the uproar there grew a resumption of the business and a tacit dismissal of the incident.

These men were then emerging from the bitterness of the Civil War. With many of them the intense emotional state thereby produced still existed to some degree. Their political problem was the reestablishment of national conditions, as all nations are now confronted with the reestablishment of order in the world. Some of the States that had seceded had been already readmitted to the Union under provisional governments. In that session Virginia, Georgia, Mississippi and Texas were asking to come back. In certain sections of the South recognized government was under negro domination, and testimony before committees was burdened with almost unbelievable stories of violence.

A most bitter speaker against the South was Mr. John A. Bingham, of Ohio. He was a nervous man, with a pale face that resembled the current pictures of Lord Alfred Tennyson. His seat was in the front row of desks immediately facing the Speaker and near the steps on which the page boys rested. We were always in for an almost dime-novel description of horrors whenever Mr. Bingham began upon the subject of the unregenerate South or the outrageous Ku-Klux Klan.

One of the most collected and methodical speakers in that Congress was Fernando Wood, of New York; seldom eloquent, never stirring that I can recall, but with an enamelled precision and accuracy, and with that almost invariable note of regretful finality that accompanies the public utterances of our own Elihu Root.

Garfield's style was orotund, authoritative, Mid-Western and homely. He talked easily, often with one hand in his pocket, and generally with a kind of good humor in his manner that would have been completely winning except for the suspected presence of a condescension not easily separable from any genial reception of grave topics.

One member who never spoke but was always pointed out to the visitors was the ex-champion prize-fighter, John Morrissey, of New York.

Mr. John F. Farnsworth, of Illinois, who wore a long beard and had the prairie tone in his vowels, was a mixture of revivalist and barker. If he hadn't preferred to be a statesman he could have taken a couple of beaded squaws and a band wagon and made an equal success anywhere west of the Mississippi with patent medicine.

And speakin' again of Injuns, it is interesting to note the debate pro and con on the measure passed at that session to send the Indians from Kansas to other reservations and to remove the Osage Indians to a territory that is now Oklahoma. According to current reports, in the present year of 1921, each of these Indians, owing to the oil struck in their territory, is individually worth thirty thousand dollars. I have recently seen numbers of them riding about in their own automobiles. Another legislative landmark which will help measure the rate of our progress is the law passed at that session to put a tax on brandy made in this country from apples, peaches, or grapes.

I heard Proctor Knott deliver his celebrated Duluth speech in January of that session. It was unquestionably the most famous speech of the Forty-first Congress. Mr. Knott had decidedly the Mark Twain manner of the conscious humorist. As he proceeded with his speech and gained the confidence that palpable success brings to a speaker, he grew even more at ease and his mannerisms more pronounced. In appearance he had what might be called the Civil War make-up—plenty of hair, worn fairly long, parted on the side, and a mustache. The Duluth speech ran about five thousand words, and punctuated as it was by the laughter of his great audience, laughter growing more prolonged and hysterical as he progressed, must have in his slow manner easily consumed an hour. My sponsor, Mr. Wells, sat very near to Mr. Knott and the two were friendly. The men in that section of the House probably had some advance information on the effort, because shortly after Mr. Knott began to speak page boys were sent in various directions to call in absent members and even to notify the senators at the other end of the Capitol.

A trip to the Senate was among my assignments, and I made it in great haste in order to miss as little as possible of the speech. Ten minutes after the speech began more than half the senators were in the Representative chamber; clerks, and employees had left the committee rooms and supply departments and crowded into the cloakroom. The galleries were full.

Mr. Knott pronounced the name "Duluth" with a caressing coo that was funny the first time and grew irresistible with the repetitions, of which there were some forty-two. The Speaker interrupted him when his time had expired, but there were loud calls from all parts of the House for him to go on, and in the absence of objection he did so.

His ridicule defeated the measure against which he spoke, which was to construct a St. Croix and Bayfield railroad, but his ironical references to the future of the city in a territory of wonderful resources, its beauty and future greatness, read now like prophecy instead of ridicule.

There was also a touch of antiquity for present-day readers when in his reference to possible future amendments to the Constitution that should cover the growing greatness of this Duluth he enumerated supposititious Seventeenth, Eighteenth, and Nineteenth Articles, but said of a Sixteenth: "It is, of course, understood that it is to be appropriated to those blushing damsels who are day by day beseeching us to let them vote, hold office, drink cocktails, ride a-straddle, and do everything else the men do."

None of these privileges is longer in debate.

James G. Blaine was a greater man at that end of the Capitol Building than he ever became in the Senate. The active work of the larger body gave finer opportunity for his extraordinary power. I have seen many presiding officers, but not any who was his equal for promptness of decision, clarity of its statement or vigor of its defense, if needed. On two or three occasions, when a legislative measure was before the House on which he wished to express himself more fully than would have been becoming to a presiding officer, he called a member to the chair and went upon the floor himself. I don't recall his equal in that body for swift and forceful statement of his views and aggressive attack upon the opposition.

Of all the orators in that brilliant galaxy, however, the idol of the page boys was John A. Logan, whose speeches did not read so well as those of more than one other, but he was personally so picturesque, and the fact that he was descended from Black Hawk and showed it in his tawny skin and jet-black hair, gave him a romantic interest that no other had. He had a fine voice and an earnest intensity we liked to believe characteristic of the Indian, with the added fire of a Spaniard or an Italian. And then we knew of him as Fighting John Logan too.

How many of those men were to us colossal from the nation's use of them as symbols of power! General Thomas was the Rock of Chickamauga; when Blair joined somebody it meant that food for an army had arrived; when Banks was to move against Mobile it was thirty thousand men that were moving, not alone that tall, scholarly-looking man in the second row to the Speaker's left; when Logan joined somebody near Champion's Hill, a division thereby arrived; the enemy's retreat was cut off. There were giants in those days; men more interested in the conformation of the continent and in the majesty of the Constitution than in the distribution of garden-seeds.

When I left Washington at the end of that July and started back for Missouri I said good-by to my uncle-grandfather, A. W., never to see him again. I have always been curious to know what prompted his parting gift to me. It was made with considerable impressment —a plate of copper about eight by ten inches in size, holding in bas-relief in the smallest agate type the full text of the Declaration of Independence set around a miniature circular medallion reproduction of Trumbull's picture of the signing of the document, and holding in an open margin of about an inch below the text almost microscopic but most accurate bas-reliefs of the autographic signatures to the document. A delicate raised moulding of the same copper framed the entire plate. This work of art must have been the combination of several mechanical and manual processes, and is evidently one of several copies. Perhaps there are elsewhere in the United States other men who possess this passport and by its virtue belong to my lodge.

When I got home I found that my father estimated more highly than could any boy of my age the events with which I had had such modest association. The more bitter rancor of the Civil War was gone; I had witnessed the long session of the Reconstruction Congress; the seceding states had come again into the Union.

I wonder if there is really a world spirit brooding over all, and if the seemingly disconnected events are more wisely associated than we surmise. A mystic that autumn walking through his quiet path at Concord, from which a specific fruit takes its name, wrote in his private diary not meant for publication but for his own refreshment only, "The grape is fruitful this year that men may be genial and gentle and make better laws."

V

GROWING UP IN ST. LOUIS

In October of 1871, three months after my return from Washington, the St. Louis papers were filled with mounting reports of the Chicago fire. Extras issued; the people of our older and larger sister city, moving leisurely in their dominantly Southern fashion, slowed down a little further to discuss the alarming news of destruction in the lake-shore town, and then waked up to a rescue as characteristic in its impulsive generosity and dash as a cavalry charge by Early. My interest was local and my contributions of curiosity principally obstructive.

One idol of our St. Louis boys was H. Clay Sexton, the head of the fire department. Sexton was the typical fire chief of that time: red leather helmet with white-and-gold escutcheon; flannel shirt; broad belt and buckle; trousers in high boots. He carried a silver speaking-trumpet presented by admiring citizens and insurance companies. But behind the picturesque make-up and inside the burly body there was a real man with a brain. Ahead of the newspapers the telegraph brought to this chief constant news of the fire's progress and the work of the fighters; and then suddenly the alarming report that the flames in the acres of wooden houses that made the Chicago of that period had got beyond control by the local department. The water system was unequal to the drain upon it. Engines able to work and men eager to do so were without hose enough or water.

Somewhere over a St. Louis engine-house Clay Sexton was working like a co-ordinating marshal, anticipating the ultimate call—his firemen, his material, his machines and hose reels, the broad-breasted, long-legged horses, the stock cars ready for them at the chutes, the flat cars with skids and blocks and ties for the machines, the fastest passenger engines, the ablest engineers all at readiness and attention. Then the call.

Daily express-train time from St. Louis to Chicago was nine hours. Clay Sexton, with his train of stock cars and flats, with nine fire-engines, reels, horses, and firemen, went up there in a fraction over five hours. The gallant feature was the readiness and the run. The work after arrival was prosaic enough, though vital. The visiting engines dipped their suckers into Lake Michigan and fed water by constant relay to the local men more familiar with the ground. The fact that two hundred and fifty persons met death in that fire and ninety-eight thousand were rendered destitute I heard many times. The oral message was tame, however, and fleeting in effect compared with the picture of the old General Lyon Number 4, our neighborhood engine, swinging out for her part in that enterprise of relief.

Another outstanding feature of those days is a noon-hour book of weekly newspaper illustrations of the Franco-Prussian War, none now definite but all making a vague mental frame and background somehow inseparably tied to an otherwise unconnected statement of General Phil Sheridan's. The general had seen somewhat of the French and German conduct in that war. As the result of his observations he thought that the German soldiers could, on equal terms, conquer those of any other nation except the American; that the American's superiority lay in initiative. Other soldiers seemed to act only upon command; the American also obeyed, but added to his obedience the individual activity of starting frontier fashion every night to intrench or to build or to do other essential things for himself without waiting for the word. In Sheridan's belief, political freedom and its responsibility had produced a better unit. Phil should have been at Château-Thierry. Perhaps he was. At any rate, his commendation of individual initiative gave it lasting importance in my small decisions.

I hope I may tell of another trifle that will amuse a million boys, perhaps mar a thousand jackknives and determine one or two embryo James McNeil Whistlers. Halfway up the steps to the Capitol dome in Washington there used to be a door, sometimes ajar, letting to a room wherein were the batteries of the simple electric system of 1870. If a boy dipped his knife-blade into one of the many jars of copperas solution that stood on the low shelves, and let the blade dry without wiping it, the steel in appearance turned to copper. When I philanthropically tried that on father's knife at a neighborhood battery in St. Louis my pride was tempered by his explaining that the color was acquired, not unlike many a later luster, by the copper's eating into the steel and to that slight degree dulling its edge.

With a tolerant wisdom that untiringly tried to steer my destructive impulses into productive channels, he took a clean blade on my knife, patiently rubbed it in different directions with a piece of lithograph crayon until it had a full coating of dense black grease over it; then with one point of a broken steel pen he had me write my name through the black field.

To this writing he had me apply a few drops of the

fluid and let it stand till the shining letters of steel bubbled into crusty copper. When, after two or three minutes, both crayon field and copper ashes were washed off the written name was there, etched into the blade of the owner's knife.

That year in the high school I bit a score of autographs on schoolmates' knives. Among the beneficiaries in the senior grade was a boy named Will Harlow. Harlow had literary ambitions, a hand-printing press with a six-by-eight chase, and possessed a curling, back-blown pompadour that should have had an Eton collar with it. He was a typical Rollo. Aware of my ability to do outline drawings, such as they were, and seeing in this litho-crayon-and-copperas combination a way to simple etching, Harlow proposed the publication of a magazine. Together we undertook it. The magazine was named *Scratches and Sketches*. We issued five numbers, I think, at irregular intervals, approximately a fortnight, with some paid ads—eight pages of short stories, verse and local comment, all furnished by Harlow, and three or four pages of alleged etchings made by me.

These etchings were done on zinc plates bought at the tinsmith's, laboriously burnished with a hand burnisher by me, coated with lithograph crayon, drawn with a pen and bitten with a saturated solution of copperas. The prints were made on superior paper as inserted etchings should be, at a professional shop, and then pasted into the letter-press stuff.

Subscriptions were few despite our courageous proclamations, but enough copies were issued to embroil Harlow and me. His playful comment upon our acquaintances in North St. Louis met with several demands for retractions and apologies. Some real enmities were established.

One bellicose warning delivered to me to transmit to
Harlow, who was keeping out of sight, as grown-up editors are said sometimes to do, carried a descriptive word
for our magazine that stuck. The complainant was one
William F. Putnam, a fine youngster, who became in
early manhood an influential miller in Cleveland, where
he had as a side line a stable of trotters, one of which in
fraternal recollection he called Gus Thomas. Billy in
our St. Louis days was a handy boy with his fists; a good,
clean, upstanding, handsome lad, looking the world in
the eye as I am sure he still does.

Holding my lapel after our second or third issue he
said, "You tell Mr. Harlow that if he ever mentions my
name in his damned almanac again," and so on.

I never recovered from "almanac." Nine years later
in the playlet of "Editha's Burglar" I had the burglar
refer by that term to the paper of Editha's papa, and I
spoke the burglar's line myself some four hundred consecutive times, but with no ultimate relief.

The rector of Grace Church in our district also found
some ethical flaws in our unripened policy. These and
similar incidents, and the expense account, decided Harlow's mother, who was a widow in modest circumstances,
to withhold further financial support. Some years later,
when for a partner's guaranty to a theatrical manager
the sheriff took our printing office in Kansas City and the
ill will of a weekly paper that languished therein, the
funeral wasn't nearly so depressing as our farewell to the
"almanac."

In writing one's recollections for publication the experienced advise cautious utterance concerning living
persons, and a news sense that shall choose as subjects
men already in the public notice. I am unaware of any

notorious interest in Frederick W. Ruckstull, though I am not ignorant of his claim upon Fame herself. Mr. Ruckstull, who to-day is still young and a few years my senior, is the author of that Victory monument in Jamaica, Long Island, against which from four directions sober motorists used to drive on foggy nights until the city authorities, after the manner of ruling minds in normal democracies, concluded that four iron lamp-posts were cheaper than numerous rosewood coffins, and thereupon set up a cordon of strong lights.

That Victory identifies Mr. Ruckstull for the sporting New Yorker. The tourists will recall his beautiful female nude of Evening in the American Hall of Sculpture in the New York Metropolitan Museum. Pennsylvania has his equestrian Hartranft in front of her capitol; St. Louis his decorative Mercury and eagle in Portland Place; and the Southland his cavalier, General Wade Hampton, and four or five Confederate monuments. Washington and other cities have from his studio other mature and classical performances.

Ruckstull, an Alsatian by birth, was brought to St. Louis by his parents at the age of two. Fifteen years later he attracted the attention of my father. Into the profound talk of this wise man of forty-three and that positive philosopher of seventeen I gradually won my way. My father respected me—either already or still; I had to prove it to Ruck. I wish to mark the boy Ruckstull now in this year 1871, when he first comes into my ken, because he still is there in 1921, the least deviating note in this revolving rug of life. Whenever after any sentimental vertigo I can first get my feet on the floor and partly retard the vibrating patterns in the carpet and on the wall-paper, as soon as I can locate Ruck amongst them the rest begin to orient and grow less vocal.

In appearance he is now as gray as Senator Lodge and as bald as Sir Oliver. When I first saw him he was black-haired, black-eyed, athletic. It may be that some slight changes have also taken place in my make-up. In 1894, when the caricature of him facing p. 326 was drawn in our guest-book at New Rochelle by lamplight, he was still dark-haired, but had lost some locks, as indicated.

Dear old Frederic Remington, who sat by on that Christmas night and looked on and laughed all through the execution, said: "You're not only getting a portrait of Ruck but of Ruck's opinion of Ruck."

Father had heard young Ruckstull speak in what now would be a Boy Scout debating society, but was then an Episcopal attempt to divert the gang spirit of our North St. Louis incorrigibles. Concurrently with this Grace Church Debating Society there was organized a Marion Place Dramatic Club, for which I wrote my first full evening's play, named "Alone." Our leading lady was Mittens Willet, who subsequently became the juvenile lead for John McCullough and the wife of Henry Aveling, a leading man of the late seventies. While Mittens was with us her leading man was Robert Cornell, earlier mentioned as a Jefferson City page boy. Cornell did not become the greatest real-estate agent in St. Louis, but he would have been an ornament to the American stage.

That year to the old Olympic Theatre in St. Louis—not the present spacious house on the same site, but a Douglas Jerrold type of playhouse, with pit, elevated horseshoe dress circle, family circle and gallery—there came a fine old character actor named John Dillon, husband of Louise Dillon of later fame. Dillon played *O'Cal-*

lahan in Bernard's play, "On His Last Legs," manifestly adapted from Molière's " Le Médecin Malgré Lui." Dillon's performance was a masterpiece of finish in technic, rich in byplay and pause, and as liberal an education in what added expression can give to mere lines as is Frank Bacon's "Lightnin'."

Both Cornell and Mittens, superior in serious work as they were, insisted that this comedy part of *O'Callahan* was for me. The play was even then a fifteen-cent yellow-back, available to any buyer. We gave it many times in parlors, in the parsonage, in the hall over Sturgeon Meat Market, and on the road. I shall recur to that compact little two-act farce; once when it pays a company out of Canada and once again when in ample disguise it rescues Mr. De Wolf Hopper from a temporary lapse and restores him to Broadway and opulence and matrimony. And when I do so perhaps such of my youngish readers as continue to trail may note a connection between those grown-up enterprises, running in the Hopper instance into a fortune, and these small beginnings, like learning in amateur days a good play well. They may infer that the money side of the return is of the lesser worth; that the big value is the self-expression obtained; that the debating society, the dramatic club, the singing school, the art class, the pursuits that invite brain to the finger-tips, and to become articulate, are the interests that make life eloquent. They may even come to have opinions and to believe that the amount of self-expression encouraged and protected in any country is the measure of liberty in that country.

I shall tell stories of these adolescent years only when the incidents are influential in later results, not simply important to me privately, but with some color of general

interest or possibility of serviceable application. All
children of parents in modest circumstances have their
trials. It is only the little rich who have the right to say
with a great American:

"Am I not too protected a person? Am I not de-
frauded of my best culture in the loss of those gymnastics
which manual labor and the emergencies of poverty constitute?"

Therefore, that I took a job to write and deliver freight
notices to St. Louis consignees for the Vandalia office,
and had to be in East St. Louis to receive waybills from
an incoming train at 7 A. M., is not important. Many
another boy of fourteen years, three miles from work,
to which he must go on foot, is called an hour and a half
before the shop time. If the call is 5.30 and the season
winter, he will dress by candle-light; the kitchen will
glow with the genial presence of the stove; and the smell
will be domestic and stimulating, to the capacity of the
family purse.

But not every boy will have a frozen Mississippi to
walk over, with the Great Dipper half upside down in
the sparkled sky, holding its long pointers to the North
Star on his left, and underneath on the massive ice an
endless train of coal-wagons with four horses to each,
crunching its way to the Illinois side, while off to the
right of his path the piers of the Eads Bridge, then to
be the eighth wonder of the world, are as yet only a few
feet above the river's level, their great dam breakwaters
prowed like battleships against the frozen current, whose
first flying charges of winter have piled like sculptured
foam, deck high, against these defenders. Half-way out
on that mile-wide ice was a barroom with a red-hot cannon stove, where a cold driver could run ahead of his

team, which would keep its place in the plodding train, and get a drink and a thaw and pick up his wagon as it went by.

To see the chance for that squatter barroom, to foresee that endless train of wagon traffic, and a day after the ice quit moving to be out there with boards and nails; with that degree of skill and attack and the sporting willingness to wager this lumber and labor and a stock of whiskey against the changing elements, indicated a vanguard imagination quite kindred to that which planned and set up the cantilever double span at St. Louis or devised and drove the jetties at the Delta below New Orleans. The difference was the trained engineer's mathematics that Eads possessed and that Kelly had never had the chance to get.

James Buchanan Eads, who died in the Bahamas in his sixty-seventh year, was born on the Indiana prairie in 1820. When he was forty-one he designed and built that Mississippi fleet of ironclads and monitors without which Grant's western campaign might not have been so successful. I met him when I was a young man and he about sixty. I remember his modest and gentle bearing, and the deference that the important men of that occasion instinctively paid him.

The years between that date and the earlier winter when I trudged twice each day past the looming piers of the Eads Bridge had been wonderfully filled with incident for me. To relate those incidents would be unpardonable trespass upon type and eyesight. An earlier writer recording his landlady's appeal to sympathy by a recital of her history says, "It was as though a grain of wheat that had been ground and bolted had tried to individualize itself."

But flour that grades up to the market sample might quite properly, if it could, say whether the way of grinding had been of the old upper-and-nether millstones kind or the roller system, and might with equal propriety claim the nutritive percentage obtained by the process.

I recently heard a Yale professor refer to newspapers as destructive of thought. He had in mind the gossipy hours spent in their reading, and the dissipation of nearly all serious attention on the part of those addicted to them. Some day an equal censor may attack the weeklies, and if we guilty contributors and readers can here and there point to a paragraph of right intent and perhaps helpful issue, we may quit the field retreating in good order and not in panic rout.

Will it not be an orderly method if, reporting myself a man at nineteen and omitting the hurtful things, I tell those physical experiences that built a margin of muscular gain; and if, eliminating the wasteful lures and attractions, I recount the better mental interests that won out for such equipment as has served in a profession that is without curriculum or diploma; and if I can find the skill to do so without offending, may I not imply or hint the developing factors in that third element of human tissue which we call spiritual?

Somebody said that the military victories of England were won on the cricket field. I believe a right American soldier is as much better than a similar English soldier of equal training and experience as baseball is better than cricket. I wish some alchemy could give us the percentage of baseball that was in the Argonne victories. I think the training that equips a boy on the diamond, with all the bases filled, to pick up a batted grounder and without a fraction of a second's wait to put it to the right spot is as fine a preparation for the market, the bar, the pulpit, the forum, the surgical clinic—especially the surgical clinic—and the battle-field as any physical exercise in the world; and yet if I had to choose as one who knew both between baseball and boxing I'd tell my boy to box—and I'm writing these recollections for boys. I hope the girls, too, will like them, but I know a good deal less about girls. With the fellows past forty—yes, say past thirty—I don't expect to change a vote. Mr. Franklin Haven Sargent, president of the American Academy of Dramatic Arts, asked me some years ago to suggest any additional course for his pupils.

I said, "Teach them to box."

Mr. Sargent was then past thirty. Before I offered that advice I had found in several years of professional rehearsals that men and women, self-conscious on the stage, were so principally on account of their hands. There is the same embarrassment in some public speakers. The boxer is free from that; to see his hand in front of him in an instinctive gesture does not fill him with sudden fear, and if the hand as placed stands for some mental attitude he is at ease in leaving it there as long as he asks attention to that fact. The most graceful man in the use of his hands on the stage thirty years ago was Maurice Barrymore, who had been the champion amateur boxer of England. One of the most graceful to-day is Eddie Foy, another boxer. I have never in many talks with William Faversham mentioned the subject, but I am confident that he was a skilful boxer in his younger days.

My father was a boxer, and despite mother's most feminine protests he began to teach me the art when he had to sit on a low chair to make my level. After I was fourteen there was never a time when I was not at least part owner of a set of boxing gloves. Father's persistence in teaching me may seem trivial, but will it take on value if I can show a valid connection between it and the important diplomatic communications of others? I fancy I shall do that a little later.

There were two youngsters with whom I learned much in sparring. The first and most constant one was Charles A. Beamer, now a merchant in St. Louis and a man active in high Masonic circles. Charley had a very effective right, and two or three times a week used to leave my face looking like an August sunset. But better than his right was his great good humor, and I learned from him as much as from all others that the control of one's temper, a prevailing good-nature, was one object of every bout.

From the Vandalia office when I was fourteen and the St. Louis Transfer Company when I was fifteen years of age, I went to the old St. Louis, Kansas City, and Northern Railroad at sixteen. The work was principally on the freight platforms and in the freight-yard as a clerk. The platform men, the switchmen, the engineers and firemen of that period were almost exclusively Irish. The play of our resting intervals was boxing. As I developed and grew in the exercise my opponents were truckmen, trainmen, coal-shovellers, and mechanics— none of them spoiled by pampering. In that K. C. & N. yard was the second lad I refer to, one Ollie Crockett, as handsome and as continually smiling as a lithograph of Douglas Fairbanks.

Once in the switch shanty in my nineteenth year this debonair youngster, half a head shorter than myself, knocked me out with an eight-ounce glove. A report of it can be defended as a reply to the gentlefolk who decry the brutality of the sport. On that occasion nothing described my own sensation so accurately as a line in the George Ade pugilistic Fable in Slang, that "somebody turned off the daylight." When I came to I was looking into Crockett's smiling face and wondering only what had interrupted our fun.

In later years and fuller manhood I had some professional mates. I never got any medals, but I received consoling compliments. Bob Farrell, a lightweight who had fought a couple of good old-time bare-knuckle matches with Billy Edwards, the champion whom the old Hoffman House patrons will remember, was among the number. Let me join these references pertinently. One night after he had lost the championship to Fitzsimmons, Jim Corbett was one of fifty guests at a dinner to Mr. Otis Skinner in a Chicago hotel. Both he and I had been called upon and had spoken and Corbett had temporarily taken a seat next to Otis for a laughing exchange with him.

Seeing the intimacy of the two men, I took the same chair when Corbett left it and expressed to Otis my admiration for Corbett's talk. I finished my comment by saying with stage-manager bumptiousness, "I could make a speaker of that fellow."

Mr. Skinner laughed more immoderately at this than either its conceit or its improbability called for, and then explained that Corbett had come there the moment before to say of me, "I could make a fighter of that fellow."

Mr. Corbett was unaware both of my stale years and my timidity; but that my estimate of him was right his finished and artistic ability as a public speaker to-day is proof.

Professional baseball of the middle seventies differed materially from that of to-day. It was not less rigorous or less athletic; in some respects it was more so. The old-fashioned pitched ball, which had more speed than would be believed by one who had not seen the professional pitcher deliver it, was giving way to the underhand throw, which was probably quite as fast as the best delivery now. No catcher, however, wore a padded glove or mask. Little red-haired Miller, the first catcher of the St. Louis Browns, wore on his left hand an ordinary buckskin glove with the fingers cut off; his right hand was bare. His face had no protection; there was no padding over his body or guards over his shins. During the second season, facing Bradley, he introduced the use of a rubber wedge about the size of a domino, which he held between his teeth and let protrude slightly from his lips. This was suggested by a catcher on another nine having had the dental processes broken by a foul tip, and taken by the Harvard College catcher, Horatio S. White, later dean of the university.

In those days a batter had the right to call for a high or a low ball, and the pitcher was required to put it above or below his waist, according to his demand. Moreover, a pitcher once in the box went through the nine innings, or if changed was changed for some other member of the nine whom he replaced in his position from the in or out field. Generally a third baseman or a fielder was engaged for his ability as a change-pitcher. One or two substitutes attended the game, but they went in only when a man was put out by a physical injury, as they come in now in a football game.

We were very proud of our St. Louis Browns, and equally jealous of the Chicago White Sox. One never gets this partisanship out of the blood. Only last Sunday the sculptor, Ruckstull, now sixty-eight, and sunk deep in the hollow of a library leather chair from which he was freely reading Montaigne's archaic French, paused at some mention of memory and said: "What a heaven-sent gift a good memory is!" And then, with an accusing challenge, "Can you name the whole nine of the first St. Louis league team when they won that first series from Chicago in 1874?"

And trying to beat each other to it, we alternated and interfered and reached a flushed crescendo in a run of competing explosions, telling: "Bradley, pitch; Miller, catch; Dehlman, Bannon, Hogue on bases; Dickey Pierce at short; and in the field? Cuthbert, Chapman, and—and Haight."

But we couldn't remember Chicago. We remembered the whiskers on some of those Lake Front athletes, as luxuriant as those now worn only by the Cough Drop Brothers. And all the time the sculptor was commanding attention with a hand on which the hypnotic feature was an ossified contusion of the first phalange of the little finger, pitched to him on our old railroad nine of that epoch.

A third gymnastic field is one to be noted but not recommended. In the seven years amidst the freight-cars and switch engines one acquires the average brake-man's ability to get on and off a moving train. Twenty years after I had left the service I was still annoyed if a street-car stopped or even checked its speed to let me either board or leave it, and then one day in New York as a Broadway car passed the Empire Theatre, which was my destination, I stepped from its platform onto the wet asphalt as gracefully as the president of the conductors' brotherhood could do it, slipped to a sitting posture, ruined a pair of fifteen-dollar trousers, and broke my record. After thirty-four it's a good plan to watch your step. Right here I could possibly say something analogous about political platforms, but the times are hard enough as it is.

VI

ARTS AND THE THEATRE

My interests and ambitions were threefold—poetry, painting, and the theatre. Let us try to agree about poetry. Poetry is the feeling that there is soul behind all form; such feeling is not religion, but it is the source of religion. The difference between poetry and fact is like a sailor's difference between the North Star and lighthouses. The lighthouse marks the irregular and charted coast. The North Star fixes a permanent direction. Now wait a minute! You boy in Cheyenne or Manistee or Talladega, and you men with blue pencils, I'm trying to tell something; nothing too highbrow for a boy that is allowed to sit up after supper—and the something is useful.

A capacity for poetic feeling is the receiving end for all those messages throughout life that the recurring seasons, the grass and leaves, the winds and clouds, the stars, the nostril-dilating odors of the fields, the hum of insects and the sound of ocean waves are trying to get through to us. The fogs of the rough surfaces on which we ride obscure and hide the polar direction of the poetic call, and we move along the prudent shore line and soundings of supply and demand and cent per cent, but the refreshing reaches are when the star is now and then in sight.

This occasional glimpse through the clouds, which is poetry, has been appraised by William James, our de-

lightful philosopher. It is worth getting a little closer
to the lamp; reading very carefully; pausing to look up
at the framed photograph of mother and father when
they were first married; and then slowly reading again.
It is from his chapter on the "Mystical Faculty":

"Most of us can remember the strangely moving power
of passages in certain poems read when we were young,
irrational doorways as they were through which the mystery of fact, the wildness and the pang of life, stole into
our hearts and thrilled them. The words have now perhaps become mere polished surfaces for us; but lyric
poetry and music are alive and significant only in proportion as they fetch these vague vistas of a life continuous
with our own, beckoning and inviting, yet ever eluding
our pursuit. We are alive or dead to the eternal inner
message of the arts according as we have kept or lost
this mystical susceptibility."

During the years leading to and including my nineteenth I not only read poetry; I learned it by rote when
it appealed to me, and I recited it. There is no wish to
compete with Jean Jacques Rousseau in self-abasement,
but I did recite it, in public, at church festivals and the
like. I don't defend the term "festivals," but the historic fact is that they were so called. Once when my
friend James Whitcomb Riley and Bill Nye were jointly
lecturing, Riley, who was nervous at the game, peeped
through the curtain before beginning in a little Minnesota
town, and then hurried to Nye, who was still adjusting
his white tie in the dressing-room.

"Bill!" he exclaimed. "There are only about twenty
people in the house!"

"I can't understand that," Nye answered. "We've
never been here before."

And now with the confession that I recited on these church occasions I want to plead that I was paid to do so, and that sometimes I got return dates.

Noting this disposition to memorize verses, my father said to me, "What you fill your head with in that fashion now will stay with you for a long while. It is a good plan to select the best."

I tried to keep his advice in view. The old McGuffey School Readers, it seems to me, were well-chosen selections. They ranged from Shakespeare to Patrick Henry and Webster, and included such sonorous stuff as Macaulay's and such gentleness as Whittier's. In the full editions of the poets I devoured Tom Moore, Scott, Burns, Longfellow, Bryant, Tennyson, Keats, and others. The inference might be that this crowded out the trash, but it didn't. Nothing is so omnivorous as the mind of a growing boy bitten with the theatre and romance.

Before we quit the subject of poetry I want to say to those who admired "Ivanhoe" and "Marmion," and other thrilling things by their author that Sir Walter Scott once said nothing had so influenced him throughout his life as four lines of verse in a poem called "Cumnor Hall," by William Julius Mickle, a Scot, who died when Walter was seventeen years old.

> "The dews of summer night did fall,
> The moon (sweet regent of the sky)
> Silver'd the walls of Cumnor Hall,
> And many an oak that grew thereby."

For Walter Scott those words never became mere polished surfaces, but remained always alive and held their strangely moving and beckoning power. "And many an oak that grew thereby." Change that line to

"And twenty oaks that grew thereby," and see how the fact of the definite numeral clips the wings of your invited fancy. That suggestion is to the boy and girl. Dear papa, whom the angels must excuse because he is so busy that he cannot leave the store, is asked to remember the regretful words of that successful scientist, Charles Darwin, who, looking back in his seventieth year, said

If I had my life to live again I would have made a rule to read some poetry and listen to some music at least once every week; for perhaps the parts of my brain now atrophied would thus have been kept alive through use. The loss of these tastes is a loss of happiness and may possibly be injurious to the intellect and more probably to the moral character, by enfeebling the emotional part of our nature.

Some great editors have read those lines of Darwin, and grown thoughtful about them.

In my wish to write for the theatre, my father thought I would meet with fewer obstacles in the degree that I knew the theatre itself behind the curtain. I saw no betraying twinkle in his eye as he talked to me about it, but he was a person of cultivated self-control. He reminded me quite seriously how Shakespeare had been an actor, and had begun to write his plays from that standpoint. He told me of Molière and of others that I have forgotten, but particularly of Boucicault, so that he built up a fair determination in my mind to get all the experience I could. In the absence of a professional association he approved of the amateur work, always cautioning me that it would have some features that would have to be unlearned.

Our St. Louis amateur theatricals soon took on a semiprofessional tone. Those were the days of the Jay Gould ownership of railroads. The enginemen were already organized in discontent; the trainmen were following their example. The managements were anxious and conciliatory. So whenever the conductors, looking for ways and means, invited our club to play for their "benefits" at Moberly, the headquarters of our division, the superintendent promptly passed our little company; some other influence fixed us with the Pullman people. Great occasions, those, with all expenses paid; a full house secured by the tickets the trainmen sold weeks ahead; the local volunteer band at the depot when we arrived; the big posters on the opera-house walls; the selected orchestra that had just doubled in brass; and in front every shopkeeper, barber, saloonist, hotelkeeper, attorney, and family doctor who wanted to hold his railroad clientèle, each with his lady. Add to that a brave representation from the local fire department in uniforms; two policemen and the waitresses from the hotel, all crowded into that second-story uncushioned auditorium, impatient for the curtain to ring up, and you have a combination equalled only when the state standards mass round a national nomination to make it unanimous.

The freight agent at St. Louis, Captain P. Flanigan, who had to deplete his force of some twenty clerks for the day by excusing Matt Cooper, Fred Naylor, and me for each of these rural assaults, was an able transportation man who had learned his business on the Mississippi. He was of quite the better class of river captain, considerably travelled and by no means unread.

Matt Cooper had a tracing department shut off from the main office. The captain unfailingly visited him the day after such a trip and heard every detail of it. I found

Cooper in a gale of laughter after one such visit.   He closed the door to impart the joke to me in confidence. The cue had been Cooper's narrative of the play of which I was the author.

The proud captain had taken it seriously and his side-splitting line—from Cooper's view-point, not from mine —was "Why, if Gus can write that he may some day be as big a dramatist as Boucicault."   Cooper had controlled his mirth till the captain left the room, and now he was pounding me on the back to force me to see it.

The first steady job I got in New York was twelve years later, when A. M. Palmer at the Madison Square Theatre engaged me to take the place of Mr. Dion Boucicault, who wished to retire.   I tell it now in no prideful flush whatever, but mainly in a gentle retrospect of dear old P. F., and partly for its associative value: in the beginning, my first boyish writing, a frank forage on Boucicault's *Rip;* in the middle field that ridicule that Cooper, of course, passed out for me to our little company; and the finish—Boucicault's desk.

It was during this period that I got my first long coat. There is nothing now extant by which with one indication it can be pictured.   It was not so long as a Prince Albert, nor so closely joined below the waist; not so cutaway as the English morning coat of recent years, but something between the two.   Fashion dictated that it should be made of what then was known as basket-cloth, a prominent weave looking like a diminutive checkerboard with squares of one-half-inch.   The material was black, and when made-up was bound with the broadest possible braid.   With its arrival the women of the household thought I was entitled to an evening at a theatre in company with some nice girl.   My preference was for a piquant young person of about fourteen years of age named Dickey B——. It had been an unexpressed fear of my mother's that I would so choose. Dickey was a bit the neighborhood soubrette in her way. She had an elder sister, neither so good-looking nor so lively, whose name I think was Louise. I don't remember inviting Louise to go with me. That was arranged through some conferences between the families; all now confused in my memory perhaps because I wasn't aware of them. No ladies went into the parquet of those days; I bought two seats for a dollar each to the old Olympic dress circle, which was sufficiently lifted at centre to allow patrons of the parquet to pass through the gangway beneath it. There was only one opposition theatre so the choice was not wide, and the other attraction was a burlesque of some kind to which a very young man with his girl couldn't go. I can remember no occasion on which my embarrassment was so great as when I sat in that thin audience, the only man in the front row of a dinky dress circle, and saw a performance of the serious history of "King John." The poor girl and I tried to make conversation. I think she was depressed by the fact that she had been wished onto me. I was depressed by the same belief, and the much more overshadowing tragedy of my basket-cloth coat which looked well in front of the tailor's mirror but came up unpleasantly behind the collar when I sat down; and persons looked at us in the street-cars on the trips both ways. It was many years before I was able properly to assess the memory of that evening. It gradually turned from bitterness to indifference and then to a comic recital, and as time went on to a veritable treasure, as I found I was one of the very few Americans who had seen a performance of "King

John," by Junius Brutus Booth, the elder brother of
Edwin, with his new wife Agnes Booth playing *Constance*,
and that sterling young actor of those days, Joseph
Wheelock, playing *Faulconridge*.   I never met Junius
Brutus Booth, but his son, Sydney, and I are friends.
Mrs. Agnes Booth and I worked in more than one play,
and on her last appearance in Boston, in 1892, in a one-
act sketch called "After Thoughts" which I had written
for her and Ed Bell of the Madison Square Theatre, I
was her leading man.   Joseph Wheelock I came to know
very well and rehearsed both him and later his son,
Joseph Wheelock, Jr., now both dead.

Those were the transition days in the professional
theatre.   The local stock company engaged to support
the visiting stars was gradually making place for the
visits of entire organizations.   A local company might
work three or four weeks with as many different stars,
and then be laid off a week while Shook and Palmer or
Augustin Daly came in with a full cast for some successful play from New York; or Tony Pastor brought a full
variety company.   Some stars came with one or two
supporting actors for the second rôles and filled the remaining parts from the resident stock.   The uncertainty
of such a broken season quickly weakened the local companies in both ability and number, so that at times in
St. Louis the house manager had to wire a hurry call to
Chicago or Cincinnati or in an extremity use even some
available amateur.

My first professional calls were of that origin, and
were soul-stirring occasions.   I have in later years, as
have other authors—for themselves—gone on in some
New York emergency in some play of my own to replace
Maurice Barrymore or other actor of note in a stellar

green whiskers and egg-sized lumps raised on bald heads by cave-man shillalahs; after which the Irishman in turn gave way to the stage Jew.

The most popular Jewish character actor of those days was M. B. Curtis, who sprang into sudden popularity in a drummer-salesman character called *Samuel of Posen.* This play had the same progressive history of commercial struggle that one gets glimpses of in "The Auctioneer" and "Potash and Perlmutter," which play and dramatization were both made by that talented Jewish author, the late Charles Klein, and in which respectively appeared David Warfield, Barney Bernard, and Alexander Carr. The rise of Curtis financially was a phenomenon of that time. The play had been done in the East, and when it came to St. Louis its arrival was heralded by lithographs which showed Curtis as *Samuel of Posen* mounted on a racing horse taking hurdles over the field. These hurdles grew in the number of bars as the horse progressed. Each hurdle had on it the name of the city, with the bars carrying the advertisement of the gross receipts of the play. We had often had in plays the Jewish character, both sinister and comic, but aside from the classical Jews, as *Shylock* and the *Jew of Malta,* I do not recall the Jew as being a dominating character of a play before that. Following *Samuel of Posen,* there was an invasion of Jewish impersonations. This character bids fair to continue his comic tenure, because his present exponent, engaged by a Jewish manager, is himself Jewish, and has his material furnished by observant male and female writers of his race.

To go back just a little farther in the period we are considering: The first time I ever sat in a dress circle without my father was when my boy pal, Charley

Beamer, bought the tickets. The attraction was Lydia Thompson's "British Blondes." We were in the front row of that horseshoe as one would be to-day if on a depressed balcony. The burning, the unforgetable feature of that Christmas matinée was the appearance of six girls in tights. To-day I should know it was a bum-front scene with two baby spots arranged to let the carpenters set the stage behind. Then it was an intoxicating illusion with calcium lights that never were on land or sea. Three of those robust ladies I have forgotten, but Lydia Thompson, Pauline Markham, and Eliza Weathersby I remember.

In the matter of stage effect that sextet of substantial femininity in a double cross current of prismatic splendor is my lost chord. Now and then at Easthampton, with the motor headlight making a profiled tunnel through a lane of pines at 2 A. M., there has been a heart-throb of a former incarnation that I have been able to connote as that Christmas matinée, but it was ephemeral, tantalizing, fugitive, and mocking. The perfect ecstasy of that holiday disclosure will never come again. Lydia Thompson was playing *Robinson Crusoe* in a ballet skirt and shako of snow-white goatskin, the rest of her costume, skin-white tights of silk.

The man *Friday* was the wonderful Harry Becket, whose picture as one of its first officers now hangs in the Lambs Club, New York. *Friday* was in brown. He carried a large flappy valise and a dictionary, which, at every moment of linguistic doubt, he threw himself on his stomach and consulted violently. Each coveted stage prop was picked up, and with a repeated "put it in de bag" dropped into that insatiable receptacle. The climax came with the arrival of the rescue ship, a stately frigate quite satisfying in stage perspective as it rode into view on the third set water cut in profile. *Crusoe* was lyrically happy at the arrived relief; *Friday* studied the distant, full-rigged boat a moment and then, striding by easy hurdles over the interposing waves, said "Put it in de bag," and did so. Is there such wholesome stage fun anywhere?

It will be impressive and perhaps valuable to set the stage of that earlier amateur and professional environment. Let us rapid-living, swiftly going, flying people of to-day try to realize that then there was not in all the world a telephone or electric light or trolley-car or automobile; not even a bicycle had yet been evolved or invented. There had been the velocipede, a tandem two-wheel device with a saddle on which one wearing side-whiskers could sit in a high silk hat and other singular garments and propel himself by pushing along the ground with his feet and then lifting them for a glide of a rod or two; but nothing speedier or more automatic. There were no typewriters. The newest illumination was coal-gas; the quickest local communication was a longhand letter sent by a boy. All watches wound with a key; the stem-winder was not yet offered or introduced in our section. But goldsmiths were not idle; each proper shop tempted the ultra-fashionable by a tray of gold toothpicks.

These fascinating implements, in a variety of decorations, some even jewelled, were composed of a thin cylinder of precious metal three-quarters the length of a modern cigarette and half the diameter, from which by turning the base of the tube one could cause to emerge a piston fitted with a thin spearhead of gold, designed to dislodge stubborn remnants of food from dental inter-

vals. After such an interesting service the harpoon, on
its disappearing gun carriage, moved into the cylinder
again and the implement was replaced in the right-hand
vest pocket. And for that meal, as they say in diplo-
macy, the incident was closed.

Occasionally a young man in some older and more
established family inherited one of these toilet acces-
sories.

At the Centennial Exhibition in Philadelphia in 1876
the Bell telephone was regarded as a toy. Visitors permitted to listen to the voice of a friend speaking from
the next room examined the legs of the table to find the
tube which they were sure Mr. Bell had concealed to
convey the sound. The first arc light in St. Louis was
a few years later. This was a spitting and sparking
and blinding globe suspended outside of a Budweiser
beer bottler's on Sixth Street near Locust, and pedes-
trians were astonished at the magic silhouettes of themselves that it cast on the pavement. Street-car parties
were organized like the rubberneck auto deputations of
to-day to ride down-town and view this wonder. In-
candescent lamps came later still.

All that was but five and forty years ago. Statesmen,
ministers of the gospel, bankers, and boys all wore boots,
the leather legs of which reached halfway to the knees,
either under or outside the trousers. Lincoln, Johnson,
Grant, Hayes, and Oom Paul were inaugurated in such
gun-cases. Before sending trousers home, the tailor or
merchant of the ready-made faithfully obligated himself
to press out the creases down the front now regarded as
so desirable by the well-dressed. The well-to-do river-
men, the romantic survivals from the Jack Hamlin
period of Bret Harte, had soft-bosom shirts with wide

plaits fastened by gold or jewelled buttons held in a set by a threadlike chain of gold, festooning from stud to stud outside the shirt-bosom. The average man, however, had his shirt buttoning down the back to permit an unbroken expanse of impenetrable front, garnished by one large diamond mounted on a substantial crown of gold, and anchored to this linoleum breastplate by a tight-wormed spiral of the same metal. Tom Nast's old cartoons of Bill Tweed show that Tammany chieftain wearing one of these sparklers. Hotel clerks and negro minstrels competed and specialized in this single shirt-stud adornment. That the fashion had some intellectual approval is indicated by a comment of Colonel Robert Ingersoll when in 1880 our city went Republican while the State had gone Democratic.

He said, "St. Louis is a diamond stud on a dirty shirt."

Let me make now one inclusive declaration of independence in belief. I wish to write through these memoirs now and then of spiritism, clairvoyance, telepathy, and other psychic phenomena; and in order to forestall any apprehension on the part of those at all gun-shy on these subjects, to say that I am not a spiritist, although possessed of a very avid curiosity on all that authoritatively relates to spiritism. I am not a hypnotist, but am intensely interested in the phenomena of hypnotism. I have no second sight, no clairvoyance, no abnormal or supernormal powers of any nature; and yet I think that perhaps more than the average man I have been in contact with *soi-disant* possessors of such powers.

My father was one of the sanest and best-balanced men I ever saw. He had had many chances to observe the table tippings, rappings, levitations, and the like of spiritists. He was reluctant to characterize all of it as fraud and equally unwilling to accept it as any demonstration from the so-called dead. The most experienced investigator of this class of phenomena that I personally know, outside of those actively interested in the work for psychical-research societies, is my present friend, Hamlin Garland. Mr. Garland conducted a series of investigations some years ago for *Everybody's Magazine*, and wrote one book upon the subject, masquerading as a novel, under the title of "The Tyranny of the Dark." Garland has seen and experimented with the so-called materializations of spiritism. If I remember rightly, he thinks the power may be but an undeveloped psychical attribute of the race; that the so-called materializations are psychically induced emanations from the operator's own body, and that it is all a part of what we might call unexplored biology.

Between the years of my father's cautious dictum and the equally conservative conclusions of Mr. Garland I have read publications of the psychical-research societies of both England and America, talked extensively with the late Doctor Hyslop, and had been asked by him to write of some personal observations. That I never did so was due to a congenital disposition to procrastinate. My mother shared my father's agnostic attitude, although surrounded by an atmosphere of the belief. My dear old grandmother, of whom I have written somewhat playfully but with great reverence, had no doubts on the subject. As a young woman she had been rebuked for her opinions by her friend, Archbishop Purcell, who took the safe and wholesome attitude of the Catholic Church that the whole subject was an excellent thing for the simple layman to avoid. Personally, grandmother overrode this advice; she firmly believed that she was in communication with a spirit world. This was not an obtrusive or offensive or disquieting position with her, because she seldom talked of it. But there were occasions at home, some half-dozen notable instances, when, with sickness somewhere in the brood of children and the puzzled doctors in conference disagreeing, the old lady had not hesitated to give a definitive diagnosis of the trouble and prescribe a remedy. This she did with all the solemnity of a traditional oracle, quietly seated in her chair, but with none of the described theatricality of the cult except that she closed her eyes.

On those remembered occasions there are no data for verifying her diagnoses; but her recommended remedies were completely curative, and although these were resorted to as a rule without my father's consent, and sometimes against his opposition, their unbroken record of successes gradually won his silence and apparently his respect. This therapeutic assumption of grandmother's was her only spiritistic claim. She had no visions or pretended auditions; she told no fortunes; she attended no church or circle of spiritists; nor had she with their professed believers any relations whatever of which I ever knew. Years after the last of A. W.'s letters she announced one day that he was dead. To use her own words, she "just received a feeling of it." We had then no acceptable way to verify her conviction. On my last visit to St. Louis during her life, when in her eighty-fourth year, she was but a shadow of the substantial and militant grandmother of the Civil War period, she held my hands as I bade her good-by for my return trip to New York, and she talked of her approaching departure to another world with the serenity of Socrates.

I know how one's prudent friends advise against any

discrediting admissions of this kind. Our greatest men
are not free from fear of the ridicule it risks. Colonel
Henry Watterson once told me that, taking Joseph Jefferson to a dinner in Washington City which he was giving to John G. Carlisle, then Speaker of the House, and
Chief Justice Fuller of the Supreme Court, and knowing
as he did Jefferson's predilection for all things spiritistic,
he had felt it wise to caution Joe against showing that
side of his credulity in the company that evening. He
had explained that Carlisle was a hard-headed lawyer,
trained in the presentation of evidence and not given to
any vagaries unsupported by material testimony; and
Chief Justice Fuller, of the Supreme Court of the United
States, was eminently of the type of mind that his position required, and that any spiritistic statements would
probably be prejudicial.

The dinner had hardly started; the rain outside induced a serious atmosphere. Something was said that
made an easy approach to the subject, when Carlisle
himself introduced the question of spiritism, supporting
it by a most extravagant story of his own experience.
When Carlisle finished, Chief Justice Fuller followed
with something from his recollections that topped the
Carlisle story.

Colonel Watterson relates, "I then threw up my hands
and said, 'Joe, the bars are down.'"

On the day that I was dictating my recollections of
this story, in September, 1921, I had a telephone communication from a mutual friend telling me that Colonel
Watterson was confined to his room with a slight attack
of bronchitis in the Prince George Hotel in New York.
I went to see him. Our friendship has existed since 1888.
I am happy to say that I found Colonel Watterson's

confinement to his room more cautionary than imperative. In our rambling talk I reverted to this story of
Jefferson, and Colonel Watterson verified my recollections of it.

I told him that I was writing it in a contribution to a
paper, and said, "Why wasn't that in your own fine
book?"

He said: "There was so much to tell that most of that
kind of stuff was crowded out; and besides, my dignity
sat on my pen."

Perhaps by this implication, stimulating or restrain-
ing, according to one's interpretation, dignity should
drag a little here. But I feel the need, which Colonel
Watterson did not have, of laying a foundation for some
fuller expressions on the subject later on, all of them
relating to experiences that culminated as far as I believed the theatre then permitted an intelligent summary in my play "The Witching Hour." Besides, a
very wise counsellor once said: "We should be generous
even of our dignity." And so, with what I hope was a
cautious approach to the subject, and this explanation
serving as a rear-guard, I leave my psychical preparations
temporarily between them.

My interest and practice in drawing were advanced
by some experience nearly every day. Almost mechanically I filled the margins of car reports and chance newspapers with pencil sketches. During some winter nights,
as late as two or three in the morning, huddled in the
switch shanty in the railroad yard, waiting for the
double-decked hog trains that were arriving at half-
hour intervals, we used to get fun out of chalk or charcoal caricatures of some member of the crew, drawn on
the walls of the dismantled box-car that served as our

refuge. Now and then a switchman of undeveloped taste would intrust to me a photograph to be enlarged in crayon.

It may be because we young men were so much in the midst of it that I got the idea that there was a considerable art interest in St. Louis at that period. Pictures of three painters whose reputations led and which in later years I had a chance to see again bear out the estimate in which they then were held. James M. Tracy, a painter of landscapes and animals, came afterward to New York, and made a considerable stir with his pictures of hunting dogs in the field. There was a time when the important magazines were glad to reproduce these canvases. J. R. Meeker, a man of heroic mould physically, had made a study of Southern landscape with its hazy atmosphere, hanging moss, and brooding cranes. Few men before or since have been so able to get the spirit of the hazy regions of Pontchartrain. W. S. Marple handled landscape bits with the affection and delicacy if not the superlative skill that mark the gentlewomen that our present Thomas Dewing paints. About these three men were a score of lesser popularity, with here and there in the number men of equal craftsmanship. Carl Gutherz was a Munich graduate, as was also Paul Harney.

At the Washington University there was a completely equipped and well-organized art school, founded by that administrator of international fame, Professor Halsey C. Ives, who later directed the art exhibit of the World's Fair in Chicago. In one of the university departments was the usual life class, and for the benefit of young men who were obliged to work in the day some of the sessions were held at night. In North St. Louis a little nucleus met in the rooms of the brothers, George and Edward Snell. A third companion there was the late Sylvester Rawling, who subsequently became an important member of the editorial staff of the New York *World* and an authority upon music.

Four or five of us used to come together once or twice a week immediately after supper at George Snell's rooms, and start for our walk of two miles to the Washington University for the night class, and when that was over foot it home. We came back through the streets of sleeping and shuttered houses toward midnight, laughing and singing, as we knew from the stories of our elders the students laughed and sang in the Latin Quarter.

Gutherz, one of the teachers in the life class, was a master draftsman. Howard Kretchmar, the sculptor, lectured on the skeleton and the muscular structures, and made them vastly interesting. I recall the astonishment with which I learned that a piece of sculpture in the making was built up and not chiselled out of some solid mass. This fact, so familiar to us older ones, now comes as a helpful surprise to most beginners in art. I recently saw a friend's wife who has considerable talent for modelling struggling to obtain a form by cutting clay from a sufficiently inclusive mass. She is a lady of thirty-two and fair general information, yet she came with astonishment to know that the sculptor in making a draped figure sets up first the frame that somewhat simulates the skeleton, and adds a sufficient outline to approximate a nude before he puts over the final drapery.

About that time, encouraged by the three old artists first mentioned, we organized a sketch club in St. Louis with some thirty active members. I have been in many organizations since then, from labor-unions to academies;

but none for sheer good fun, for emulation, for real progress, for general education, and for generosity has equalled that old St. Louis Sketch Club. We met twice a month, each member bringing in a sketch upon a subject announced at the preceding meeting. The host of the night obligated himself to furnish some sandwiches and a keg of beer, and became the owner of the sketches.

The principal art firm of the city gave us a rear gallery in which to have our fortnightly gathering, where the sketches were tacked up on the wall or placed upon proper pedestals, seriously discussed by all, constructively criticised by the men competent to judge them, and always applauded when at all deserving. When we had talked ourselves out about the exhibition, sandwiches were opened up, the beer keg was tapped. Kretchmar, Meeker, or some other positive personality presided, with the beer mallet as a gavel, and there was such impromptu entertainment as the vivacious spirits of our little artistic membership could give. The next day our commercial house had the place cleaned up; the art men on the local newspapers came in and wrote helpfully of the exhibition and for a week following it was open to the public.

The entertaining character of our meetings gradually drew privileged citizens, and after a while it was our custom to have as special guests, who came in after the play was over, visiting actors of distinction. I made at such meetings my first acquaintance with Robson, Crane, Raymond, Wyndham, Florence, and other men. On her first visit to St. Louis, when she brought with her own art works, her little canvases and bronzes, the reception to Sarah Bernhardt was under our auspices, and her works were exhibited in connection with our own. We had a special meeting in the afternnon for the divine Sarah. She stood in the salon of our little club to receive three or four hundred honored with invitations. I remember her little flat but jaunty and beplumed hat of that period, set high on her shapely head, and her tight-fitting gown of purple velvet, more like a riding-habit than any other style that would in a word describe it.

Local interest in this little organization grew. Philanthropic and discriminating men picked from our membership the boys they thought capable of a career. George Snell went as the protégé of a syndicate to Paris. A year or two later Ruckstull followed. About the same time Will H. Howe, the eminent cattle-painter, who now lives at Bronxville, where he may show his three medals that make him *hors concours* in the National Salon of France, and who wears in his lapel the red ribbon of the Legion of Honor, was another.

George Snell and Rawlings both are gone; a younger brother, Henry Bayley Snell, with medals from Philadelphia and Paris, the Buffalo and St. Louis expositions, and from Panama, is now president of the New York Water Color Club. One distinguished patron of art and an honorary member of this sketch club was Mr. John P. Colby, father of Bainbridge Colby, Secretary of State during the last year of the Wilson Administration. When our little gang in St. Louis said good-by to George Snell the night before he started for Paris, with a real sense of loss and more emotion in the Godspeed than one finds anywhere outside of a college commencement break-up, the parting ceremony was at John Colby's beautiful home, with the future cabinet officer and his younger sister tucked safely away in their beds.

These gentlemen who financed the Paris studies of

some of these boys made me a similar offer, but affairs at home were not in a condition that permitted my leaving. I had had some training for the disappointment three years before, when, after a competitive examination, and by the help of the local Methodist minister, who upon grandmother's appeal tutored and brushed me up for the contest, I had won an appointment to West Point. This had been declined for the same domestic reasons. I write of both seeming deprivations to record an unmanly self-pity, although I hope I didn't openly confess it at the time.

There were no appointed Spartan preceptors in the railroad yard to teach us to be calm above the aggression of our hidden foxes, but there were stoical traditions. In those days we used to injure in some degree or other an average of a man a month, and it was the sporty thing, with a foot that had just been mashed in a frog or a hand that had been caught between the bumpers, to sit tight, and while admitting it was tough luck to smile as gamely as one could. A sturdy freight conductor, Alex Beecher, with both legs run over and crushed at a siding some fifty miles out, had rallied his demoralized crew, made tourniquets of a couple of belts to stop the hemorrhage, cut out all but his engine and caboose, telegraphed for a clear track, sent a call to the St. Louis surgeons, and when he pulled into the terminal to meet the ambulance was sitting stoutly upright in his rude bunk calculating his run. Heroic examples of that kind shamed the spirit that could repine even to oneself over a disappointed dream. But art and Paris could not have had for me the varied experience that a catch-as-catch-can grapple with the world enforced for the work I was ultimately so glad to do.

VII

NEW FRIENDS AND YOUTHFUL EXPLOITS

I referred in the last chapter to the number of men injured in the railroad yards before mechanical protections had been invented. The absence of safety devices on the crude railroads of that day that made possible these frequent physical accidents, the keenness of the railroads to get the injured men to sign waivers of damages or to take mere settlement of surgical and hospital fees were among the many things of which the men complained. They had just passed through a period of payment by scrip; that is to say, paper promises by the railroad instead of the paper currency of the United States. This company scrip was discounted at the neighborhood groceries, which further reduced the compensation of the men. Discontent was not local but nation-wide.

Terence V. Powderly, the labor leader, visited each section of the industry and organized assemblies of the Knights of Labor. I was not yet of age, but men in the freight-yard closed their eyes to my disqualification. I became a member of the Missouri Assembly No. 9 and a subscriber to its oath. This assembly had about two hundred members recruited from the trainmen and the freight platforms.

Their attempts at conducting business in parliamentary fashion were frequently confused, and after I had been called upon a number of times because of my page-boy information to decide some point, one of those practical foremen whose object was not office or decoration, but to get the work done, said: "Why do we waste time asking this kid what to do when we know that if we put him into the chair we can get through with our business and get home to bed?"

There was no dissent even from the incumbent officer, and with no outspoken opposition I was elected to the place of master workman. As a man, according to the laws of the organization, had to be twenty-one years of age, and I was two years shy of that, it is probably a fair assumption that I was the youngest master workman in the order. I went through a protracted local strike at that time with our men, and sat in councils that decided rather fateful questions.

In any secret organization an oath with the accompanying ceremonies and surrounding paraphernalia is an impressing thing. Although not a joiner, I have seen two or three kinds of initiation; but never an equal solemnity to that of those men, who felt they were uniting in a life-or-death class struggle.

At that time it was not the avowed policy of organized labor to keep clear of politics. I think the leaders among them felt that to influence legislation was the way out of their difficulties. At any rate, in my twentieth year the Labor Party of St. Louis determined to make an organized protest, and although moving to an unquestionable and thoroughly foreseen defeat in the elections, they decided upon the count of noses. In that forlorn hope, as an ineligible candidate for clerk of the circuit court, I made my first out-of-door, cart-tail speeches. The atmosphere was pretty thoroughly surcharged. The great railroad strike had swept the country. In Pittsburgh the strikers had been victorious over the local militia. They had driven the Philadelphia Grays into a roundhouse upon which they trained their captured cannon, and into which they ran a car of burning oil. The Grays were many of them trampled to death. Millions of dollars' worth of property was destroyed, and order was restored only when General Phil Sheridan, with United States troops, took charge of the situation.

John Scott, the first Earl of Eldon, Lord Chancellor of England in 1821, is quoted as saying, when he was eighty years of age, and protesting against the rapid disposition of anybody in the possession of three acres and a cow to become conservative, "If I were to begin life again, I am damned but I would begin as agitator." I had not read Lord Eldon, but I began as agitator.

Through all this perilous time I had at my elbow my dear old father, wise in political and military fashion; and it may be that much of our organized activity was tempered by thoughtful things I was able to say to my men and of which father had in serious discussions informed me.

We talk now of persisting forces that work at the foundation of our civilization either for its upbuilding and its support or its renovation or its decline; it is proper to be briefly serious concerning them. Associated as I was with men who were working with their hands and were constantly risking their lives, I have no apology for a sympathetic alignment with them in what was decided class feeling. In my immature and impulsive measurement of the field it seemed that money was heartlessly exploiting the people. My father didn't believe that to be so desperately the case. Working as a printer at that time, he joined an assembly of Knights of Labor with whom the printers were affiliated; then had a transfer card to the lodge over which I presided. I took this to be a paternal desire to augment our roll. But since then I have had a boy of my own, and I know it was the supervision of an affectionate parent who felt that he must move somewhat cautiously to influence a rather impulsive son.

Somewhere in his reading father had picked up the statement that when Arkwright invented the spinning-jenny there had been six thousand hand spinners in England, and that fifty years after the machinery was in fair operation the man-power of the machines represented the work of six hundred million spinners. He had a statement, probably gathered from the same source, or one similar, that when the hand spinners were undisturbed in their work the land of England had been under two hundred and fifty thousand separate owners; that after machinery had been in use fifty years the land of England had been concentrated into the possession of thirty-two thousand individual and corporate ownerships. I wasn't able to make any profound deduction from these two facts, but I remember my father saying to me:

"Suppose we both were hand spinners competing, and that I suddenly came into the possession of a machine that could do the work of two hundred and fifty men, where would you be? Suppose I made money enough to buy a second machine, and I had five hundred man-power to oppose against the output of your two hands."

Somehow he felt that the dominance of the machine was a factor in its present status that threatened civilization. He wasn't sufficiently Chinese to wish to destroy the machine, nor was he statesman enough or political economist enough to know the proper answer; perhaps there isn't anybody at Washington or Westminster that can give it now; but he thought he saw a gleam of promise in an income tax that could be wisely used. I had a groping apprehension of what he was trying to work out, and in my cart-tail speeches advocated an income tax.

I talked it in every political campaign thereafter to which I was admitted or tolerated. America could not have played her part in the recent World War without an income tax which enabled her to take excess profits.

To jump ahead chronologically, I remember meeting Mr. Charles Schwab in the foyer of a theatre when at his wife's solicitation he was taking a half-day off from his strenuous work in the war.

With the utmost cheerfulness, he said to me, apropos of the government assessments, "I have to make one hundred dollars for every eleven I want to use for myself."

There was no color of complaint in this, but rather a pride in the resourcefulness of his country. But leaving the question of income tax aside, I wonder now if the insensate machine, still encroaching where it has not yet subdued, isn't largely responsible for part of the international industrial mess. I wonder if our trouble is altogether a friction between capital and labor—a matter only of production and markets; or if there is not more obliquely and obscurely some trouble still in that old menace that my father thought he sighted.

One clause at that time in the constitution of the Knights of Labor provided that no lawyer should be a member of the order. The constitution was an emanation of Mr. Powderly's council, and I shall leave to him or others equally wise the reason for this precaution.

But by the automatic action of that clause, when I entered the law office of John Colby to study law I had my Washington's Farewell to that assembly.

John Peck Colby was born in Nunda, New York. He was the son of Luke Colby, a Baptist clergyman, prominent in educational movements of the day and identified with several institutes of learning which had their origin at that time.

Young John, enlisting in the Union Army in the Civil War, attained the rank of captain. At the close of the war he married an Elmira girl, Frances Bainbridge, related to Commodore Bainbridge, of Mediterranean fame, and became instructor of Latin and Greek in the local academy. After he was admitted to the bar he came to St. Louis with his bride to establish a home.

My acquaintance with him had begun, as I have said before, in the circle of artists and his first interest in me had been along those lines. At that time his son, Bainbridge, was not quite ten years of age; his little daughter, Lisle, was younger. Mrs. Frances Bainbridge Colby's father also was a clergyman—the Reverend Doctor Bainbridge, then of Elmira.

As John used to say, "It was seldom that one saw such eminent piety concentrated in one family."

In the law office I found the books unattractive, but I read Blackstone's "Commentaries," "Parsons on Contracts," and the other ponderous furniture of that sombre place.

If, after my grandmother and my own parents, I named the most definite personal influence I had known, I should say it was probably that of Mr. John Colby. With the habit of his scholarly precision, he was very much more interested in the style of anything I had to

JOHN PECK COLBY. 1865. FATHER OF MRS. THOMAS.

E. B. THOMAS, FATHER OF AUGUSTUS THOMAS. 1865.

compose in or out of business hours than he was in its legal accuracy. In both art and letters he was a patient advocate of standards, and he had a sensibility natural and cultivated that made him aware of any influence having a tendency to depress them. He had a love of simple Anglo-Saxon and a sense of fitness in its use or propriety in its elaboration. His reading was wide and selectively renewed, and he had that capacity for quick association or analogy that the psychologists note as a prime element of genius. In writing of his influence upon me I feel that I may claim as an effect of it only an "attention" on my part, and not a "forward march."

His son, Bainbridge, was a sturdy boy with a well-balanced interest in books and play, and in the first days of our association intensely interested in my railroad activities and his occasional chance thereby to get among the cars and locomotives. A characteristic quality of the boy was his interest in affairs and his capacity for sustained attention. The shipping cards on the side doors of the cars indicating destinations and contents interested him. He had to know the reasons for these supplies going to certain places; the original shipping points of their production; the interrelation of the sections of the country; and he took such information as I was able to give and made such pat application of it and such thoughtful associations of its parts that it was a source of constant astonishment to me. His father, who was a wise educator, had in the library of their home a large-sized terrestrial globe, so that the children had no distorted ideas of the relative extents of the different countries such as most of us get in school from the inadequate systems of maps. Another characteristic of the boy was in the kind of questions he used to put to his father. I remember Colby, Sr., showing a good-natured generalization of these attacks by replying to the first of an expected bunch of volleyed questions by a prompt resort to the established stencil.

He said, "The gentleman of whom you ask is in the woodenware and cooperage business; he makes barrels and buckets; he sends them to all sections of the country; he is at the head of a very reputable firm; I think they do a large business." And the father finished with a hearty laugh at the boy's reception of this short circuit on his intent.

All that delicate culture could give to him Bainbridge was getting from that household and its atmosphere; personally I was anxious to make him familiar with the rougher edges of life. My attempts at this often ran counter to the family's ideas. The Fourth of July was not then safe or sane, but their careful mother kept explosives from the Colby children. There can never be any world conflagration in which Bainbridge Colby, however active politically, will create such a sensation as he did on our first Fourth together when we came back from the corner grocery, young Bainbridge astride of my shoulders and holding in each hand, by the tail of its plaited fuses, a package of exploding firecrackers, which of course very safely released themselves from the string before they fell and went off at our feet.

At that time in Kansas City there were two girls to whom George Snell and I used to write from St. Louis. One Sunday we planned a visit to them, and by some relaxation of the rules I had persuaded the Colby parents to let us take Bainbridge along. He was then a kid of ten, and roughed it quite manfully with us overnight in the chair car. The nearest station to our destination in

Kansas City was a stop that as we neared it we learned had, for our train, been cut out; but we felt that we would not go by at a speed that would prevent our getting off. Snell took his place on the steps of the car in front of us; we—Bainbridge and I—were on the platform immediately after. Following instructions, he had his arms wrapped around my neck and his legs around my waist—I had a waist in those days. I dropped on to the platform all right with the boy in the greatest glee; but the speed was too fast for Snell, who prudently stuck to the train as he blew us a kiss and went a mile farther on. My excuse for this foolhardy act is that I was as ignorant as Cæsar's boatman of the freight I carried. Bainbridge's recital of this experience didn't make the hit at home we had looked for.

My father had taught me boxing while he sat on a chair. I began in like manner to teach young Bainbridge the art. This was as contrary to the church precepts ruling that house as can be imagined; but at irregular intervals we persisted. When Bainbridge at sixteen left for his freshman year at college he had pretty well outgrown his tutor. I don't remember whether reports were satisfactory as to studies, but on the freshman field-day my pupil with soft gloves knocked out two men. I have seen him since in legal and political contests, and have had no difficulty in persuading myself that the stamina there invariably shown had in it some element of our earlier work together. In 1916, when Mr. Roosevelt tried to lead the Progressive Party back into the Republican fold, it was the fighter Colby who resisted that unattractive persuasion; and in the ensuing campaign, when Colby, as the principal unterrified Progressive, canvassed the West for Wilson, I think the three deciding votes from California were more a response to the pugilistic antecedents of the oratory than to any theological recollection. Also in the smoothly lucid and unmistakable diction of his diplomatic communications I thought there was the firmness of the lad who knew how to keep his balance and to put up his hands.

Colby, Sr., was very sympathetic with my scattering interests, and especially with my play-writing ambitions. Before I went into his office, and as a sequence to my experience in our North St. Louis dramatic club, I joined the larger McCullough Club. This organization of amateurs, while resembling the present Comedy Club of New York and the Mask and Wig of Philadelphia, had certain distinctive features that are worth considering. The old McCullough Club had about five hundred members, of which fifty or more were on the active list. Each member paid ten dollars a winter, and for that received two admissions to each of the five performances in a season. The plays for these were carefully chosen, and were as thoroughly rehearsed as amateurs can rehearse, taking two or three nights a week for a month. A regular theatre was rented for the single performance. The mechanical force back of the curtain was of professional hands from the regular houses.

Shortly after joining the club, because of my semi-professional and considerable amateur experience, too, I became the stage-manager of the organization. Any one who has sympathized with my allusions to financial embarrassment hitherto will feel a sense of relief at learning that I received fifty dollars a performance for rehearsing and presenting each play. As this work was done outside the hours of other employment, it was what was then and may still be called velvet.

A number of actors who achieved fair prominence, though not stellar distinction, were graduated from that club. William Beaumont Smith, son of General A. J. Smith, of Vicksburg and Red River fame, was one of our members. He later went on the professional stage and was for many years a popular leading man. Guy Lindsley, who has been Mr. Robert Mantell's leading man, was another McCullough Club boy; Mr. Edgar Smith, for many years librettist for Weber and Fields, and now still successful as dramatic author, was another; the late W. G. Smythe, who was the first manager for William Collier, and thereafter for many years, up to the date of his death in September, 1921, the booking manager for the Belasco attractions, was a McCullough Club actor; A. G. Robyn, the composer, had his first musical work presented by members of this company.

In those days there was an old play called "Mrs. Waldron's Bachelors," a fifteen-cent book available to any amateur and without copyright. From it Mr. Joseph Bradford had made the play called "Our Bachelors," in which Robson and Crane were starring. There is an anecdote of this author, Joseph Bradford, who was a very able Boston journalist, that should not be lost. There will be no better place for it than this.

Bradford, who wrote of and for the theatre, had a wish to play, and when Adelaide Neilson came to that city in repertoire the management arranged for Bradford to go on in the small part of *Paris* in "Romeo and Juliet." In the abridged version his only appearance was as the bereaved bridegroom at the tomb of *Juliet*, where he encounters *Romeo* forcing the door to the vault. *Romeo*, interfered with, kills *Paris*, who falls and speaks the line, "O, I am slain!"

Bradford was so occupied with the technic of being stabbed and falling that he forgot his line. He not only forgot to speak it, but he forgot what it was, until some minutes later, when *Romeo* has taken the poison and is dead, and *Juliet*, kneeling over his body, is bewailing him.

At this point the interested audience was astonished to see the corpse of *Paris* rise to its elbow and, as if resenting the sympathy that was being showered upon the unhappy *Juliet*, exclaim, "O, I am slain!"

The house, which had utterly forgotten the unimportant man up stage, burst into a chorus of laughter which brought down the curtain on the unhappy Adelaide.

When the McCullough Club announced "Mrs. Waldron's Bachelors" the attorneys for the Robson and Crane enterprise endeavored to enjoin the performance legally, but the amateurs won out. Another attempted injunction was when the club put on "Esmeralda," by Mrs. Burnett and William Gillette. This they had rehearsed from the published text of the play in the *Century Magazine*. Our present copyright law was not in existence then. Legal action taken to protect a play was based upon property right under the common law, but the courts were reluctant to say that plays printed in magazines had not been printed subject to any use that any buyer might care to make of them. In both of these unauthorized performances I had the leading part.

"Esmeralda" was played by the club only a few weeks before the regular Madison Square Company came to St. Louis with the drama. One of the local papers, the *Spectator*, in criticising the professional company, said that the performance of old man *Rogers* by Mr. John E. Owens had not been so good as that of the same part by

Mr. Thomas of the amateurs. John E. Owens, the famous *Solon Shingle*, was one of the foremost comedians of the country, and this treatment of him was not to be tolerated by the management. A controversy ensued which lasted while the company was there, and was then forgotten. I rather egotistically make a note of it because years later it was the basis of a pretty act of generosity on the part of Mr. Owens.

A moving spirit in the McCullough Club—in its organization, its management, and in its active expression—was Wayman McCreery, now dead. I am sure that ten thousand of his surviving contemporaries in the city of St. Louis will remember Wayman McCreery. Few men are so physically and intellectually equipped as he was. There was nothing that an athlete could do with his body that in a notable degree Wayman McCreery could not do. He was boxer, wrestler, fencer, runner, and swimmer, and all-round athlete. In addition to these he was a graceful step dancer. Intellectually he was equipped with a college training and had an interest in everything that interested the intelligent people of his day. He sang well enough to be a leading tenor in a fashionable choir. He wrote music of good quality. He was the author of the opera "L'Afrique," which was first done by amateurs in St. Louis and subsequently produced in New York, although with not very great success, by Jesse Williams. McCreery will be remembered by the sporting world as the inventor of the three-cushion game of billiards, of which he was at one time the national champion. As *Hugh Chalcot* in Robertson's comedy "Ours" it would have taken a professional to equal him. Another part of McCreery's was *Captain Hawtree* in "Caste," by the same author.

The Colby children, like all youngsters, were attracted by such knowledge of the world behind the curtain as our home talk developed and as an occasional peep behind scenes would emphasize. As is commonly the case also, the little girl's interest was the greater. One day she brought to me a copy of *St. Nicholas* with Mrs. Burnett's story of "Editha's Burglar."

"Don't you think," she asked, "that would make a pretty play?"

With the addition of the dramatic element by having the burglar be the child's father, it did make a pretty play, the first of mine to be done professionally and to be produced in New York.

Theatricals, amateur and semiprofessional, gradually claimed more and more attention, so that when I finally told Mr. Colby that I thought the cast in the law-books was too short, that nothing could be done with John Doe and Richard Roe, and that the love interest was entirely lacking, he made no objection to my accepting the offer of Mr. Charles R. Pope to go into the box-office of his new theatre.

Charles R. Pope had been a partner with Mr. Charles Spalding in the ownership of the old Olympic. The men had separated for some reason, and Mr. Pope had built Pope's Theatre on the site of the late Century Theatre in St. Louis. Pope's Theatre was rather economically constructed by making a playhouse out of a church that stood there. Mr. Pope was without capital; he financed his enterprise by the issuance of a number of subscribers' tickets which admitted the holders to two performances a week at a reduced rate. These tickets were not unlike the old-time commutation tickets on a railroad, with margins of serial numbers to be punched as the tickets were used. Visiting companies objected to this bargain-counter finance, and these tickets were the occasion of endless trouble.

Before managing the Olympic with Spalding, Charles Pope had been a tragedian of considerable prominence, especially in the West. He was a man of heroic figure, stentorian voice, and a method plainly founded on Edwin Forrest's. At both the Olympic and Pope's Theatre he continued to appear when the opportunity offered or the emergency required. His wife was Margaret Macauley, a member of the well-known Kentucky family of that name. Her brother, Daniel Macauley, the senior of the family, had been a general in the Union Army and won distinction. A second brother, Barney Macauley, was one of the foremost actors of his day. A still younger brother was John, who ultimately became the sole owner of Macauley's Theatre in Louisville, in which all the brothers had been jointly interested.

Mr. Pope's financial troubles in St. Louis were not confined to the commutation reductions which he was occasionally required to make up, and the men in his box-office had an intimate acquaintance with the amusing financial finesse then customary in theatrical circles. Then, as now, among bills paid by the resident manager were those of the bill-poster. Our St. Louis bill-poster was a rough, truculent, good-hearted person named Cottrell, who might have stepped out of that group of pirates in "Treasure Island" as far as his appearance was concerned, and very often Pope wished he would go back. Besides his bristling mustache and black beard, he had a gin-and-fog voice that would have frightened any nursery. It was the duty of us men at the window, when we saw Cottrell coming to collect his bills, to flag the owner, who would then flatten himself against the inner wall and stay out of sight.

On one occasion, however, Cottrell was too quick for the manœuvre, and caught Mr. Pope on an early afternoon when—as we knew—there was no money in the bank, none in the box-office, and no prospect for the evening. Cottrell wanted his bill. Pope's histrionic training stood him in stead.

Pushing the treasurer aside, he leaned on the box-office window-sill and said: "Where are those stands and three sheets, Mr. Cottrell, for whose posting you are demanding payment?"

Cottrell made the expected reply that they were on the billboards throughout the city.

"Well," said Mr. Pope, "I want my paper to be put on the walls where the people are and where the car lines run."

This metrical diction into which Pope in his blank-verse training always drifted in his moments of dignity elicited from Cottrell the reply that the bills were there in the places Pope had described.

"I want to see them."

"Well, how can you see them?"

"I can see them by your getting a horse and buggy and driving me over the route."

Cottrell belligerently agreed to do this, and the trip was made. When the two men came back it was past banking hours. Pope proudly gave him a check that could not be offered for payment until an evening had intervened, in which he could scout among his friends for cash.

As theatre manager, the old tragedian, not always in the best of health, made a gallant fight, not only against the burden of the cut-rate tickets he had discounted but against Spalding and Norton of the two competing houses, who combined against him. He finally won out and sold his theatre at a profit on his time and trouble. When Harrison was elected to the presidency, Mr. Pope became our United States consul at Toronto, where his fine presence, his dignified bearing, his knowledge of modern languages, and the bonhomie of the old trouper made him as fine a national representative as we had at any European court.

There was not always good business at Pope's Theatre. As in other playhouses, we had idle times, when a man in the box-office had little to do. In those days there was not in St. Louis any rapid-fire photo-engraving establishment. Any pictures wanted quickly for a newspaper could be turned out more promptly by the local wood-engravers, of whom there were several. Many otherwise idle hours in the box-office I was able to occupy profitably on such occasional illustrations.

There are few occupations more fascinating than to draw upon boxwood. This material, which comes in blocks type high and varying from the width of the newspaper column to four or five, as desired, is made of little sections, each not more than a square-inch in size, dowelled together more tightly than marquetry in furniture is joined. The surface of this assembled block is pumiced to a delightful smoothness, having enough grain, however, while imperceptible to the touch, to take a pencil-point without slipping. As it comes to the draftsman, it has the natural-wood color not unlike the tint of freshly planed pine. Over this one throws a light wash of water-color white. The surface then is good for either pencil or brush.

When one has finished his drawing by either of these methods, the wood-engraver cuts out all the portions of the block that are meant to be white in the reproduction —that is to say, meant not to print at all—and leaves the rest. If he left the rest unchanged, however, it would print a solid black silhouette. The engraver's skill lies in so breaking this surface as to get by the use of alternating black and white lines the various shades the artist intended. The simplest understanding of this will be by considering an outline drawing only, but done in pencil, which of course is gray and not black. If the engraver left this line unbroken it would print black, however, and resemble a pen stroke and not the mark of a pencil. But wishing to give the pencil effect, he traverses the line on his block with a sufficient number of tiny cut-out spaces to get resemblance to the pencil mark.

As an example of a pencil drawing upon a piece of box-wood so treated that the gray reproduction resembles the pencil, there is given here an outline cut that has a story. At the time of which I am talking there was a young man in New York named Freddie Gebhard, who came into sudden prominence through his admiration for and attentions to a world-renowned actress then visiting America. As I remember, Mr. Gebhard's enthusiasm did not have the approval of his father, and nearly all the newspapers felt distressed about it. Despite these solicitudes Mr. Gebhard joined the lady in her various professional engagements throughout the country. The people called him a dude.

Few of us now remember what were the distinguishing characteristics of a dude forty years ago, when the name was adopted. The principal ones were that he should wear very tight trousers, a black cutaway coat, the beetle tails of which protruded some six inches below a short tan-colored box-cloth overcoat of very easy dimensions. Besides these sartorial marks, a dude was supposed to be somewhat of a sapling and lacking in manly fibre.

A morning paper in St. Louis had on its editorial staff at that time a man named Cunningham, reputed to be a person of physical courage and a dangerous man to provoke. Some of the things that Mr. Cunningham wrote about Mr. Gebhard's St. Louis visit displeased that gentleman. Gebhard inquired concerning the writer, learned his name and reputation, and then, before a considerable group of spectators one evening just after dinner in the corridor of the Southern Hotel, walked up to Mr. Cunningham and very soundly slapped his face. Something in the way in which he did this convinced the observers that it had been intentional and premeditated, and had respectable force of character behind it. Nothing was done about it except some extended reports by the rival papers.

Mr. Gebhard stepped into a kind of public respect. It was not possible to get pictures of him. He didn't want notoriety. As the story above would indicate, he rather resented it. A weekly paper in the city asked me to get a drawing of him from memory. It wasn't a good plan to ask him to pose. It was learned that Mr. Gebhard had for the week a certain seat three rows from the orchestra rail which he occupied every night his friend the actress played. This seat was on the right aisle of the parquet near the trap drummer. By an arrangement with that member of the orchestra I got a chair in his corner from which I could see Mr. Gebhard, and in that manner the pencil drawing was made. It is offered now as a *point d'appui* for this story, and as an example of a wood-engraver's line that looks like lead-pencil.

A really fine wood-engraver is an artist of a very superior type, excelling in real technical knowledge his brothers of the brush or chisel; but he is becoming increasingly rare, as the photographic and autographic processes of illustration drive his work from the magazines and papers. Fifty years ago, when Blanchard Jerrold, son of Douglas Jerrold, wrote his "London Pilgrimage," in 1872, and Gustave Doré illustrated it so splendidly, there were three or four wood-engravers working upon the illustrations, whose production deserved and gained as much if not more praise than the work of Doré himself.

The last of the great American wood-engravers is the veteran Timothy Cole, now living at Poughkeepsie, New York, and in his seventieth year still working importantly at his profession. The superlative skill of Timothy Cole won for him membership in the American Academy of Arts and Letters. The best collected records we have of the old masters of Italy, Holland, England, Spain, and France are his wood-engravings, for which he has had gold medals at the Paris, Chicago, and St. Louis expositions. It would be impossible on the printing-presses that run off our great weekly and daily editions, going into the hundred thousands in one issue, to show the finest example of a wood-engraver's art. Such pictures, delicately printed on Japanese paper, and properly mounted, enrich the collection of connoisseurs.

The most simplified process of reproduction available to draftsmen of St. Louis became common about this time. It employed paper overlaid with starch in solu-

CARTOON DRAWN BY MR. THOMAS FOR THE ST. LOUIS WORLD IN 1880.

From a photograph by Strauss, St. Louis.

JOHN W. NORTON.

tion. The paper was toothed or pebbled to take the mark of the greasy lithographic crayon. A drawing made upon it was turned face downward upon a lithographic stone and passed beneath a hot roller under considerable pressure. The heat and pressure transferred the greasy crayon to the lithographic stone, which was then used as if the drawing had been made directly upon it, and produced the ordinary lithograph with but a slight loss of value from the drawing made upon the paper. This process was used in the production of the cartoon of which a reduction is shown.

There are two or three interesting facts connected with this cartoon. To the best of my belief it was the first political cartoon printed in St. Louis of Mr. Joseph Pulitzer, the eminent publisher and organizer of the present New York *World*. Pulitzer, in 1880, the date of this cartoon, had not yet purchased the old New York *World*, and had but recently acquired the St. Louis *Post-Dispatch*, of which he was proprietor and editor.

He and others in St. Louis were joining in an attack begun by Major Emery S. Foster, editor and proprietor of the St. Louis *World*, against a political conspiracy known as the Dark-Lantern Ring, engaged in the sale of political nominations.

The directing mind of this conspiracy was said to be a politician named Lancaster. He was assisted by an aggressive little attorney named Frank Turner and a blacksmith named Edward Butler, who was at the head of the political machine. Lancaster, Turner, and Butler are in the front row of the cartoon in the order named, and Butler is pictured as knocking out of the ring State Senator Cable, one of the beneficiaries of their combination, who had indiscreetly talked too much about it.

Outside of the ring and looking in are depicted Colonel William Hyde, then editor of the Missouri *Republican;* and Mr. Joseph Pulitzer, who with Colonel Hyde was endeavoring to correct the corrupt conditions.

Major Emery S. Foster, who had won distinction in the Northern Army, was a modest but very notable figure in St. Louis. In the Civil War he had been captured by Quantrell's Guerillas and was said to be the only Union prisoner released by this band, who made a practice of giving no quarter.

His escape was due to one of those border romances which the public are apt to think inventions of the novelist and the playwright, and a fine example of which was interwoven in Mr. William Gillette's war play, "Held by the Enemy."

In the Quantrell group of James boys and Younger brothers was one man who knew the captured Foster, as he and Foster were rivals for the hand of the same girl. With her in mind, this Quantrell guerilla had asked for the life of Foster, and being granted this by Quantrell had conducted Major Foster outside the lines and given him his liberty. This particular Southerner still lives; and the lady in question, now his wife, is also living.

Major Foster, at the close of the war, became the editor of the St. Louis *Journal.* A very personal editorial attacking him appeared one morning in the St. Louis *Times,* of which ex-Confederate Major John Edwards was the editor. Foster immediately challenged Edwards, and the two men met upon the Illinois side of the Mississippi, some few miles above St. Louis. At the first shot Edwards' bullet went wild; Foster's bullet went through Edwards' hat, grazing his scalp.

While the seconds were reloading the pistols Foster

walked over to Edwards and put out his hand, saying, "Edwards, you and I are a pair of damn fools."

Edwards conducted Foster to a log near by, sat down with him, and then told Foster that he had nothing whatever to do with the editorial; that he had gone home and was in his bed when Stilson Hutchins, the proprietor, himself had come into the office and written the objectionable publication. Edwards, however, true to the ethics of the time, had accepted the responsibility of his chief.

Another group of readers will remember Major Foster as the man who in that same St. Louis *Journal* first made and repeated the charges that led to the exposé of what was known as the Whiskey Ring, in Grant's Administration. That was not a band of bootleggers engaged as now in supplying a thirsty community, but was a combination contriving the evasion of the internal revenue tax upon spirits. In the prosecution of that ring General Grant appointed as attorney ex-Senator John B. Henderson, previously referred to in connection with incidents at Jefferson City. As the investigation in court proceeded and involved General Orville E. Babcock, who was the President's private secretary, Henderson, boasting indifference to where the investigation led, said that he was not among those "to bend the pregnant hinges of the knee that thrift may follow fawning." Over his implied defiance Grant had promptly removed Mr. Henderson from his position, and General Babcock, on a deposition from President Grant, was acquitted.

At the time I was making these drawings for Major Foster in that campaign he was a soldierly-looking figure in his early fifties. He had a fine face, good brow, clear-cut, aquiline nose, fine open eyes, perhaps accentuated in their gaze, and sharpened slightly in appearance because of the gold-rimmed spectacles which he always wore. The lower part of his face indicated a substantial modelling beneath his short beard and mustache. He looked in every turn and expression the thoughtful, cultivated, amiable gentleman that he was, with an ever-present suggestion of proper determination.

VIII

THE THEATRE AGAIN

It is difficult for a reader to measure the happiness of a young man for whom the theatre has been the objective when he finds himself ensconced in a quasi-administrative position in a genuine playhouse. As assistant treasurer it was my duty to open up the box-office in the morning, to see that the bill-poster and his assistants received the paper which the advance man brought in his bill trunk; that the boys connected with the theatre had their supply of hangers, lithographs and half sheets that were to go into the windows of saloons, barber shops, and hotels; to see that the scrub-women reported on time and were at work; to sort the mail for the visiting company and send that of the players to the stage door. These duties carried one all over the building after the treasurer arrived to relieve the assistant, and excuses might even be made for visiting and looking over the paint frame. Every theatre at that time had its resident artist. His shop was in the fly gallery; his studio was a bridge at the back wall of the building, against which a movable frame carried his colossal canvases up and down. This artist was expected to get up each week the scenes for the coming attraction. It must not be supposed that he made a complete production in that time. He had at his command a more or less sufficient stock of scenery always stored away in a room adjoining and accessible to the stage, with an opening between, high enough to admit the flat scenes riding upright; this storeroom was called the dock. It properly contained the more usual scenes of the mid-Victorian drama; the parlor or centre-door fancy, kitchen, baronial chamber, castle interior and exterior, pents flat, a street, a garden, cut-wood, forest, and horizon drops. To hold and change these scenes the stage was arranged with runs and grooves. These were sets of wooden guide tracks on the stage and adjustable grooves corresponding some eighteen feet above, arranged in groups about four feet apart, beginning at the curtain line and numerically designated. Their terminology still governs in the theatre. An actor entered or made his exit in One, Two, Three, or Four, right or left, as the case might be, or up centre. He still does so, although the grooves with their old sliding scenes that were pushed on to meet in the middle, and separated to be quickly drawn off for a change of scene, have disappeared.

It was upon this customary stock of scenery that the scenic artist depended, supplementing it from time to time with some new scene, of which sufficient warning would generally be given, painted upon new canvas and construction, or painted over one of the old scenes that was seldom called for.

At the time of which I'm talking the old runs and grooves existed in Pope's Theatre, but were beginning to disappear from other houses projected at about that time. They gave way to the clear stage with boxed scenes now so common and which are supported in panels by stage braces set behind each panel, with the panels held together by lashings hung from the top and falling over alternating cleats on the two joining edges.

Our paint frame at Pope's Theatre was presided over by Ernest Albert, an artist to-day, both in the theatre and in the gallery, of international reputation. His assistant was a blond and gentle lad named Frank E. Gates, son of the old Si Gates who for many years was in charge of the stage at the old Olympic. Frank Gates is now at the head of one of the largest scenic studios of New York.

The brilliant artist, Ernest Albert, was not much, if any, older than myself. He was a member of our St. Louis Sketch Club, and there was always between us a real artistic sympathy. It is probably because I knew what Albert was trying to do and what he succeeded in doing when physical conditions permitted that many of the hours during which I was relieved from my watch in the box-office I was allowed to put in on the paint frame, where with an eagerness that equalled any protégé of Tom Sawyer's I found delight in spreading flat colors on the immense canvases.

Before the speculators and the agencies intervened, and when the patrons of the theatre got their seats at the box-office by a diagram on which they were permitted to make their choice, there were few places of business so interesting to the occupant as was the old box-office. In ordinary times, from the hour that it opened up until the window was pulled down for the day, there was no such clearing-house for gossip, not even excepting the celebrated rural sewing circle.

Pope's Theatre at Ninth and Olive streets was outside the important business district, although upon a street of the smaller and more exclusive shops. Also the most fashionable car-line of the city was double-tracked past its doors. Across Ninth Street to its left were a post-office and custom-house, in their fine new granite structure, grand for that time. Facing the theatre immediately across Olive Street was Pierre Lambert's three-story

French Restaurant Porcher, with its iron balconies along the front in Southern fashion and its wide stairway with ornamental railings of cast-iron grape-vines leading to the first porch.

Hancock the Superb had just been defeated for the presidency, and sought a semi-retirement in one of the two or three apartments run in connection with this Restaurant Porcher. At the hour of nine, when we were to open up in the morning, the picturesque general, wearing his Ben Butler hat, was often coming in leisurely fashion to the sidewalk from this building. Men who remember the Hancock campaign will recall Tom Nast's cartoon of Hancock seated on a platform with a placard on the wall behind him—A Tariff for Revenue Only. Hancock was depicted as leaning over to his neighbor and privately asking, "Who is Tariff and why is he for revenue only?"

The country was then laughing at Hancock's declaration that the tariff was a local issue. The subsequent alignment on the tariff question of widely separated communities as soon as they became interested in some local manufacture indicated that Hancock was more nearly right than were his critics. Perhaps it was his courage that inspired Andrew Carnegie, one of the tariff's greatest beneficiaries, to say, somewhat later, that "the tariff was the mother of the trusts."

At the theatre business men of some degree of leisure and independence walking down from the residence districts in the morning would stop in for their reservations. Others would hurriedly drop off a car for the same purpose. After the first run of buyers for the ordinary attraction, and when the lobby had then quieted down to the occasional straggler, the early afternoon newspaper men came by. They were followed by the bill collectors and local advertisers. About eleven the fashionable women, married and unmarried, made their calls. It may be that the visiting actors showing up at about that time had some determining influence. During the lunch-hour there would be a run of the clerks and bookkeepers who tucked a call at the theatre into the noon recess. After 2:30 big boys and girls from the high school came into the lobby to look at the pictures. Later the brokers walking home and the ladies combining a call with their other shopping would drop in. Then there were always members of the half-idle contingent who found the lobby an excellent place to waste some portion of every day.

I don't know why it is, but there has always seemed to be a strong affinity between the young men in the box-office and the snare drummer in the orchestra. There were two drummers of considerable reputation in Pope's orchestra during my time. One was Le Grand White, the first husband of Minnie Maddern Fiske, married romantically in St. Louis during her first starring engagement. Miss Maddern had met Mr. White through her uncle, Dick Maddern, who was then the conductor in Pope's Theatre orchestra. The other drummer, who succeeded White, was Frank David, who came to the lobby every afternoon to give comic imitations and practise dance steps on the tiled pavement. A few years later Frank was for a short time the most prominent comedian on Broadway, having made a phenomenal hit in the comic opera "The Pyramids." Another orchestra leader at Pope's was William Witthers, who had been the conductor of the orchestra at Ford's Theatre in Washington on the night Lincoln was shot.

Opposite the theatre, a little farther up the same block with the Restaurant Porcher, was the photograph gallery of Mr. Fox. Mr. Fox was the father of two daughters. Lily Fox, the elder, then about sixteen years old, was one of the prize beauties of the city. She had a face that would have delighted Neysa McMein as a model for a magazine cover, and I am sure still delights her husband, Nat Roth, the general business manager in New York for the Shuberts. Lily came to the theatre in the daytime chaperoning her little sister, Della, then about ten years of age, and available to the visiting or local attractions as a child actress. Della's first appearance on the stage, I think, was at Pope's Theatre in "A Celebrated Case," with James O'Neill. After Charles Thorne, James O'Neill was then perhaps America's favorite romantic actor, but as modest and lovable at the height of his popularity as he continued to the day of his recent death. His son, Eugene, author of "Emperor Jones" and "Beyond the Horizon," promises to surpass his noble father in enduring fame.

John Raymond was a great box-office visitor. He would patiently stand through five minutes of ticket-selling or longer to get a half minute in which to match silver dollars with the treasurer. This form of gambling was a passion with him. Frederick Warde brought with him as leading man Henry Aveling, who married our amateur heroine, Mittens Willett, and brought also a juvenile man calling himself Hallet Murray, who turned out to be my old boy friend, Palmoni, of Washington City.

Palmoni on that visit told me of the death a year or two before of A. W., our old actor preceptor, as grandmother had intuitively reported it. Palmoni himself was a disappointed man. He had an ability that in legitimate parts could have overcome his lack of stature, but he had a tendency to be stout enough to make him undesirable in the rôles.

Two years after the time of which I am writing he died in New York City. With this confirmation of A. W.'s death and the news of Palmoni's end a sustaining interest passed from grandmother's horizon, and the dear old lady began to fail more perceptibly than was warranted by her advancing years alone.

In the box-office one made a fairly extensive acquaintance with the men employed in the local departments of the newspapers, and now and then with some of the editors. Most prominent among the reporters who used to visit the front of the house, and certainly the one best known thereafter to the American reader, was young William Marion Reedy, who later became the editor and owner of the St. Louis *Mirror*, which for so many years he conducted with such distinction. In the early '80's Reedy was a slight lad with a face noticeable for its intelligence. He was interested, as most young men on newspapers are, in the playhouse; and there began then a friendship which was cemented when I went on the newspapers myself a few years later, and which continued to the time of his death.

Among the men in the editorial department with whom I enjoyed an intimate friendship was the gifted Colonel John Cockerill, then acting as managing editor of the *Post-Dispatch*. Colonel Cockerill was also president of the Elks' Club, another member of which was his fairly intimate friend, Alonzo W. Slayback. In a political campaign of that time it became necessary for the paper to speak critically of Slayback, and Slayback, who was a Southerner, served threatening notice upon Cockerill in the event of any further publication. The next afternoon the *Post-Dispatch* followed its first article with a second reference.

The paper was hardly upon the street when Slayback, accompanied by a mutual friend by the name of W. H. Clopton, passed through the *Post-Dispatch's* local rooms, and entered Cockerill's private office. As he advanced he drew a revolver, but before he had time to use it Cockerill had taken his own weapon from the table in front of him and fired. Slayback was instantly killed. Cockerill drove to the police court, surrendered himself and was locked up.

The news of the shooting was telephoned to the theatre. I was on duty at the time. Mr. Pope considerately took my place at the window and I went across the town to the jail. I was the first man in Cockerill's cell, and remained with him until Johnny Norton, who was his boon companion, came there. In the few minutes that we were alone together Colonel Cockerill was self-controlled, but plainly alive to the tragic character of his act and the seriousness of his own situation. His only reference to it all was when in commonplace I had said: "Sorry, Colonel."

He nodded slowly as he answered, "Too bad, but it couldn't be helped."

Colonel Cockerill was released on bail and the case was dismissed without being brought to trial. Whether the tragedy terminated his usefulness in St. Louis or not, it made continuation of his work there unpleasant to him. He removed to New York, where he took charge of the editorial page of the *World*. I saw him frequently after 1889, when I came to make my home in the East.

He became the president of the New York Press Club, and gathered about him a small circle of agreeable and influential friends, but it was my opinion that the Slayback killing clouded the rest of his brilliant life.

One outstanding recollection of that time at Pope's is of William Gillette's first visit as a star. He came in his own play, "The Professor," to my mind the most charming of the long list from his pen. Gillette was then under the management of the Madison Square Theatre, his tour directed by Gustave and Charles Frohman. An indication of the dignity with which affairs theatrical were treated is in the advance illustrations by Kelly printed in the newspapers and the programmes of the day. These drawings, designed for clearness on rapid printing presses, had as much artistic merit as the process permitted. The two facing p. 138 show the character of the work; give an idea of the costumes of 1880 and fairly epitomize the story of "The Professor," an attractive but mature person beleaguered by lovelorn applicants and challenged by younger and envious rivals. The garments of the young men in the picture, especially the lad with the short jacket buttoned tightly to the neck, are worth a glance; the entangling trains of the women, the Watteau pleats, their stays and bustles will make the modern girl thank heaven for her freedom.

Another welcome visitor at the box-office was W. J. Florence, familiarly known as Billy Florence, who with his wife was jointly starring in the phenomenally successful comedy, "The Mighty Dollar." Florence was the projector and organizer of the Mystic Shriners, that post-graduate playground of the thirty-second-degree Masons. He and the elder Sothern, *Lord Dundreary*, were boon companions.

One week when Sothern was playing at the Olympic Theatre and Florence was at Pope's, Florence took a carriage at the first intermission in his play, drove rapidly to the stage door of the Olympic, which was half a mile away, passed the doorkeeper and went onto the stage, where *Lord Dundreary* was in the midst of a scene. Waddling down from the centre door with his unctuous laugh he grasped the hand of the astonished *Dundreary*, and wished him health "by a large majority." The crowded house, watching "Our American Cousin," immediately recognized the star from the other theatre. This prank occasioned a good deal of merriment at Pope's when Florence got back and reported it. Its perpetration had extended the intermission but slightly.

Florence and his wife were in the middle of their big scene in the succeeding act when, to their great astonishment, but to the equal delight of this second audience, the lisping *Dundreary* minced in through the centre to announce that he "had just had a letter from Sam." He greeted both Florences effusively and departed. This good-natured interchange has had many imitations since that day, but I believe it was original with Florence.

One story of Florence concerned his first endeavor on any stage. When as a lad engaged to keep out of sight behind the scenes and on a given cue to bark like a dog, which he could do, an actor asked: "What will you do, Billy, if you get stage fright and can't bark?"

The boy answered, "I'll wag my tail," which showed a ready sense of character.

Perhaps more than any other man in the theatre, with maybe the exception of Joseph Jefferson, Florence numbered among his friends the important politicians of the country. This may have been the consequence of his

TWO SCENES FROM "THE PROFESSOR," IN WHICH WILLIAM GILLETTE
APPEARED. 1882.

admirable burlesque of a congressman as the *Honorable Bardwell Slote*—and he had political ambitions himself. After Cleveland's first election the belief was general that Mr. Florence would be appointed ambassador to France. Colonel Henry Watterson was the man who brought the question to the attention of Cleveland. Although Cleveland was numbered among the personal friends of the actor, he was obliged to explain to Watterson that the church members of the country would not forgive him if he appointed to an office of such prominence a member of the theatrical profession.

James H. Hackett, the father of our present James K. Hackett, lately made chevalier of the Legion of Honor for his performance of "Macbeth" in Paris, was considered by playgoers the greatest American *Falstaff*. But I have heard men who saw both claim the supremacy for Ben De Bar. This old actor required very little padding to realize the rotund knight, a favorite character with him. De Bar also excelled in most of the low-comedy parts of that repertoire. He was unsurpassed as *Toodles*, and was the best *Dogberry* I ever knew. I saw him walk away with the honors in an all-star performance of "London Assurance" that was given for some charity in which the brilliant Edwin Adams played *Charles Courtly*. A good leading man of that time, one Metcalf, played *Sir Harcourt;* Charles R. Pope was the *Dazzle*, and Ben De Bar the *Mark Meddle*. I doubt if the play had had an equal presentation in its first production in England when the then young Dion Boucicault, its author, wrote to his mother in Ireland, "I have London by the throat."

Adams was then starring in "Enoch Arden" and some Shakespearian parts. I saw his "Hamlet" that week.

Many men of judgment in the theatre preferred it to all others.

I have seen some thirty *Hamlets*, including Booth and Barry Sullivan, but I think Adams the most thrilling of them all in the scenes with the ghost, probably because of his more melodramatic methods.

The boys in the box-office were always happy to have C. W. Couldock come along, as he did in "Hazel Kirke" and "The Willow Copse." We went with the old gentleman one night after the play to the Elks' rooms for supper. The order had been given when the uneasy veteran asked if there was not some place to which we could take him where there would be sawdust on the floor, and he could get an order of finnan haddie. There were just such conditions in a room at Tony Faust's, two blocks away, where we spent the rest of the evening with the coveted smoked fish and some bumpers of beer.

Couldock at that time divided popular support as the first old man of the country with James H. Stoddart. He had spent his life in the theatre, been one of the most prominent exponents of *Louis XI* and similar legitimate parts, and could fill all the evenings of a week with stories of the old days before we had fallen upon the degenerate times, as he then measured the one in which we were.

Another very agreeable acquisition that came to one in a box-office was the fraternity which it established with the men in the other box-offices, and the information that came through them concerning all current theatrical happenings. At the Olympic Theatre the treasurer was Mr. Dunn, who is still called Eddie, though he must be within a few years of my own age, and has had now the responsible position of general-manager for Mr. George M. Cohan. I don't think I ever saw a more uniformly courteous and even-tempered person than Mr. Dunn has been in a number of trying occupations. In the old days the only railroad in the country that advertised a four-track roadbed was the New York Central. Eddie, who has always been a careful dresser, was then the leader if not the misleader of fashion. He used to wear in the box-office what he called his New York Central shirt, which had four very decided stripes down the bosom.

I think that both Mr. Dunn and I, as well as all others that were ever in the theatre offices of St. Louis, will accord to old George McManus credit of greatest popularity. There is scarcely any man who came into the profession as early as twenty-five years ago who will not remember him as a pleasant acquaintance and delightful friend. After saying that he was the father of the present George McManus, the talented artist who runs the comic stories of "Bringing Up Father" and similar humorous drawings in certain syndicate papers, it will be interesting to the members of the Eugenics Congress to note that this humor that has blossomed out in young George through his illustrations found expression in the father in an unbroken series of harmless practical jokes of legitimate kinship to the absurdities depicted by young George. A few of these are worth telling, because of their character and the light they throw upon the mind that got entertainment out of the disproportion between common expectation and events.

On the wall of George McManus' box-office at the Grand Opera House there was a strip of wood equipped with what appeared to be four tenpenny nails on which some coats and hats might be hung. Two of these nails were usually occupied by garments. One of the remaining two, although a tenpenny nail in appearance, was a very artful imitation made of black car-spring rubber. A regular nail had first been driven into the wood, then withdrawn, and this rubber counterfeit substituted. McManus got an average of one laugh a week out of this by hanging his own coat on the good nail when it came time to count up, and then watching the business manager of the visiting company try to make his coat stay in midair by passing the collar over this rubber nail. It seemed to be a law of the human mind to assume that the overcoat's fall to the floor was the result of a failure to encompass the nail, and it sometimes took two or three repeated attempts for the victim to discover the deception.

Just over the office table, and affixed to the wall, was an ordinary electric push button in its hard wooden plate. When the laugh was over about the overcoat and the two men were going to count up George would say, "We'll have a drink on that," or a cigar, and ostentatiously push this electric button. A moment or two after an aproned waiter from the adjoining barroom would enter and inquire the pleasure of the gentlemen who had summoned him. He really came because McManus had arranged with an usher to go after him. The button on the wall had no connection with anything except the plaster.

Twenty-four hours would go by before McManus could realize anything on this investment, and then upon the second night the visiting agent would in his turn say, "Shall we have a drink now?"

George would assent, and the next half-hour would witness the mounting irritation of the visitor as he intermittently punched this dummy call-bell. There were many of these devices, and some were being constantly replaced. Just inside the box-office window was a gigantic thermometer of the kind sometimes displayed for advertising purposes outside the corner drug-store. It was about three feet in length. When an agent of a coming attraction arrived and began his preliminary talk through the box-office window with McManus he would be puzzled by George's turning to his assistant and saying "Forty," or "Sixty," or some other number; the explanation for which the agent would find a few days later when he got the run of the office and saw the decimal degrees on the thermometer variously marked with the customary phrases of boastful advance men, such as "Capacity in Cincinnati"; and "When I was with Booth"; and so on. It was a salutary shock for a pompous individual to find that he had fallen into a tiresome category.

In the early '80's there was an impression still current in our sober city that economy is wealth. McManus used to be annoyed by that section of the opera-house patrons who, moved by this precept, lighted cigars during the first intermission and then carefully left their half-smoked butts resting on the wainscoting of the lobby when the curtain went up and they were called inside. McManus would then come from the box-office with a squirt bottle of tabasco sauce, from which he carefully shot two or three charges upon the chewed end of each cigar. In the second intermission the man first to recover his cigar was generally sport enough to try to control his sensation. But a dozen frugal patrons looking their mutual confessions to each other made an amusing *ensemble*.

In the contraband literature of our kid days Ned Buntline or some equal author used to write of Buffalo Bill. One day an advance agent arrived at Pope's and the paper went up for this hero in his romantic play "The Prairie Waif." The next Sunday night I had the great happiness of meeting the Honorable William F. Cody. I found that my admiration was shared by the preceding generation. He and Pope were already great pals. During that engagement, in a buckskin suit which Buffalo Bill lent him, Pope and the famous scout—boys grown tall—were photographed together seated over a stuffed deer which the property man carried over his shoulder to the gallery across the street.

This hero-worship is a great tendency. One of Cody's engagements overlapped that of Nate Salisbury, who had his little company of five sprightly people—John Webster, Nellie McHenry, John Gourlay, Rae Samuels, and Salisbury himself—known as Salisbury's Troubadours. Nate Salisbury came to be a figure of international reputation. At that time he was fixed in my mind principally by a story that John Norton used to tell of one Charles Salisbury, with whom I had confused him.

This Charles Salisbury as a young man had written from Chicago to Cincinnati asking an engagement for utility business in the stock company of Bob Miles, who ran a theatre in that city. Miles had sent a negative answer. Salisbury replied with an offer to go for forty dollars a week. Miles refused this. Salisbury then telegraphed him, the situation being urgent, that he would accept the place at thirty dollars a week.

Miles, thoroughly annoyed, wired back: "Mr. Salisbury, I don't want you at any price."

Salisbury answered: "Terms accepted. Will be on in the morning." And he came.

An equal push and energy, which manifested itself in everything that Nate Salisbury did, was in harmony with much that Cody had. Shortly after the two men got together their great enterprise of the "Wild West," which ran for many years, was organized and launched. Salisbury, knowing my railroad experiences, wished me to take charge of its transportation department, moving its large collection of animals and men. At that time, however, I was filled with the project of a theatrical company of my own, and, wisely or unwisely, declined.

Toward the end of our second season in Pope's Barney Macauley came to play a week in "The Messenger From Jarvis Section." He had with him a little girl named Lizzie Evans playing the part of *Chip*, of which I believe the child, Minnie Maddern, had been the original. His leading man, Mr. Charles Mason, a very sterling actor, still in the profession, was leaving him, and at Mr. Pope's suggestion I went in on short notice to play the part of *Sandy Mitchell.* The character of *Keppler*, a German barkeeper in the play, was being played by the stage manager, a young fellow about twenty years of age, with remarkable eyes. They had most soulful and pathetic appeal. This actor was a good comedian and a most excellent stage manager. His name was Charles Klein. He was even then interested in the subject of writing plays, and was acting to get the experience so helpful to a playwright. Before he went down on the ill-fated *Lusitania*, Charles Klein had won his way to the foremost rank in his profession. Readers will remember his "Music Master," "The Lion and the Mouse," "The Third Degree," and other plays.

In an earlier chapter of this record I referred to the discreet treatment of living persons by one writing that is advised by men of experience. A decent respect for this advice and such conferences as it has made desirable have invited a few time-to-time advisers. One of these is an attorney, old enough to serve upon any pardon board, experienced, grave, dignified, and scholarly, and not so much my senior in years as to be out of touch with all my impulses. He frowns discouragingly at such glimpses as he has had of my doings thus far. He wishes that I would write with the restraint and gravity of John Morley or Sir George Trevelyan, though of course not curbing my genius to the mediocrity of either; that there should be no audible laugh in the sessions, and that the greatest relaxation should be only a genial glow indicative of good-nature. He tells me that I am not on a witness stand; not under any compulsion to make a revelation that will not read always to my advantage; and moves further, upon my silent reception of this, by an alarm for the interest of the helpless sensitive persons whom I may involve.

That my father, who at the age of fifty, having met with an accident that for a time prevented further pursuit of business, resumed the study of medicine interrupted in his youth, and won his degree in an established medical college, my counsellor submits is an unnecessary statement, even though father's course in the college required my co-operation at home, and to that extent attached itself to my activities. Well, my adviser is right; that is an unnecessary statement; but so is any other statement in this whole performance. My own present needs are not such nor is the financial return for the promised output large enough to furnish me with even the sordid excuse of *Romeo's* apothecary when parting with the poison that "my poverty but not my will consents." It is only fair to the publishers, however, in this connection to say that a middleman, previously indicated, has assured me that "they will come across stronger next time."

But I think I could resist that inducement, too, if it were not my belief that my father if living would himself take pleasure in the recital. He lived to practise his profession thirty years; to know his colleagues and his clientèle in that helpful, expanding, increasingly interesting way that a physician's calling opens and the agreeable atmosphere that it provides. He radiated what he so acquired, and the studio in which I write and the summer places of which our domestics so fully approve would lose much that makes them magnetized and restful if the repeated visits of the sweetly aging doctor were unremembered.

When father was compelled to quit his work we had as neighbor a Doctor Kent, member of the faculty of the Homeopathic College, who approved of the suggestion for father to resume the study of medicine. There were some serious family discussions which narrowed down to a talk between father and me. I found an increase of income by undertaking to do more drawings on boxwood for the engravers, and with this in sight father consented to start in on his four-year course. Looking back at that time over an interval of more than forty years, I don't believe that I am exaggerating the human interest of it. The positions of father and son were in one respect completely reversed. He started off to school with his books in the morning and came home after his day's session and devoted his nights to study. About him were the domestic problems. The important thing was to meet these with the least call upon him, and at the same time to keep up his spirits to the heroic thing he had undertaken. I won't attempt the proper tribute that belongs to the women of the family for their part of this; they were unwavering in the brave front they presented to father and the atmosphere of content that they created.

My job in addition to that already indicated was to establish a comedy view of the thing; to call the medical student to account for implied truancy and theatrically to assume the rôle of a grouchy stage father bringing up an incorrigible son. About once a week I pretended to get favorable reports from the teachers, and would reward their pupil with a visit to the theatre, on which I accompanied him during the time I was in the law-office and in which I joined him when we had counted up at Pope's after I had gone there. As a matter of both economy and companionship he and I used to walk home— two miles. My interests were theatrical; father's experiences were largely so; and the talks that started as far as I was concerned in a deliberate intent to divert his thoughts always finished in a real abandonment to the subject, with both of us in the happiest earnestness.

The last attraction at Pope's Theatre during my employment there was the celebrated Vokes family. At the end of their week they separated; the girls, Victoria, Rosina, and Jessie, and the brother, Fawdon, going back to England. Fred Vokes, however, the principal member and manager of the enterprise, had a play in mind which he wished to try in America during the summer; a farcical contrivance which he called "In Camp." He engaged me to undertake the part that had been originally intended for Fawdon Vokes. When the new company, which immediately assembled, found itself together in Buffalo, all rooming at the old Mansion House, the principal members were Pauline Hall, later the comic-opera star; Minnie Schultz, a soprano, at that time the wife of the talented Louis Harrison; and Miss Helen Dingeon, a soprano of power and reputation. The principal men were Owen Westford, a very excellent comedian, and a young man named Byron Douglas, who later became an established leading man.

When rehearsals should have begun we discovered that Vokes had no script whatever, but only an idea for a play. All of us boys thereupon sat down with pen, ink, and paper to help him. Together we finally ground out a hodgepodge not unlike a modern musical play. All that is important to note of that engagement is that in one of the off hours, in a wrestling bout, Westford had the misfortune to break an ankle, so that his Buffalo engagement was played on crutches.

Our next important stand after Buffalo was Chicago, where we arrived on a rainy Sunday, none of us with any money. Westford, Pauline Hall, and I, forming one little coterie, went on foot in the rain in search of a hotel. The old Matteson House, later the Wellington Hotel, was situated on Wabash Avenue. The desk was approached by a corridor some sixty feet in length and twenty wide. A pompous clerk glared at our party as we came in from the drizzle and stood at the front door. Westford being on crutches, I went up to the desk to negotiate for quarters. The hotel was on the American plan.

I said, "What is the rate for board and room?"

The clerk answered, "Three dollars."

"What is your professional rate for actors?"

Looking over my head into vacancy, the clerk answered, "Three-fifty."

We went a few blocks farther on to a little rooming-house called the Windsor, with a second-floor office, where one could get a comfortable room at a dollar a day. When the Chicago engagement was fairly launched my colleagues in St. Louis were far enough advanced with their plans for a company of our own for me to quit the Vokes enterprise and go home.

In the early days of his popularity as a singing tramp, Walter Jones, our prominent *farceur* of to-day, used to recite some verses written by Ben King of the old White-chapel Club of Chicago, expressing the tyranny of the preposition. As I remember, the first lines ran:

> "Nowhere to go but out,
> Nowhere to come but back,
> No place to stand but on,
> Nowhere to fall but off."

In my few essays at a career up to the time of which I am telling there had uniformly been no place to come but back. I never came back, however, with more eager-ness than from my experience in that summer season with Fred Vokes; or with more welcome or greater hap-piness upon my arrival. My father, who had got his diploma from the college, was now set up as doctor and building a little practice that made it possible for me without excessive selfishness to try somewhat for myself. In our leisurely review and stock taking as I sat with him that midsummer, he now the breadwinner and I the adventurer, we talked over the period covering slightly more than a decade since I had come back from Washington. How full the time had been! What pros-perity the country had had! What a growth in its activ-ities! What a reaching out of its markets! What a turmoil in its political agitations!

A syndicate of newspapers, the Scripps-McRae League, had established a penny paper in our city, among others; copper coins were really beginning to circulate west of the Mississippi and south of the Ohio; merchants were marking down goods from five dollars to four-ninety-eight; newsboys were making change for less than a nickel; my old friend, General Benjamin Butler, by some turn of the whirligig found himself politically associated with the sand-lot agitator, Dennis Kearney, of California, who originated the slogan, "The Chinese Must Go!" with whose blatherskite ambitions I felt a perhaps reprehensible but not inexplicable sympathy; what was called the National Party had been organized with strength enough to pass the Greenback Bill for fiat money; the bill had gone through both Houses of Congress and been stopped only by the stubbornness of Grant, who vetoed it; our own corn-tassel statesman of Missouri, Richard Bland, far outrunning the subsequent vision of the peerless leader of Nebraska, had put through a bill making silver the sole basis of our national currency; Grant had vetoed this also; and then for the first time since 1862 gold, gradually dropping, had reached par and the country was again on a bi-metallic basis with specie payment resumed. The negroes had achieved civil rights; probable war had been averted by the patriotism of Tilden, who counselled patience and the submission to arbitration of the contested election between himself and Hayes, which put the latter in the presidential chair by a vote of eight to seven in the commission organized for that hearing; Garfield had come into the presidency and been assassinated by a madman, Charles Jules Guiteau, of Chicago; Guiteau had been tried, convicted, executed; the great Eads Bridge had been opened; the Father of Waters was no longer the barrier to the railroad communication of the two great longitudinal sections of the country.

In my own little personal world there had been an almost commensurate exfoliation of events and hopes; far beyond my most vivid expectations I had been given an inside knowledge of the theatre in all its departments as much as any city in the Union other than New York could provide such initiation. Besides the actors I have mentioned, I had been permitted to witness repeated performances by the beautiful Mrs. Scott Siddons; I had seen the incomparable Marie Geistinger, equally excellent in opera, drama, and comedy; had seen and become acquainted with the famous Bostonians, with Tom Karl, Henry Barnabee, Will McDonald; had seen Salvini in his heroic work with such splendid support as Lewis Morrison and Marie Prescott gave. I had studied the perfect work of the well-balanced New York companies, from the Union Square, Palmer's, and the Madison Square theatres; had become personally acquainted with Steele Mackaye, with whom I was to have a profitable friendship until his death, when the acquaintance would be carried on with his gifted and poetic son, Percy Mackaye, also a playwright; had made and begun a lifelong friendship with the matchless Robert G. Ingersoll; had made friendships that lasted till their death with many others that have gone, and friendships that still continue with many who remain. Among the departed are Digby Bell, Joseph Arthur, George R. Edeson, father of our present Robert Edeson; Stuart Robson, McKee Rankin, Frank Mayo, Charles Wyndham, Harry Pitt, Dan McGinnis, and a host of others. Of those still playing I had come to know William Gillette, Francis Wilson, the sturdy

William Muldoon, De Wolf Hopper, William Crane, Forrest Robinson, Henry Miller, the veteran Charles Stevenson, who along with John Drew is one of the few survivors of the older and classic school, now flexibly adapting himself to the later methods. I had met nearly all the responsible and irresponsible players who still play and were then travelling. I had come to know the ablest managers of the time, and the younger men that were to succeed them. One particular friendship to which I owe so much was with the late Charles Frohman, who dominated the American theatre until he was lost on the torpedoed *Lusitania*.

IX

THE DICKSON SKETCH CLUB

In the summer of 1883, when I had come back from the Vokes Company hoping to start organizing what ultimately proved to be the little theatrical company called the Dickson Sketch Club, I had a fair knowledge of the kind of material of which actors were made, and some measure of audiences too; but I felt that the experience to be had in a tour would give a knowledge of audiences in general most desirable to a playwriter. He would learn the kind of line and business that would please not only the people with whom he had been brought up but all kinds to whom he would be fortunate enough to play and ultimately to write for—the altogether American audience and the one that would be a mixture of many nationalities.

With this in mind I began my last season in Pope's box-office, having several months ahead for preparation of material and enlistment of help. The task in detail of getting material, organizing a company, playing in it and going with it in a trial through small towns was a varied experience, of which an intimate telling will probably interest others besides equally ambitious amateurs.

Looking for some one who could play the child in "Editha's Burglar," our attention naturally went to Della Fox, who was the professional infant around the theatre, and who a few years later became the light-opera prima donna with the Comley Barton Opera Company, and still later the featured lead with De Wolf Hopper in "Wang" and other Broadway successes. She also introduced the Della Fox curl in the middle of the forehead, which became the fashion from Maine to the Pacific.

Edgar Smith, now the prominent playwright, was at that time working very rebelliously in a gas-fixture establishment in St. Louis, a branch of a New York house in which his father was a partner. Edgar had been launched upon this attempt at a commercial career by his father in order to get him away from Daly's Theatre, where he had been a minor member of the resident company and a fairly important one of a company that went on the road. With us amateurs of his own age this gave him authority. At that time he was a slight and distinguished-looking person about five feet eleven inches tall, and as fine a young man physically and facially and in deportment as one would wish to see. His profile was regular, and his expression had the high, open-eyed, self-confident quality of a French marquis. He sang acceptably; he spoke with well-bred pronunciation and tone. The idea of a little company that we could call our own appealed to him thoroughly. He became a third owner in the enterprise. His choice as the exponent of anything romantic that we might play was conceded and fixed.

Frank David, the drummer I have referred to as often dancing in the lobby of the theatre during the hours he was off duty, was naturally mimetic. His work in the orchestra had required that his attention should at least be synchronized with the slap-stick and knockabout element of the performance in which his drum and cymbals assisted. Mr. Wilton Lackaye once remarked that repartee was largely a matter of repertoire. It may be that many entertaining personal properties have the same origin. David, as drummer student, had a repertoire; he was our principal comic.

Another possible member of our company, a product of the business, was William Sullivan, whom we discussed as a second comedian. He had been brought up around the theatre, being successively errand boy, usher, and bill-poster. Memory, when at all associated with genius, is selective. Sullivan's memory had fixed for him every trick of every Irish player that had made a week's stand in the city of St. Louis during his time. His particular model had been that fine Irish actor, Hugh Fay. Sullivan could give an imitation of Fay, not only in the things he had seen Fay do, but in any new material that he imagined Fay undertaking. These men— Smith, Dickson, David, Sullivan, and myself—had many conferences over our plans. We felt that "Editha's Burglar" was a sufficient *pièce de résistance*. But this playlet represented only twenty-five minutes. With a ten-minute intermission added, it still left two hours of entertainment to be devised.

Smith and I set about together to devise a comedy that would contain songs and dances and an equal opportunity to put into the show-window what we thought we and our associates individually and collectively possessed or could develop. We turned out a two-act concoction which we called "Combustion," and which we all thought up to our dress rehearsal was a very funny and sufficient vehicle to carry the last half of our evening; but it was neither. To this rehearsal, which was held in Pope's Theatre on the Sunday evening before our opening, which was to be in the little town of Mexico,

DELLA FOX AND THE CURL SHE MADE FAMOUS.

Missouri, we invited enough of our acquaintances comfortably to fill the parquet.

"Editha's Burglar" did all that we had expected of it. The audience was enthusiastic. Our two acts of "Combustion," with an ample intermission, went less than an hour and a half. Our comedy wasn't very good, and it was thirty minutes too short. After the play we knew enough of the theatre to call the company for a rehearsal at noon next day. Edgar Smith and I met in the morning for heroic work. While merely trifling and waiting about at moments during the weeks of preparation it had been the occasional practice of David, Smith, Sullivan, and myself to get together and sing what were known in those days as barber shops—quatrains from the popular songs, with very close harmony at effective points, all marked out and rehearsed by David. We would do one or two of those. In one of the Vokes comedies Fred had a table scene in which he endeavored to carve a tough fowl. This was an old stunt with him, thoroughly elaborated and filled with all manner of tricks, from shooting the resisting bird into a lady's lap to pursuing it with his knife up and down the legs of the table, where he led it with his fork. As there was a dinner scene in our piece, we resolved to introduce that foolery, with which I was perfectly familiar. Three or four other interpolations convinced us that we could pad up the evening to something like the required length. We cued in these few turns and got ready to leave town, a very apprehensive bunch of inexperienced barnstormers.

On the day of our departure from St. Louis we were in a higher degree of excitement than even young people can attain for the ordinary embarkation. We had spent a morning patching equipment, and it was therefore only by crowding appointments that I was able to respond to a call from George McManus to be sure and see him at the Grand Opera House before leaving town. I had only five minutes at his window, but he said he could deliver his message in even less time. A great many companies were coming to grief at that time in the West—organizations with New York records and indorsements—and here we were, a little band with not even a St. Louis pronouncement of our complete product, with no reputation as an organization, and not any as individual members, almost asking for disaster.

With the most serious face in the world, and of course with all these facts in mind, McManus said to me, "What is your first big stand?"

I told him Minneapolis. He took pad and pencil, put down relatively two dots, one marked St. Louis and one marked Minneapolis. He then drew an arrow between them, indicating general direction. "You see," he said, "going up you are going northwest." He drew a parallel arrow, but reversed, and then added, "Coming home you will be going southeast; just remember that."

With this pessimistic implication to be shaken off, I joined my friends and made the train.

Our first stand, Mexico, Missouri, was then a railroad town with probably three thousand inhabitants, but enough surrounding population to justify its little wooden opera-house. The audience was not critical. We were delightfully surprised, as theatrical people often are, to discover that the material added hurriedly as afterthoughts was of the most effective. Our little barbershop quatrains went so well that we had to repeat them. The next day, moving to the next town, we added two or three encores. In a week we were giving a smooth performance of what simple people of the Middle West called a good show.

The little playhouses of that time were more inadequately equipped behind the scenes than they were in front. Sometimes, not often, a curtain had to separate the dressing-room of the men from that of the women. In one little town whose name and locality I have forgotten there was no dressing-room at all, nor room for one. We were expected to do what every company that visited the town did: We dressed in a shop that was occupied by a cobbler in the daytime and lent to the theatre at night. It was some forty feet from the stage door, and on the night I have in mind we all of us—men, women, and the little girl—covered the distance between these two places in the rain.

In Muscatine, Iowa, a pretty little town on the west bank of the Mississippi, the theatre was a second-story room, built over some stores on the main street. It was lighted by coal-oil lamps, three or four of them behind tins for footlights, and a large one, a circular burner, hanging permanently above the middle of the stage. The machinery of these lamps was not in the best condition, but the audience felt perfect confidence in the watchfulness of the janitor, who sat in the front row, with his attention divided between the play and these coal-oil burners.

Smith and I had reached the most effective and dramatic part of the Burglar sketch when this tall figure rose from the front row of kitchen chairs and said with irresistible authority, "Wait a minute! Wait a minute!"

We stopped. There was no laugh in the audience, no protest. The man climbed onto the stage, which was only about three feet high from the floor, pulled his kitchen chair after him, set it in the middle of the scene, stood on it, turned down the lamp overhead, very carefully regarded it a moment with the eye of an expert, got down, took the chair, retired to the floor of the auditorium, turned and waved to us with a peremptory "Go on!"

We went on. The audience was evidently used to this as a regular feature of the visiting entertainments. It was, however, pretty hard for Smith and me to look each other in the eye and proceed with the lines, especially with the wheezy laughter of the company half smothered in the wings.

Our various stays, measured by hours, in these little towns differed of course, being governed as they were by the time of the arriving and departing trains and the distance to the next stand. Often we got in comfortably late in the forenoon, had time to see that our scenery and baggage reached the theatre and was properly placed, and then found ourselves with an entire afternoon at our disposal in some picturesque little place, full of interest for the visitor. There might be a lake or a little stream with rowboats; there was always a stable with acceptable saddle-horses, and if one were a walker two or three minutes took him into the lanes and fields outside.

My own interest in every part of America had been stimulated by early political associations. The men I remembered with admiration had come from little districts such as these all over the country. The features that characterized these districts, to some of which we now were going; the products that made them valuable in contributing to the welfare of the commonwealth; the relation of the plain, wise, sturdy people to the tasks upon which these products depended; the human capacity of the individual to be interested in the work at hand, and kindred things, were always as entertaining as a storybook.

After we had been out a short while we were joined by Will Smythe, who came to us in the capacity of business-manager. The late William G. Smythe—or as we knew him familiarly, Billy Smythe—remained in the theatrical business as manager or producer until he died in September, 1921, while occupying a position as David Belasco's booking-agent.

They treated us rather well in Minneapolis. The papers, morning and evening, were complimentary. But I have always attributed much of this to the influence of W. C. Edgar, editor of the *Northwestern Miller*, published in Minneapolis and at that time owned by Charles Palmer, who subsequently became business-manager of the New York American.

One night after the play Smith, Smythe, David, and I went to Edgar's and played poker. I think some one in our party must have won a little, because we were coming back in excellent good-nature. As we neared the Hennepin House, the hotel at which we were staying, we became aware of some excitement about the place, and a gathering of fire-engines, one of which was still working, indicating that we had come in at the finish of a fire. This proved to have been in a small building to the rear of the hotel. The crowd that still remained was intensely interested in an excited individual who was looking from one of the small windows under the eaves on the topmost floor of the hotel, which was about six stories high. This person was calling in a most complicated German dialect, asking if he should throw his trunk from the window; calling for somebody to put up a ladder; making all kinds of appeals to the crowd that was hooting at him from below. It didn't take our party long to recognize this excited roomer as our Irish comedian, Billy Sullivan, who had not been invited to the poker party, but had met much more entertainment at home.

In the hotel corridor we found one of the clerks complaining of this performance and that the door was locked and he couldn't get into the room. Sullivan, answering our calls over the transom, admitted us. He was highly elated over the attention he had attracted, and was a perfect hero in the eyes of little Della, who had come across the hall in her wrapper to prompt him in this escapade. Papers reporting the fire the next morning carried a serious account of this frightened German, who was saved from jumping only by the cries of citizens below.

On this first trip it was a great happiness for us to meet such able men writing for the theatre as George Goodale of Detroit, Elwyn Barron, Teddy McFeelam, and Biff Hall of Chicago, and the men of equal seriousness in the other cities, all of whom without exception spoke of the comedy, "Combustion," as being entertaining, clean, full of fun; commending it more or less in the vein of one writer who said: "The only wonder is how and where so small a party collected such a budget of amusing nonsense." These criticisms were valuable not only in addressing the public when we were again on tour the following season, but they were influential with theatrical owners everywhere in getting time. It must be remembered that in 1884 there were no theatrical syndicates. Men who owned theatres had not delegated

THE DICKSON SKETCH CLUB, AT MINNEHAHA FALLS, MINNESOTA. 1884.

Standing: Edgar Smith, William G. Smythe, Pearl Dudley, Augustus Thomas, Della Fox.
Seated: Sydney Haven, Frank David, Nellie Page.

to any central authority in New York or elsewhere the task of putting attractions in their theatres. They were not linked in a chain. Each manager selected his own attractions and each company corresponded by letter and by wire voluminously to organize suitable tours.

The regular bill of our company was "Editha's Burglar" and "Combustion." We had, however, two or three other little things, such as Gilbert's "Sweethearts" and Bernard's "His Last Legs." "His Last Legs" had a longer cast than we were well prepared for. We met this by having Smythe come from the front of the house and play old *Mr. Rivers*, and by changing the footman to a housemaid and giving that part to little *Della*; and she was very cute in it too. Our second comedian, Sullivan, had to be cast as a walking gentleman, one *Doctor Banks*. This was a rôle quite within the capacity of any utility man in the world, but as he had to wear a high hat and gloves and present *O'Callahan* with a card in the front scene and speak a serious line or two about looking for a long-lost daughter, the pretense of it was so far afield of anything Sullivan had ever imagined himself doing that he was almost panic-stricken with the assignment. This was in no wise relieved by the conduct of Della, who considered it her business on the tour to regard Sullivan as her particular play boy of the Western world. In and out of the theatre these two were given to guying each other and to practical jokes.

Della had a little sand jig to do in "Combustion." It was quite good enough and up to the standard of that time, and I am sure Sullivan thought well of it; but he made it very difficult for the little girl by standing in the wing when nobody in authority was around and dramatizing the insufferable torture that it gave him to witness her pretended skill. Della's turn to get even came when Sullivan had to walk on as a gentleman in the part of *Doctor Banks*. Her scenes followed closely upon his own, and during all his time on the stage Della was in the prompt entrance with clinched fists and agonized looks to heaven.

After his first performance of the part Sullivan declared that he would never go on for it again; but there was no choice between doing so and leaving the company. With each added performance his distress mounted, until by the time we had finished the season *Doctor Banks* was a nightmare with him. He studied the route ahead in his effort to figure out where we might possibly want to put up that bill. Will Smythe, a good deal of the joker himself, would occasionally invade the smoking-car with a forged telegram from some manager ahead asking for this comedy of "His Last Legs," and read it to me or to Smith loudly enough for scraps of it to reach Sullivan across the aisle.

The name of the character, *Doctor Banks*, finally passed into Sullivan's vocabulary as descriptive of any inadequate person in life. Occasionally when he lost his temper about something else and had exhausted the polite and impolite expletives at the command of the average tough he would finish by adding that the party under condemnation was a regular *Doctor Banks*. Language could convey no more.

The theatre all over the country at that time was suffering from the competition of roller skating, which was then a craze. The rinks throughout the country made as much of a bid for persons who would otherwise have gone to the theatre as the motion pictures now make. Though as actors we disapproved of this fad, we were not superior to it, and many an hour in the afternoons was used up by visits to the rink. Mr. Smythe was generally busy during these times with his books or his other business duties. Sullivan inferred from this that Smythe was afraid of the roller skates, and he thought it would be fine fun to lure him to a rink and then laugh at his mishaps when he had been equipped with a pair of skates. Smythe evaded these attempts for a time, but finally consented.

I must confess that all of us had more or less indirectly assisted Sullivan in his plan. We were all present on the afternoon in mind; we stood about while Sullivan carefully strapped the skates onto Smythe. We restrained our laughter as Sullivan and David with difficulty helped him from his seat to a prominent place on the smooth floor of the rink, and then left him alone and unsupported. To the surprise of all, however, Smythe's first move was to go into what is called the spread-eagle, a difficult figure, with the heels together and the toes pointing in opposite directions. From this he passed on to cutting a few figure eights, and finished with a pirouette on his toes that would have done credit to any professional. We had all coaxed an expert with medals into this intended exhibition of a tyro!

Little Della Fox was a pupil of Nellie Page, who was our leading woman. The Fox and Page families were neighbors and friends, and Della was placed in the care of Miss Page during her tour with us. One of the conditions of her being permitted to go with us was that she was to carry her schoolbooks, and her studies were not to be abandoned. The rôle of pedagogue was mine. As we weren't paying salaries with any regularity, and as her money went home anyway, the usual theatre fine for a breach of discipline meant nothing, but to fine her one extra lesson was effective.

Outside her studies she had a child's curiosity in all questions raised by the features of our shifting environment. This was generally satisfied by some member of the company, but not in the spirit of seriousness that should guide an education. There was a disposition, especially on the part of the men, to tease rather than to inform. For example, meeting the word frequently on the bills of fare, Della wanted to know, "What is a veal?" Everybody tried to describe it to her in terms of elimination; it wasn't as large as a cow; didn't have wings like a chicken, and so on; and all so seriously that Della went through the season, hurrying now and then to the car window, but always too late to see a veal that we had just passed. In the beautiful little city of Madison, Wisconsin, business was bad because there was a meeting of the alumni that competed. Della wanted to know what an alumni was. Smythe was trying to tell her in the usual way, eliminating colors, wings, and the like. Della, hoping to make better progress by combining ideas, asked if it was anything like a veal. Smythe told her it was very much like a veal, only it didn't know so much.

It was not always possible to get first-class trains. On more than one trip we had to be content for a short jump with the company huddled in with the trainmen in their caboose. One awkward booking forced us into that kind of travel overnight. We reached our hotel early in the morning. Della walked to the hotel desk.

The clerk, noticing her dishevelled appearance, said: "What's the matter, kid?"

Della answered: "I've been in a calaboose all night."
She looked it.

I think I should tell of our advance man, Frank Hamilton, because in some other important business ventures and episodes growing out of them Hamilton and I were intimately associated. He was not quite thirty years old, but looked a bit older. You could safely call him colonel or judge in any group without risking doubt of your seriousness. For a short time he had been an actor; for a shorter time an unsuccessful star. He had the most unbounded confidence in himself and his capacity to carry out anything that he undertook; but as soon as Hamilton filled in all the outlines of any sudden conception, and was able fairly to communicate the figure to one or two other minds, he was ready to abandon it for some newer and more inviting dream. Sometimes where there was a gap in the route the duty to get a date for us fell to him. His optimism concerning the business we would do at any place he selected and thought about was sufficient for him to feel guaranteed in the required railroad journey, however long. My only venture as the owner of a newspaper was following one of Hamilton's will-o'-the-wisps. The only time I felt I was sharing the lease of a theatre was when we went arm in arm after another prospect.

Getting home from this try-out trip of ours as we did late in June, with the intention of beginning a regular season toward the end of August, left us players with not much more than six weeks' vacation, which we employed leisurely improving material we had as to text and in getting new songs, and the like. The trip had been vastly interesting and educational, but there was salary owing to the company, and unpaid paper bills at the local printers', the Springer Lithograph Company. Whatever our trip had proved besides, it had certainly shown that we were not a paying enterprise in a spring season over small time in the Middle West.

X

ADVENTURES ON THE ROAD

Those were sad vacation days, divided as were our hopes and our actual prospects. Mr. Dickson bravely argued that we had done all that we had any reason to expect in the way of business. We had a perfected entertainment and a scrap-book of notices that many a New York manager would have given thousands of dollars rightly to own. Furthermore, the offers for return dates in the regular season were most reassuring. One menace lay in the fact that nearly every member of the company had received some flattering offer from other managers who had seen our work in Minneapolis, Milwaukee, or Chicago.

My first meeting with A. L. Erlanger, for so many years the head of the syndicate that later controlled the business of the American theatres, and still in that position, was at the end of this summer. Mr. Erlanger, then a young man, probably younger than I was, as he is now younger than I am, was managing the first financial venture of magnitude on his own account. This was a play called "Dagmar," of which the star was Louise Balfe. I had been in to see it on Tuesday night of its early week at Pope's, and was in the lobby of the theatre during an intermission when Dickson called me and introduced us. The young manager said that he would like me to replace his leading man, an actor by the name of William Harris, not related to either of those prominent managers of New York, the late William Harris or the present

William Harris, his son, and that he would pay me seventy-five dollars a week, a large salary for a road leading man at that time. I declined the offer and went on my errand to the near-by café. He met me again during the following intermission and raised the offer to one hundred dollars, which I also declined.

During the last year of the World War, 1918, I was at Mr. Erlanger's dinner-table in New York with a number of men who were discussing some war aid in which the theatres were interested. To my astonishment he referred to that first meeting at Pope's thirty-four years before. He asked me if I remembered my reasons for refusing to go with the company, and told, to the amusement of the company, that I had said: "I won't go, because I think you have a bad play which should be in the storehouse." And the Napoleon of managers laughed heartily at this freshness.

"But Thomas was right," he added, "and I should have saved money by taking his advice at the time."

I then told him of a reinforcement that had been given to my estimate of the play. Before I had gone into the theatre on that Tuesday night I had met our Dickson Sketch Club comedian, Billy Sullivan, whose anguish at having to play a straight part I have related. The week before Mr. Erlanger's engagement in the theatre the attraction had been one Ada Richmond, a rather indifferent type of burlesque woman in as bad a performance as could be imagined.

I said to Sullivan, "How is the 'Dagmar' piece?"

With a seriousness that intensified the unconscious humor of his remark, he answered: "Why, Gus, it's a case of Ada Richmond with a whole cast of *Doctor Bankses!*"

My refusal to go with "Dagmar" at a hundred dollars showed me how truly at heart I preferred our little home company. My own wavering was over, and the other boys fell into line for a big try at a real tour. As I looked over Dickson's route sheets for the coming season, fairly filled as they were for the early months, and for later ones marked out with indicated points of importance between which we should manœuvre the tissue of connecting engagements, I had a great eagerness, inspired by the prospect of such a season in a little commonwealth company wherein were no stars, where the proprietors were comrades and where baby-girl and impecunious owner and accomplished manager got each the democratic salary of forty dollars a week, with no guaranty and infrequent realization. You can't go far wrong on forty dollars a week; but if you are willing to waive its collection and transmute the debt into railroad tickets with an intermittently encouraging patronage you can cover a lot of ground.

Starting on this regular season, we naturally recovered the territory of our try-out. The people remembered us and we did not do badly. One of those filling-in jumps referred to as sometimes made by our advance man carried us from Stillwater, Minnesota, to Winnipeg, Manitoba, broken only by a stop at St. Cloud, about seventy-five miles north of St. Paul. The round trip was all based on Hamilton's hopes of Winnipeg, inspired by some glowing description by a local manager. Stillwater is a beautiful little town on the St. Croix River, almost due east of Minneapolis. We were playing there Friday night, and made St. Cloud for Saturday, and then had Sunday to get into Winnipeg and prepare for the week. To do this we were to make a very early start from Stillwater and change cars at St. Paul. We left a night call with the hotel proprietor and went to bed. I waked in the morning about fifteen minutes before train time, ran along the hall where we were quartered, roused the company and without breakfast made a dash for the station, but too late. The next train would get us into St. Cloud at about the time we should ring up for the play, with no margin for getting the scenery to the theatre or making ourselves up for the characters. The hotel proprietor thought that we might drive across country in time to get the train scheduled to take us out of St. Paul. But after consulting with the livery-stable man this was found to be impracticable. The scenery and baggage had gone on the train.

On a quick decision it was agreed that Sullivan and I should try the cross-country drive. The stable keeper sent us a double surrey, with two ordinary-looking horses, and a boy of fourteen to drive. We started. The boy handled his team with the knowledge and composure of a veteran. Sullivan and I complained of the slow pace we were taking. The boy figured that the drive could be made in time to give us a margin of ten minutes on the train, somewhat over two hours, as I remember; that to rush the horses would be to tire them out and not make the connection. We thought that more speed could be safely tried; but the lad insisted that he was in charge of the expedition and that he would conduct it to suit himself.

At last on a little lift in the rise of the landscape the boy, pointing to a distant cloud of smoke, collection of chimneys and roofs, said: "That is St. Paul."

The horses had increased their speed little if any, but were now moving with great regularity, and under the guidance of this little tow-headed North American we went up to the proper station in St. Paul fifteen minutes ahead of the time. We were able to get sandwiches and some coffee at a stand in the terminal and make our train, on which we had the satisfaction of seeing the car with our scenery and baggage already hooked. This put Sullivan and me into the town of St. Cloud early in the afternoon. We had the scenes set and the baggage distributed for the company that arrived at eight. We also had time to get out some hand-bills and explain to the little community, who had seen no company arrive upon the morning train, the situation as it stood, and promise them the plays as advertised in the evening.

When we got into Winnipeg we were astonished to find that it was winter. It was late autumn in the States. But in this city of Manitoba the ground was covered with snow. All vehicles had been taken from their wheels and were upon runners; the roads were already packed. The hotel at which we stopped was fitted with storm sashes outside the working windows, closed in for the winter siege.

Despite the optimism of Hamilton and the genial hopes of the local manager, we didn't open to much business. There is always an excuse in a little town for bad business; the local manager has alibis. They begin about a quarter of eight, when the house is not promising, by his assertion that the people come late; and finish by his suddenly remembering that there is a church sociable or gathering of equal importance, or some local political excitement that explains the lack of patronage. The saddest excuse that you can get is that the people are saving their money for the attraction that is to follow.

In Winnipeg a local malefactor had broken jail a day

or two before our arrival and made his escape. He had been recaptured and brought back. The lieutenant-governor of Manitoba, resenting this criminal's failure to respect the iron bars, had caused him to be flogged; and the free Englishmen of that fine little city were discussing this punishment. They had finally come to the conclusion that a man in jail was justified in dismissing any moral restraint that bars were supposed to imply. His right to escape was by implication just as inalienable as his measure of beer by the London quarter guaranteed by Article XXXV of Magna Carta. The debate of this flogging order had slowly mounted into indignation, and finally into something very like rebellion.

As we were ringing up on our first performance the lieutenant-governor was in the midst of a banquet at the Windsor Hotel. The after-dinner speeches were interrupted by a crowd of Englishmen that was rapidly gathering outside, looking for his excellency. The hotel proprietor had been forced to lock his doors, guard his windows, and finally the lieutenant-governor, after an hour or two of this menace, was covertly conducted out the back way, in disguise, and spirited off in a sleigh in order to save his skin. When we came home from the theatre the police had to help us to get through the mob, and we had to be identified before we could be admitted to the hotel. The women were frightened; all of us men were impressed. But one thing about which we agreed was that that was the largest audience out there we had seen for some weeks. Somehow this suggestion caught in the tinder of my political recollections and preparations. When we reached the second story I went out on a little iron balcony, while Will Smythe and Edgar Smith stood behind me in the doorway.

It was impossible for the people below to distinguish this figure silhouetted against the lighted but curtained windows. To them it seemed to be some messenger from the fugitive official they were hunting. With the fool-hardiness of twenty-seven I addressed them as fellow citizens, lifted my hands for silence, which came quickly, then leaned on the rail and spoke as I fancied Blaine or Logan would have addressed them.

The night was cold and clear; the houses opposite made a fine background; it was as good a place for a political address as a man could ask for. I began with a paragraph or two about the rights of Englishmen, the guaranties of their great unwritten constitution, the elaboration of that in tradition and practices; spoke of the reason for their coming to the hotel doors; told them that among the rights of every Englishman were those of self-expression and the pursuit of happiness; and then mentioned the Dickson Sketch Club playing at the opera-house, where the most pleasure for the least money——

Bang! A shower of snowballs caught me and my friends standing behind and broke a number of windows. I was dragged inside and some man, speaking more directly to the facts from the door below, finally got them to believe that the lieutenant-governor had escaped.

The next day the agitation in the community kept up. The people didn't know the man who had been whipped; they didn't care anything about that. Their rights had been invaded by an appointed official. The thing that impressed me in their behavior was the way they went about their self-assertion. Instead of being perfectly satisfied with getting something on the editorial page in the public forum signed by a Lover of Liberty, they had moved promptly to direct action. I am not even at this date prepared to advocate their methods where there is a judicial machine capable to redress, but there is fine value in tradition and in its authority with an unmixed stock.

Despite this advertising, our business on the second night was no better. The local manager thought our entertainment was not so hilarious as his patrons expected. He advised a change of bill. We were ready with "His Last Legs," and in order to present a full evening of new offering we decided to try "Muldoon's Picnic," which we had been discussing for some time. Sullivan was thoroughly familiar with the play from watching two or three engagements in which Barry and Fay did it for a week each time. David also had watched it from the orchestra, and little Della had played the child for Barry and Fay when they were in St. Louis. I had some familiarity with it from having got in occasionally from the box-office.

The plan was to put this on Thursday night. In the old days, twenty years before the time of which I am writing, it was not unusual to pitchfork pieces into a production in that hurried way, and experienced variety people even as late as 1900 would get together and put on an afterpiece with very few rehearsals and relying more upon tradition than upon script. It was necessary, however, for us to have a prompt copy, or we thought it was. Edgar Smith and I sat down to tables with pens and paper, while Sullivan, David, and Della dictated to us the play as they remembered it. Smythe, the third of our scriveners' department, set to work copying parts for the women. Della required no part. She was herself an authority. Smith and I preferred to copy our own, because that was an excellent method of study. David and Sullivan knew the play.

A principal member of any "Muldoon's Picnic" company is the donkey. We found one on a farm, guaranteed his full value to his owner, and hired him for the last half of the week. Our auditorium was reached by a winding staircase, making an ascent of some thirty feet. The donkey refused to follow or drive up this, so we carried him to the parquet and down the side aisle and up five steps more to the stage. We played "Muldoon's Picnic" on Thursday evening. All the work I have indicated—writing the play, writing some parts, holding the rehearsals implied, getting the donkey, getting our own costumes—was accomplished in thirty-six hours, during which we had also given one performance of our original bill. "Muldoon's Picnic," with Bernard's farce, "His Last Legs," drew enough money for us to get our railroad fares back to the States and resume our tour in northern Wisconsin. Sullivan's agony at having to play *Doctor Banks* the first half of the evening was assuaged and almost compensated by his chance to do *Muldoon*, which was really a star part.

There is a comic episode connected with another presentation of "Muldoon's Picnic" by this company. It occurred in New Orleans. We weren't in the best theatre. The only piece of local scenery that would serve as the required picnic-ground was a back drop representing the Lakes of Killarney. This was very old and wrinkled and was suspended from the gridiron. To take out the wrinkles, the carpenters pulled the canvas taut and nailed its lower batten, or wooden rail, to the stage. David as *Mulcahy* had to mount the donkey at the usual moment in the second act. The New Orleans donkey was not only sulky but reactionary. He backed up against the Lakes of Killarney, and—cheered rather than deterred by this opposition—backed through the rotten canvas and disappeared in the waters. Nothing during the week had pleased our audience so much as that vanishing act, and nothing that could be said condemnatory of theatres in general and donkeys in particular was omitted by David, whose voice from behind the Killarney Lakes was fortunately muffled by the canvas of a reunited Ireland and drowned by the screams of the house in front.

One day soon after our return· to the States I found our boys in the smoking-car roaring with delight over a little comedy in *Harper's Magazine*. I joined them and listened to the smart dialogue of "The Elevator," by William Dean Howells. That was my first knowledge of him as a dramatist. The effects that he achieved in that little play, "The Elevator," and in the others that followed soon after were very educational suggestions to a young writer as to what could be done in the theatre with restraint joined to precision.

There was a tidy little opera-house in Fort Wayne, Indiana, fixed in my memory by the clatter of tinware that began in front of the curtain some time before the overture and grew to a deafening charivari in a few minutes. This noise was a result of the gallery rule in that house that every boy had to carry with him to his seat a tin spittoon from a stock piled at the doorway where he entered.

The effect is associated in my mind with election night. It was from the stage of that little opera-house that we announced the returns of the presidential election in 1884, as was then the custom in the theatres, and of course still is. These returns were read during intermissions, but as the excitement mounted the interest in them more than equalled that in the play, until as each

fresh telegram came an actor stepped down in character
and read its contents to the audience—such and such a
vote for Blaine, or this or that State indicated for Cleveland.

At one point in the burlesque that closed our show
Ned Smith appeared as a spinster of the Directoire
period, poke bonnet and curls. In this costume, toward
10.30 in the evening, he got the laugh of the night by
reading this telegram:

"Us girls seem to have got left at the post.—Belva."

This revives the fact which many, even those rather
well informed politically, never fixed in their minds—
that in that year a woman, Belva A. Lockwood, ran for
the presidency of the United States as the candidate of
a regular accredited political organization, the Equal
Rights Party.

We had a half-day in the city of Washington in the
early winter of 1885; not playing there, but changing
cars on a jump from Pennsylvania to a Southern town.
It was my first return to the city of magnificent distances
since my term as page-boy fifteen years before. Pennsylvania Avenue looked impressively broad but depressingly
shabby, with its little four-story houses, five-story hotels,
and dingy shops, all even smaller than I had remembered. But the fine old Capitol stood at the head of the
avenue, inspiring in its grandeur and symmetry, its form
and color and satisfying balance. Neither House of
Congress was in session. I roamed the corridors and
rotundas, renewing youthful impressions, and on the
ramble drifted into the Supreme Court room. I found
that I had insufficiently estimated the impression of the
General Butler rebuke for my boyish caricatures of him,
as I felt a nervous tingling up the spine at sight of the

old warrior seated at the table, his chin resting on his hands and his eyes closed, while the solicitor-general or some representative from his office addressed the court. As near as one could gather, sitting with the three or four spectators listening to the uninteresting case, the issue was a claim against the United States for certain cotton owned by a loyal citizen and destroyed as a tactical necessity by some Northern general during the war. The solicitor for the government, indulging in forensic elaboration and effects, tired his listeners in the lobby, who were evidently waiting for Benjamin F. Butler to speak. When the solicitor finished Butler slowly opened his eyes, turned his head with an inquiring jerk, lifted his chin as he directed his gaze to the members of the court, rose with deliberation, and said:

"If it please the court, I have but one point to submit: If the court overrules me I have nothing further to offer; if the court sustains me I have won my case."

And then he submitted his point, a very brief one, too technical to make an impression on my mind; but the thing that did strike me was the old gentleman's running true to form—brief, direct, condensed, significant.

When I was first drawing, my father who taught me to sharpen a lead-pencil with a penknife—and, by the way, that is an art I should like to describe if space permitted—inculcated the habit of filling in odd moments, even those of some preoccupation if one's hand were free, by making short parallel strokes upon any convenient piece of paper, and then later by equal and similar strokes crossing them at angles. Each new layer of pencil marks deepened with definite degree the effect of shadow that the earlier marks produced. As we left Pennsylvania and later left Washington, and then moved south upon our route the increase of the percentage of colored population had very much the effect of a cosmic draftsman recrossing his crayon marks on his continental carton.

As we got deeper into the black belt I was puzzled to understand the authority that our comedian Sullivan had over the boys whom he engaged to help him handle baggage and do other work behind the scenes. Even when the work was done, one often saw him in control of three or four full-grown negroes who were dancing in violent contest, all the while watching him in terror.

He was playing upon their superstitions in this way: No full-blooded African south of the Ohio River is free from the fear of a rabbit's foot. To wave one across his face with malign intent is to put over him a black spell that only a strong voodoo practitioner or the possessor of the rabbit's foot himself can remove. In the theatre rouge is applied to an actor's face by a hare's foot, upon the ball of which the long soft fur is like a short camel's-hair brush impossibly broad. There was such a hare's foot in Sullivan's make-up box. Having discovered the darky's susceptibility, he carried this thing in his pocket as an object of authority and a magic wand; but ignorant of the negro psychology beyond this first experimental stage, Sullivan was in the habit of going away with the company and leaving those poor fellows under their depressing delusion.

Nothing that I could say to the black boys when I found this out altered their obsession. But I was able to devise a white spell that they believed curative and magically potent.

As far as they knew the power was entirely in the cabalistic words with which I accompanied the gesture of rubbing them slightly under each eye with a white silk handkerchief. But as the spell worked and the tears ran involuntarily from their eyes, they never doubted its efficacy, and I never told them that I had concealed in the silk handkerchief the white button of a menthol pencil. Perhaps I should be ashamed to confess it, but in the interest of efficiency, as well as occasional entertainment, Sullivan and I finally came into a working agreement by which he covered our local assistants with the black spell during the time of their required services and I released them by the white spell before we went away.

In 1885 every local community in the South had its military organization of whites, trained to the utmost efficiency of militia. We met the members of one such company in the jointly incorporated community of Winston-Salem, North Carolina. Salem was an old Moravian settlement of simple dwellings, flanked by its cemetery, in which this religious sect, consistently with its belief that death was a democracy in which all were equal, permits above the graves of its dead only the little uniform cubes of stone. Winston, in contrast, is the new town, with everything therein apparently erected since the Civil War, and a graveyard in which the most ostentatious are welcome.

Our engagement was for one night. The house was very thin, but, as the favorable notices say, most appreciative. When the curtain fell two or three young gentlemen came behind, introduced themselves, expressed their approval of the plays and apologized for their townspeople who had not patronized the entertainment; and then, with a refreshing ignorance of theatrical arrangements, suggested that we stay another night. It obviously never occurred to them that theatrical arrangements were made in advance, and that we could not prolong a visit anywhere simply because our hosts were agreeable.

The sequel, however, almost bore out their innocent assumption. The Winston militia, the local name of which I forget, overrode our excuses and explanations with a disarming hospitality that one doesn't meet north of that latitude. We were to play the next night in the town of Salisbury. We couldn't ask the manager there to release us. We would be under pecuniary obligation and liability. All of this these young men quickly accepted, assimilated and transmuted into energy. With our consent, they got hold of the Salisbury manager; they arranged, in what manner I do not know—they hadn't had time to send our next morning's notices—for his consent to our cutting out his town, and they gave us, as they had promised, a fine house and a jolly audience on the second night. They also gave us a supper and a dance in their armory.

The spirit of entertainment spread through the little town. The hotel keeper, with a couple of two-horse rigs, showed us the surrounding country. When, in the glow of this give and take and quite family intimacy, Mr. Smythe felt called upon to speak some farewell words of thanks before the curtain, his enthusiasm outran his information, and he spoke in most glowing terms of their wonderful little hotel. A roar of mocking laughter answered him; even local pride knew this hotel to be rotten; and the next morning the hotel proprietor, who—also knowing his own hotel—could not be convinced that Smythe's compliments had been sincere, forced an apology from him by threats of personal violence. We left, unanimously admitting that the hotel was bad, but that we thought the home folk didn't know it.

My travelling bag with its contents was a standing joke in our company. It weighed about fifteen pounds. One side of it was filled with a tightly rolled steamer rug and a pair of five-pound iron dumb-bells. The other side held the usual toilet articles for a night away from one's trunk. Although we had plenty of exercise on the stage in our rough dances, I was fearful at that time of losing the strength I had acquired in the railroad yard. In my anxiety to avoid that I packed this pair of dumb-bells, weighing together ten pounds, and I conscientiously used them every day in the bedroom. The steamer rug, which somebody had given me, I continued to carry because of its value now and then as protection to little Della. There used to be a blacksmith in St. Louis who sold somebody's horseshoes. His attractive advertisement read:

"No frog, no hoof; no hoof, no horse."

That could have been paraphrased in our organization by writing:

"No Della, no 'Editha's Burglar'; no 'Editha's Burglar,' no show."

Except to those acquainted with the country at that time, it will be a surprise to learn that the most penetrating cold was sometimes in the Middle South. The people there had not yet recovered from the impoverishment of the Civil War. Many hotels were poorly heated. Railroad cars were often cold. Some junctions at which we had to wait had only a frame house, with no fire in the stove. At such times we rolled Della up in the steamer rug. There was one hotel to which we returned from the cold theatre in what the local people called a norther, which corresponds to a Western blizzard. At the late hour nobody in authority could be found about the hotel. The two or three half-frozen negro servants we were able to arouse brought us a small armful of wet wood. The women members of our company were really suffering. Miss Page had a singer's sensitiveness to atmospheric and temperature changes. We had come to a pass where it meant not only a temporary incapacity of these more delicate ones, Miss Page and Della, but it might be a question of serious illness; and a company stranded a thousand miles from home.

Assigned to rooms according to the apparent importance of our members, Edgar Smith had been given a room with an open fireplace. Miss Page and Della, wearing their street wraps, got into the bed in that room; Edgar and I sat up fully dressed and wearing our caps and overcoats. But the blasts of this norther came through the badly joined windows until the water on the washstand was freezing. The hard wet wood fetched up by the shivering darky wouldn't ignite. Heroic measures were necessary. We men took the pine sides and backs from the drawers of the washstand and the bureau and the shelves of the wardrobe, broke them up with a dumbbell, and kept the fire going. We left the hotel before dawn, according to railroad requirements, after having some thin coffee and corn muffins given us in the chill dining-room. We told the man who came on duty about our necessity to use the cheap furniture as fuel. We had probably caused a damage of ten or fifteen dollars. Whether from indifference or from belief in the justification of our emergency measures, the hotel proprietor never communicated with us about the matter.

We had a wonderful week in the city of Charleston.

The owner of the theatre where we played was the fine old actor, John E. Owens, whom I have already mentioned, celebrated for his *Solon Shingle, Caleb Plummer*, and *Doctor Pangloss*. He came in to see our performance on the first night, and every night after that came in to see only our Burglar sketch; but after the play each night when we got home to the hotel we found Mr. Owens waiting for us at a table reserved by the chimney corner in the bar. About the middle of the week Mrs. Owens, who was an austere lady—I have the impression that she had been a player too—sent for us. Although she was somewhere near the age of her husband, who was then sixty-two, her hair was jet black and combed in a heavy fold on each side, completely hiding her ears after the manner later popularized by Cléo de Mérode. This *grande dame* asked for Mr. Smith, for some reason considering him the chief offender, and while Smythe and I stood by she told us we should be ashamed of ourselves to keep an old gentleman like Mr. Owens up at the bar to the small hours every morning.

She was right. But what eager youngsters in their middle twenties would have lost the opportunity to sit with this convivial veteran as he filled the hours with an uninterrupted series of anecdotes and recollections of the theatrical experiences so attractive to their fancies?

Toward the end of the week, in one of these sessions, he asked me, "Are you the Thomas that the St. Louis papers said played old man *Rogers* better than I did?"

I told him that I was, but that I had had no part in the controversy.

He answered: "Neither had I, and I haven't spoken of it since. But now that I've watched you play the

Burglar this week, I think the St. Louis papers were probably right."

The hour was late, there had been some alcohol, but
the tears sprang to my eyes as they would come now to
the eyes of Rollo Peters if John Singer Sargent were to
say to him, "I think the portrait you painted is better
than the one I did."

On our way from Atlanta, which still bitterly remembered Sherman, we passed through Talladega to the
busy little city of Birmingham. A story that Mr. Owens
had told us of a night in Talladega, the beauty of the
town as we saw it, and especially the sight of a razed
gateway to one old estate, impressed me. I laid there
the scenes of the first play that I wrote some six years
later for Mr. A. M. Palmer. Also, I named the play
"Talladega," but Mr. Palmer thought that too exclusive
for the theme, and we agreed upon the title "Alabama."

New Orleans! Every member of the company had
been looking forward to the visit for different reasons.
To walk around the old town after we had been there a
day or two and located its points of interest was like
hearing my father talk about it as he had talked when
he came back to St. Louis bringing the bananas and
mocking-birds in 1865. The same quaint personages;
the same French market with its early coffee; the excellent restaurants; the wide-open gambling-houses; the
walled gardens; the graves built above the ground because excavations of a foot or two developed water; the
beautiful women; the men in broad hats and linen suits;
the descendants of the proud old aristocracy—all were
there.

Our little company put up at Victor's on Bourbon
Street. We ate on the westerly side of the street, where

Victor officiated in his own restaurant and brought us the stuff hot from the grill; we lived in a Madame Delphine garden on the easterly side, in rooms each letting to a common gallery reached by a stairway; each room furnished with a window fitted with Venetian blinds and a swinging door of fixed slats like the summer doors of an old-time Missouri barroom. The darkies brought us our black coffee in the morning; for *le petit déjeuner* at table across the street the coffee was served from a pot with a straight ebony handle projecting on one side and an equal spout from a right-angle face.

Two blocks away on Royal Street one when passing could locate the gambling rooms by the rattle of the keno balls in their wooden roller. I liked keno. It took only ten minutes to wait through a turn, and even in an afternoon of scattered attendance one stood a chance of winning some four or five dollars by an investment of ten cents.

In our New Orleans week we were all of us so short of funds that to risk even ten cents seemed dissipation. But partly for the reviving passion, partly for the sake of local color, partly wishing to try everything once, I went from the theatre one night into the crowded keno room on Royal Street with thirty cents as my limit, picked what looked like a good card, and on the second roll won eighteen dollars. This was too much of a windfall to be risked at a game of chance, so I cashed in and carried my winnings back to the company. We stocked up on a number of needed articles that eighteen dollars could provide.

During this engagement in New Orleans, Charles Frohman, then an advance agent ahead of some Madison Square company, came in to see the performance, and later arranged for the production of "Editha's Burglar" by Eddie Sothern in New York at the old Lyceum Theatre on Fourth Avenue. This chance for the one-act play in New York and something Mr. Frohman said made me begin to think of its value as a full evening's entertainment if elaborated. My leisure time during the rest of the season was devoted to that work, and before we closed I had written a four-act drama which was subsequently called "The Burglar."

Among the towns on our way home was Louisville, where I had a week again with John Macauley, whose acquaintance I had made so favorably while with the Norton company. We had many pleasant hours together and John was complimentarily anxious to have me meet Colonel Henry Watterson, the editor of the Louisville *Courier-Journal*. We called at the editorial room one afternoon together, and were told that Colonel Watterson was at the Pendennis Club. We followed there. As we entered the large living-room on the ground floor a handsome, black-haired, soldierly person, apparently in his middle thirties, was seated at the piano, his shirt collar unbuttoned and thrown open as by a hero of romance. He wore a seersucker coat, the sleeves of which were pushed well up from his turned back shirt-cuffs, and he was absorbed in playing a medley of operatic arias, Foster folk-songs, and improvisations.

Macauley stopped me in the doorway. The conditions were not unknown to him. It was Watterson's frequent practice at that epoch to repair to that room and that piano and play himself out of some overshadowing perplexity. After Macauley had led me outside of the clubhouse he explained this and his unwillingness to intrude upon the mood and its expression. It was not

until four years later that I met my good friend Marse
Henry. But that room in the Pendennis and that ability
to improvise were to witness and to mark for me a very
memorable moment some years later.

We reached St. Louis deeper than ever in debt, to
players and printer. Smythe went East to be a manager;
Ed Smith went to New York, where as a writer he was
to win reputation and comfort; Della became a star,
David a Broadway hit; I was stranded in a St. Louis
summer.

XI

JOURNALISM IN ST. LOUIS

When younger men have asked me what to do to fit themselves to write plays I have advised three pursuits: The study of good modern plays, both on the stage and printed; acting professionally for a while; reporting on a metropolitan newspaper. The first two occupations explain their own relation to the business of playmaking. The reason for reporting is not so obvious; but the reporter learns news values, and the climactic situation for a play would be almost always a first-page story in a newspaper office. He also learns dialogue from his interviews, and he learns character-drawing in his daily work.

None of these considerations, however, influenced me in the summer of 1885, when I found myself out of a job and in debt and in St. Louis. I was looking for work, and I looked for it amongst the men I knew. M. A. Fanning, a running mate of William Marion Reedy, and later secretary and adviser of fighting Tom Johnson of Cleveland, was for a few weeks in that summer acting as city editor of the St. Louis *Post-Dispatch*. Mike and I were theatre-lobby and summer-garden acquaintances. He thought I could write; he knew I could draw a little.

His word to Henry Moore, the managing editor of the paper, got me a job at twenty-five dollars a week, which was five better than I could have done by going back to Pope's box-office. I took it as a stop-gap and went to work hoping from day to day that "The Burglar," a four-act play I had written, would find a producer. I had a second play on the stocks which I called "Pittsburgh," dealing with the big Pennsylvania strike. It contained the Philadelphia Grays, a burning roundhouse, a cannon fired on the stage, a fire-engine and four horses, a burning tank car of oil, a runaway hansom cab, the interior of a rolling mill with a red-hot steel rail made in full view, an attic, an abduction, a bank robbery, a fight with bowie knives, a picnic by a flowing stream, a strike of mill hands, a man on horseback with rattling chains like the fellow in the "Barnaby Rudge" Gordon riots, a rusty, ruined mill-wheel that turned over and drowned an escaping villain, plenty of sentiment, political economy and several light-comedy touches. I still have it; and some day, when the Hippodrome becomes a dramatic house and the United Steel Trust goes into the theatrical business, I mean to produce it. Charles Pope seriously considered it that summer.

Years later Joseph Brooks, after some interest in "Ben Hur," also read it, and said: "I'd like to do it, but, thank God, I can't!"

But in the summer of 1885 my hopes were pinned to "The Burglar." Will Smythe had a copy of "The Burglar" with him in New York trying to place it, and E. H. Sothern, who had another copy, wrote that he would be in St. Louis soon and discuss it with me. The job on the *Post-Dispatch* therefore seemed the most temporary assignment imaginable. But even at that there were daily duties, and there were editors.

I was not a stranger in newspaper offices. As an amateur actor looking for show publicity, as a man from the box-office going with visiting advance men to the editors for two years, and also in the theatrical travel earlier described, I had become familiar with the local rooms. It was another matter, however, to report in the early morning as one of the force.

My first duty on my first day—and for that matter my first duty every day for many weeks—was to condense items from the morning papers to paragraphs of proper relation for our afternoon issue. At that time in St. Louis the newspaper practice was to cover by reference or by full report everything that happened in the city, from a drunk and disorderly to a burning barn in the suburbs. There was not the selective system now followed in metropolitan journalism, and there was no central news agency or flimsy. Each paper was expected to get its own information, and if possible to get it exclusively. The scoop, as a beat was then called, was evidence of a journal's efficiency and enterprise.

As the cub reporter in service, not in youth, I drew the simplest and most tail-end assignments. My first morning, after condensations were over, was devoted to a chicken show; not such a chicken show as would now fill Madison Square Garden, but a very unpretentious collection of coops and cages put into a twenty-five-foot vacant store. There were perhaps two hundred and fifty birds in this collection, ranging through the various breeds from Bantams to Cochin Chinas, and through the various specimens from new-hatched chickens to roosters with criminal records.

On this first day of the poultry show no awards had yet been made. As far as I could see, there was nothing to write about but just chickens and farmers with goshding-it whiskers. Quite disgusted with the assignment, and seriously revolving in my mind an impulse to quit the business, and feeling strange at any kind of writing except dialogue, I hit upon what I thought was the outrageous notion of interviewing a young cockerel from Belleville, and letting him talk of the exhibition. I turned in several pages of this kind of copy with a feeling of defiance. My astonishment can be imagined when I found that the report was considered a hit. The acting city editor read it aloud to men at the near-by desks, who laughed at it in chorus and regarded me estimatingly.

I was conducted into the art department and introduced to a German draftsman by the name of Steitz, who was instructed to make illustrations for the chicken interview under my direction. Irvin Cobb just back from Flanders with a portfolio of special stuff probably didn't make any relatively greater sensation than this first article of mine turned in at the *Post-Dispatch;* and to my mind there was a distinction about the issue of the paper that afternoon that I had never seen before. I carried extra copies home to my family. I reread the article with detached astonishment. The only reaction I didn't include was a lecture tour.

There is an introductory line in a book called "The New Hyperion," written in the early '70's by a Philadelphia newspaper man, I think named Strahan. It was his second book, and it began with this phrase that has stuck in my memory: "The man who hits one success by accident is always trying to hit another by preparation." That fully expresses my condition thereafter. I wanted with careful intent to repeat a performance which was the outcome of a rebellious explosion. Other assignments on subsequent days, however, did not lend themselves to dramatic dialogue, and from a candidate for the magazines I dropped suddenly back into the routine of hotels, real estate, justices of the peace, a school board on its vacation, architecture, and weekly art notes.

It was a depressing experience to have the paper come out day after day with only one's condensations of the unimportant morning articles; depressing to see the other fellows with fatter departments grab the first copies that the office boy distributed as they left the roaring presses, and scan their stuff ostensibly for errors but really for that authority which formal type seems to lend to gelatinous contributions, giving a satisfaction not unlike the sculptor's joy as the disappearing piece-mould reveals his permanent bronze.

The first important assignment alone grew out of a morning paragraph relating an inquiry at police headquarters concerning a young girl who had been absent from her mother's home for forty-eight hours. Was it to be rewritten or to be reprinted as it was, a simple emanation from police headquarters? It was impossible to condense it. City Editor Magner said:

"Colonel Thomas, the reason that item is so brief is that it came into that morning newspaper office too late to be expanded or inquired into. It is now your pleasant duty to discover that young lady and her family and write an extended report of the case."

I went immediately to the girl's home, a rear apartment well out on Cass Avenue, one of the poorer quarters of the city, where I found the anxious mother, her eyes red from weeping, confined to the little apartment by her domestic duties. She confirmed the item, answered my questions, gave me a photograph of the girl. Beyond this there was nothing upon which to proceed.

The girl's intimate friends were near at hand and had all been seen. There was no young man in the case, so far as mother or friends knew. There was at home no particular disappointment further than the daily grind of poverty.

I started walking down Cass Avenue in the direction of the nearest police station, which was to be my next call. It was about ten o'clock of a summer morning. A dingy street-car with two lazy horses jingled past me, going in the same direction, the conductor lolling on the back rail. Seated in the car were two laughing girls, the only passengers. As I caught their expression I smiled in the involuntary human response that is perhaps still a trick with youngish people. Then something familiar in the face of one of the girls fixed my attention and hooked up with the photograph I had in my pocket.

I ran after the car and boarded it. The girls grew serious with resentment of this procedure, which seemed more than they had invited. I addressed the one in particular: "Is your name Mamie Kelly?" and saw at once by the expression of both girls that I had found the missing daughter. I sat down, told Mamie of her mother's unhappiness, of the police hunt for her, the item in the morning paper. The girl was contrite for her truancy and immediately ready to go home.

The car was stopped, we took one in the opposite direction, and a few minutes later I turned Mamie Kelly over to her mother, who wrung my hand and patted my shoulders with the inarticulate gratitude of a rescued animal. I stayed long enough to get the girl's story, which was one of a simple temporary revolt against the hard conditions of a monotonous life. I returned to the office, a fortunate full-fledged detective journalist, to

make my report. There were only two or three of the
ten or twelve local men still in the rooms.

"Well?" said Magner.

"I found her."

He called into the next room, "Hey, Moore, Thomas
has found that Kelly girl!" The managing editor joined
us.

"Where did you find her?"

"On a Cass Avenue street-car."

"Where is she now?"

"At home."

"How did she get there?"

"I took her there."

With a look of disgust, Magner turned back to his
corner.

Moore went into his room.

"What shall I write about it?" I asked.

Magner said: "Not a damn thing! But who ever
told you that you belonged in the newspaper business?"

Out on the deserted route between the justices of the
peace I met Bicycle Hicks, one of our reporters, who had
rather taken me under his wing in the office. Bicycle
Hicks was so called because he was one of the few men
in the city and the only one on a newspaper who possessed a bicycle, which at that time was a machine with
a front wheel sixty inches in diameter and a Hogarthian
spine that ran from the saddle above the big wheel to
a little trailer wheel behind, perhaps a foot high. His
department was churches and the sterilized edges of
athletics. Among my male acquaintances he was the
original woman suffragist, prohibitionist, and anti-cigar-
ette advocate; a staring, ingenuous enthusiast. When

I last heard from him he was editing the *Army and Navy Journal.*

At the street meeting I speak of I asked Bicycle Hicks what had been wrong with my report; what it was that the newspaper had expected me to do with that lost girl. He said he didn't know, but thought it was something extraordinary that would have furnished the paper with exclusive and worth-while news. He then told me, as an indicative incident, of a reporter who had been highly commended for having carried the body of a dead man which he found on a deserted street into a near-by empty building, so that after writing understandingly concerning the inquiry which the disappearance of this man occasioned he was able as a representative of his paper wisely to reason out and discover the hiding-place of the body, and to clear up the mystery which he had created.

Hicks told me also of another enterprising reporter, who had obtained indirectly the stolen minute-books of a St. Louis grand jury that was investigating some political bribery cases and had then carried these books to a near-by town in the State of Illinois outside the jurisdiction of the court to which they appertained, and from this safe retreat had sent in daily installments transcribed from their records, to the great embarrassment of the machinery of justice, but to the renown of the paper to which the reporter was attached.

Thomas Jefferson, writing from Paris to Mr. Edward Carrington in 1787, said: "Were it left to me to decide whether we should have a government without newspapers, or newspapers without a government, I should not hesitate a moment to prefer the latter."

It seemed to me that to take the stolen records of a grand jury and print them defiantly was a practice which if persisted in would soon reduce a country to the alternative that Mr. Jefferson had preferred. I felt also that the desirability to have something to print scarcely justified its manufacture at this excessive cost to the subjects; but as I went on in the business observation convinced me that newspaper men who go to unethical extremes in the manufacture of news are in a very decided minority, and that many of the enterprises which they inaugurate in order to have something to print make the newspapers not only organs of publicity but frequently great constructive factors.

One rule on that early Pulitzer paper, the parent of the present New York *World,* was that nothing was to be printed reflecting or commenting upon any man's nationality or religion, whether for comic purposes or otherwise. It would be difficult successfully to deny the wisdom of this requirement or the justice of it.

One day a despondent German in the northern district of the city, self-persuaded that the future life held nothing hotter for him than that St. Louis August, killed his wife and four children and then shot himself. The scene was three miles away, and the hour was nearly three in the afternoon. In the rickety hack that billowed us over that distance of rutted macadam dust and oblique hurdles of street-car tracks, Johnny Jennings, the senior of our group, assigned to each man his proper department, such as cause of the crime, description of scene, neighbors and comment, police and coroner. I drew neighbors and comment. Each reporter, as he got his information, hunted a near-by telephone and talked his stuff to a relay man in the office. It was exciting at the time, but my collaborator on the office end was a matter-of-fact person with a passion for extracts. And when

I read the finished and assembled and printed product an hour later the whole tragedy, as far as I was concerned, was a disappointment and a waste of material.

That incident relates immediately to the lesson one learns early on a newspaper—that all material must adapt itself to the hourly changes in the paper's requirements. Oscar Wilde, being asked slightly to shorten "Lady Windermere's Fan," sighed as he took his blue crayon to comply, "Who am I to trifle with a classic?" But for the newspaper, classic, epic, and *chef-d'œuvre* watch their step, move up in front or change cars at command of city editor and make-up man.

One other thing I learned was that material good elsewhere might never be of value on the paper. In addition to the daily work expected of each man certain of us were supposed to turn in what was called a special for the weekly edition, an elaborated and extended write-up of some department, or now and then a more frank attempt at fiction. One such contribution of mine was a little dramatic sketch called "A Man of the World." Magner laughed at the form, and the sketch did not appear in the paper. Months afterward, when George Johns, during Magner's vacation, was again acting city editor, he dug this sketch from a drawer of dusty discards and returned it to me, saying he thought it too good to be lost.

In 1890 Mr. A. M. Palmer, at the Madison Square Theatre, produced a short comedy called "Aunt Jack," in which the principal members of his company, including Agnes Booth and James H. Stoddart, were appearing. Maurice Barrymore, on the salary list, was, however, out of this bill. After two or three curtain-raisers had been submitted to him and found unsatisfactory, he carried this sketch to Mr. Palmer, and it was put on ahead of "Aunt Jack." I received a royalty of fifty dollars a week for it the rest of that season, and when "Aunt Jack" went on the road the following year Mr. Joe Haworth played Mr. Barrymore's part in my curtain-raiser. Mr. Barrymore also played it in vaudeville, where successively his sons, Lionel and Jack, each made his first appearance in the theatre in one of its minor parts. I should roughly estimate my receipts from it at three thousand dollars. Of course the adaptability of the materials to their respective demands must be taken into consideration, but the incident is an example of the disparity between the early pecuniary rewards in the two professions.

If forced to choose, however, between the royalties for "A Man of the World" and the things I learned as a reporter I'd promptly take the training. To write of the events of interest in that training would fill a book. This article may not even identify them. An obligation exists, however, to tell clearly such experiences as put permanent dents into my articulating mentality. These experiences fall broadly into two departments: The technic of the game and the incidents it dealt with—the first central, the second environmental. I don't think the *Post-Dispatch* made that ostentatious claim to good English that the *Sun* under Charles Dana was supposed to make, but its editors were educated and exacting men. A reporter soon quit writing "those kind," and his objective cases gradually made fewer and less ambitious tries at the active; but I don't remember so much fuss over split infinitives as some nouveaux purists make. Maybe our editors had somewhat of that deeper culture which made the late Thomas R. Lounsbury of Yale and the American Academy defend the divided infinitive not only as scholarly and time honored, but as often the more expressive form.

We reporters also learned a concentration of attention which gradually calmed down from frenzied resistance to a self-respecting exclusion. The typewriters that make such a bedlam of modern offices were not then installed. But as the hour approached the make-up the rush in the office was the same as the modern rush: boys calling for copy; men from the current sensations arriving with their verbal condensations to the city editor; shouted consultations; and perhaps another element in that smaller city that may not be present now—the invasion of the room by men who might be affected by the news calling to secure its modification or suppression; these and the dozen other confusions all were there, surging around the reporter who was to have them accelerate rather than retard his part of some report that he was scratching on the cheap print paper. More than once since then at a dress rehearsal and its attendant hubbub I have been thankful for such of that control as was then acquired, which has helped me to sit at a music-stand in the orchestra pit and patch up some limping scene.

Let me tell of certain influencing contemporaries on the *Post-Dispatch*. Although it is preferable to deduce character from revealing incidents, just as it is amusing to infer the outline of the lady on the barn door from the scars made by the knife-thrower, some facts concerning our regular city editor, John Magner, cannot possibly be inferred and should therefore be told, because a city editor more than any other man on a paper determines the relation of a new reporter to his business.

Some congenital or youthful calamity had seriously

crippled one side of him, arm and leg. This affliction, as is not infrequently the case, had produced a compensating, and therefore gratifying accompaniment of increased intellectual acuteness, a mental scalpel and bistoury attack of every problem, and carrying a touch of acid. But the dissecting and cauterizing qualities were salved by a never-failing emollitive humor.

I can see Magner now sitting at his desk in that second-story room, from which three windows looked on Market Street and across to the façade of the Grand Opera House, turning in his swivel chair for some pointed instruction or corrosive inquiry, his blue pencil in the left hand, by which he had to operate it, and his swift gesture as with the same hand he agitated a reddish pompadour that looked like a brush of rusty iron.

The desk that I used for a year or more was immediately behind this swivel chair, and faced the middle window—for neither reason a coveted location. To Magner's left on the right-angled wall was Mike Lane, our sporting reporter. Lane was an able person not insensible to approval and with a great respect for Magner's opinions. I recall a colloquy which gives a touch of both men. Lane had just put a bunch of copy on Magner's desk.

He said: "There's that stuff, John. I don't think much of it myself, and I don't believe that I am writing as well as I did two years ago."

Magner made an unnecessary display of the excisions that he immediately began as he loudly answered: "Oh, yes, Mike, you do! You write just as well as you ever did. But your taste is improving," and then the blue pencil slashed out another half-page before he quickly swung to me.

I was bending over my own work, naturally amused, but I had not laughed aloud. His attention had been prompted solely by accurate suspicion, and here is his speech to me—I give it because it contains an expression which has multiplied more prolifically than the Biblical grain of mustard-seed:

"Colonel Thomas"—Magner always conferred a military title on a prospective target—"Colonel Thomas, you have a very sensitive dial. Sometimes you smile, sometimes you lift your eyebrows, sometimes you only shift your wrinkles. But you always register."

The chorus in that quadrangle of desks gave him the response he had played for. But his dial illustration impressed me, and the word "register" was indelible.

In 1891 at the rehearsals of "Alabama" at the Madison Square Theatre, and with Magner vaguely in mind, I found myself using "register" to the members of Mr. Palmer's company, whom Mr. Eugene Prestrey, the stage manager, was rehearsing, with occasional conferences with me. Presbrey consciously or unconsciously adopted and worked the word until it became a matter of playful comment with the people he rehearsed then and afterward. It was repeated by him and others more and more frequently through the years, until now that it has entirely saturated the nomenclature of the movies both seriously and in burlesque I am wondering if its inundating start was not back at that rivulet from the corner desk in the old *Post-Dispatch* rooms on Market Street

Except for the anodyne of intervening years it would be depressing to go on recording one's repeated failures to measure up to editorial expectations. But at the expense of my vanity I must tell of my first political convention and therein of two ineptitudes, or, in modern parlance, of two bones that I pulled. This nominating convention was held in Jefferson City. I attended as one of the *Post-Dispatch* corps of reporters, some three or four altogether. The permanent chairman of the convention, a clean-shaven man named James Hagerman, was elected about noon of the opening day. His resemblance to an amateur theatrical friend of mine in St. Louis was so striking that a person knowing both might address either as the other one. I persuaded Jennings of this fact and got him to wire Magner at the St. Louis office to get a photograph of Dan Bordley, of a well-known wholesale tobacco company on Vine Street, and print it as a portrait of Hagerman. This was enterprising, and should have been scored to my credit; but when the newspaper of that afternoon reached Jefferson City, and circulated in the convention next morning with its alleged portrait of Hagerman, it was ridiculous, because Bordley, not understanding the requirement, had furnished the paper with a character portrait of himself wearing a huge mustache. It was hopeless to try to point out the resemblance in the uncovered features of the face.

This said convention was meeting in the Representatives' Hall, where I had been a page. In the big room nothing seemed to have been changed; the colossal portraits flanking the speaker's daïs were there; the run at the back way to the document room; the large, resounding cuspidors under the individual desks. I felt disarmingly at home. The nominations had progressed to a vote upon the candidate for attorney-general. Our choice was a *bon vivant* by the name of Nat Dryden, whose free-handed fellowship had made him a favorite in nearly every newspaper office in the State. Representatives of these newspapers sat about the tables, where we were some thirty in number. Our private tally of the roll call in strokes of five like little garden gates told us the ballot before the clerk was ready officially to announce it. It was undecisive. The newspaper men were anxious for the outcome.

In the interim occasioned by the count I was conscious of no impropriety in getting up and saying to the convention that they would be called upon to vote again in a few minutes, and that the entire press of the State was in favor of Nat Dryden. As the entire press of the State had been somewhat critical of all of these small politicians now convened, my statement was not helpful, nor was it in order, as the pounding gavel of the smooth-faced Mr. Hagerman informed me.

This oratorical ebullition, coupled with the substituted picture, decided the man in control of our staff. When the next bundle of longhand copy went east to St. Louis I carried it, and resumed my patrol among the real-estate offices, the school board, the empty studios, and tired hopes of a call from the New York play market.

XII

TWO PULITZER PAPERS

In all these times and amidst these duties I never quite lost sight of the theatrical objective. Any mail might bring word of the sale of "The Burglar" in New York. Any week might bring Eddie Sothern and his company to St. Louis, where there would be a possible consultation about it; and always just across the street were the inviting doors of the Grand Opera House, with George McManus in its box-office and John Norton on its stage. How cool its classic shade! How respectable and dignified its purpose!

One week Mary Anderson came there after her triumphant visit to England. She brought with her a company of Englishmen headed by the present Sir J. Forbes-Robertson. Mary's earliest triumphs had been in St. Louis, and her first supporting company had been that of Johnny Norton, though before my time as his leading juvenile. There were still thousands of people in the city who were her admirers, and hundreds who were her personal friends. The paper decided to make a spread on her opening performance. I was detailed to get behind the curtain and report the first night from that view-point.

As the order came late, the best way was to go to the super captain, pay the fee already agreed upon to a super who would let me take his place, and also pass a small tip to the captain himself. At the proper time I found

myself in a hauberk, a pair of dirty woollen tights, and
otherwise arrayed as one of the retainers in "The Winter's Tale."

Miss Anderson's stage-manager was an Englishman
named Montgomery, to whom I had often given his letters
at Pope's box-office, and who I feared would recognize
me; but he did not. I was herded with his fifty-cent
roughnecks, some of them making their first appearance; and once when told to stand "clowser," and I
had not moved fast enough to suit Mr. Montgomery he
had given me an admonitory touch with his toe on the
fuller side of my trunks.

This was a good deal of an indignity for the representative of a great daily paper, parent of the New York
World, said representative an American leading man and
ex-star in disguise, and author of two unproduced dramas
—a great indignity to take from a visiting Englishman,
forty years of age and out of condition; but remembering what was expected of me in the newspaper office and
the dying Nelson's statement of England's general expectation from every man, I stood "clowser," and got
ready for the second act.

Just then General William Tecumseh Sherman, who
was an old friend of the tragédienne, came from the side
door toward Mary's dressing-room with both hands out-
stretched. The star met him on the stage and took his
hands, and the general kissed her in good round fashion.
This kind of greeting was not new to General Sherman,
who was then arriving at that privileged epoch in which
the French describe a man as *gaga*. Montgomery, in
the centre of the stage, with us super men lined up and
waiting, whispered to little Napier Lothian of Boston,
travelling with the company in some advisory capacity,

"Who is the old gentleman in uniform who just kissed the star?"

Lothian answered in a whisper, "General Sherman."

"Schirmer?"

"No! Sherman—great general."

"Ow!" Montgomery looked critically at Sherman, turned back to Lothian and asked, "As great a general as Wolseley?"

"Wolseley!" said Lothian with disdain. "Why, Wolseley isn't a patch on this fellow's trousers!"

"Now down't you say that, my boy! Down't—you —say—that!" And Montgomery extended his hand in a gesture of caution which meant, "Go no further."

This incident was the tenderloin of my written account next day, and was especially acceptable to Magner. Frequently after that, during my stay on the paper, when we had a new spectator or auditor in the room Magner would demand a verbal report of this colloquy, and insist upon a dramatical imitation of both men. Magner was as anti-British as Judge Dan Cohalan.

During the dull spells in local news the paper increased the number of its illustrations. This was partly because it would occupy some of my time, as I was put to helping the artist, Steitz. I have described in earlier papers the method of making pictures on boxwood by cutting out the white parts of the wooden field, and have referred to photo-engravings which were made by washing out the white parts from a gelatin field affected by the chemical action of light. The pictures in the *Post-Dispatch* were made by a third process, in its kind a reversal of these two methods. This was called the chalk process. The artist drew his lines with a sharp point through a deposit of specially prepared chalk precipitated upon zinc plates, which were then used as moulds upon which stereotype metal, poured hot, hardened into plates that printed exactly as the ordinary letter type. The method was hard on the draftsman, because the chalk, which turned to dust under his strokes, had to be blown away after each mark in order to let him see the shining metal of the exposed plate, which after all made a poor contrast to the white field.

Both Steitz and I used to look with envy and covetousness at the daily copy of the younger paper owned by the Pulitzer company, the New York *World*, which came to us fresh each morning and was spread on our carefully guarded files, generously supplied as each edition was with illustrations made by photographing the artist's unimpeded pen work, and having the further advantage of reduction from large originals, whereas our chalk plates had to be drawn to the exact size and limits of our column.

It was the custom of the New York paper at that time to illustrate its current news with little run-in cuts made by its admirable autographic process; little outline illustrations sometimes taking less than half the width of the column, but so pat and referable to the text carrying them that they were a pleasure to the reader. Something in policy or process has now banished these little pictures.

In that winter of 1885-1886 there was going on in the city of New York the trial of General Alexander Shaler, charged with accepting bribes while a member of the militia board of New York from the owner of certain parcels of ground selected as sites for armories. The New York papers were treating him and his defense with a levity that made amusing reading even in the Middle

West, where there was no other interest in the trial. Experts in our St. Louis office were divided in their guesses at the writer of these excellent reports, the weight of opinion being for Joseph Howard, Jr., a writer then frequently signing exclusive and syndicated stuff, and held up by all editors as an example to the local men.

Referring to these reports years afterward, to Joe Howard himself, he disclaimed their credit and pointed to Henry Guy Carleton, who was sitting with us. Carleton was then receiving congratulations for his play "Ambition," which Nat Goodwin was doing at the Fifth Avenue Theatre, a block above Valkenburg's Café, in which we were. Thus prompted, Carleton told of Shaler's indignation one morning at the descriptive phrase, "His eyes looked as though they had just been taken from the oven and buttered." With the paper in his hand, Shaler had left his place in the court-room and, shaking his finger in the face of the *World's* routine man at the reporters' table, denounced the whole reportorial tribe, while Carleton, the guilty writer, was safely seated among the spectators.

But the New York *World* of that time held for me each day an interest transcending those comic reports. Robert Mantell was winning praise in "The Marble Heart" at the Fifth Avenue Theatre, and a letter to me from Will Smythe said that he was considering the advisability of following that drama with "The Burglar." Pauline Hall, who had been in the Vokes company three summers before when we played "In Camp," and had been refused the transient hotel rates along with Westford and myself at the Matteson House in Chicago, was now starring jointly with Francis Wilson at the Casino in "Erminie," which had reached its three-hundredth performance on Broadway.

Rosina Vokes, who had left Fred before his tryout of that same piece while she went to England, was back with her own excellent little company, playing "The School Mistress" at the Standard Theatre. "Muldoon's Picnic," the comedy our company had appropriated for performances in Canada and New Orleans, was crowding Tony Pastor's Theatre, with Barry and Fay in their proper rôles. Salsbury's Troubadours, after which we had modelled our now disbanded company, was playing "The Humming Bird" at the Star Theatre.

James O'Neil, with whom Della Fox had made her first appearance in "The Celebrated Case," was beginning at Booth's Theatre in New York his run of "Monte Cristo," which was to serve him as a vehicle for some twenty years thereafter. Sarah Bernhardt, who had been our Sketch Club guest at the picture gallery in St. Louis, was giving for the first time a farewell tour which was to be repeated at intervals for the next thirty years. Minnie Maddern, in whom I felt more than a passing interest because she had been such a favorite at Pope's Theatre, and because Tom Davy, who had been in partnership with my father in New Orleans when I was a lad, had subsequently become her father, was playing "Caprice," by Howard Taylor, at the Bijou Opera House.

Robson and Crane, friendship with whom I had formed in the old art-gallery days, and who had done much to inspire me and my companions in our theatrical ventures, were playing Bronson Howard's record-breaking comedy, "The Henrietta," at the Union Square Theatre. Will Gillette had quit his amusing play, "The Professor," and with "Held by the Enemy," the first and best of the war plays, was rivalling the concurrent success of Bronson Howard.

But the most interesting item of all if I had had the gift of prophecy would have been the fact that Edwin Booth and Lawrence Barrett were beginning their joint starring venture under the management of Arthur B. Chase in the tour that was to have as one of its incidents, as already hinted, my own elimination as a budding newspaper proprietor.

These theatrical events in New York, distracting as they were to a would-be dramatist in St. Louis, were helped in their irritating insistence by their summary that our then theatrical man, George Sibley Johns, now managing editor, made every week for the Saturday edition.

Many big newspaper stories broke that year, carrying valuable material for a would-be playwright. I got the backbone of "In Mizzoura," in which Nat Goodwin starred in 1893, from the Jim Cummings express robbery. Cummings, whose right name was Whitlock, had forged an order upon a Missouri Pacific express messenger to carry him deadhead from St. Louis to Vinita, and had climbed with this authority into the express car as the train was leaving the Union Station. He had helped the messenger sort his packages until a good chance came to poke a gun into his cheek and tell him to be quiet while being tied. Then Cummings had stepped off in the dark at a water-tank with a suitcase packed with one hundred and twenty-five thousand dollars in currency.

When Cummings was finally arrested, and in the same cell in the Fourcourts where I had gone to visit John Cockerill after the shooting of Slayback, he and I became well acquainted. Two features of his exploit that I admired were his motive for it and his rehearsal of the performance. The motive was to get four thousand dollars to lift a mortgage his mother had put on her home to start him in the coal business.

Knowing that he would reach this water-tank and drop off in the night, his rehearsal was to go over the route of his escape, about twelve miles of rough country to the Missouri River, twice—once in the daylight to determine it, and once at night to master its difficulties under that condition. It was only when later he got to extemporizing that he fell into difficulty and was captured. For a successful run full rehearsals are necessary.

Another celebrated case was the murder of an Englishman named Preller by a fellow Englishman, Maxwell, who needed the money, and who left a trunk containing Preller's body with the hotel as security for his board-bill. I made an incidental use of this in the "Earl of Pawtucket" for Lawrence D'Orsay in 1903.

Other incidents, character bits, and situations in that newspaper work, too numerous and detached for present description, helped pack a mental record upon which I drew more or less for some sixty plays, big and little.

Along in this first *Post-Dispatch* winter came what was called the Great Southwestern Railroad strike, handled from the labor end by the consequently notorious Martin Irons. This started over the discharge of one union man. When manifestations at the Missouri Pacific yards between Grand and Summit Avenues in St. Louis required a second reporter to help cover them I was sent to the scene. Among the captains handling the labor forces I met two of the old K. C. & N. Railroad men who had served as junior officers in the Knights of Labor assembly over which I had presided as master workman some ten years before. By them I was enabled

to sit in the back room of a little cake and ice-cream shop
on Chouteau Avenue and write up all the big events of
a physical nature in that district some hours before their
occurrence; to send these reports to the newspaper and
have them on the galleys ready to put into the forms and
print upon the telephonic release. Some sensations happening as late as four o'clock in the afternoon, with the
paper held for their promised performance, and then
able immediately to go upon the street with a detailed
account of them, took place two or three miles away
from the quiet crossing patrolled by the police and fellow reporters.

I was never at liberty to tell my sources of information, but the paper, after the first confirming result, gave
me its confidence. The only concession I had to make
for this exclusive information was not to give the strikers
the worst of it. For two weeks the *Post-Dispatch* led in
this privileged fashion; and then one morning, getting
off the train, which usually slowed down at Summit
Avenue, but on this particular occasion, avoiding an
expected assault, pumped up a speed of some thirty miles,
I stepped onto a crossing covered with oak planking worn
to bristling splinters. One of these ran through a break
in the defective half sole and lining of a shoe and pinned
me long enough to retard my technic. It also sent me
to the hospital. Another man took my job at the crossing,
and there was a turnover in the paper's treatment of that
local situation. When I came back to work, these exclusive reports, bunched along with the good work of
the staff, had taken me a little out of the awkward squad.

I wish that what I have next to record could be written
in the third person; wish that I were writing of somebody
else or that the yarn didn't sound so like the small-boy

stories of the despised bush-league pitcher called from the big-team bench to save the deciding game of the championship series. And, as it is, I'm going to hamstring every dramatic trick in the telling of it. I'm going to draw all the climactic fizz from it now by saying to start with that one Saturday afternoon I was the low-score man on the local staff of the *Post-Dispatch*, and that twelve days later, because a talented and honest and earnest woman happened also to be vain enough to pretend to a knowledge of elementary Latin which she didn't have, a committee of politicians and bankers and otherwise sane citizens were trying to give me in fee simple a going newspaper and fifty thousand dollars in cash under the misapprehension that I was responsible for nearly all the business success of Joseph Pulitzer, to whom I had never spoken.

I have referred to the prominence in the journalistic world at that time of Mr. Joseph Howard, Jr., the New York *feuilletonist*. Either Johns or Jennings had in a generous moment of attempted encouragement mentioned Howard's name in connection with my own, observing of course the proper interval between the two. This mention had been seized upon by Magner as material for pleasantry, but there may be some truth in the maxim that every knock is a boost, because his ridicule fixed it in the mind of the managing editor, Moore, even though in distorted form. One morning about the latter part of March, 1887, Moore came into the local rooms with a telegram which he slowly handed to Magner. Magner read the telegram and looked at Moore, who waited expectantly. All of us reporters were watching both men covertly. Moore cautiously indicated me. Magner threw up his hands with an incredulous laugh, went to his swivel chair and again swung into the consultation. Moore laid the telegram in front of me. It was from Mr. Ballard Smith, managing editor of the New York *World*. It read:

On Tuesday, April 5th, the women of Kansas will for the first time vote in the local elections. Send your best humorous writer and an artist at once to make a tour of the State to describe and illustrate conditions in principal cities. Have them arrange with local men in each city to report by telegraph to a central point, say Topeka, on election day, from which place your reporter will telegraph us summaries of the results.

When I had read it I looked over at Magner, who was grinning derisively, and then up to Moore, who stood beside me with a quite uncertain expression.

I said: "Were you thinking of sending me?"

Moore nodded.

"In what capacity—humorous writer or artist?"

Moore answered, "Both."

When I didn't faint at his reply he told me to follow him into his private office, where the arrangements were completed. It must be told in partial explanation that, as far as affairs on the paper were concerned, Moore was noted for his extreme economy. The chance to save the expenses and salary of one man on this proposed trip for two must have been a consideration.

On the daylight run from St. Louis in the parlor-car, which had few passengers, a lady came from a chair at the other end to take away her little daughter of five or six, who she thought was annoying me. On the contrary, I was much interested, as the child had said her home was in Leavenworth. The lady herself was a sister of Mayor S. F. Neely of that city, who was a candidate for reelection. She was going home to vote for him.

During the afternoon I got from her a better insight into the politics in the State from a woman's point of view than I could have got perhaps by two or three days' unaided reportorial inquiry. Getting to Leavenworth that night, I made Mayor Neely's acquaintance under these favorable conditions also, and after a day there started over the State. I made the prescribed tour, sent in stories and drawings to the New York *World*, and it was fun to be able to draw freely with a pen for publication for the first time without an interfering medium.

On Saturday, April 2, I returned to Leavenworth, and called at the house of D. R. Anthony, brother of Susan B., to see Mrs. Helen M. Gouger, the militant suffragist who had organized the Republican women of Kansas. Mrs. Gouger was in good spirits, because it was felt by her party associates that they would carry the State and that Mayor Neely, the Democratic candidate in the city of Leavenworth, would be defeated by three thousand majority. The mayor himself privately conceded an expected defeat by twenty-five hundred.

I had chosen Leavenworth as my headquarters for election day because of its nearness to Kansas City for one reason, and largely because of my new friendship for Mayor Neely and the comfortable quarters at the Hotel Delmonico, kept at that time by two Italian brothers named Giacomini.

For herself, Mrs. Gouger said that she was there because Leavenworth was the Sodom of America. I called her attention to the significance and the gravity of this characterization, both of which she said she knew and stood for; told her the statement was to be printed in the New York *World*. As it would not appear before Tuesday morning, she gave her full permission for its publication. Answering further questions, she said Leavenworth deserved that characterization because the upper strata of its female population had been corrupted by the proximity of the military post of Fort Leavenworth, with its officers. I knew that both these statements, the Sodom characterization and the charge against the military, were loaded, and hesitated to repeat them even with her permission. Back at the hotel I inquired of Neely if there was ground for the statement, and, in the slang of the day, he hit the ceiling.

My room that night was invaded by consecutive committees of citizens asking me to confirm this report which Neely had rather liberally passed on. In one of these committees, unknown to me, was a reporter for the Kansas City *Times*. That paper appeared on Sunday morning with a vivid article calling upon the citizens of Leavenworth to defend their homes against this slander, and a free copy was laid at every door in the city. As I was comfortably taking a late breakfast in the hotel dining-room Monday morning a square-toed visitor touched me on the shoulder and told me he had a warrant for my arrest.

Remembering Don César de Bazan, Elliott Gray, Sir Francis Levison, and other theatrical leading gentlemen of self-control, I tried to emulate them. Not allowing this startling news to seem to interrupt my breakfast, I asked why I was to be taken, and was shown a warrant for my arrest upon the charge of criminal libel. The constable consented to wait in the doorway and watch me finish my meal. While I Fletcherized everything and ordered more, I sent for a proprietor of the hotel, and he and his brother despatched messengers to find Mayor Neely.

As the constable and I approached Judge Plowman's court policemen had to make way for us through a crowd which was threatening. One tough individual with an unshaven jaw close to my face asked if the *World* had sent me to Kansas to fight the Knights of Labor. Without speaking, I gave what had been the secret signs of membership when I was a master workman of the Knights of Labor. It seemed these signs had been superseded, and my use of them rather increased his anger and that of his gang. I got into the court and in front of the judge, however, unpunched. It was a serious situation for the artist and the humorous writer for the *World* and *Post-Dispatch*. To paraphrase Mansfield's *Prince Karl*, "I was two men, and she arrests me both."

I looked about for Mayor Neely. No friend was in sight. I began to write a telegram reporting the situation as briefly as possible to the St. Louis office. As I wrote, the prosecuting attorney addressed the court. He was asking for an adjournment of the case until Wednesday. The judge asked if that was agreeable to me. I answered that it was, but as I spoke a card was put on the telegram I was framing.

The man holding it said: "I am your attorney."

The judge announced, "Then this case is adjourned until——"

My new friend of the card interrupted him.

"Pardon, Your Honor, we demand immediate hearing."

"But your client has asked for an adjournment to Wednesday."

I, too, begged His Honor's pardon and said I had not made any request. Personally I wanted to be agreeable; but my attorney, Mr. Thomas P. Fenlon, would conduct my case with no interference on my part. After another interchange by the lawyers a recess was taken by the State.

Except for its mere outline, this was all rather meaningless to me until I was again through the threatening crowd and safe in the office of ex-United States Senator Lucian Baker, associated with the Honorable Thomas P. Fenlon. Then I learned that the prosecution hoped only to get the case over and beyond election day, and that the town was already being covered with handbills containing an account of the criminal proceedings against me and announcing that the slanderer was in jail.

The news of the *World* man's arrest had followed the morning papers to Fort Leavenworth, where Mrs. Gouger's published charges against the army officers of that post had released a hornet's nest. Those officers could take no immediate action in defense of their own good repute and the reputations of the Leavenworth ladies who had received them socially, but they were not unable to show their colors. When Judge Plowman's court came to order after recess the equal crowd that packed it was of another complexion than that of the morning rabble of political strikers. Closely around its sides stood a row of commissioned officers, every one in his best dress uniform of the old army blue and gold; and they were grim of face, those fighting fellows.

The case opened. Mrs. Gouger, on the stand, didn't wish to deny her statement that the upper strata of Leavenworth's female society was corrupted by the Leavenworth post. She had been decided upon her charge against me by my exaggeration in changing "strata" to "stratum." When she found under the ironic cross-examination of Baker that "stratum" was the singular not the plural, of her Latin noun, the poor lady burst into tears.

The case was dismissed and in a little while Leavenworth was again covered with handbills issued by the Neely camp, saying, "Mrs. Gouger repeats her slanders in court."

It is difficult at this distance of time and territory to appreciate the agitation that this charge of immorality and corruption made upon that social section. That afternoon and again next morning, election day, both the Leavenworth and the Kansas City papers dwelt sensationally upon the gravity of Mrs. Gouger's accusations, with the result that when the lines formed at the polls there was the unusual sight of the finest women in the city pleading with their humbler sisters who worked for them as laundresses, maids, or in other domestic relations to come to their rescue and resent this slander.

It was an exciting day, and when the polls closed everybody knew that Neely had not lost by any twenty-five hundred. At 7.30 the report came in that he had lost by only thirty-one votes, and then, a half hour later, after some intense scrutiny, the final result was announced.

Neely winner by a majority of sixteen!

Neely had represented the liberal tendencies of the community and of course the municipal organizations, and when the sixteen majority was a settled fact at about 8:30 that night fire bells rang, engine companies turned out, their red-shirted crews came to the Delmonico Hotel and in a kind of Mardigras excitement ran their hose through all the building. I don't know just what that symbolized, but along with their yelling and the brass bands and the military on leave it was one more variety of emotional outlet. As the excitement mounted there was a call for the representative of the New York *World*, and despite protests I was carried by those firemen and Mayor Neely's managers to the balcony of the hotel, from which I was refused egress until I had made some sort of speech to the crowd.

This whole thing has a Munchausen ring to it; but it is in the musty files of those old papers, and I can't escape it if I am going to tell truthfully the things that have seemed to affect my course, guided as it was, like that of the beetle, principally by collisions. Wednesday was another large day, and on Thursday evening there was a victor's banquet organized by the local banker, Mr. M. H. Insley, who with Mayor Neely owned a majority of the stock of the afternoon paper, the Leavenworth *Standard*. There were about forty of the principal business men of the city at the table. In their speeches they explained the secret of the great Pulitzer successes. It was having priceless men like me beside him and making it worth-while for them to stay there. The next day Mayor Neely and Mr. Insley and two others who made up the big four came to the hotel and offered me *The Evening Standard* and fifty thousand dollars with which to get additional equipment if I would stay in Leavenworth and edit the paper in the same vigorous way in which I had just won the recent campaign. As we talked about it a telegram came from Ballard Smith of the *World*:

"Go at once to Fort Gibson, Indian Territory, where James G. Blaine is seriously ill at the home of his son-in-law, Colonel Coppinger. Send full reports."

My good friend, Mayor Neely, and his banker partner said they would hold their offer open for me until my return, and they did. I gave the banker a draft for railroad fares to Gibson.

CHAPTER XIII

NEW ENTERPRISES IN KANSAS CITY

In the spring of 1887 James G. Blaine was an important figure in the field of national politics. Less than three years before he had been defeated by Mr. Cleveland by a very narrow margin. The State of New York had been lost to Blaine by a little more than one thousand votes. Shortly preceding the election the Reverend Doctor Burchard, a member of a committee of visiting ministers, had made an address in which he spoke of the opposition to Blaine as a party of Rum, Romanism, and Rebellion. This phrase, unnoticed by Blaine at the time, and unchallenged or uncorrected until it reached the public, had undoubtedly alienated at least the five hundred and odd votes in the State of New York upon which the election turned.

But the two years and more between that time and May of 1887 had in the public mind relieved Blaine of any responsibility for this utterance, and in a spirit of fairness there was a disposition over the country to give another chance to this gallant candidate. That he should be dangerously ill at an out-of-the-way military post in the southwest territory was of interest.

Fort Gibson is nine miles from the little railroad siding and telegraph office of Gibson. Instructed by the *World* to go to this place from Kansas, where I had been reporting the State elections, I found it necessary to make two round trips between the station and the fort each day, a total of thirty-six miles, on a little cow pony hired for the service. Along the trail the grass and spring flowers were showing profusely. The ride was pleasant, and during the week's stay in the quiet place it was agreeable in the saddle to think over the offer by the generous citizens of Leavenworth, under a total misapprehension on their part, to give me an afternoon newspaper. The prospect offered immeasurable possibilities to a man of thirty, not unfamiliar with politics and in thorough sympathy with the people of the section. But to accept the offer would mean the abandonment of a long-desired association with the theatre. It was a difficult choice. On one side was a property established and in the hand; on the other, a dream.

In Gibson town, besides the station house, a dinky shed, at once passenger and freight depot, there were exactly two houses. One of them was occupied on its first floor by a small general grocery store and post-office, with two family rooms above. The second red frame of four rooms sheltered a squaw man and his full-blooded Cherokee wife, besides three or four small children and his handsome half-breed daughter, aged eighteen. There was no hotel, no boarding-house. In the squaw-man's house I shared one ground floor room with a great Dane watchdog. Before my coming he had had the bed to himself. He was a particular dog, and during my week there never grew fully reconciled to my using half of the bed. If I turned over in the night too vigorously he growled, but perhaps because I stopped promptly each time at his first growl he never bit me.

The window was open. There was no lock on the door. Two or three times each night at irregular intervals the dog suddenly bounded through the window with terrifying barks, and, as I judged by their diminuendo, regulated some distant intrusion into what he held to be the home district of that wide prairie. After a while he would come grumbling back and resume his place on our bed, and like an English tourist turn around and over as much as he liked. Each morning I washed my face and hands in a tin basin on a bench outside the kitchen and combed my hair by the help of what reflection I could get in the window glass of the open door, while the Cherokee half-breed daughter asked me how I liked my eggs.

That half-breed girl was one of the prettiest, best-mannered, best-educated girls I had seen anywhere. She was home at that season because the female seminary at Tahlequah had temporarily been put out of commission by a fire. She had a senior high-school knowledge of English literature and its accompanying studies of that grade, and she specialized in French. Of the Indian mother I had only an occasional glimpse. The white father was busy with his planting. I was the only person at table for twenty-one meals, and this dusky beauty stood opposite me at each meal and talked down at me on all subjects wherein my dependence was upon books. About Wednesday she started in to improve my mind. There was a phrase in the Cherokee tongue that she wanted me to learn. I got it perfectly, although I forgot it years ago; but I shall never forget her roguish eyes, or the perfect teeth as she smiled in its repetitions.

Women unchaperoned are the same the world over. She wasn't bold and she wasn't timid, but she wouldn't tell me the English of it. I did all I could with it in Cherokee, however, careful of course to let nobody else overhear me. I gave it all the insinuation a man could give any phrase of whose meaning he was still a bit uncertain. I repeated it while on the little buckskin pony so as not to forget it. An old Indian fighter at the post with whom I got friendly couldn't translate it. Friday night I resolved to take a chance. Two squaws were buying sugar at the grocery. The big storekeeper was speaking Cherokee to them. After they left I got near the door, because there are things a pretty girl can say to a stranger with more propriety than the stranger can claim in saying them to a general grocer with whiskers and a flannel shirt and a gun.

I said, "Mr. Brown, will you translate a sentence in Cherokee for me?"

"Certainly."

I can see him now tidily wiping out the big sugar scoop on the scales with a soiled towel. The sun had gone down. Outside it was dark. He waited. I repeated the speech just as the girl had pronounced it to me, but without the teeth-and-eye business or any coquettishness, of course. I didn't want him to plead my impertinent manner as an additional excuse for violence.

As I finished and he shook the sugar crumbs from the towel he said: "Oh, yes, that means, 'The Lord is my shepherd; I shall not want.'"

The next day Mr. Blaine was sufficiently recovered for me to leave him to local reports. Getting back to Kansas City I met by appointment our old advance man, Frank Hamilton. Hamilton was the owner of a weekly paper recently started, called the Kansas City *Mirror.* He was also the owner of a lease of a proposed theatre to be called the Warder Grand Opera House. He offered to give me one-half interest in both if I would help him in their management and would decline the Leavenworth offer. I returned to St. Louis, closed my relations with the *Post-Dispatch*, left it flat, and contrary to the advice of my father, who thought the Leavenworth opportunity was the greater, joined Hamilton in his enterprises.

As editor and half owner of his paper I had a drawing account of thirty dollars a week, partly commuted into a room and dinners at Hamilton's home. Breakfast and lunch I got outside. By Hamilton's advice, and following his sturdy example, my breakfast was uniformly a cup of coffee and a quarter section of pie. I had heard that certain real intellectuals in parts of New England had pie for breakfast—apple pie, I thought—but Hamilton explained that with its crust, its fruit, and its meat, mince pie had all that the human system required. I often recalled the story of the dyspeptic gentleman who to the maxim, "You can't eat your cake and have it too," replied that he could do just that; and to my own feeling of possession the generous alcoholic content of the mince pie in that locality and time added the vague feeling of a banquet the night before and a surviving aroma of popularity.

The Kansas City *Mirror* was an eight-page paper of a somewhat larger sheet than the *Saturday Evening Post*. Four pages of what is called patent inside came to us already printed with matter about equally divided between inferior fiction and national advertisements not entirely devoid of that element. The four outside pages I filled each week with original and selected matter, and some illustrations. I had an editorial column and a dramatic department. I was more interested in the latter. The local news, wherever possible, was manipulated to forward the opera-house enterprise. The dramatic notes and gossip gave preference to the attractions that we had arranged for and others that we hoped to get.

As the editor of the paper I met many old theatrical friends who came as members of the companies that visited Kansas City while the Warder Grand Opera House was being built. I also made new acquaintances. Among those the most lasting and agreeable was that with Edwin Milton Royle, since author of "The Squaw Man" and other dramas, but then playing juveniles with Booth and Barrett. Royle's play-writing inclination was a strong bond between him and me.

Kansas City was organizing a great exposition. President Cleveland came to the town with his bride for a visit of two days, during which municipal activities— public reception, a grand ball and the like—made such demand upon the local papers that I was called in to help the reporters of the Kansas City *Times*, and began in that two-day engagement a valued acquaintance with the author, Roswell M. Field, brother of Eugene Field.

The opening attraction of the Warder Grand was to be a week's repertoire by Booth and Barrett under the management of Arthur B. Chase. They were to play six nights and two matinées, and were to receive a guaranteed share of three thousand dollars a performance, a minimum total of twenty-four thousand dollars. Each man was a favorite in Kansas City; Booth was a popular idol. The Warder Grand was to be a good-sized house. We had plenty of publicity. Prices were more than doubled. There was no reason to doubt returns far in excess of the twenty-four thousand on the week, and Mr. Hamilton had no difficulty in giving the bond that Manager Chase required. Things looked fine.

As the summer waxed and waned, and as the theatrical season came upon us, it grew painfully evident that the opera-house was not going to be completed in time for

EDWIN BOOTH AS HAMLET.

the Booth and Barrett opening in November. L. M. Crawford, who had a chain of theatres through Kansas towns, offered to take the contract off Hamilton's hands, as its terms permitted it to be assigned. But in his mind Hamilton saw a completed opera-house, and no logic availed against that vision. A week before the date the sale opened at the down-town library, and every seat was promptly subscribed. But the opera-house itself was a shell. There wasn't a chair in it. The stage was not completed; it had no roof. There wasn't a stitch of scenery. The carpenter in charge of the stage was a youngster then, but one of the best stage mechanics in the world, Claude Hagen. He promised to be ready with the stage, but foretold the impossibility of opening without scenery or equipment. Hamilton had felt sure of being able to rent sufficient scenery from the opposition houses, but it was impossible to get any.

On the Thursday before the opening I went to St. Louis and explained the dire distress of our enterprise to Mr. Pope. Pope knew Hamilton and liked both him and me. I started back Saturday morning with a baggage-car full of scenery attached to a freight train. We reached Kansas City Sunday afternoon and had the scenery on the stage Monday morning. But there was still no roof. One stubborn beam that swung from the overhanging derricks was still to be put in place. The Booth-Barrett company called for rehearsal, walked about the cold stage in their fur coats and looked through to the threatening sky that showed above the entire auditorium.

This auditorium was empty except for some men who were filling it with temporary camp stools in rows. The rehearsal was dismissed, and as a matter of form the

company reported in the evening; but during the afternoon a snow-storm had fallen, and at night there was
an inch of snow on the streets and much inside the
theatre; no roof on the Warder Grand Opera House,
and no heat. Hamilton and I, two Craig brothers who
were interested in the enterprise, a stenographer, and
two men from the *Mirror* office met the arriving patrons
and explained the postponement of the performance
until the following night.

There was a good deal of grumbling then and a great
deal of confusion at the ticket-office the next day. During that Tuesday, however, Hamilton got some tarpaulins
put over the roof and brought four large cannon stoves
into the theatre. These stoves were set up in the private
boxes with pipes leading to the nearest outlets and kept
red-hot during the day. At noon Mr. Booth and Mr.
Barrett, with their fur collars turned up, were on the
stage again looking at the still-forbidding conditions.
As there was no other assistant who knew anything about
moving scenery, I was in a suit of overalls to help Hagen
on the stage.

One green hand trying to take a wing across the back
of the stage got it wabbling on its forefoot and then let
go of it as it started to fall. If it were to drop flat-sided
it would come down easily as a kite falls, and without
much damage; but edgewise, and dropping as a knife-
blade, it had lethal possibilities. There was no time to
talk. I jumped at the two stars whose backs were toward
this menace, pushed them violently apart, just as the
scene fell between them, striking the stage where they
had been standing, splitting the wood of its two-inch stiles.

Mr. Barrett, in real tragedian fashion, said indignantly,
"Don't put your hands on me, fellow!"

Mr. Booth lifted his gaze from the broken scene and said, "Thank you."

I was pretty hot at the Barrett rebuke, and told Hagen, who was also cross about it, that it would make a fair story for the *Saturday Mirror*. That night during one of the intermissions Mr. Barrett thanked me for pushing him out of the way, explained that he was very nervous and his irritable remark involuntary. I had no difficulty in believing this. The whole plexus of events was trying on everybody.

During the day there had been a conference between the stars, their manager and attorneys on one hand, and on the other hand Hamilton, his bondsmen and their attorneys. This conference resulted in a decision to stand by the guaranty and to open with "Macbeth." There was no dressing-room in which anybody could have with safety disrobed, and no ordinary theatrical costume would have kept out the freezing temperature of the building. To shut out drafts, the stage was boxed as a baronial hall with a set ceiling. Mr. Booth wore his heaviest costume, a robe in which ordinarily he played *Richelieu*. Barrett as *Macduff* wore a long quilted gown which had served in "Francesca da Rimini." Minna Gale as *Lady Macbeth* had some equally warm and equally incongruous attire. After the first act of the play the audience, that had been freezing in their wraps —the men retaining not only overcoats but hats—began to move toward the boxes where the cannon stoves were. Those already near these furnaces made way and perishing ladies row by row approached the heat. Men stood in the outer circle stamping their feet. After two or three minutes of this there was a general readjustment of camp chairs, moving from their alignments toward these thermal centres that suggested Birnam Wood on its road to Dunsinane.

Some prudent or habitual gentlemen had brought flasks with them. Others went to the nearest places of supply, and the close of the intermission took on a convivial even if precautionary color. The greatest enthusiasm of the night—not excepting Mr. Booth's reception —was for a line which perhaps in all the previous history of "Macbeth" had never called for more than a giggle.

In the third scene of Act Two the *Porter*, roused from his slumber by the knocking at the gate, says, "But this place is too cold for hell." This was greeted with a laugh and successive rounds of applause, and then recurrent ripples as the audience waited and congealed. The hardier ones stood through the whole play, but the house was half empty when the play was half over.

Through the balance of the week conditions were improved, but it was weeks before the house was a finished theatre. The total receipts on the week were eleven thousand dollars short of the company's promised share. The manager of Booth and Barrett properly called upon Hamilton's bondsmen for their guaranty, and our weekly *Mirror*, with its editorial and dramatic department, went into the general liquidation.

One happening during that editorial incumbency that closed in such summary fashion is worth telling as a coincidence. The business men of Leavenworth had wished to have something written about their section that would call attention to it and yet not look like an advertisement. I wrote a story which they approved and which carried the facts, and yet which seemed to be a bit of romantic fiction. Under an arrangement at regular space rates it had been printed in the New York *World*, and that paper had sent me a generous commission of something over a hundred dollars. One October day a young man brought to me a pen manuscript which he wished to sell. I promised to read it, although I told him the Kansas City *Mirror* was not buying fiction. After a fortnight he came again. Ashamed of my neglect, I read the story as he sat there. I was prepossessed by what I thought was its easy introduction.

As I read on I said to myself, "If I had to state that case that's the way I should like to write it."

Another paragraph and I said: "Well, that's the way I did write it."

I looked hurriedly through the script and asked the young man if he was the author of the story. He said he was. He was not a large person, and behind my desk were two compositors standing at their cases and another working on the stone.

So I felt courageous enough to say to the young man, "You're a liar!"

He sprang to his feet with fine indignation. I repeated my characterization and added: "That story was printed on Sunday, May 1, 1887, in the New York *World*, under the title of 'A Leavenworth Romance.' "

The fellow was so astonished that he could only gasp an assent.

I said: "If you will go home to the paper from which you copied this you'll find my initials, G. T., at the bottom of that story."

He said "Yes" and went out, dazed at the mischance which had made him bring to an obscure person sitting in a Western office a yarn he had copied verbatim from an Eastern daily, only to discover that he had placed the stolen article in the hands of its author. There were ninety million other citizens of the United States.

Of course the lines of communication on this little

planet of eight thousand miles diameter must occasionally intersect at points that seem supremely significant; and it may be that we should wonder at the absence rather than the occasional presence of a coincidence. But as they have their interest, I would like to jump ahead and tell the only other remarkable one that is in my own experience. I rehearsed and produced a play called "The Other Girl" in 1903 with Lionel Barrymore at the Criterion Theatre in New York. It was in three acts. Effective ending of the second act depended upon the involuntary laughter of a parson, prompted by a wink from a prize-fighter who was in the room with him. On the opening night the effect fell short. I had to leave the next day on the steamer *Kroonland* for Paris. Walking the deck of this boat four or five days later I still tried to analyze my failure at that point. It occurred to me that certain business between members of a group on the opposite side of the stage had made a stronger appeal to the attention of the audience than the quiet minister and prize-fighter on their side had made, and I mentally kicked myself for my stupidity in not discovering this. I went at once to the wireless room and sent the following telegram to Mr. Charles Frohman:

"Have the kid touch the parson before the wink."

Mr. Frohman rehearsed this business. The action attracted the attention of the audience, who thereupon saw the wink which was the provocation for the laughter, and all that I had hoped for was secured.

About a month later Mr. Bainbridge Colby was dining with the Thomases in their apartment in the Latin Quarter. He said: "This strange thing happened: On the steamer *Cedric*, when I was crossing last month on my way to London, I was in the wireless room. We were a day out from New York. A message was relayed from the *Kroonland*. The operator was Italian and a little uncertain with English, and he asked me if I thought the message could be correct. It was from you to Mr. Frohman, and read: 'Have the kid touch the parson before the wink.' I told the operator it was all right and he transmitted it to New York."

Aside from Mr. Frohman and the members of the company, Mr. Colby was the only person on earth who could have given that answer to that operator out on the Atlantic.

With our failure to get the company's guaranty on the opening of the Warder Grand, the lease of the opera-house in which I had been promised a share was forfeited, and with a winter fairly set in I was in a city where I was almost a stranger, and again without a job.

Friends have asked why in this emergent situation I did not try to recover and pick up the offer of Mayor Nealy and his banker associates to install me in ownership and direction of the Leavenworth *Standard*. But as I remember it the thought did not once occur to me, my ideas were so definitely turned to the East and to the theatre. Except for the fact that I was subsequently successful in that field, one might with apparent justice make some animadversions upon being stage-struck. But stage-struck I was not; neither then nor afterward have I felt any insistent wish to act. Playing was a means to the ultimate acquirement of play-writing, and I think it worth while now, with whatever weight anything I write may carry, to say a heartening word to the persistent young man in the neighborhood of thirty years who, despite the wishes of his prudent friends, feels a call to follow his private bent.

In 1863, at sixty years of age, Emerson wrote in his journal: "Tremendous force of the spring which we call native bias . . . whose impulsion reaches through all the days, through all the years and keeps the old man constant to the same pursuits as in youth!" Nearly twenty years before, in a similar mood, he had written in the same journal: "Men go through the world, each musing on a great fable, dramatically pictured and rehearsed before him. If you speak to the man he turns his eyes from his own scene and slower or faster endeavors to comprehend what you say. When you have done speaking he returns to his private music."

And his private music is his self-expression, the most important function in this personal hypnosis that we call life.

After a few days of uncertainty I began work for a couple of weeks as the artist on Willis Abbott's afternoon paper, the Kansas City *News*, and from there went as the resident artist to the Missouri *Republican* in St. Louis.

Mr. Sothern came along about this time with the promised interview concerning "The Burglar." No fledgling author could ask for a more complimentary opinion than Mr. Sothern had of the play. But as a star he felt that it would be prejudicial to his hopes to undertake a drama from which he was absent during the entire second act. He wanted me to rewrite it so that he might appear in that section. But though the burglar was out of the second act physically he was very much in it as problem and menace. In my stubborn insistence upon the script as written at that time I left myself, as far as theatrical prospects were concerned, still stranded in St. Louis.

One other notable incident for me during that time is that I then made my first acquaintance with Colonel Henry Watterson. The paper wanted a picture of him. Marse Henry didn't care to sit for a sketch, but when I saw him two days later he was very complimentary about the one I had made from memory after my talk with him. As a stunt that caused our mutual acquaintance I have more than once repeated it since that time.

I worked steadily on the *Republican* from the end of 1887 until August of 1888. The time was filled with interesting experiences; few of them, however, pertinent to my career as a playwright, although my duties as artist threw me now and then into touch with events that were dramatic. In the mind of a playwright it made a grisly front scene to be called out of bed at two o'clock in the morning and driven hastily to the levee, and with the light from one lamp taken from the side of the hack that had conveyed him there to sit astride the body of some murdered roustabout and get a memorandum sketch that would transfer to a chalk plate in time for the morning edition.

I suppose it was my exaggerated enjoyment of the dramatic element in any happening that lent zest to my good-by to the *Republican* and to the newspaper business. Charles Knapp, the proprietor of the paper, was a man liked by all the employees. Frank O'Neill, the editor, was a promoted reporter who had deserved his advancement. A new proprietor who came to us that summer with revolutionary ideas, none of which I recall as subsequently justified, was Mr. Charles H. Jones, a small, emphatic, laconic person, with extraordinary side-whiskers and an entire absence of the personality that appeals to the Western product. He changed the honored

name of the Missouri *Republican* to the St. Louis *Republic*
and started in upon his campaign of economy and re-
trenchment. When he reached the art department he
instructed the city editor to tell me that my thirty dollars a week had been cut to twenty-five.

The information came the afternoon of a day which
brought a letter from Will Smythe stating that Ariel
Barney offered me the position of business manager in
the season soon to begin, with a young actress whom he
hoped to establish as a star. The name of this young
person was Julia Marlowe, and Barney and others who
had seen her had a high opinion of her ability and a firm
belief in her future. I was therefore able to say to the
city editor that instead of submitting to a cut of five
dollars I would demand a raise of fifteen if I stayed on
the paper.

This did not indicate a wish to remain, but as the work
on the paper had grown the management had engaged
as assistant in the art department a young draftsman
from the Washington University by the name of Paul
Connoyer, and I felt that a Parthian demand for an increase of salary would operate as a defense against any
assault upon Paul. Connoyer took over the department
when I left and they got some man to help him. He
later came to New York, where as a painter of landscapes
and street scenes he took high rank among artists.

At that time the St. Louis Baseball Club, owned by
Chris Von der Ahe, was under the personal management
of Al Spink, the present dean of sporting writers assisted
by George Munson. Munson was a free lance, ready to
try almost anything, and in his experience, which ran from
newspaper work to management of a swimming school,
we had met and were friends. Al Spink had a Pullman

car with twenty-four berths in it which was leaving in two days for New York with the ball club. Three of these berths were unoccupied. He gave me my choice of them, and I left St. Louis the ostensible historian of that party. Railroad fare and Pullman to New York in those days totalled about thirty dollars. It exactly bridged the gap from journalism to management, as my duties began when rehearsals did.

In that old ball club I had several friends. One still in the public eye was Charles A. Comiskey, or as he was called then, Commy. He was playing first base and acting as captain of the team. Arlie Latham, probably the greatest fun maker in the history of professional baseball, was on third. Years after Latham had ceased to play ball he was engaged as a coach because of his ability to entertain grand stand and bleachers. This was a natural gift with Latham, and its exercise was irresistibly spontaneous. The Harrisburg station on the Pennsylvania Railroad is inclosed at its west end by an iron fence about nine feet high, separating its tracks and platforms from the streets. That same fence, or one similar, was there in the summer of 1888. Our train made the usual five minutes' stop. Men were stretching their legs under the sheds of the station. Outside this iron fence a citizen of Harrisburg, with an old-fashioned set of whiskers, was passing. Latham screamed at him, and then as nearly as he could vocally reproduce the noise he dramatized a tornado, theatrically implying in the slang of the day that the wind was blowing.

The owner of the whiskers was of Celtic origin. He turned upon Latham and looked helplessly along the fence for some gateway by which he could reach him. None was there. Latham, thus protected, grabbed the iron bars of the fence, went along a section of it like a caged chimpanzee, violently shaking the bars and repeating all the time the whizzing noise that had so angered this inoffensive citizen. Through the man's anger there shot a more intelligent gleam and he started to run for the brick station house itself. Latham made a dash for the train, which fortunately pulled out as the belligerent citizen burst past the ticket taker and into the inclosure. A witness of the whole performance might have called Latham's attack unwarranted hoodlumism, but it wasn't that; it was simple exuberance of animal spirits, and very much the kind of vitality that when the offering is more a matter of personality than of intellect finds a market in the theatre. Latham himself had a successful engagement later in vaudeville, after which he came back to the ball field as a coach.

For men who are trying to write for the theatre and are impatient at the unavoidable delays it is worth while to take stock of my first arrival as a man in New York. I had in my trunk two long plays and five or six short ones. I was thirty-one years of age and had had an intimate acquaintance and relationship with the theatre nearly all my life. I had played many years as an amateur, three or four years as the occasional member of a repertoire company in the legitimate, and had more than a year of consecutive travelling with a company in which I had an interest. I had produced four plays that I had written, had had two years in a box-office and had shared for a few full minutes the lease of a theatre, while never losing sight of dramatic authorship as objective. I had refused to rewrite a play for so promising an exponent as Mr. Sothern. And yet, in order to keep in touch with the business and do something that would occasionally put me at the producing centre, I found myself in a forty-dollar job to count tickets for a young actress upon her first trip as a star.

In the thirty-three years that have passed since that date my observation has built up the opinion that the American playwright does not generally make better headway. There have been one or two brilliant exceptions; but as a rule the public is not interested in a man who has written from books, and to write from life requires that some time should be spent in living it. If there is somewhat in that statement that is depressing it is more than offset by the fact that hardly anything happens to a man or woman during this probationary wait that is not directly or indirectly serviceable in the playhouse. Everything is fish that comes to that pond.

CHAPTER XIV

JULIA MARLOWE AND OTHERS

Julia Marlowe, our young star, had played as a child. As a young lady she had been carefully coached in a number of parts by Ada Dow, who shortly after the season of which I write became the wife of the present veteran actor, Frank Currier. Miss Marlowe called Miss Dow Aunt Ada. Of the several parts in which she was prepared Miss Marlowe had been seen only in "Parthenia," in which she unquestionably excelled any actress that her generation remembered. Colonel Robert G. Ingersoll had seen her performance in this part, and had been moved to write a letter of such high praise that Mr. Barney had sought and obtained his permission to have it reproduced on his large printing. Barney as advance agent had visited St. Louis twice while I was at Pope's. My engagement was the outcome partly of the acquaintance then made. He had with him as adviser an advance man, Fred Stinson, who had conducted more than one tour for Mme. Helena Modjeska.

Stinson was very wise in the matter of arranging legitimate repertoire and in getting public attention for a female star. Barney had been a newspaper man; Stinson was himself a writer with an ambition to do plays. So the association of us three men was at the start an agreeable one. Except to get the names of the company and be told the salary that each was to receive, it wasn't necessary for either Barney or Stinson to lose any time

on my theatrical education. With all the duties of this
position I was familiar.

In St. Louis I had gone with Barney to the critics and
more than once helped him on his publicity. Notwithstanding that fact, and knowing my job, I was compli-
mented when Barney asked me to participate in the
councils of policy with him and Stinson. There was a
hitch about the matter to go upon the first three-sheet.
Barney and Stinson were comparing adjectives to describe the supporting company, and for one reason or
another hesitating over all the trite descriptions. "Splendid," "excellent," "distinguished," "adequate," had
each some recommending and some objectionable feature.

Happening to know that in certain sections of the
country there had been some regret over Mary Anderson's revisiting her old territory with a company that
was exclusively English, I suggested dismissing all their
adjectives by using the word "American." This so
caught the fancy of both men that they used it not only
to describe their company but to describe their star.
There was an implication of rivalry about it; but fine
as Mary Anderson had been, Barney had a star who
would stand comparison, however invited. All the parts
that Miss Marlowe played that year I had seen played
by other actresses. In nearly all the plays I had played
some part myself. I felt qualified to form an opinion
not only of Miss Marlowe's work but of the business
which Miss Dow had devised for the other members of
the company, and to which she held them with an in-
flexibility relaxed only when the opinion of some equally
experienced person, such as Charles Barron or Mary
Shaw, convinced her of its value.

Julia Marlowe had every requisite for success in star parts on the stage that a girl could need—youth and health, with their attractiveness; facial and physical beauty; stature, poise, carriage, voice, diction, proper pronunciation, mobile expression, definite and graceful gesture and competent, well-shaped, responsive hands. Her mental equipment included gayety, hospitality for humor, self-reliance, ready emotions under fair control, a capacity for attention. One great value was that her beauty of face was of the kind that the stage enhances. It is not unusual for a parlor beauty to be lost in a stage frame; but Marlowe's features were of a scale that fitted that larger canvas. This harmonious ampleness of feature, the bone structure underlying it, was one foundation of her voice, then as now the best woman's speaking voice on the American or English stage. I had heard Charlotte Thompson and others in "The Hunchback," but none who by sheer variety and charm of tone lifted from mediocrity and made memorable such lines as "I've seen the snow upon a level with the hedge, yet there was Master Walter."

As a beginner, meeting admiring callers in her hotel parlor or behind the scenes, and even on the railway trains with the company, there was about the girl a slight self-consciousness, a willingness to look to Aunt Ada for moral support, that was altogether girlish; but on the stage that near-timidity was transmuted into an archness quite devoid of embarrassment. This archness hovered over every playful line and inhalation—perhaps inhalation especially, as inhalation is the tide of what the Scot called the come-hither influence.

In those early days, watched by her studious support, it was a question how much of her effect was the girl herself and how much the imprint of her instructress. Some there were who thought that a servile imitation and obedience were the full depth of the possession. And in that first year this belief was encouraged somewhat by Miss Dow's watchfulness in the wings and frequent critical comment right after a scene. For myself, however, not unpractised in estimating such work, and with the better vantage of seeing all from the front, there was evident an exuberant personality of Marlowe's own, a personality thinking and implying and conveying a most bewitching overlay around all the set and studied business of the teacher. Nobody I ever saw on or off the stage could put into two words the challenge and the retreat, the winsomeness, the temptation, and the clean innocence that Marlowe, as she sat on the log near Orlando, put into the words: "Woo me."

During that period Miss Julia was most jealously guarded. No señorita had ever a sharper-eyed duenna, and I thought then that the balcony and the Forest of Arden were both gainers because of that background of repression.

What a national possession a generation has in such a woman as Marlowe! What a change could be wrought on our national speech if one such exponent might be in every great centre where the girls of America could come under her repeated spell.

Besides Stinson, as playwright, there were in that first Marlowe company Mary Shaw, Edward McWade, Albert Bruning, and Dodson Mitchell, all interested in playwriting, and all still prominently before the public. Miss Shaw and Bruning were wise in the maxims of the art. McWade and Mitchell subsequently became skilled and successful. Mary Shaw was easily the intellectual centre of that theatrical family, not only concerning things of the theatre but literature in general. Miss Shaw had been a school-teacher before she became an actress, but had not served at it so long that she in any way tired of giving information. She had also been the leading support for Modjeska, which equipped her with many of the traditions of her chosen profession, but better yet, as far as her companions in the Marlowe company were concerned, gave her a fund of anecdote that made that season a joy. Mary's particular hero as a *raconteuse* was Maurice Barrymore. I had not met Barrymore at that time—did not meet him until nearly a year later; but when we did meet I felt pretty intimately informed of his professional and private career through the stories of this generous biographer.

Albert Bruning is among the prominent players of New York at the present time. Previous to that Marlowe engagement Bruning had played Shakespeare in German, winning considerable praise in the part of *Hamlet*, and in that excellent and American company he was a notable actor. In "Romeo and Juliet" he played the part of *Tybalt*. As attractive as *Juliet* was, and as magnetic as Taber was in *Romeo*, and as Barron was in the part of *Mercutio*, when Bruning was on the stage as *Tybalt* he carried such a quiet and intense air of menace that he was the centre of attention. Theatregoers of the last year or two will remember the fine impression he made as *Polonius* to Walter Hampden's *Hamlet*.

The first time we put up "Romeo and Juliet," I think in Washington City, the company was short one member for its long cast. An actor who was expected from New York to play *Benvolio* missed the train that would have let him arrive in time for the performance. It was

JULIA MARLOWE AS JULIET. 1889.

too late to change the bill, and at Miss Dow's suggestion I agreed to go on for the part if we could find a costume. One member lent me a pair of tights, another a pair of shoes, and so on. I definitely remember that Frank Currier furnished the doublet. He was a slighter man than I, but by dint of compression I got into his garment.

Benvolio's most important office is to catch *Mercutio* when he falls wounded by *Tybalt* in their duel. The scene went remarkably well up to this point, but when sturdy Charley Barron, wounded, dropped into my arms, this tight doublet of Currier's split up the back like a roasted chestnut, and with a ripping noise that defied neglect by anybody in the audience. I doubt if the death of *Mercutio* ever got so good a laugh.

Charles Barron had supported the greatest actors in the American theatre. He was a product of the old Boston Museum stock and had been at times a star himself. He was an acceptable *Ingomar*, a good *Mercutio*, a fine *Master Walter*, and an excellent *Malvolio*. Few actors of his day, and none of the present, had better diction on the stage; but in private discourse he was singularly uneven, at times almost inaudible. It amused the other men in the company to compare notes and see which of them had understood most of some speech of Barron's as he stood with a group on the street corner or at the stage door, mumbling as he mouthed his tobacco pipe and emitting now and then some staccato explosive that served as a stepping-stone through the maze of his unintelligible recital.

Stout Billy Owen, another Modjeska favorite, was at that time a tower of strength in any legitimate company. When he played *Sir Toby* and Frank Currier was *Sir*

Andrew Ague-Cheek, with Barron's *Malvolio*, Taber's *Duke*, and young Ed McWade—the best double Miss Marlowe ever had to her *Viola*—playing *Sebastian*, with Mary Shaw and Emma Hinckley in her other women rôles, the public was offered about as good a cast of actors as America gets at any time.

Robert Taber, our leading man, had been a Sargent pupil and had learned his business with Modjeska and Charles Coghlan. When he had been with Modjeska the leading man had been Maurice Barrymore, and consciously or unconsciously Taber's leads with Marlowe strongly followed Barrymore. It must be said that he could not have found a better model. Taber came of fine family. His sister, who survives him, is the wife of Henry Holt, the publisher. He had had a good education and fine associates. While I was with the Marlowe company he was my nearest friend among its members. Taber liked a good laugh, but his bent was essentially serious. His happiest hours were after the play, when Miss Shaw would let him and me have supper in her room, while Rob persuaded himself and me—perhaps rightly—that he was really discussing philosophy. I would not doubt it now but for memory of Mary's laughter.

When Rob and I were alone he talked much of the star for whom in that first season he protested positive dislike and fortified his feeling by many minute fault-findings. I was some fourteen years older than the girl and a good half dozen older than Rob. The phrase "protective coloring" was then not yet invented, but I was not astonished some two years later to read of the Taber-Marlowe marriage.

We were to leave Trenton one morning for some place

farther south where we had a guaranty—and needed it. The only train that would make our connection left at ten o'clock in the morning. Miss Marlowe, Miss Dow, their maid, Frank Currier, and myself, who were to go to the station in the carriage, met in the hotel lobby at the proper time. After a wait of a minute or two, when the carriage didn't appear, we telephoned the liveryman, who said that the order had been for the same hour in the evening, which was absurd. His rig wasn't ready and there wasn't time to get it.

Currier and I gathered up the baggage and our mixed quintet went to the street. No passenger conveyance was in sight anywhere. To miss the guaranty in that next town meant disaster. I stopped a man who was driving a covered milk wagon. After loss of much precious time he declined to consider the proposition that I made. We moved on to the corner, hoping to find one more willing. On the side street at the intersection stood two large furniture vans with pictures of George Washington on their sides and large letters announcing their ability for long or short hauls with furniture. No drivers were in sight, but a shout into the saloon on the corner produced one. I asked him what he would charge to take the five of us to the station, about a mile away. He said two dollars. I promised him five if he got there in four minutes.

He got onto his box. Currier and I threw the luggage in over the lowered tail gate, helped the two ladies and the maid in after and climbed in ourselves. It was almost a straight run to the station. Certain obstacles in the street necessitated our crossing the car tracks once or twice, in which manœuvres the greatest living *Juliet* ricocheted between the thin mattresses that lined the two sides of the van.

As we neared the station we saw one of our company pleading with a nervous conductor who was running his left thumb over the heavy crystal of his watch after the manner of railroad men. Currier and I whistled shrilly, the actor saw us and explained to the conductor. A minute later we swung tail end to the railroad track like an emergency ambulance and the day was saved as Currier cried, "Out, you baggage!" The train was rocking under way as we went down the aisle to our seats, the sympathetic company full of questions to the agitated ladies.

Currier, the first man coming after, explained, still in mock heroics, "We had to drag her on a hurdle thither."

How often the human mind accepts intellectually a fact long before ever dramatically or emotionally acquiring it. Thereafter for the much-amused Marlowe the angry *Capulet* had a magnified reality when he scolded the cringing *Juliet:*

> "Thank me no thankings, nor proud me no prouds,
> But fettle your fine joints 'gainst Thursday next,
> To go with Paris to Saint Peter's church,
> Or I will drag thee on a hurdle thither.
> Out, you green-sickness carrion! Out you baggage!"

In the theatre, as far back as I remember, when salaries were paid the old actors called it the ghost walking. Our first old man was a youngish actor named Jimmy Cooper. At that time it was customary to pay salaries Tuesday night. One Tuesday, however, the money had to be conserved to move the company. As I neared the door of Cooper's dressing-room on my way back-stage he watched with hopeful eyes my coming. When on the return trip I again passed him without leaving the pay envelope I heard him quote in melancholy tone *Horatio's* line:

> "But, even then, the morning cock crew loud;
> And at the sound it shrunk in haste away,
> And vanish'd from our sight."

The average man must always envy the well-stocked memory of the cultivated player. What a delightful element in the bright talk of John Drew, for example, are the pat quotations that sparkle through it from its remembered backing.

Ariel Barney, proclaimed on the bills as presenting Julia Marlowe, had business ability. Marlowe had genius. There came a time in the association of these two factors when success impaired Barney's sense of proportion. The persons who felt the consequence of this misconception most were Stinson and myself, who had been on intimate and friendly relations with him. I think, however, that I would have gone through the other two months needed to finish the season if it hadn't been for a trick hat.

The American theatre was less a business and more of an institution thirty-three years ago, and Marlowe's audiences in the cities were the nearest in formality to those of the grand opera. Therefore in the cities her business staff dressed. I had a fur collar and this accordion hat as I stood at the door. One form of Barney's solicitude for the star was to carry to her dressing-room door a bottle of Guinness's stout. This ministration didn't occur often, and when it did Miss Marlowe didn't like the tonic. On the first night of our second engagement in Philadelphia the lobby was filled with Marlowe's local admirers.

In one group were Colonel McClure, the publisher, and two of his friends. Barney, who was tossing a silver quarter in his hand, at a break in their conference called to me at the door, "Thomas, Thomas!" Ordinarily we spoke to each other by our first names. In the surroundings referred to and under my silk hat the peremptory "Thomas!" had an office-boy sound. I joined him. With some display and without leaving his friends, Barney extended the quarter and said, "I want to get a bottle of stout for Miss Marlowe."

I heard myself answering, "I'm a stranger in Philadelphia, Mr. Barney, but if I were you I'd try a saloon."

Colonel McClure and his friends laughed.

The day I got back to St. Louis out of a job again I called on John Norton at the Grand. He was talking to John Ritchie, who had formerly managed Mrs. D. P. Bowers, and was then handling the thought reader, Washington Irving Bishop.

Norton said to Ritchie, "Why, here's your man!"

It was Tuesday. Bishop, who was having a week's engagement in St. Louis at Exposition Hall, had to open the following Monday in Minneapolis, and his advance agent had left him without notice. I went that evening to see Bishop's work. It was astonishing, and as I came to be more and more familiar with it afterward it made upon me a profound impression. It deserves to be described at length; but as I am trying to write here only that which affected my ultimate vocation, I shall tell but two stories indicative of his peculiar power. In other articles not included in these remembrances I hope to write special and extended accounts of psychic phenomena. But I explain my wish for brevity if not my achievement of it here.

The Bishop experiment that impressed me most that first night was his finding while blindfolded an article carried from the stage and hidden somewhere in that vast audience. To do this the volunteer who had hidden the article down a side aisle was making his second trip from the stage behind Bishop, who was eagerly dragging him. The volunteer, determined to give no help to the blindfolded telepathist, was not only hanging back but was looking at the ceiling of framed glass in a refusal to indicate in any manner the location sought.

Near the hiding-place Bishop halted, and after a fretful waver turned to the audience and cried: "This man is not complying with conditions. He is not thinking of the place where this article is hidden. All that I get from his mind is a picture of skylights." In a spirit of fairness the audience burst into a round of applause, regarding that reading by Bishop as more revealing than the finding of the article, which immediately followed.

On Wednesday Bishop was ill. Ritchie and I sat by his bed for our interview. I engaged to leave town that day as his advance man. I took with me nothing but some newspaper clippings. There wasn't a sheet of paper or a single lithograph or anything of the usual equipment of the man ahead. Ordinarily for a visiting attraction in a city like Minneapolis the advertising paper is on the walls on Thursday morning. The advertisements are in the newspapers, and such space as the dramatic men are willing to accord the agent has already been partly used. None of these favorable conditions was mine.

I have had occasion to say before that I wish I might write some of these stories without letting everybody know what a devil of a fellow I am. But the experience

I am about to tell would lose whatever value it has if I depressed it below the level of simple statement. I told it once in New York in the middle '90's, when as a more or less arriving playwright I was the guest of an organization of theatrical business men, predominantly advance agents, numbering about two hundred. Their taking it as qualifying for honorary membership is the most expert rating I can quote to justify my belief that it is worth telling.

At St. Paul, a half hour before my arrival at Minneapolis, about eleven o'clock on Thursday morning, I got a Minneapolis paper in order to see what opposition Bishop would have in that city. The front page was covered with sensational accounts of preparations for a double hanging to occur the next day, and extended reprints of stories of the crime, the trial, and futile efforts for rehearing and for executive clemency. Two boys named Barrett, employed by a street railway, had been convicted of the murder of a passenger at a terminus of the line. One claimed to be innocent; the testimony of his brother supported him. It was plain that in regular course Friday's paper would be filled with this same kind of news, and that it would be Saturday or Sunday before the papers would print anything about Bishop with a chance of attention. The biggest possible distraction was the sensational hanging. To be noticed at all we would have to get on the band wagon; have to go with the hanging and not against it.

Arriving in Minneapolis, I had a cab driver take me to the principal evening paper. I asked the city editor if there was anything new in the matter of the Barrett boys.

He said, "Nothing."

Would he print any news concerning them? If it was news, yes. I said I had a letter to the governor of the State from Washington Irving Bishop, the thought-reader, asking him to postpone the execution of the boy claiming to be innocent until Bishop could reach Minneapolis on Sunday, when he would agree to read the mind of the young man, reënact the crime, and define the boy's association with it. The editor asked for the letter. Searching through my pockets, I was unable to find it. Search through my bag also failing to produce it, I told him that it must be in my trunk, but that having originally written it I could accurately reword it.

When the afternoon paper appeared its first page carried a ten-line scare-head beginning, "Hope for the Barrett Boys! Thought-Reader Washington Irving Bishop Asks a Stay of Execution." And then followed more descriptive lines, scaling down to the written introduction and a copy of the letter I had composed; also the important fact that Bishop was to arrive Sunday and that his arrival was preparatory to his week's engagement at the theatre. That afternoon all Minneapolis had the information. I went to the jail, explained my call to the captain of the police, was permitted to see the two boys, and convinced them they had little to lose in permitting this experiment by Bishop.

I wish to say here that my confidence was based upon the fact that Bishop in Portland had made a similar visit to a criminal's cell and dramatized his crime. Both boys were glad to sign what I set down for them, which for purposes of brevity and dramatic value read simply: "We are willing to wait."

When I reached the office after leaving their cell in the jail I was confronted by a dignified, martial-looking man who as soon as the captain indicated me opened fire. He knew the object of my call; thought I should be ashamed of myself for trying to play upon the hopes of these two boys in order to get publicity for a showman. I was able quite truthfully to deny this as my sole purpose, because I had then and still have a belief that Bishop would have made good on a test. But the attorney interrupted with a loud "Rot! Remember that you are not talking now to two poor, ignorant boys, but to an attorney-at-law."

I said: "General, my knowledge of you as an attorney is confined to the records of this case. As both your clients are condemned to death, you must excuse me for not being impressed."

The two or three reporters followed me to the door in order to get the line right for the morning papers.

From the jail I went to the Capitol in St. Paul and handed a copy of the letter to the governor, told him of the Portland experiment, and dilated upon Bishop's ability. He was considerate and non-committal.

The regular edition of the morning papers carried full reports of all I have told, and when the Barrett boys were hanged some two hours after these early editions extras issued beginning with the statement that the drop had fallen at eight minutes after six. In these extra editions the proposal and appeal of Bishop, the scenes at the jail, and the governor's declination were included. The matter had been telegraphed to St. Louis also, because I received a wire from Ritchie:

"Good work. Your salary is one hundred dollars."

This was a lift of twenty-five.

Bishop arrived on time and we had a sensational opening.

The other example that I wish to report of Bishop's work is worth while, as an attempt to repeat it that spring in New York resulted in his death. We played one night in Jefferson City, Missouri. Honorable David R. Francis, recently United States ambassador to Russia, was then governor. Mike Fanning, already referred to, was his secretary. The governor, who was unable to come to the theatre, sent an invitation to Bishop, Ritchie, and me to take supper at the mansion. Besides the five men named, there was present only the governor's sister, Miss Francis. After supper, when the governor wished to see a demonstration, Bishop asked him to go alone to his library and select a word from any book. When the governor returned we all followed him again into the library. Bishop went in an ordinary walk to the proper bookcase, took down without hesitation the proper book —there were perhaps two thousand in the room—opened this heavy law volume, turned without hesitation to the proper page, went down the page, put his finger upon a certain word.

Governor Francis said, "That's it! That's it!"

The whole proceeding occupied but little more time than I have taken in its dictation.

A few days thereafter Ritchie, Bishop, and I went to New York. Bishop and J. Levy, the great cornetist, had met and agreed upon a joint tour for the following season. Ritchie and I were to be equally interested. It looked like a good business proposition. The Sunday night after our arrival in New York Bishop was a guest at a Lambs Club Gambol. He repeated this exhibition that I have described. Doctor J. A. Irwin, a member, came in after midnight, was sceptical about what he had heard, urged Bishop to repeat that test or perform one similar, and although Bishop had been cautioned against overwork of this kind by his physicians, he repeated it successfully and fell into a cataleptic fit.

On Broadway the next day a man said, "Your star is sick at the Lambs."

I found Bishop in a little hall bedroom on an iron cot, where he had been for twelve hours, a tiny electric battery buzzing away with one wet electrode over his heart and the other in his right hand. He was unconscious. Two doctors sat smoking in the adjoining room, tired with their watch of the night. I looked at the handsome face of Bishop and sat beside him for some minutes. Although he was to every appearance dead, a deeper solemnity suddenly came over his face. I stepped to the doorway.

"I think there's a change in your patient, doctors."

They came into the room and said at once, "He's dead."

In half an hour I was on the way to Philadelphia to break the news to his wife. Five hours later I was back in New York with Mrs. Bishop.

With Bishop dead, I was again out of work, this time in New York. Will Smythe was also there and our meeting, together with the fact that Maurice Barrymore, who had just closed a highly successful engagement in "Captain Swift" at the Madison Square Theatre, was willing to undertake a summer performance of "The Burglar," embarked us all upon the production of my first four-act play in the East.

CHAPTER XV

MAURICE BARRYMORE AND "THE BURGLAR"

In the early summer of 1889, finding myself in New York and unemployed, I was glad to accept the offer of Mr. William G. Smythe, who had associated himself with another young manager named Charles Matthews, to produce a four-act play, "The Burglar," which I had built up from the sketch "Editha's Burglar." Maurice Barrymore had just closed his engagement at the Madison Square Theatre in a successful run of Haddon Chambers' Australian play, "Captain Swift."

Barrymore at that time was not only the matinée idol but was the favorite leading man of most of the theatre-going men of New York. My first meeting with him—in fact, my first identifying sight of him—was in an office on the second floor of a converted dwelling on Broadway near Thirty-first Street, where Smythe and Matthews had desk-room. Will Smythe introduced us.

As this smiling, keen-eyed, handsome, athletic fellow shook hands with me and looked me over as critically as I was regarding him, he said: "Somewhat of a husky, eh?" and, still holding my right hand, jabbed in playful burlesque ponderousness at my ribs with his left. As I instinctively stopped him he added: "Know something about that, do you?" I have seen boys of ten begin acquaintance in similar pretense.

That meeting characterized the intercourse between us that covered the next twelve years or more—the last of his active life. He had an army of friends, but that during that final period I was the nearest to him I believe none informed will dispute. During that time he played in six pieces of mine, "The Burglar," "A Man of the World," "Reckless Temple," "Alabama," "Colonel Carter," and "New Blood," his parts in all but the first two being written for him.

I never saw Harry Montague, but I have seen numerous portraits of him. All the other popular idols of the American theatre from 1880 to 1900 I saw in person. Barrymore was easily the finest-looking and best-carried man of them all. His features were in drawing almost identical with those of his son Jack, with the difference that for Jack's poetical expression and fibre the father had the challenge and the sturdiness of a Greek gladiator. Physically he was five feet eleven inches tall, with a shoulder breadth accentuated by the smallness of his head. and weighed about one hundred and seventy pounds. In romantic costume or in evening dress on the stage he had the grace of a panther. On the street or in the club or coffee-house he was negligent and loungy and deplorably indifferent to his attire. In the theatre a queen could be proud of his graceful attention. Outside, a prize-fighter or a safe-blower was of absorbing interest to him unless some savant was about to discuss classical literature or French romance.

At that time the stationers' and jewellers' windows displayed silver frames containing photographs of him as "Captain Swift" in a dress suit, standing in a conservatory, holding in his hands a saucer and demi-tasse from which his attention had just been sharply distracted.

MAURICE BARRYMORE IN 1888.

AUGUSTUS THOMAS IN 1888.

Some observer, Wilton Lackaye, I think, said not long
ago that Barrymore in transmitting his traits had definitely separated two personal and principal characteristics. The teacup quality he had bequeathed to Jack
and the prize-fighting excellence had gone to Lionel.
There is enough truth in the comment to justify it, although both the boys are much more protean than it
suggests.

Mentally Barrymore was capable of interest in the
most abstruse questions, but as far as I was qualified
to judge he did not care to seem profound. He was vastly
more amused in surfaces, but to the depth that facts
and theories, forces, events and expression in all forms
did interest him his was the quickest, most alert, the
most articulate, the wittiest, and most graceful intelligence that I ever knew.

Once, describing to me a fight between a pet mongoose
that he owned and a cat, he said: "All you saw was an
acrobatic cat and a halo of mongoose."

The line could have been paraphrased to describe any
tilt in repartee in which I ever heard Barry himself take
part. And yet I never heard him speak a line that left
a scar. It is hard to quote some of them and convey
this conviction, but his smile and manner, true declara-
tions of his intent, made the most acid speeches amiable.

I was delighted, of course, to have him chosen for the
lead in my first big play in the East. These young managers were considerate of my wishes in getting the entire
cast. Other prominent artists engaged were Emma V.
Sheridan, who had been playing leading business for
Richard Mansfield; Sydney Drew, then in his early
twenties, but already a favorite as a comedian—he had
been featured in a play of Gillette's and was regarded as

starring material by more than one manager; John T. Sullivan, a prominent leading man for second business; and Gladys Rankin, the beautiful daughter of McKee Rankin. I went into the company to play the old man and to understudy Barrymore in the part of the burglar. Willie Seymour, later the general stage-manager for Charles Frohman, was engaged to rehearse the play. Mr. Seymour was an experienced producer—as a matter of fact, had been in the theatre all his life, having gone on as a child with Edwin Forrest in "Metamora."

The managers had little money and were staking all on our trial in Boston. As a matter of economy the organization was taken there by the Fall River boat. Nobody in the company had any important money. Salaries at that time were not what they are to-day. The largest on that list was Barrymore's at two hundred dollars.

On the palatial *Plymouth* at the dinner-table we sat down somewhat a family group. Barrymore took the head of the table, with Miss Sheridan to his left. The rest of the company strung along on the sides. There arose somehow a pretended dispute over the honor of ordering dinner for Miss Sheridan.

Drew said: "We'll toss for it."

A cube of sugar was marked on its six sides like an ordinary die and given to Sydney for the first throw. It was an anxious moment, the comedy of it irrepressible to his temperament, and as he shook the cube in his hand and looked at the other derisive men before throwing he said, "High man out." Barrymore had to remind him that the stake was the honor of ordering dinner for a lady, but Sydney's line had revealed the situation. Before all had finished throwing, Joe Holland, who was with another company on the same boat, noticing the hilarity of our party, joined us and wanted to know what the gambling was for. Sydney, who had lost, told him it was dinner for the entire party. Barry added, "A large stake."

Joe threw and lost, and after the order was given, being also in an actor's summer, made a tour among the members of his own company, borrowing for the prospective bill. When the checks came Barrymore paid for all the dinners. But Sydney's line of "High man out" passed into the company's quotations, and on all occasions was used to exclude anybody from polite or generous enterprises.

Our rehearsals were in Boston. Knowing how much depended upon the result of the venture, I was especially watchful, trying to detach myself and look at the presentation objectively, as a critic in the theatre. I could see nothing but success. As a touchstone for my estimate I had of course the rather full record of the little play which was now the third act of the big one. Naturally the story mounted to that, and the fourth act, which was a logical sequence, did not seem to drop.

Our first night was not more short of its endeavored effects than most first nights are. The nervousness of men and women in a new play is such that at a first performance they never give their best interpretation. At this opening the calls were sufficient, the applause and laughter were great. Behind the curtain we thought we had a success. The thing that chilled us was the failure of the inexperienced management to say so. They had been in touch with the men from the papers, and we felt that they reflected the opinion of those men.

Most actors have a light dinner around six o'clock and a supper when the work is over. That night in Boston we men were all too excited to think of going to bed even at the actor's hour. Four of us, Barrymore, Drew, John Sullivan, and I, decided to sit up for the morning papers. We were joined by dear old General George Sheridan, the silver-tongued Republican spellbinder, father of our leading lady. He had been with us during our four weeks' preparation.

The impression upon a sensitive author may mislead me, but as I remember the morning papers they had very little to comfort any one. Barrymore's indignation and revolt were magnificent. He consigned all the critics to the bowwows, and was disposed to send the audience with them.

His finishing line as he slapped me encouragingly on the shoulder as daylight was breaking through the window was: "Boston, my boy! Why pay any attention to it? What is it? A city of Malvolios."

Sharing my first faith in the piece, trying to analyze and weigh the elements of success against everything in the other scale, he was sympathetically bracing me up.

Sydney Drew, who lacked Barrymore's ability to do this, but who had an equal good-will, broke in by saying: "Now, Gus, I've been in too many first nights——"

His brother-in-law said playfully, "You have, Mr. Drew, you have," and pushed him out of the conference.

Sydney, with his comedy smile and a gesture of recovery, added: "Well, I'm a wonder."

"You do yourself an injustice—you're a freak," Barry said, and returned to lifting my soggy spirit.

Two or three managers had come down to Boston to see our opening, among them Joseph Grismer, at that time a favorite actor on the Pacific Coast, where he was starring jointly with his beautiful and talented wife,

Phœbe Davies. Grismer had an option on the Western rights to the play. That he had disappeared at the end of the performance was an unhappy augury in the mind of the management. I was staying in the old Clark's Hotel, a place for men only. At six A. M., I turned into bed in a room on an upper floor with a door at right angle to a room occupied by Smythe. The weather was warm, the transoms were open. I was waked about nine o'clock by Matthews calling upon Smythe. Through the open transoms I could hear the dejected conference between the two managers.

A bell-boy knocked at the door. Matthews took the card.

From Grismer! Each man tried to pass to the other the painful duty of going below to interview him. Matthews finally went.

After a considerable interval I heard his steps come quickly to Smythe's door, a sharp rap, an entrance, and his excited tone as he reported to his partner: "Why, he still wants it!"

Further sleep was impossible to me. I dressed quickly, and as soon as I could do so diplomatically confirmed the meaning of the report. Later I saw Grismer himself. With the ease of the veteran he had dismissed the unfavorable notices. He had seen the play; he had watched its effect upon the audience. He saw himself in the part.

I shall never forget his hearty laugh or the strong, soldierly face as he said: "Why, my boy, it'll make a fortune for everybody!"

That was a hard Tuesday for me. The day before I would have bet upon my ability to brace up under any conditions. But when I found Smythe and Matthews discounting also Grismer's optimistic opinion and acceptance, and regarding both as peculiar to his isolated territory and his personal needs, I was a demoralized author. One thing that hurt me much was what I thought injustice in important press comments. In the first act of the play my burglar was a man in refined surroundings, speaking good English; in the third act he was talking thief jargon. I had believed that subtilely effective, because in my railroad experience I had seen educated men quickly adopt the ungrammatical and slangy speech of the man on a box car. Mr. Clapp, then the principal critic of Boston, cited this departure as a mark of my immaturity. The opinion marked only his own inexperience with actual life in that stratum and environment. Two or three days later some other paper took issue with him upon the point, but on that Tuesday I was submerged by that and other objections equally valueless.

During a walk alone in the afternoon I found myself looking into a shop-window with no accurate consciousness of my surroundings or recollection of how I had acquired them. It was only a dazed minute or two before objects fell into their proper categories and I was able to get my bearings, but the lapse alarmed me. A half block farther I met Mary Shaw, whose home was Boston. Mary had seen the play and was enthusiastic in her approval of it and of the work of the company. This, however, was to me unimportant in the presence of the lapse of consciousness I had just been through. In frightened fashion I told her of it.

Mary put back her head and with her contagious laugh of those early days, said: "Good old-fashioned biliousness, my boy, nothing more." Mary's diagnosis was correct.

Our Boston engagement was for two weeks. The business showed such healthy signs that we were regretful that it was not for a longer period.

On Wednesday after the matinée Wesley Rosenquest, managing the Madison Square Theatre for A. M. Palmer, proposed to Smythe and Matthews that the piece be brought to New York for as long a time as it would hold up in the summer. His terms were for the theatre to take each week the first two thousand dollars. It was of course possible to play to much less than this on the gross, and for the management also to be stuck for salaries and advertising.

As they hesitated Barrymore said: "Take it! If the money doesn't come in you'll owe me nothing, and I think I can answer for most of the company."

This decided the managers. As they started to thank Barrymore he interrupted them: "I'm not doing it on your account. This is for Thomas."

The New York opening was a night of almost equal anxiety to that of Boston. As one of the cast I had only the actor's biased opinion as to how the play was going. I was heartened during the first intermission by a visit of the comedian, Louis Harrison, who came to my dressing-room with a message from Bronson Howard, commending the workmanship of the act just finished; and when the play was over Harrison came again to Barrymore's room and mine to bring us good news and to give his own opinion—by no means an unskilled one—that we had the best melodrama offered in New York since "The Two Orphans."

Bronson Howard was then in New York with his production of "Shenandoah" at the Star Theatre, where its great success was so substantially the beginning of Charles

Frohman's fortunes. Other attractions running at that time were Rosina Vokes with her little company at Daly's in repertoire, including "My Milliner's Bill," "The Rough Diamond," and the song "His 'Art Was True to Poll." Maude Adams was making her first hit at the old Bijou Theatre in Hoyt's "A Midnight Bell"; Francis Wilson was playing "The Oolah" at the Broadway; Sothern was rehearsing "Lord Chumley" by Belasco and De Mille to go on at the Lyceum on Fourth Avenue, the beautiful little second-story theatre managed at that time by Daniel Frohman and supported by a clientèle second only to Daly's. The McCaull Opera Company, with Digby Bell as principal comedian, was in the midst of a run at Palmer's; Lillian Russell was playing "The Brigands" at the Casino; "Ferncliffe," by William Haworth, was at the Union Square, and Helen Barry had in rehearsal "Love and Liberty" to follow. Denman Thompson was in the midst of his popularity with "The Old Homestead" at the Academy.

"The Burglar" was a success in New York, and after its first year on the road played with two and sometimes three companies throughout the country almost continuously for the next ten years. I report this to record a fact which may be useful to other writers. When I was in St. Louis Will Smythe had written to say that forty dollars a week was a fair royalty for a four-act play by a beginner. In his own inexperience he had consulted Howard P. Taylor, then somewhat in the public eye as a dramatist. That royalty was agreed upon. I was sure that Smythe had been misinformed, but the terms were adhered to. The lowest royalty that a beginner of a play worthy of production should have received would have been 5 per cent of the gross receipts, amounting on "The Burglar's" average business to more than ten times forty dollars. Smarting under what I felt to be the injustice of the arrangement, and yet declining to ask anything not in the contract, after the first few weeks I sold my rights for twenty-five hundred dollars. The piece did, as Grismer had prophesied, make small fortunes for all owners associated with it.

When "The Burglar" went away for its first season, however, its royalty of forty dollars a week was my total income. I don't know what decree of fate led to such a general agreement upon this figure as my value, but with certain obligations in the West economy was essential. Smythe relinquished a second-story front room at 205 West Twenty-fifth Street, over a parlor that was occupied by an Italian who gave a table d'hôte dinner for thirty-five cents with a pint of red wine thrown in. That was the dinner to which I treated Barrymore and asked him if it wasn't a fine offering for the money.

Barrymore said: "Great! Let's have another!"

This second-story room was let for three dollars a week. I engaged it when Smythe left toward the end of September. It was a fine room for the money, being nearly twenty-five feet square and having three windows at the front. Among its few drawbacks were the simplicity of its furnishing and a rich, permeating odor of Italian cooking, never absent and especially high at the flood of the gastronomic tides. Barrymore thought that anybody ought to be able to write in such rich and redolent quarters, away from all distractions and calls, and when the rear room on the same floor, separated from the front room only by the customary wardrobes and marble wash-stands of that period, was vacant he rented it at the same price.

On his first day as a tenant he brought in two reams of soft printing paper, typewriter size, and two dozen plain wood pencils already sharpened and made of a grade of plumbago suggesting stove polish. They had retailed at ten cents a dozen. He declared his intention of starting in the next morning to write a play. But he didn't come that morning or any other morning. His wife predicted that such would be the case. She said their own apartment, wherever it happened to be, was strewn with stray leaves on each of which was written, "Act One, Scene One. A Ruined Garden."

Some five or six years later, when I had built a home and was living at New Rochelle, Barrymore came out one night to read a play he had completed. We had to explain the burst of laughter that greeted him from my wife and me as he began to read, "Act One, Scene One: A Ruined Garden." Not only did Barrymore never work in that Twenty-fifth Street room, but as far as I know he never came to it but once.

This failure to use the room is not astonishing when we remember Barrymore's way of living then. Rather than store his four or five trunks of valuable costumes which he was apt to need at a moment's notice, he kept them in a little hall bedroom on Twenty-eighth Street in a house managed by a Mrs. Higgins. The room also contained a little iron bedstead and washstand. Barrymore never occupied it, but to disagreeable persons he gave it as his address. Mrs. Higgins was instructed to say always that Barrymore had just gone out, and occasionally some wastrel transient, on an order from Barry, slept there. In conjunction with one or two actor friends he had a flat on Fourth Avenue. I think this was really the place where he preferred to sleep and to get his breakfasts. Mrs. Barrymore was travelling with the Crane company at that time, and when she came to the city Barrymore took an apartment with her at some hotel. During one of these engagements their joint address was the old Sturtevant House, so that with the room back of mine Barrymore quite honestly had four private addresses.

One blizzard night, walking away from The Lambs Club on Twenty-sixth Street, I was stopped by a shivering boy of twenty who asked for a dime to get a bed. I took him with me, showed him into this back room. The boy looked at the sofa.

"There?"

I said "No," pointed to the roomy and well-furnished bed and left him stammering his thanks. About three o'clock in the morning I was waked by somebody striking a match and turning on the gas. Barrymore, dripping from the storm, stood in the middle of the floor.

He nodded to the back room and said: "What's all this in there?"

After collecting my thoughts a moment I said: "That's a little philanthropy of mine."

"Well, where am I to sleep?"

"What's the matter with the Fourth Avenue flat?" There was some friend there. "What about the Sturtevant House and Georgie?"

Barrymore said: "Ethel is over from Philadelphia to visit her mother, and I've been turned out."

"What about the room at Mrs. Higgins'?"

"King Hall has that this week."

I couldn't help laughing at the picture of America's favorite and best-paid actor, with four apartments for which he was paying rent and no place to sleep.

I said: "I don't know what you're going to do, old man."

"I do."

He shed his outside clothes and got into bed with me.

Barrymore at that time was playing my one-act piece, "A Man of the World," previously referred to as the contribution refused for publication when offered during my reportorial duty on the *Post-Despatch*. Somewhat dissatisfied with his opportunities at the Madison Square Theatre, he was considering an engagement to star under the management of J. M. Hill. I was casting about in an effort to devise for him a play that would show to best advantages the Barrymore qualities. My association with him and the little circle about him at this time put a decidedly new twist into my way of thinking of the theatre.

Barrymore had written and produced for Helena Modjeska a story of Russian life called "Nadjesda," which in the opinion of many had been handicapped by the intensity of its dramatic incidents. It was drama of that kind that he wanted from me. Somewhere from the South there was a newspaper item of two men who had fought a duel by drawing lots from a hat with the understanding that the man who got the marked card was to suicide. This and other incidents coming to our attention at that time, all equally unusual or bizarre, combined to make a story which, under the title of "Reckless Temple," I submitted to Barrymore and Hill, and, urged by their enthusiasm, wrote in that Twenty-fifth Street room.

CHAPTER XVI

GATHERING PLACES OF THE ACTORS

I had now become a member of The Lambs. At the clubhouse I passed more than half the time I permitted myself away from my writing. The Lambs was then in its fifteenth year, and contained the best element in the profession. It was a great honor, privilege, and education to be received on equal terms by its then membership, a total professional number of one hundred, which included such men as Lester Wallack, Dion Boucicault, Steele Mackaye, Mark Smith, Robert G. Ingersoll, Otis Skinner, the Holland brothers, George, Edmund, and Joseph, and others worthy of the standard that these names indicate.

A table d'hôte dinner was served for fifty cents at the large club table, where the men were like members of a family. There was a notable musical contingent and often between courses the popular songs of the time. The gayety of such youngsters as Harry Woodruff, Cyril Scott, Fritz Williams, Francis Carlyle, and Ned Bell was as memorable as the wise talk of such elders as Steele Mackaye and Frank Mayo. Fun was spontaneous and unconstrained. At one of these small dinners I began my real acquaintance with Otis Skinner. He had come in from a trip on the road, was greeted with shouts and lifted glasses, and because the place on the impromptu programme fitted it he stood in the doorway, and answering the men's demand recited Béranger's "When We Were Twenty-One." I shall always remember the

romantic picture of that virile, Moorish-looking youngster, and the sentiment with which he read "Flo, my
Flo, was a coryphée."

The Lambs was then at 34 West Twenty-sixth Street,
between Broadway and Sixth Avenue; the house an
old-fashioned five-story, twenty-five-foot-front brownstone dwelling with high stoop, under which was a basement entrance. It was like its adjoining houses in external looks and faced similar buildings on the north side
of the street. Those respectable neighbors eyed it with
distrust. Leaving The Lambs and walking east to Broadway you passed the St. James Hotel on the corner. On
the other side of Broadway was Delmonico's, running
through the short block to Fifth Avenue. The block was
and still is short, because these two great thoroughfares
wedge sharply three blocks farther south. East of the
long plaza made by their intersection is the park called
Madison Square, a plunger fountain in the centre and
the Saint-Gaudens bronze of Farragut on the northwest
corner.

Facing this square on all four sides in 1889 were beautiful and impressive buildings, each with its history fairly
mellow and all with their uniform sky-line that could
be enjoyed without suggesting curvature of the spine.

To have eyes and never to see the sky is to be slowly
and unconsciously immersed in matter. Where no vision
is the people perish, and the vision of this nation is born
and nourished and reinforced and sustained from modest
houses that are detached and which face four ways to
the weather and from which men and women look in
easy angle at the sky. Some one has gone further than
this and said that a view of the horizon is necessary to
the sanity of the eye. In thirty-three years Industry

with a capital I has torn down the old Delmonico's, the old St. James, the Worth and Hoffman houses, the Fifth Avenue Hotel, and the handsome homes of modest height, and replaced them with cubes of the towering kind that make central New York City a gridiron of box cañons.

In 1889 Madison Square had just won from Union Square, nine streets farther south, its claim to be the theatrical centre. It was the smart and modern spot, although many of the actors of the comic-page, fur-trimmed intensity still haunted the older Rialto. And at Fourteenth Street there was still considerable theatrical power and vibration. Under the old Morton House J. M. Hill still managed the Union Square Theatre. One street farther south was the Star, where Crane's long run in David Lloyd's and Sydney Rosenfeld's "Senator" and other plays was to occur before the passing of that historic house. North of Union Square, where now stands the lofty Century Building, was the stately, hospitable Everett House; while to the east was Riccadonna's, famous for spaghetti and the patronage of the Salvinis, father and son. These, with the Academy of Music, then run by E. G. Gilmore, and Tony Pastor's own theatre just behind it, put up their ancient claim for attention. But the fashionable town was moving north.

At Twenty-fifth Street two tides of easy promenaders joined in their down-town drift, and returning there divided for the northerly walks. Every fine afternoon other than matinée days members of the stock companies of Daly's, Palmer's, and the Lyceum theatres, and members of other combinations of nearly equal importance, moved in leisurely manner and almost small-town neighborliness through the comfortable throngs of well-dressed and fairly intelligent Americans, to whom all of them were known by sight. Fashionable New York was out in private rigs with liveried coachmen and tigers; there were no trolley-cars, no motors. The busses on Fifth Avenue were drawn by slow-plodding horses.

Life itself had a gentle pace, social intercourse a more genial temperature. Friends, meeting, stopped to exchange a word; men in groups told stories, laughed; policemen did not ask them to move on. The moulds of form, the glasses of fashion were John Drew and Herbert Kelcey, Robert Hilliard and Berry Wall. Equal centres of interest and prompters of good-nature were Barrymore, Coghlan, Goodwin, Hopper, Digby Bell, Dixey, Charles Stevenson, and Frank Carlyle. A certain challenge went with Ted Henley or Lackaye.

Some day it will be as respectable to write historically of the fine barrooms of that time as it was for Dickens in his day to write of the tap-room; and even now I must venture something, because to leave them out is to attempt a portrait with half the face concealed. Any one of those important men just named could be stopped in that parade, and under the pretense of business or pressing communication enticed for a moment's misleading conference into one of those convenient snares.

In the St. James Hotel, behind and above the glassware, was a picture of three dashing cavaliers, plumed hats, flowing cloaks, swords, and all; portraits in costume of Billy Connor, hotel proprietor and erstwhile manager of John McCullough; of Charles W. Brooke, distinguished lawyer, orator, and *bon vivant* of the day; of Louis N. Megargee, newspaper writer of Philadelphia and New York, all initmate friends of the talented Moses P. Handy of Clover Club celebrity. This picture had the kind of draft and influence of Maxfield Parrish's Old King Cole,

painted in after years for the late Knickerbocker Hotel
café, with the difference that *King Cole* came from the
nursery with the reputation of having quite shamelessly
and in *haute voix* expressed his preferences, whereas the
St. James trio depended entirely upon the law of associative suggestion.

One habitué was Jerry Dunn, a handsome fellow
strongly suggesting in appearance former United States
Senator J. Hamilton Lewis, though Dunn was rather a
silent person. He had, however, killed a man with a
revolver. Another sport was Pat Sheedy, who managed
John L. Sullivan. It was in that saloon, the story ran,
that when Sullivan proposed to beat up Sheedy with his
fists, Sheedy, not unprepared for the attention, had
pushed a derringer against Sullivan's body and asked him
not to do it.

Some politicians came there. General Sheridan—
Silver-tongued George, as his Republican friends called
him—lived in the hotel.

On the next block south from the St. James was the
Hoffman House café, perhaps the finest in the world.
The proprietor was the handsome, melancholy, gray-
haired Ned Stokes, who had killed Colonel Jim Fisk on
account of the notorious Josie Mansfield. It was said
Stokes always slept thereafter with the light burning in
his bedroom. In this café, guarded by brass rails and
plush ropes, hung an heroic canvas by the great Bou-
guereau, a painting of several nymphs trying to throw
a fighting satyr into the water. This prophetic symbol
was years before the general adoption of woman suffrage.

In the theatre the prizes are to magnetism quite as
much as to ideas or antics. Of the three factors, magnetism is the hardest to define. To call it attraction is

but to change the substantive. To call it personality is only to befog it. To recite the reasons for my own explanation of it or to support my case adequately in the controversy those reasons would provoke would take half a volume. I therefore omit reasons, and avoiding controversy issue only my belief that the force is electrical; that its possessor is not its generator but its medium, and that the voluntary transmission of it is exhausting. The truly effective actor cannot simply wipe off his grease paint and turn in to slumber.

Our Favershams, our Hacketts, our Marlowes, our Cohans, our Drews of three actor generations, our Barrymores of two, with the admixture of the Drew strain, our like artists of repute, as well as those yet undiscovered and uncelebrated, cannot after a night's play set the psychical brakes and come to a dead centre. Like a machine before the stop, the human organism before the normal nerve rate must slow down. For this retardation the ample apartment with trained butler or equally trained maid and the presence of understanding comrades who quit at the first suppressed yawn is ideal.

For an income unequal to such provision the proper restaurant, the club, the café of the Hoffman kind, is invaluable. Let us not chide that immortal coterie at the Mermaid Inn, nor Chris Marlowe, nor Ben Jonson, nor Will Shakespeare, nor criticise too severely that other at the Cheshire Cheese of which Garrick was so often the centre and Doctor Johnson the mentor.

Into that old Hoffman House café from the Madison Square, the Fifth Avenue, the Lyceum, three theatres within a radius of two blocks, actors easily drifted. Those of Palmer's, Daly's, and the Bijou had but little farther to come. The writers met them. For some obscure reason—as slightly higher price or the watchful eye of the house man, Billy Edwards, ex-champion prize-fighter —only the better element of the men about town frequented the place. A group of players and playwrights at a table were uninterrupted. Men nodded to them, or joined them if invited, but they did not intrude.

What wise conferences were many of those expert discussions of current or projected plays; what condensed experience; what discovered and tested rules; what classifyings of situations; what precedents and likenesses; what traditions, conventions, experiments, suggestions; what a winnowing of ideas by what vigorous, original, challenging, prolific fellows; and in what free interchange in an atmosphere and temper stimulated to just that degree of exaltation that can bridge and blend and give an overtone and group consensus! Truly, "Wisdom is justified of her children."

For more private and smaller conferences, among other places, there was also Browne's famous old chophouse on Twenty-seventh Street just off the Broadway corner; one stone step to the hallway and a turn to the right for the parlor dining-room with its little tables, to which a third chair could be drawn; the hot-water dishes for the mealy Welsh rabbit and the pewter mugs for the musty ale.

I first saw Paul Potter there, rewriter of French comedy at the time, but afterward author of "The Conquerors," "Trilby," "Under Two Flags," and adapter of a half score of farces. He looked an oldish young man then as, thirty years later, after the unmanageable cropped hair turned white, he looked a youngish old one. Barrymore made him join us, and then rallied him on his theories until daylight. Paul Potter was always a bookworm. Why study life when it is all so thoroughly written and pigeonholed and catalogued by men so superior to any of us? And Paul knew all the indexes, including the Expurgatorius. Diderot was his guide, and his laws were immutable. Paul remade plays as an Italian worked in mosaic, or he thought he did.

After that first meeting he met me at long intervals in America, in London, in Paris, and without astonishment in a seemingly uninterrupted intimacy, with both hands out in greeting and with perplexed eyes; but whether in luck or in trouble, always with the self-deprecating, boyish, white-toothed smile. At Foyot's on the Rue Vaugirard, the French senators from the palais opposite, equally with the bowing waiters, saluted him as Monsieur l'Américain.

I saw him last in New York in the early spring of 1921, one afternoon in a Turkish bath on Forty-second Street. I first inquired quietly of the attendant, and having made sure of the solitary sleeper talked loudly enough to rouse him. The grave, emaciated face, simple as one of Shakespeare's forest rustics, took on its waking smile as he asked "Gus? Gus?" and sat up in his sheet, as sunny as a boy at a swimmin' hole.

"How are you, Paul?"

He chuckled with the merriment of it.

"Why, Gus, old friend, I'm dying!" And then he laughingly told me how desirable diabetes was as a way to finish. One had to go some time. The doctors gave him only a few weeks longer. "See? It's the swelling of feet and ankles that keeps me in here most of the time, but the boys all know me and don't mind me lying around. Soon after this stage one goes into coma and—it's all over." And he laughed again, his forehead wrinkling under his thick white hair. The next day they couldn't wake him.

I hate to jam old friends into their coffins this way, but with only twelve of these articles one has to do it or hurt some of their feelings by leaving them out. But back in Browne's in 1889 Paul told me that, as Diderot had printed for him, our plays are written backwards; that is, constructed like a mystery story, from the solution backward to the enigma. Of course, it was helpful to know that, and I've told it to dozens of youngsters. Who was it said the unpardonable thing, the one base thing in life, is to receive benefits and to confer none?

There came into New York that winter a typical Southerner in speech and appearance named Colonel Edward Alfriend. His home had been Richmond, Virginia. Other citizens of that place reported that because of his courtly manner he had been called Count Alfriend. The colonel was about sixty years of age, tall, suddenly portly at the meridian, with prominent features, and a walruslike white mustache, which with the important consciousness of an English guardsman he stroked to hold the floor in the pauses of his discourse. His ambition was dramatic authorship. His most prominent friend in the theatre was A. M. Palmer, above whom in physical stature he towered some seven inches. He spent many hours in Mr. Palmer's office when it was evident to other callers that Mr. Palmer was not insisting on it.

Reporting these interviews outside, the colonel frequently said: "I am very close to A. M. Palmer."

After a couple of years, with the assistance of Mr. Augustus Pitou, who signed as joint author, he produced a play under the title of "Across the Potomac." His second play, the only other from his pen as I remember that was produced, was "The Louisianian," played by Mantel. In Palmer's office Alfriend met Barrymore; and Barry, amused by the old gentleman's punctilious manner, his pomposity, and a mediocrity that warranted prediction, carried Alfriend about with him in many leisure hours. One of Barry's gentle friends wishing to embroider a sofa pillow, a Penelope activity then not fallen into neglect, asked me to draw in outline on a square of silk a profile of herself and one of Barrymore. After I had drawn her own profile I said: "How close to that do you want the profile of Barry?"

The lady said: "About as close as Alfriend is to Palmer."

Barrymore introduced the colonel to me and insisted on my sharing for the new acquaintance his own enthusiasm. Later Barry found a furnished flat, fourth floor, on Thirty-fourth Street between Seventh and Eighth avenues, with three bedrooms, a little parlor, dining-room, and kitchen. The tenant wanted to sublet it furnished for forty dollars a month. Barrymore thought it would be an ideal arrangement if we three—he, the colonel, and I—should take this flat and live there. We entered upon its occupation. A rotund, matronly negress, the janitress for the building, did the housework and prepared our breakfasts. Other meals we took outside. I don't remember a happier period.

When the spring came and the fish were running so thick in the North River that one could buy a five-pound shad with roe for thirty-five cents, General George Sheridan, having sent old Sarah word the night before, would appear in time with such a fish in a brown paper; and as Sarah, under his instructions, prepared it and put it on the breakfast table he would discourse upon it and the expert way to separate the fibre from the bones with all the savory interest of a Colonel Carter.

During those five months in the Thirty-fourth Street flat I wrote two plays, both under arrangements with Manager J. M. Hill; one for Sydney Drew, which was never produced; another adapted from the German, which was produced more than a year later under the title of "A Night's Frolic," with Helen Barry, an English actress of more than masculine stature, in the principal rôle, which fortunately required that most of her scenes be played in the uniform of an officer of the chasseurs. That event lives principally by the association of one of its least important members at that time, a singularly active, optimistic, dark-haired lad of some nineteen or twenty years named John L. Golden. It is difficult to avoid his name now among the Broadway white lights with his presentations of "Turn to the Right," "Lightnin'," "Thank You," and so on.

After a while Barrymore's enthusiasm for the flat subsided noticeably, and with the coming of the summer we abandoned our arrangement. We were the only theatrical ménage in the building, so I doubt if we could have maintained our occupation much longer, because during our last month there I heard the colonel, whose point of view old Sarah understood perfectly, tell her to ask the lady on the floor above what the devil she meant by moving furniture around at eleven o'clock in the morning. The colonel seldom slept more than six hours, at that. He wrote his plays from books of the vintage of the "Deserted Village." They were pitiably short, but filled with long soliloquies, and all of them written for Barrymore. Barrymore listening to one of these, and looking to me for help would have been an inspiring subject for "When a Feller Needs a Friend"; but with his diplomatic skill he always protested himself an unworthy exponent. One spring day on Broadway Barry and I, walking together, saw Wilton Lackaye approaching us with menace in every lineament.

When we met him he said: "See here, what do you fellows mean by sicking the colonel onto me?"

After leaving the Thirty-fourth Street flat which we three men had leased I roomed at The Lambs Club until I left it to take an apartment with my wife at a hotel. The sojourn at The Lambs was rich in experiences which would fill a volume of small talk, smaller even than this. One item that, notwithstanding its diminutive proportions, I feel justified in describing, was of a parrot. Parrot stories do not amuse me, because as a rule so palpably invented; but as Maeterlinck has written some association between happiness and the bluebird, I will tell of this green one's occasional power.

The club at this period was not prosperous; in fact quite the contrary, and the newly organized Players had begun to draw from it many of its best members. The only other permanent lodger in the house in that fall of 1890 was the owner of this parrot, John B. Miley, a graduate of Dublin University. Mr. Miley's business was to sell wholesale, on commission, fine liquors handled at that time by the old-established house of Roosevelt & Schuyler. Miley was proud of his business and of his wares, and as self-respecting as if a discerning monarch had just given him the knighthood recently conferred upon an eminent English distiller. The parrot had been with him in many years of convivial associations that may be inferred, but it had learned nothing demoralizing—no profanity, no greetings, no call for biscuits; but laughter of every variety, from a complimentary chuckle to the hysteric and pained abandonment that needs help.

Miley occupied the little hall bedroom, second floor front, in which Bishop had died. He was an industrious person, and went early to his business. Alone in the club, down-hearted for important personal reasons that must not take attention here, each morning as I reached Miley's room I was greeted by a formal, complimentary little laugh from the parrot. It was my custom to push the door farther open, speak to the bird, and sometimes sit on the bed and invite his specialty. That little formal laugh of his, encouraged by my echo, voluntary only at first, would grow in volume and expand in character until it revived somewhat of all the merry and maybe dissolute hours of exhilarated companionship that Miley's trade and temperament had won; laughs of a superior clientèle, but punctuated occasionally by guffaws of chance and cheaper acquaintances, and by concerted crescendo effects spraying into broken vocables as some falsetto, tearful enthusiast regurgled the point of the story. I was a poor amateur compared to Polly, but together we could fill all the windows on both sides of Twenty-sixth Street with matrons and housemaids, sympathetically agrin and curious as to the disorderly convocation at The Lambs. It was a great way to start the forenoon, and required several unpleasant letters of efficiency experts to dissipate Polly's fiat sunshine.

In the spring of that year the reputation of "The Burglar" on the road and "A Man of the World" at the Madison Square Theatre had influenced Mr. Palmer to ask me to become connected with that fine playhouse. Dion Boucicault was then under a regular retainer to patch or adapt for Mr. Palmer any imported play that might need it, and also to give him first option on any original work, subject, of course, to usual royalty terms. Boucicault wished to retire. After a study of the rather limited field, still more limited in approachable material, Mr. Palmer offered me the Boucicault desk at a salary of fifty dollars a week the year round. He had been paying Boucicault one hundred, and told me I could follow the theatrical custom and say outside I was getting the same; but that never became necessary. It was stipulated that I was at liberty to produce "Reckless Temple" and "The Correspondent," which J. M. Hill had respectively for Barrymore and Sidney Drew. This Madison Square engagement was a substantial addition to income, was good publicity, and a fine business address. I was then thirty-three years old.

I wrote at Mr. Palmer's request "A Constitutional Point" for Mrs. Booth, who needed a one-act play. Mr. Palmer thought the public wouldn't understand it. Eighteen years later I expanded it to four acts and called it "The Witching Hour." For Mrs. Booth's immediate need I wrote another one-act play called "Afterthoughts," which she did successfully.

"Reckless Temple" did not succeed in New York, and after sixteen weeks on the road Barrymore came back to Palmer's Madison Square Theatre, where, anticipating both those events, I was at work upon a play with parts in it for all the company, including Barrymore. About making that play there is in my opinion a story of some psychological as well as pathological interest.

Men differ in degree, perhaps in kind, in their capacity mentally to see forms. My ability to draw faces from memory leads me to think that I have at least the average faculty. Sometimes in the dark, with no external claim upon the optic nerve, these mental pictures seem faintly objective. Their definition is not perfect. Against the reddish-gray background that closed eyelids bring there will appear in contrast lines of a lighter gray. These lines are not fixed. They move. At times, when they take on resemblance to a face, imagination running just a little ahead of the vision will muster them into proportions of perfect drawing, and memory can manage them into portraits. It is a fact in pathology that under fever nearly everybody sees these shapes. In drowsy daylight figures of the wall-paper grow fantastic, move, and have expression. In his most excited moments, Martin Luther, it will be remembered, could not banish the image of the devil from the wall of his cell, and there used to be shown a spot where he had thrown his inkwell at this negative invocation, become objective.

After the production of "Reckless Temple," and some attendant dissipations and demands upon me physically, and when I was in a run-down condition, this faculty of such seeing was feverishly augmented. Under the doctor's orders I had resumed strictly regular hours, not the easiest recovery in The Lambs. One night before the club was completely quiet I was trying to go to sleep in the dark. At the piano down-stairs E. M. Holland was playing a melody, then popular, called "Down on the Farm." These lines in the dark of which I have written assembled into definite shape, and I could see before me more plainly than many a stage set shows in theatrical light two posts of a ruined gateway, one standing, the other fallen, crumbled. I recognized the picture as of a gateway I had seen in Talladega some six years before, but had not consciously thought of since. As I looked at it with some amusement an old man walked through it, stood a moment, and was joined by a young girl who took him by the arm and led him obliquely out of the picture. Two or three times this little action was repeated so definitely that it was impossible for me in any way to connect it with imagination, although the association between Holland's tune, with its rural, sentimental color, and this picture is fairly evident.

There was nothing unpleasant about this visional intrusion, nor was there such persistence that I felt driven to Luther's protest. This little gateway and its two figures played somehow through my dreams. In the morning I found myself interested in the relationship of the two people, partly trying to divine, but rather drifting with, their story. After a day or two the result was a one-act sketch. This I had typed, and carried it to Mr. Eugene Presbrey, stage-manager for Mr. Palmer. Presbrey was enthusiastic about the little piece, but told me it was a mistake to play it in that form. He reminded me that "The Burglar" had some of its New York effect dulled by having first been done as a one-act play, and insisted that I had in my possession the nucleus of a fine big story. He saw at once in the characters a part for Stoddart and another for little Miss Agnes Miller, who was the ingénue of the company at that time. There were other parts for Barrymore, Ned Bell, and Harry Woodruff.

Under Presbrey's encouragement, using the sketch as a third act, I wrote the four-act play "Alabama." I had fun with the Southern colonel in the piece, whom I called Colonel Moberly and whom I endowed with all the formality and pomposity of our Colonel Alfriend. There was a boy's part for Harry Woodruff, and a fat squire for Charles L. Harris, the splendid comedian who had been with us in "Reckless Temple." At my suggestion, after hearing the scenario, Mr. Palmer added Harris to his company and used him in two or three plays that were produced before we finally reached "Alabama."

Ed Holland liked the idea of the colonel written for him, and as he and Woodruff already had some hint concerning certain scenes in which they were together they soon began to greet each other in Southern dialect and manner. The membership of The Lambs, ignorant of the reason for this assumption, but amused by it, caught its contagion, and in a little while the club was apparently an organization of two hundred Southern colonels all shooting cuffs and stroking phantom but magnificent mustaches.

The play was finished under pressure in January and read to the company on the stage. Presbrey, familiar with it, was not of that group, but in his little office near the entrance to the dressing-rooms.

As Mrs. Booth left the theatre she leaned over the closed lower half of Presbrey's Dutch door and whispered to him, "Rotten, thank you!"

When we reached rehearsals she declined to play the part written for her and it was given to May Brookyn, from whom she reclaimed it shortly after the piece was produced. After rehearsing "Alabama" a week Mr. Palmer lost faith in it and replaced it with one of his English plays. This attack and retreat were repeated twice. But after there had been three English failures the rehearsals of "Alabama" in a spirit of desperation went on to its production on Wednesday, April 1, 1891.

In these varying moods Mr. Palmer lost faith not only in the play but in its author, and one dark day told me that when the year of our contract ended, which would

be in May, my engagement as dramatist extraordinary
—that was my title; I don't know why—would cease.
But he added that he was sending on a first tour through
the country Mr. E. S. Willard in "The Middleman,"
and that if I liked I could go ahead of him as publicity
man. He would pay the salary I had earned with Bishop,
one hundred dollars. It felt like a slip backward, but
as a newly married man I took it. The plan was for me
to leave New York Sunday, March 29, and have two
weeks in Chicago before Willard opened.

By earnestly protesting that I didn't need all that
time I got Mr. Palmer's permission to wait until early
Thursday morning, and thereby on Wednesday night
see "Alabama" open.

Shortly after his installation as Vice-President of the
United States Theodore Roosevelt was one of six men
who came to the home of Brander Matthews to meet at
lunch Mark Twain, recently returned from a trip abroad.
Colonel Roosevelt was most entertaining throughout the
luncheon with reminiscences of Cuba.

Pertinent to one of these he turned to Mark Twain
and said: "As an old Confederate soldier, Mr. Clemens,
you must have noticed the nervousness of the bravest
men upon going into battle."

Mark took his cigar from under his white mustache,
and with a dreamy squint replied: "Oh, yes, I know that
nervousness of brave men going into battle, and I had
the quality of maintaining it all through the engagement."

The playwright never gets so experienced that a production is not an occasion of nervousness. An inexperienced one whose play has been set aside three times because of the manager's distrust has more nervousness

than the brave man going into battle. On the first night of "Alabama" mine was augmented by an almost panic condition of Mr. Palmer. Although quite unknown to anybody that mattered, I sought a further obscurity by standing behind a post in the gallery. A similar timid figure in the shadows across the aisle attracted my attention. It was Mr. Palmer. When the first curtain fell with mingled laughter and applause, the most desirable response a company can ask for, Mr. Palmer looked at me, his eyebrows lifted in an inquiry mixed with astonishment.

Friends of Mr. Palmer will remember his regular features and intellectual and distinguished expression; also his large, pale eyes. He also had rather full gray side whiskers, decorations not so uncommon then as since the introduction of the safety razor.

These facial forms and effects, his white lawn tie, and his look of shocked surprise carried the uncomfortable suggestion of some interrupted mortuary function. Four or five curtain calls and the mood in which the audience had taken this blandest of our four acts gave me courage to go to the balcony for the second one.

With similar but more pronounced responses after that, and finding that Mr. Palmer had also ventured down to my level, I threw all caution to the wind and said: "I'm going to see the rest of this performance from the ground floor."

When the play was over it seemed to me we had been in the presence of a success, but Mr. Palmer was not able to lift his spirits from the depression of the disastrous season, so that despite the congratulations of many friends I went to bed uncertain.

My wife and I at that time were in our first apartment

in the old Oriental Hotel, opposite the Casino. As we had to take an early train for Chicago, we agreed not to look at any of the papers until we should have had an undisturbed breakfast and were alone together on the train, speeding from police detention. I gave her the paper in which I felt I would get the most considerate treatment, and took myself the one I believed most hostile. Its very head-lines disarmed me. I looked up and met an enthusiastic glow imparted by the notice she had read. We hurriedly went at the other papers. The press was unanimous. "Alabama" seemed the surprise of the season, and was characterized in terms almost too laudatory to refer to except by proxy.

In Chicago, as Willard's advance man, my calls at the newspaper offices were exciting, owing to telegraphic reports about the New York first night, and the dramatic men were kind. But that day an ailment that had been threatening became acute, and I had to submit to an operation under ether that put me in bed for the next ten days. During that time the men on the Chicago papers gave me all the help I could take. I was told that whatever I got to them concerning Willard would find space. Thus encouraged, I dictated to my wife long specials for each paper, which she carried to the offices, and I doubt if any theatrical attraction ever went into Chicago or any other American city with better publicity than those generous fellows handed us.

Presbrey kept me informed of the play in New York, where it was doing capacity business, and the royalty checks made me think of the first time I had ever sat in an overstuffed chair. We got the New York papers every day; the ads and paragraphs were fine, and some of the papers carried editorials about the play, inquiring

CHARLES L. HARRIS AND E. M. HOLLAND AS SQUIRE TUCKER AND COLONEL
MOBERLY IN "ALABAMA."

if New York managers had not made mistakes in leaning on the imported article when native subjects seemed so acceptable. And then in the midst of all of it came a long telegram from Nat Goodwin asking me to write a serious play for him, to choose my own subject, and offering a royalty of 10 per cent of the gross receipts, with an advance of twenty-five hundred dollars. I agreed to do it.

With the Willard company Mr. Palmer came into the city, delighted with conditions in New York and heartily approving all those he found in Chicago. I passed the credit for the display to the men to whom it belonged, especially to a young writer named Kirke La Shelle, whom Mr. Palmer engaged that week to take the place with the Willard company, which for sufficient reasons I was giving up. La Shelle later became a theatrical captain, and produced for me "Arizona," "The Earl of Pawtucket," "The Bonnie Briar Bush," and "The Education of Mr. Pipp." Mr. Palmer asked me to forget his terminating our contract and to go on under the old arrangements for another year. He consented to my writing the play for Goodwin, which he expected from the optional claims of our Madison Square agreement.

There were more checks from New York, and this twenty-five hundred dollars from Goodwin. I was able, with a cane, to get about comfortably. I had been away from St. Louis for twenty months. We went home to see the folks. Crossing the Eads Bridge in the morning I got to thinking of Whitlock, alias Jim Cummings, who robbed the Missouri-Pacific express-car to cancel the mortgage on his mother's home, and I felt ashamed of myself. My mother then lived in a rented place. I didn't tell her my inspiration, but we went together and picked out a house.

CHAPTER XVII

SOME NOTABLE MANAGERS

In the middle of April, 1891, after Mr. E. S. Willard, for whom I was serving as publicity man, opened his mid-Western tour in Chicago as *Cyrus Blenkarn* in Henry Arthur Jones' play "The Middleman," with Marie Burroughs as his featured support, my wife and I went to St. Louis, and afterward to the Minnesota lakes and the Northwest. We returned to Chicago in the middle of May to see the Western opening of my play, "Alabama," which had been forced out of New York by a summer sublease of the Madison Square Theatre. My father and mother came from St. Louis to see that first night and visit us a few days in Chicago, where I tramped over the crowded down-town streets with father hunting landmarks of the small town he had known as a printer and medical student in his youth. The first week in June the parents went back to St. Louis and my wife and I returned to New York.

Under my arrangements with Mr. Palmer I had rewritten parts of "John Needham's Double," a play by the English author, Mr. Joseph Hatton, produced February 4, 1891, by Willard at Palmer's Theatre. This rewrite was after I had completed "Alabama," but before that play was produced. An account of it in this place is a little out of such time order as I have attempted, but not enough to make the dislocation jar. Hatton had put into his play a supposedly Southern colonel whom he called *Silas Higgins*, or something of that kind, and who talked about nutmegs and apple-sauce. Mr. Palmer asked me to make this character proper to its section not only in name and in speech, but in view-point and relation to the story. I wrote a character which I called *Colonel Calhoun Booker*. Mr. Palmer, at my suggestion, engaged for the part Burr McIntosh, at that time about thirty years of age, fairly prominent in the Bohemian life of New York, celebrated for his good nature and his willingness to take chances, and for a pronounced mimetic faculty. Palmer knew nothing of McIntosh, but I had heard him tell stories at the clubs and was sure he had the foundation for the part. With Palmer's permission I stressed *Colonel Calhoun Booker's* importance in the play, feeling that its presentation would be a *ballon d'essai* for "Alabama," which was to follow; and I believe that the success of McIntosh helped determine Mr. Palmer to go through with it.

"Needham's Double" was one of those plays of dual personality, resembling in kind "The Lyons Mail." It was invented and unlikely, and on the first night in New York McIntosh, with his breezy manner and his welcome Southern geniality, would have walked away with the honors if the opposition had not been a star in large type. He played the part during its short run and left it to do *Colonel Moberly* in the second company of "Alabama."

After the original "Alabama" company played its New York and Chicago engagements, and before it reopened at Palmer's in the fall of 1892, it went to Louisville. Mr. Palmer asked me to go there and look over the performance. The Louisville engagement was in the fine old playhouse belonging to the Macauleys, so dear to me in memory of Johnny Norton and the more recent visit of Marlowe. Henry Watterson saw to it that our first night was a gala occasion, and the men of the company were invited to a midnight reception at the Pendennis Club. Marse Henry was in his element, ably aided by those Kentuckians who have the Southern instinct amounting to genius for hospitality and entertainment. At an effective moment in the evening he got the attention of the party—close on to a hundred men, I should say—and with his arm through mine in the centre of the floor explained the circumstances under which our acquaintance had been made, and claimed to be proud that I was a product of a newspaper office.

Then shifting his arm over my shoulder, a habit he had with any younger fellow he thought it would help, and reverting to the play, the subject of which was the reconciliation of the two great political sections of the country, he said: "This boy has done in one night in the theatre what I endeavored to do in twenty years of editorial writing."

No half-way measures about wonderful Henry Watterson, gone since I last wrote of him in these chapters.

With the opening of Palmer's at this time, the little Madison Square Theatre passed into the control of Messrs. Hoyt and Thomas. Charles Hoyt was the author of a line of comedies as distinct in their kind and for their day as the George Cohan plays are three decades later.

There was in the business department of the theatre of America at that time a relationship of forces worthy of comment here. Those forces were then functioning principally in New York. Although perhaps traceable to more remote origins, they focussed and funneled through the chanels of publicity.

The principal managers, like Wallack, Daly, Palmer, Daniel Frohman, had been accustomed to get their plays from the other side of the water. American playwrights, compared with to-day's number, were few, their triumphs not numerous; but in the '80's there had been some notable successes with American subjects: Florence had played Woolf's "The Mighty Dollar" to extraordinary business; Curtis had had success with "Samuel of Posen"; Raymond had made a fortune with *Colonel Sellers* in Mark Twain's "Gilded Age"; Denman Thompson, under the encouragement of his manager, J. M. Hill, had elaborated a vaudeville sketch into "The Old Homestead." Concurrently with these American plays on the road was a cycle of big productions of English melodrama like "Romany Rye," "The Silver King," "The World," "Hoodman Blind," "Lights o' London," and the like, the exploitation of which throughout the country had developed a school of publicity men who knew accurately what part skilful press work played in all these successes. They also had a thorough knowledge of the respective values of the patronage to be obtained in the various cities. This experience and this knowledge had come along together with the rapid growth of the country upon which both depended, and while the older managers, content with their local triumphs in New York and Boston, gave their attention to those centres, these lesser agents and the publicity men referred to were wide-awake to the value of the road.

Just back of Palmer's Theatre, both formerly and later Wallack's, on Thirtieth Street, in the basement of what had been a dwelling-house, was the office of Jefferson, Klaw, and Erlanger. The Jefferson of this firm was Charles Jefferson, eldest son of Joseph Jefferson. Klaw and Erlanger need no identification now; but even at that time A. L. Erlanger was one of the best informed of the men of whom I am writing.

At 1115 Broadway, near Twenty-fifth Street, in a rear room, Charles Frohman had his first office under his own name. He was another of these men.

Erlanger's genius was of the synthetic kind; he had the faculty of combination. Very rapidly, under his activity, there was built up the first big syndicate of American theatres controlling the best time on the road. Charles Frohman's vision was the supplementing one of producer. He also knew the country, the tastes of the people, and had an uncanny flair for what would be acceptable. But both men, and lesser ones with whom they were associated, approached the whole theatrical question along the lines of availability and salesmanship. What were the things for which there was a market, and how rapidly could the public interest in them be created, stimulated, and expanded? These two sets of managers, the Palmer-Daly-Daniel Frohman group on one side, and the Charles Frohman-Hayman-Erlanger group on the other, approached the business from entirely different points and with entirely different methods. An example of approach and method is furnished by "Alabama." When that play was produced in April, 1891, there was ahead of it in the Madison Square Theatre but four weeks. After that time Mr. Palmer had rented his theatre for Martha Morton's play, "The Merchant," and although "Alabama" immediately played to capacity and would have rapidly restored the failing fortunes of Mr. Palmer, it never occurred to him to depart from the arrangement made to sublet his theatre. To get ready money, he was therefore obliged to sell a half

interest in the play to Charles Frohman and Al Hayman.
Both these men urged him to continue its run at the
Madison Square. They argued that Miss Morton's
play was as yet untried; that other theatres as suitable
as the Madison Square could be got for it in the city, and
that Miss Morton had no right other than the most technical one, and none whatever in justice, to impair Mr.
Palmer's property by forcing it out of a theatre where
it had such momentum. As a matter of fact, the new
partners were right. Miss Morton's manager would
have benefited rather than have lost by some financial
accommodation that would have deferred their *première*.
"The Merchant" was produced in warm weather and
was not successful.

Charles Frohman knew nearly all the men then playing in the American theatre. He had travelled with
Haverly's and Callender's Minstrels, with modest ventures of his own; he was a most approachable and human person, and with his little office just one flight of
stairs up from the Broadway sidewalk, where anybody
entered without knocking in those days, his acquaintance
and his popularity rapidly grew. After "Shenandoah"
he acquired a lease of the Twenty-third Street Theatre,
between Sixth and Seventh avenues, and produced "Men
and Women," by Belasco and De Mille, on the model of
the plays they were then supplying the Lyceum. This
was followed by other dramas and a string of farces provided by the skilfully original as well as adapting pen of
William Gillette. This success built for him the still
beautiful Empire Theatre at Broadway and Fortieth
Street, which he opened with Belasco's fine melodrama,
"The Girl I Left Behind Me," in which Frank Mordaunt,
William Morris, Theodore Roberts, and others appeared
with the boy actor, Wallie Eddinger, as *Dick*.

Clay M. Greene, in a burlesque of that play, had the colonel in agony, reading news of an injury to little *Dick*, hand the telegraph tape to the major and say: "Take it. I must get back."

"Back where?"

"To the centre of the stage."

I'll talk about me.

We were friends, Charles Frohman and I, from our first meeting in 1882 until he was lost on the *Lusitania* in 1915—thirty-three years. After 1892 he produced nine plays of mine—"Surrender," "Colorado," "The Man Upstairs," "The Other Girl," "Mrs. Leffingwell's Boots," "De Lancey," "On the Quiet," "The Harvest Moon," and "Indian Summer," and five others which I had rewritten but did not sign. I don't remember that we ever signed a contract, and I am sure that we never had a difference. He was among the first men upon whom I called when I first came to New York to go with the Marlowe company, and when I returned with the thought-reader Bishop. He was the first manager to ask me for a play after my coming to the city. I wrote for him many bits not mentioned above. These little things were often written in his presence as he pushed a piece of paper across the desk when a subject came up in some related talk. He had a fashion of doing that with other play-wrights—Gillette, or Fitch, or Carleton—and it was great fun to give him some bit for one of his girl stars and hear him say, "That will go in to-night."

There was never any talk of remuneration for these little things, as the burden of obligation, if obligation existed, was always so heavily on the other side for the hundreds of little courtesies that he found one way or another of extending. Charles Frohman had a fine dra-

From a photograph by Underwood and Underwood.   Copyright by Daniel Frohman.

CHARLES FROHMAN.

matic sense, and without attempting exactly imitation had the mimetic faculty that suggested the object of his protrait quite as definitely. Men amused him much, and when he told of his last visitor the interview was likely to be vividly dramatized. I remember a report of a visit of Colonel Alfriend, the Southern author of whom I have written.

C. F., with his irresistible twinkle, said, "The colonel was here to see me," and then without another word there was the pantomime of the high hat laid carefully on the table, one finger after another of one glove carefully withdrawn, then the entire glove straightened out and laid across the hat; the same treatment for the other hand; the silk-faced overcoat carefully taken off, shaken out at the collar, folded, laid over the back of the chair; the button of the surtout carefully adjusted at the waist; mustaches stroked, and the victim, transfixed with a steady and piercing gaze. The scenario of a play was drawn from one inside breast-pocket.

But C. F., *in propria*, interrupted—"I am going to do a play by J. M. Barrie for Miss Adams. If you had brought me in something for Miller——"

Then C. F. was stopped; another scenario came from the other inside pocket. This was not exactly the kind of story that was wanted. Then, still as the colonel, C. F. put one hand over his head like the legendary Westerner getting a bowie knife, and drew a third phantom scenario from the back of his coat collar, this last gesture burlesque, but so in character that it was impossible to find the line dividing it from preceding comedy.

Charles Frohman had a bit of philosophy that he carried through life. He had learned that existence was supportable if he had one real laugh in the day. Among men interested in art and the theatre as connoisseurs and patrons the wisest that I know is Mr. Thomas B. Clarke. I was at a loss to comprehend his standard of excellence in the drama until I heard him say one time that any play which for two consecutive seconds made him forget himself, made the playhouse disappear and him to feel that he was in the presence of a real event, was for him a notable play. He said:

"One seldom gets from a studio a canvas of uniform excellence throughout. There will be one feature of it better than the others. I can prize it for that feature. And if I get a play with the scene I have indicated, I go three or four times when the scene is on to get the same pleasure from it that I get from the excellent note in a painting."

C. F. seemed to apply an equal theory to relaxation and the day's conduct. The thing that amused him he would write upon a blotting-pad, and recover somewhat of its joy by telling it to many a subsequent visitor. During the rehearsals of "The Other Girl" referred to in previous chapters we had on our third or fourth day reached the first repetition of the second act. I was on the stage with manuscript and a blue pencil, the company standing about, slowly marking positions on the parts, when C. F.'s office-boy came with an envelope carrying across its back the well-known blue display of Maude Adams' name. As the boy waited for an answer the rehearsal stopped long enough for me to read the sheet inside.

It carried in large and hurried handwriting, in colored crayon, "How are you getting along at rehearsals without me?"

Taking the inquiry at its face value from a busy man,

I wrote across the note one word, "Great," handed it to the boy, and forgot it. Two days later I stopped in at the office for some necessary conference. His letter with my comment was pinned on the wall.

He said: "That furnished me laughs for two days. I showed it to everybody."

He was also a practical joker, and would go to considerable lengths, but never with any of the cruelty or lack of consideration that practical jokes sometimes breed. When "Alabama" went on its second visit to Chicago he was interested in the management.

He said: "I'll bet you that it'll do a bigger business than it did the first time."

As it was to be in the same house and we had played to capacity the first time, I didn't see how that could be, and said so. He wanted to bet, nevertheless, and rejecting cigars and hats as stakes he fixed upon a suit of clothes. I demurred, feeling that it was unsportsmanlike to bet on a sure thing. He generously gave me that advantage, however. The business on the second trip was nearly double, because of the fact, of which C. F. was aware, and I not when he made the bet, that the play had been chosen for the local police benefit and all patrolmen of Chicago were selling tickets. The increased royalties reconciled me to the loss of the bet. The bill for the suit of clothes came in with C. F.'s indorsement. The price, one hundred dollars, amused him greatly. We must remember that back in 1892 fifty or sixty dollars was a fair sum for a suit of clothes. C. F. was fond of telling all this when he had me and some other man in his office.

Considerably later he was to open with a new play, the name of which did not please him. On his blotter he had a half-dozen alternative titles suggested by persons who had called during the day. The man who gave the winning title was to get a suit of clothes. He told me the story. I suggested "Never Again," which C. F. wrote on the blotter and said would be taken under consideration. My wife and I dined down town that night and went to a play. As we were coming up town to the Grand Central Station all of the exposed ash-barrels, boxes, and temporary scaffolds were being covered with snipe advertising of "Never Again." I went to an expensive firm and ordered their best suit; the price was one hundred dollars. I asked them if there wasn't some way to increase it, and after fastidious additions induced them to boost it to one hundred and fifteen. C. F. added that to his story.

With the success of "Alabama" the continued avidity of the public for the Southern type drew Mr. Palmer's attention to "Colonel Carter," by Francis Hopkinson Smith. The story, which had appeared in one of the magazines, was already in book form and was probably a best seller; one heard of it everywhere. I had *carte blanche* as to material, but felt a little overawed by the popularity of the book and the authority of its author. The play was only mildly successful, but it marked a very notable date in my own affairs, a friendship with that man of such extraordinary versatility, Hop Smith, as his friends called him, that lasted until his death in 1915. I have at hand no scrap-book to spring upon the defenseless reader, but I think it an act of simple justice to the author of the book to quote from "The Wallet of Time," by William Winter, America's greatest critic of the theatre:

"Coming as it did at a time when the stage was being freely used for the dissection of turpitude and disease, that play came like a breeze from the pine-woods in a morning of spring." And of the wonderful artist, dear Ned Holland, he writes: "His success was decisive. The *Colonel*—with his remarkable black coat that could be adjusted for all occasions by a judicious manipulation of the buttons, his frayed wristbands, his shining trousers, his unconsciously forlorn poverty, and his unquenchable spirit of hope, love, and honor—was, in that remarkable performance, a picturesque, lovable reality."

With the production of "Carter" completed, and with plays for Goodwin, Crane, and Charles Frohman to write, I ended my connection with Mr. Palmer and turned to the wider field. Mr. Palmer had about decided to abandon management anyway, although, with his caution over any considered step, he did not do so for two years.

During those two years he produced "Trilby" at the Garden Theatre and one or two plays at his own house, in which the beautiful Maxine Elliott made her first appearance. Mr. Palmer, who had been a public librarian in his youth, was the most cultivated manager I knew personally—I never met Augustin Daly. But Mr. Palmer's culture made him timid in a business that was fast offering premiums for adventure. I remember the melancholy of the man in his gradual retirement, as during that period he said to me: "I'm an old man"—he was considerably under sixty at the time—"and I cannot compete with these younger men who are coming into the field." He named particularly Charles Frohman and Mr. Erlanger.

It would be of interest to remember the kind of world in which we then were living in that period beginning in 1892 and covering the next five years of which I now write. The President of the United States was Grover

Cleveland. William McKinley was Governor of Ohio. Roswell P. Flower was Governor of New York. The State of Massachusetts had just elected to the United States Senate, to succeed the veteran Senator Dawes, a person comparatively young and described as a man of letters, named Henry Cabot Lodge. The national legislature was considering the favorable report of a Senate committee upon a proposed Nicaragua Canal. We had reached a decision that it was essential to have our Navy doubled. Gold had been discovered in quantities in Colorado, and there was an excited movement to that State. Andrew Carnegie and Henry Frick, declining to consult with their men, with whom they were having some labor disputes, had been responsible for the precipitation of the Homestead trouble.

On the other side of the water Charles Stewart Parnell had just died under something of a cloud. In England Gladstone was preparing to retire from the premiership after explaining his home-rule bill. Bismarck was being charged by the Socialists of Germany with corrupting the press with money improperly collected. There was a famine in Russia. In France Ferdinand de Lesseps had been indicted because of irregularity in the conduct of the Panama Canal enterprise; five deputies and five senators were under arrest charged with complicity therein. Deputies Clémenceau and Déroulède had fought a duel, firing three shots at each other, and concluded by shaking hands.

CHAPTER XVIII

THE EARLY 90'S

Thomas F. Gilroy was mayor of New York City; the community was busy discussing rapid transit and the prospect for a first subway, for which it seemed impossible to borrow money. There was a great stir in municipal consciousness all over the country. L. S. Ellert had just been elected mayor of San Francisco on an independent ticket and a promise to give clean business as opposed to the sand-lot variety of politics. Mayor Pingree, of Detroit, had won on a campaign for city lighting. Mayor William Henry Eustace of Minneapolis was closing a business administration, and although contracts with the lighting companies had five years to run, Minneapolis was resolving at the termination of that time to have her own electric plants. Chicago was hoping to elect Mayor Harrison in order to have his direction during the period of the World's Fair. And Nathan Matthews, mayor of Boston, had been elected on a ticket for municipal lighting and an extension of the transit.

For the season of '91-'92 my wife and I had resumed possession of our apartment on the upper floor of the Oriental Hotel on the Thirty-ninth Street side, overlooking the roof of the Casino. In the summer and early autumn evenings we could sit at the window or on the little fire-escape balcony thereby and see the operatic performance on the Casino roof as comfortably as if from a private box, though a bit remote. Part of our royalties that were coming in I devoted under competent advice to the collection of a small library, good for working purposes, and occasionally getting here and there a little picture that was worth having. Somebody has said that when you have once thoroughly seen a picture you may safely take leave of it; it will never again have for you its first effect.

For some reason that is not the truth for me. A picture that I have really chosen and that I like grows more and more to be a part of my environment, and I feel with Doctor Henry van Dyke, who wrote that his pictures were for him windows through which he looked out from his study on to the world.

In that apartment, thus agreeably situated and surrounded, I began to think about the story for Goodwin. He had been so successful in a sentimental bit in "A Gold Mine," written for him by Brander Matthews and George Jessop, that though he was willing to have his new play largely comedy, he hoped that it would have a serious backbone. At that time Goodwin was slight, graceful, and with a face capable of conveying the subtlest shades of feeling; his voice was rich and modulated. My problem was to find a story for a blond hero five feet seven inches tall, weighing under one hundred and fifty pounds, with a Roman nose and a steady, steel-blue gaze. I stood the Goodwin photograph on my table and looked at it until it talked to me. The slight physique couldn't explain the solid confidence of that look except there was behind it a gun. I clarified my problem a little by deciding that the gun should be carried lawfully, and as there was nothing suggesting the soldier in Goodwin, nothing of the setting-up type about him, I was urged to the idea of sheriff.

Persons interested in play-writing—and I am persuaded they are not few in number—will see how that clears the atmosphere. When you must or may write for a star it is a big start to have the character agreeably and definitely chosen. To secure the love interest, I thought of a girl who would be of a little finer strain than the sheriff type indicated, and the necessity for conflict suggested a rival. The rival should be attractive but unworthy, and to make him doubly opposed to Goodwin, I decided to have him an outlaw, some one it would be the sheriff's duty and business—business used in the stage sense—to arrest.

I have told in earlier chapters of my experience with Jim Cummings, the express robber, who had given a messenger on the Missouri-Pacific road a forged order to carry him in his car, and then after some friendly intercourse had tied the messenger and got off the train with a suitcase full of greenbacks. The need for a drama criminal decided me to make use of Cummings as Goodwin's rival, a glorified and beautiful matinée Cummings, but substantially him. This adoption rescued the sheriff and the girl from the hazy geography of the mining-camps in which my mind had been groping and fixed the trio in Mizzoura.

Newspaper experience in those days before the flimsy and the rewrite emphasized the value of going to the place in order to report an occurrence, and I knew that, aside from these three characters and their official and sentimental relationship, the rest of my people and my play were waiting for me in Bowling Green, Mizzoura. I told Goodwin of the character and the locality, got his approval of the idea that far, and took a train for Pike County.

In those days Mrs. Thomas and I used to hold hands on our evening promenades; but I think it was really our foolish New York clothes that made the blacksmith smile. At any rate, we stopped at his door and talked with him. He knew Champ Clark and Dave Ball, another Missouri statesman, and had the keenest interest in the coming convention for the legislative nomination. It was fine to hear him pronounce the State name Mizzoura, as it was originally spelled on many territorial charts, and as we were permitted to call it in the public schools until we reached the grades where imported culture ruled. The blacksmith's helper, who was finishing a wagon shaft with a draw-knife, was younger and less intelligent, and preferred to talk to Mrs. Thomas. A driver brought in a two-horse, side-seated depot wagon on three wheels and a fence rail. The fourth wheel and its broken tire were in the wagon, and the blacksmith said he'd weld the tire at 5:30 the next morning.

We went without breakfast to see him do it. He was my heroine's father by that time—a candidate for the legislature—and I was devising for him a second comedy daughter to play opposite to the boy with a draw-knife. That day I also found the drug-store window and the "lickerish" boxes that Cummings should break through in his attempted escape; and I recovered the niggers, the "dog fannell," the linen dusters, and the paper collars which in my recent prosperity I'd forgotten. I also nominated Goodwin for the legislature, which increased his importance and gave him something to sacrifice for the girl's father.

I was very happy over what I felt was the backbone of a play as I started from Bowling Green to St. Louis on the return trip. In the day coach my wife and I were the only passengers except a man who sat well forward by the heater and seemed in trouble. When the conductor, whom I knew, came along I asked him about the man. He said: "That's Nat Dryden. You must know him."

I did. I went forward to Dryden's seat. He was weeping and muttering to himself, though slightly consoled by liquor.

When I spoke to him he turned to me for sympathy and said: "Oh, Gus, Gus, Nancy died last night."

Nancy was his wife, and was known as one of the handsomest women in Missouri.

"Yes, last night! And, oh, Gus, how she loved you!"

"Why, I don't think I ever met your wife."

"I know it. But you remember that convention at Jefferson City when I was a candidate for attorney-general——"

I nodded.

"The fourth ballot was a tie between me and that blankety-blank-blank from Calloway County. You were at the reporters' table. At a pause in the proceedings you rose from your impotent and inopportune seat, and addressing that convention in which you had no rights whatever you said in a loud voice: 'I want it distinctly understood that the press of this State is for Nat Dryden.' "

I nodded.

"Dear boy, it beat me. But I went home and told it to Nancy, and we've loved you ever since."

My wife and I stopped only a day in St. Louis, and then we started back for New York. There are few better places than a railroad train for building stories. The rhythmic click of the wheels past the fishplates makes your thoughts march as a drum urges a column of soldiers. By the time our train pulled into New York I was impatient to make a running transcript of speeches of my contending people. But that is a relief that must be deferred. Like overanxious litigants, the characters are disposed to talk too much and must be controlled and kept in bounds by a proportioned scenario, assigning order and respective and progressive values to them.

Before beginning to write I submitted the story to Goodwin. He was playing at the Fifth Avenue Theatre at the time, I think, in Henry Guy Carleton's "Ambition," but I am positive about his rooms at the Worth House annex of the Hoffman House just across Twenty-fifth Street. I called by appointment at twelve o'clock. Nat had been a little wild the night before, and was now propped repentantly against his pillows. As I entered the room a German waiter was standing at the foot of the bed with an order blank in his hand. Nat was studying the menu with a most regretful discrimination. Faintly assuming my permission, he gave his order, the obsequious German responding and writing down.

"Bring me a wine-glass of orange juice."

"Vine-glass, oranch juice."

"Dry toast."

"Jez-sir, try doast."

"Piece of salt mackerel."

The waiter answered and wrote. Long pause by Nat.

"Cup of coffee."

"Coffee, jez-sir."

"Curtain."

Following Nat's appealing look, I explained to the puzzled waiter the significance of the last instruction.

Goodwin was so enthusiastic about the story that it

was an added stimulation to the writing of it. I got a little inside room near our apartment in the Oriental and began work on the play, which as far as dialogue went almost wrote itself. One night in particular, after talking in minute detail the third act to Goodwin, really playing it with him, I went to my table after an early and light dinner, but with some coffee that I had the bell-boy bring at irregular times, and other reinforcements not so deadly, and wrote the entire third act of the play before the daylight came through the windows. I was a good deal of a wreck when it was finished, and the handwriting was difficult to read; but when finally transcribed it was never altered, and the play could be prompted from that script to-day.

Early in the World's Fair time there came a chance to do the play at Hooley's. Goodwin had a fine company, somewhat miscast in some particulars, but all of ability, with handsome Frank Carlyle as the villain and a tower of strength in McIntosh, whom I persuaded Goodwin to take when he had been rather set on getting McKee Rankin, a much more expensive and older actor. We had exactly eleven days in which to produce the piece. It was one of Goodwin's greatest first nights. I had frequently been behind the curtain with Nat in other plays, but never saw him begin one. That night in Chicago he had a perfect case of seasickness, and with difficulty controlled his nausea during the acts. He told me then that his nervousness always affected him that way with a new play.

I shall never forget his pale face nor his descriptive line as during one of the intermissions he looked up at me and said: "My boy, a first night is a hoss race that lasts three hours."

After the Goodwin contract I had engaged to do plays for William Crane and for Charles Frohman. The most imperative of these was for Crane, then playing in "The Senator," and looking about for a play to follow it. Crane some years before had had a play by Clay M. Greene called "Sharps and Flats," in which he and Robson had jointly starred, and Greene had rewritten for Robson and Crane some other script. Joseph Brooks, Crane's manager, wished Greene and me to write together. It was arranged that Greene and I meet Crane at his summer home, Cohasset. Greene was to be in that neighborhood with a yachting party. My wife and I planned to stop on our way to Ocean Point, Boothbay Harbor, Maine, where Mr. Eugene Presbrey and his wife, Annie Russell, had a bungalow, to which they had invited us for part of the summer.

At Mr. Crane's home I found a request from Greene for Crane and me to come to Boston, where a yacht on which Greene was a guest was anchored. This was agreeable, as Crane had his own steam yacht, the *Senator*, and was in the habit of running up to Boston once or twice a week on excuses not nearly so good. Greene's host was Harry M. Gillig, owner of the schooner yacht *Ramona*. The *Senator* anchored near by and our party went aboard the *Ramona*, where, with Harry Gillig playing a taropatch and Frank Unger strumming a banjo, the distinguished comedian showed the boys that he could still shake a foot. Crane began professional life as a basso in a comic opera company, and went from that into Rice's burlesque, "Evangeline," in which as *Le Blanc* he had not only to sing and act, but to dance. Besides the jollity of it there was an amusing incongruity in the sight of the sedate *Senator* in yachtsman's fatigue doing a rattling jig on the deck of the schooner. After a jovial afternoon Crane went home alone to Cohasset, and my wife and I joined the cabin party of the schooner yacht under Gillig's promise to sail us up to Presbrey's, an easy cruise of two or three days.

Harry Gillig, Californian, had recently married a daughter of a California multi-millionaire. This young couple were on their honeymoon. The Gilligs had with them a Western party, including, besides Mr. and Mrs. Greene, Frank Unger, father of Gladys Unger, the young playwright of to-day; Theodore Worres, painter; Charles Warren Stoddard, poet, author of "South Sea Idyls"; Harry Woodruff, actor; and Charles Thomas, partner of Charles Hoyt, of the younger group of managers. Gillig and Unger, as members of the Bohemian Club, San Francisco, were also members of The Lambs, where I had met them and begun an intimate friendship that lasted as long as both men lived.

By the time the *Ramona* reached Boothbay Harbor, Gillig and his cabin party were opposed to my wife and me leaving for the visit to Presbrey. The amiable contest was adjusted by our spending a few days ashore while the boat cruised near by, and our then rejoining for a run to Bar Harbor and back, when our host took Presbrey aboard, too, for a sail back to New York. Any cruise so composed and dowered can fill pages with its record. I shall not write a line, but will leave all to sympathetic understanding under the embracing words of youth and fellowship, sail and song and sea and summer.

It would be with the greatest regret that I would eliminate from my experiences that summer and parts of two subsequent ones on the *Ramona*, and yet I think that nearly all the embarrassment that comes from having one's expenditures exceed his income I could trace to standards accepted at that time.

Eugene Field was wise when he refused the winter strawberries, as Mr. Melville Stone relates, because he feared they would spoil his taste for prunes; and then we people of the theatre are so easily misled by appearance, and also by a creative wish to realize a fancy. Only three or four years ago I met Henry Miller in San Francisco, where, like myself, he had come to put on some plays in that summer.

"Hello, Henry! Why aren't you on a vacation after your busy season at your New York theatre?"

"Because I was not content with a place in the country good enough for any man to live in, but being a damn fool theatrical person had to build stone walls around it, and terraces, and make a production. Now I'm still working to pay for it."

On the *Ramona*, Greene and I hammered out a story we thought would do for Crane's play. It wasn't easy, because Crane, like all the comedians at that time, wanted a comedy-drama, something that would give him a chance for the untried substantial powers he was sure he possessed. With this story in hand we had a season ahead of us in which to write the dialogue.

Although again getting a little out of the order of events, for the sake of cohesion I will jump ahead to the production of the Crane play which we called "For Money." It was a four-act construction, and with a dominant serious note. Crane played a man who had been embittered by finding in his dead wife's locket, which he had thought contained his own portrait, the picture of another man. This unhappy discovery had been made many years before the opening of our story,

and the ingénue of the play, who had come under his
protection, speaking in pride of her antecedents, showed
to Crane a portrait of her father. The unhappy star
was to regard it and say in a quiet undertone to himself,
"The man whose picture I found on my dead wife's
bosom."

Charles Thorne or John Mason or Lucien Guitry might
have got away with that line, but when Crane spoke it,
registering a startled surprise, and spreading his hands
in a manner that had been irresistible in the old-time
comedy of "Forbidden Fruit," the house rocked with
laughter.

Greene said: "Some of 'em wanted to cheer for the
man in the picture."

The performance was in Cleveland, where Greene and
I had a few friends. Sympathetic people tried to restore
the equilibrium of the play by appreciating its other
serious values, but as Greene said at our little post-mor-
tem when the evening was over: "Yes, people came to
me in the lobby and said they liked it, but they didn't
slap me on the back."

By the end of the week Brooks and I took blame for
our fall-down in equal shares. The play wasn't as good
as it might have been, and Crane didn't handle serious
stuff as well as he hoped he would.

I once made a caricature in my guest book of Francis
Wilson, under which Frank wrote, *"Du sublime au ridicule il n'y a qu'un pas,* which some years later I was able
to translate. But the fact of the easy step from the sublime to the ridculous I knew by experience. Two weeks
ahead Crane's time for his New York season at the Star
Theatre was waiting for him.

I said: "Joe, I think I can save the printing, the

scenery, and most of the company and make a farce of this thing in time for New York."

Brooks said: "For God's sake, do it!"

My wife and I went back to the Oriental Hotel. With close application to the work, with the brave use of scissors and paste-pot, I rejoined the company in four days with a new script and parts for a broad farce. We rehearsed it in Baltimore, tried it in Washington, came to our dress rehearsal at the Star in New York with a good company and everybody in high spirits. There occurred at that dress rehearsal a commonplace inquiry of mine which I have seen quoted in newspapers as an example of my brilliant repartee, when it was only the most honest-to-God inquiry a man could make. In the middle of our second act at the Sunday-night rehearsal Brooks loudly clapped his hands after the fashion of the interrupting manager, came down the aisle of the theatre, calling my name. I came into the prompt entrance, from where I had been readjusting a light.

Brooks said: "Gus, there are a whole lot of funny things that could be said right there."

Having written myself out on the rush work with the script and worked myself out at rehearsals, and willing to take help from any quarter, I simply answered: "What are they, Joe?"

When I heard the peal from the company that had been interrupted and from the few people in the otherwise empty parquet, I let the answer go as an example of agility.

"For Money" played a fine eight weeks in New York, but, as I remember, Crane never did it on the road.

My first play for Charles Frohman was called "Surrender." I believed that we were far enough from the

Civil War to take a comedy view of some of its episodes, and that after the many serious plays that had handled it the public would be glad to have the subject treated humorously. C. F. thought so too. He liked the script as I gave it to him, and it was turned over to Eugene Presbrey to rehearse in Boston. Presbrey was so appreciative of its values that he thought it a mistake to make a farce of it, and after a conference with C. F., who went over to look at the rehearsals, they decided to play it seriously, stressing melodramatically every possible point and introducing a horse. When I arrived at about the dress rehearsal the enthusiasm of those two men overbore my first conception of the story, and we went to the public with it as a serious play. It lasted on the road only some sixteen weeks.

Maude Banks, the daughter of General Banks, was playing in the piece the part of the only Northern girl. A requirement of the script and of the part was a blue silk sash on her white dress, as I remembered the young women of war days declaring their loyalty. At the dress rehearsal Miss Banks declined to destroy the effect of her white dress by putting any color on it, preferring to leave the company rather than be disloyal to her dressmaker. C. F. said it was too late to do anything about it, and the young lady's whim prevailed. I don't think she ever played under Mr. Frohman's management again.

Louis Aldrich, a stalwart actor who as a star had won great reputation in Bartley Campbell's "My Partner" and other dramas, played a Southern general with a line that I had taken verbatim from an assertion by Colonel Alfriend that the South had whipped the North on a thousand fields and had never lost except when overcome by superior numbers. Aldrich declined to deliver this speech, because personally he was a Northern man, so that altogether we had considerable trouble with our temperamental actors. There came a time in C. F.'s experience and development, however, when he was somewhat more insistent on the effects that he wanted, and when actors were not so ready to oppose him.

In the spring of 1892 we built at New Rochelle the house which is still our home. The versatile, volatile Sydney Rosenfeld at that time was among the first if not actually the principal librettist of America, and a writer of comedies. He had one or two successes on Broadway, and he and I were very closely associated in The Lambs. At his suggestion we went to New Rochelle to find land on which to drive our stakes. For some reason or other Sydney postponed his building and finally abandoned the intention. I recall our first day's negotiation with Sydney's friend from whom we hoped to buy the land. Mr. Leo Bergholz, ever since that time in the United States consular service, was showing us a little pine thicket on his own land, densely grown, the ground covered with fallen needles. He had a pretty wit, but stood somewhat in awe of the great Rosenfeld, who wrote smart dialogue for the Francis Wilson operas and had also been an editor of *Puck*.

Commenting on the seclusion of this copse, Bergholz said: "No ray of sunshine ever penetrates this gloomy fastness."

When neither of us smiled at this mediæval utterance, Bergholz repeated it. With some difficulty we continued serious. As Bergholz approached it for the third time he lifted his hands after the manner of a *coryphée*, and dancing in most amateurish fashion a feeble jig, he said again: "No ray of sunshine ever penetrates this gloomy fastness."

Sydney, looking solemnly at Leo's feet, remarked: "That's the gloomiest fastness I ever saw."

It was great fun to plan a house. In the old days on the St. Louis *Post-Dispatch* architecture and real estate had been one of my departments. William S. Eames, one of the youngest and most talented architects of St. Louis, associated with Thomas Young, a pupil of Richardson of Boston, had been a member of our old life class at Washington University. He tried to tell me something each week about the beauties of his art, and I came to believe that an essential feature of domestic architecture was a roof that could be seen. According to Eames, the house should droop its wings and hover its sheltered brood like a mother hen. A memorandum sketch that I turned over to our New York architect, and which my wife still has in her scrap-book, was drawn on the back of an envelope after many conferences as to our joint needs. When we began to build we went to New Rochelle to board in order to be near the enterprise. There was no hotel. The best boarding-house in the place was kept by two elderly ladies, one of them a Mrs. David, whose husband had been the principal merchant of that little city, and after whose family David's Island, now occupied by Fort Slocum, had been named. We were satisfied with their references, and they inquired for ours. With his permission, I gave them the name of Bronson Howard. They had never heard of him, and asked his business. I told them and named his prominent plays, "The Banker's Daughter," "The Henrietta," and "Shenandoah." They had never heard of any one of these.

I said: "He is your neighbor and owns the house just around the corner," giving them street and number. They had never heard of that.

This story of Howard's obscurity was a favorite one of mine for many years to illustrate the indifference of the general public to the men who write plays, until it was superseded by an experience of my own. In 1909 Mr. Shubert asked me to go to Chicago to overlook the performance that the John Mason company were giving in my play, "The Witching Hour," at the Garrick Theatre. I purposely stood in the lobby until the curtain had gone up, and then in my most humorous manner asked the man in the box-office if he passed the profession. The lobby was filled with posters bearing Shubert's and Mason's names, and my own, in that order of importance and display. The treasurer asked my name, the branch of the profession in which I was. I told him. He asked me the names of some plays I had written. I named four or five, omitting "The Witching Hour." He said he would have to ask the manager. The manager came to the box-office window, put me through the same questionnaire, and shook his head; and it was only when I told him how he would disappoint Mr. Shubert, and pointed to the three-sheet bearing the name I had given him, that he in any way associated the sound with the type.

At New Rochelle I became intimately acquainted with Frederic Remington and E. W. Kemble. These two illustrators had been friends for some time elsewhere, and were great companions; but the most beautiful side of their friendship needed a third for its precipitation. Kemble is universally amusing when he cares to be. Few men are his equal in putting the spirit of caricature into ordinary verbal report or comment; even his famous "Kemble Koons" do not show such sure fun. Remington responded promptly to Kemble's comedy, however expressed. Most men who know it do the same, but Remington went further. When Kemble had left him after any interview, all of Kemble's woes of which Remington had been the repository were suddenly dwarfed in the larger horizon of Remington's experiences and transmuted into side-splitting jokes. In his mind, Kemble was never grown up; and Kemble reciprocated.

Remington's throes, viewed through Kemble's prism, were just as amusing. They took even each other's art as playfellows take each other's games. There were years when much of their leisure was passed in company. Their understanding was mutual and immediate. One night after the theatre, on the train home from New York, sitting together, Remington was by the car window, Kemble next to the aisle. An obstreperous commuter was disturbing the passengers, men and women. The busy conductor's admonition had been ineffective, the brakeman's repeated expostulations useless. The men passengers seemed cowed; the rowdy was gaining confidence. On his third blatant parade through the car, and as he passed Kemble's side, Remington's two hundred and fifty pounds of bone and muscle reached out into the aisle, and with the precision of a snapping turtle lifted him from his feet like a naughty boy and laid him face downward over Kemble's interposing lap. With the spirit of perfect team-work, as Remington held the ruffian, Kemble spanked him, while the legs in the aisle wriggled frantically for a foothold. The correction, prolonged and ample, was accompanied by roars of laughter from fifty other passengers. Being done, Remington stood the offender on his feet. The man began a threatening tirade. Before half a sentence was uttered Remington had him again exposed to Kemble's rhythmic tattoo. This was enough, and when again released the fellow promptly left the car for the seclusion of the smoker.

In those early 90's my sculptor friend Ruckstull's relation to life was not unlike my own. He was working in a department of art where there was no regularity of income, and where his opportunities were the result of competition. Next to getting an order for a play and finding a story satisfactory to a star or manager was seeing Ruckstull win a commission in a competition where his sketch had been approved. When he got the order for the Hartranft equestrian statue to go up in front of the Capitol at Harrisburg it made quite a little stir in our colony. Besides myself, both Remington and Kemble were artistically interested.

After one has submitted a sculptured model sketch which is perhaps eighteen or twenty inches high, the procedure toward the heroic group that is finally to be in bronze is through what is called a fourth-sized model— say, for horse and man perhaps four feet high. Ruckstull decided to make his final clay model of the finished group in France. Studio rent, plaster-casting, and the final bronze, together with one's own living for the year that the work would require, would all be so much cheaper that such a foreign residence, with somewhat of a holiday color to it, would about pay for itself. His fourth-sized model, however, he would make in this country, and for the fun that it would be for all of us I persuaded him to put up a half shade on some open ground back of our house at New Rochelle and do the work there.

Remington, a very methodic worker himself, despite his ability to play in off hours, got up early, put in an

CARICATURES FROM MR. THOMAS'S SKETCH BOOK. 1891–93.

1. L. J. B. Lincoln.   2. F. W. Ruckstull.   3. Augustus Thomas.   4. E. W. Kemble.
5. Francis Wilson.   6. Frederic Remington.
Nos. 3 and 4 are by Frederic Remington.   Nos. 1, 2, 5, and 6 are by Augustus Thomas.

entire forenoon, and with the interruption of a light lunch worked until nearly three o'clock. Then every day during this stay of Ruckstull's Remington came over to look at the progress of the model. He once said that when he died he wanted to have written on his tomb: "He knew the horse." And that could be said of Remington about as truthfully as of any other artist that has ever lived in America. Ruckstull also knew the horse, but from another angle. It was interesting to hear the disputes of these two experts as Ruckstull's horse progressed in its modelling, Remington always arguing for the wire-drawn Western specimen and Ruckstull standing for the more monumental, picturesque horse of the Eastern breeders.

During that time I went to Remington's studio one day, where he was drawing a Westerner shooting up a barroom. That hulking figure in the foreground, however, obstructed other detail that he wished to show. Remington immediately dusted off the charcoal outline, and instead drew his gunman in the background shooting down the room.

I said: "Fred, you're not a draftsman; you're a sculptor. You saw all round that fellow, and could have put him anywhere you wanted him. They call that the sculptor's degree of vision."

Remington laughed, but later Ruckstull sent him some tools and a supply of modeler's wax, and he began his " Bronco Buster." It was characteristic of the man that his first attempt should be a subject difficult enough as a technical problem to have daunted a sculptor of experience and a master of technic. His love of the work when he got at it, his marvellous aptitude for an art in which he had never had a single lesson, are some evidence that it was possibly his *métier*. His few bronze groups and figures that rapidly followed the " Bronco Buster " and his heroic equestrian monument of " The Pioneer " in Fairmount Park, Philadelphia, are the work of one who surely would have excelled in sculpture if he had lived to follow it.

Back in those days there was a wish to improve the theatre, not unlike the general desire so prevalent now, and which has never been entirely absent; a feeling that the box-office should not so largely dominate in the selection of a play, and that its verdict should not be the final one on a dramatic offering. Prominent in this opinion was Mr. Henry B. McDowell, a young man of enthusiasm and high purpose, and, what was equally valuable at that time, with somewhat of a fortune. Mr. McDowell decided upon a winter's series of plays which should be produced under the repertoire idea and be shown in both New York and Boston. To launch his enterprise, he began in the spring of 1892 with a dinner of fifty men, about thirty-five of whom were novelists, magazine-writers, and poets, the remainder being already engaged in the business of writing plays. I remember among the literary men Mr. William Dean Howells, Charles Dudley Warner, George W. Cable, Frederic J. Stimson, of Boston; Richard Hovey, the poet; Richard Harding Davis, Edmund Clarence Stedman, Frank R. Stockton, and others.

I sat to the left of Mr. Bronson Howard, who during the meal said to me: "These literary gentlemen believe that they constitute the lost tribe of American dramatists, and that the theatre will be elevated, if not saved, as soon as they turn their attention to it."

This critical attitude startled me somewhat, as I remembered so pleasantly Mr. Howells' little comedies, "The Elevator," "The Garroters," "Register," and the like, printed in 1884 and 1885 in *Harper's*. Slightly opposing Mr. Howard, I took the liberty of suggesting that that might be the case.

Very definitely this veteran then asked me: "Thomas, what is a dramatist?"

I answered: "A man who writes plays."

"Exactly! What plays have these men written?" Then reinforcing his position he told me that the capacity to write plays invariably evinced itself in a disposition to do so before middle life. When called upon to speak, however, Mr. Howard took a sympathetic attitude toward the venture and talked encouragingly. One other speech that I remember in a general way is that of Mr. Henry C. De Mille, father of the present De Mille boys of dramatic and motion-picture fame. One line particularly had a considerable influence on my way of thinking. De Mille reported a proposition by Harper Brothers that he should write for them a set of rules for playwrights.

He said: "I at first accepted the commission, but later declined for the reason that I feared that if I once formulated a set of rules for writing a play I might some time be tempted to follow them."

It was about that time that Frederic Remington, speaking of his own art, as illustrator and painter, said to me: "Tommy, if I felt cocksure of anything about my business I would begin to be afraid of myself."

The resolution of each of these experts to keep a perfectly open mind about the things they were doing went far toward retarding my own ossification.

Mr. McDowell established his Theatre of Arts and

Letters and gave the five performances. Plays by Mr. Stimson, Richard Harding Davis, Frank Stockton, Clyde Fitch, Brander Matthews, and some other author were produced under the stage direction of Eugene Presbrey. Mr. Howard took a definite pleasure when the enterprise had closed in calling to my attention the fact that the only plays that had made any worth-while impression were one offered by a professional dramatist, Clyde Fitch, a little thing called "The Harvest," which he subsequently elaborated into "The Moth and the Flame," and Brander Matthews's one act-play entitled "The Decision of the Court." Besides a very generous subscription fund, McDowell lost a substantial sum of his own—as I remember it, thirty-odd thousand dollars.

I saw these performances, and after a lapse of thirty years I remember three distinct features: The small talk of a fashionable company waiting for the bridal couple in a church, which made up the background of Fitch's little play; a line from Frank Stockton's "Squirrel Inn" spoken by Mary Shaw, who played the part of a trained nurse applying for a position, and who when the anxious mother asked her if she understood babies answered, "I ought to, I dissected one"; a third incident wherein Joseph Wheelock, Sr., played the part of a harassed husband, whose wife was a drug-fiend. Each sympathetic friend that came upon the stage took the husband's hand and gripped it in silent sympathy. As the audience began to titter over the repetition of this business Wheelock became sensitive. He put his hand behind him when Nelson Wheatcroft, the next member of the company, came near him in a succeeding scene. Feeling that something depended on the gesture, Wheatcroft took Wheelock by the elbow, recovered the hidden hand and shook it to general laughter that almost closed the performance. It is interesting, at least to me, that out of this expensive essay these somewhat technical points should be the lasting impressions, and that all the fine literary offerings intended for the reformation of the theatre should have so vanished.

In these early 90's Joseph Brooks conceived the idea of having a play written with George Washington as the central character. This was suggested by the resemblance between the portrait of Washington and that of Joseph Holland, then at the height of his popularity as an actor. Brooks's idea was to associate Joe and his older brother Edmund. I undertook to write the play, and made a fairly thorough study of Washington's life and times. Avoiding the error of the biographical play which tries to cover too much, I confined my story to the period when Washington was a colonel of the Virginia militia, and before he had married Martha Custis. I found a character for Ed Holland in Virginia's Scotch governor, Dinwiddie. When the play was done the professional engagements of the two men did not allow them to undertake it immediately, and before both were at liberty one had fallen ill. The joint project was abandoned. Having faith in the play, I wanted to see it tried, and for that purpose went to Boston, where the Castle Square Stock Company at that time had as leading man Jack Gilmour, bearing considerable resemblance in face and figure to the traditional Washington. This stock company played a new play every week, having only five rehearsals in which to prepare.

On our first night a young actor who was playing *Bryan Fairfax*, with two scenes in the first act, was not at hand when we reached his second one. The usual

efforts to hold the stage were made, but we finally had
to ring down. The young man when found was in his
dressing-room in his underclothing, having forgotten his
second scene and begun to dress for his second act. This
was explained to the audience, but when we rang up
again the whole thing had taken on such an air of unreality that two or three other mistakes, which have a
fashion of running in groups on hard-luck nights in the
theatre, destroyed any impression we might have hoped
for. Later performances convinced me that I had a good
play, but it was never done after that week.

Brooks went to the production of a new play for Crane
called "The Governor of Kentucky," written by Franklin
Fyles. At the end of rehearsals, star, manager, and director felt they were in bad shape as to story. At their
dress rehearsal, at the request of the author, I indicated
what I thought were the weaknesses, suggested the remedies, and told them what I thought the Tuesday morning
papers would say. Remembering our quick revision of
"For Money," Brooks hoped something of the same
kind could be done with "The Governor." On Tuesday
I was waked by telephone at daylight, and at his request
came at once from New Rochelle. By arrangement we
met Presbrey and Fyles. Fyles approved of all the proposed changes, but not being in good health left the work
with Presbrey and me. Between us we had a revised
script that evening, and the version went on before the
end of the week. Brooks insisted on paying for the day's
work. When I hesitated to name a figure he suggested
the cancelling of a thousand-dollar note of mine which
he held. I agreed.

A little later than this Harry Woodruff came to see
me at New Rochelle. He had then left the stage and

been two years at Harvard College under romantic conditions. Harry had won the affections of a daughter of a wealthy family whose members objected to an actor as a husband for the young woman. They agreed, however, that if Woodruff would go through Harvard and equip himself for another profession the objections would be withdrawn. They also agreed to pay his way. While Woodruff was at his studies the family took the young girl abroad and, with a change of scene and her wider opportunities, succeeded in arranging for her an alliance with one of the nobility. With this accomplished, the family had notified Woodruff that the financial support they were giving him at the university would be withdrawn. Harry was courageously making arrangements to pay his own way through the remaining two years, and regretting that he had not secretly married the girl, as he had an opportunity to do.

This possible set of relations—a young man in college secretly married and the family trying to marry his wife to a foreign nobleman—struck me as a pretty complication for a comedy. Having a contract with Goodwin for something to follow "In Mizzoura," I developed that story into a three-act play which I called "Treadway of Yale." Goodwin accepted both the scenario and the finished script, but before the time came for production he married Maxine Elliott, of whose dramatic ability he had such high opinion that he thought the comedy gave her insufficient chance. He therefore forfeited his advance payments on it and returned the script. It was produced some time later under the title of "On the Quiet" by William Collier under the management of Will Smythe, and later revived by Charles Frohman when Collier passed under his direction. Collier went to

London with the piece. During his successful run with it there Willie had occasion to be measured for a suit of clothes. An English tailor, amused with his American manner, endeavored to spoof him, a risk that no American tailor would have taken.

As he ran his tape over him he said in his blandest manner: "I saw you last night, sir, in your very amusing comedy. Have you played that before the King?"

Collier said: "I played it before anybody. I'm the original."

Along in this epoch that I am so informally trying to describe I was one day in a dark theatre listening to a rehearsal of a song intended for Marie Cahill, at that time, I think, still with Daly, or maybe with Duff. In the syncopated accompaniment there was a hesitation not unlike that intermitting heart jump that so frightens one until the family doctor with his fingers on one's wrist says: "Too much coffee." The radiant composer-piano-player bawled above his racket to Miss Cahill: "Hear that ragtime?" She did. I was at some loss to distinguish it, but that was my introduction to the term and to the manner. Soon thereafter, a year or two, "ragtime" was a stock word. Some more years and it divided space and attention with jazz. Both are negroid. On the border-line of the back belt I had been brought up on darky music. While the melancholy of slavery was upon them the negroes, intensely responsive to and expressive in music, had found a solace in the Stephen Foster "Kentucky Home" kind of melody and a racial cadence woven into the tunes of the Baptist hymnal. Their lighter output just after abolition was of the rap-tap-a-tap-tap school of sand dance, the McNish silence-and-fun variety. When full equality got onto Sixth Avenue, ragtime, the

African tom-tom in a red vest, made its appearance. Jazz was its offspring. Jazz is ragtime triumphant and transfigured, the Congo arrived at kingdom come.

The nation's feet kept time. The two-step gave way to the fox-trot and the shimmy came along with jazz. Central Africa saw ghosts. Some moralist speaks of a certain ferocity in nature which, "as it had its inlet by human crime, must have its outlet by human suffering." Why may not jazz be the cutaneous eruption of the virus of black slavery? If Davies and Vaughan are accurate in their translation of Plato's "Republic" the idea is not so novel as the inquiry, for therein Plato says:

"The introduction of a new kind of music must be shunned as imperilling the whole state, since styles of music are never disturbed without affecting the most important political institutions. The new style," he goes on, "gradually gaining a lodgment, quietly insinuates itself into manners and customs; and from these it issues in greater force, and makes its way into mutual compacts; and from compacts it goes on to attack laws and constitutions, displaying the utmost impudence, until it ends by overturning everything, both in public and in private."

It might no doubt amuse Plato to take fifty years of musical progression in America and check its changes against our changing compacts, laws, and constitutions.

"But, say, this guy Plato—where does he get that compax-and-constatution stuff? Who wised him to anything about show business? An' lissun! This Davus and Vaughan—words by, music by—I never ketch them on no big time neither."

Frederic Remington, with a natural social philosopher's view of them as they worked not only in the theatre but in life, refused to believe that the overflowing tide of ignorance was destined to inherit the fruits of the earth. He disliked the growing influence of the unassimilated immigrants. He hated the political herding of them. He loathed all politicians because they talked. He loved the soldiers because the military acted promptly and without debate. In his day in the West the local advent of troopers meant sudden and inflexible order. He saw humanity's future safe only under military discipline. We differed, but I liked his mettle and his impatience with conditions. At Remington's I met several of his soldier friends, among them General Nelson A. Miles, then the commanding major-general; also Captain Francis Michler, decorated for gallant service against Indians in Arizona in 1872 and 1873.

When finally confused with the rewrites and inventions for the theatre in which I was then becoming involved, I resolved again to go for a subject to the plain and primitive things as far as one could find them. Encouraged by Remington, and definitely interested by his enthusiasm, I took a mandatory letter that Remington got from General Miles to all commandants in the West instructing them to give me information and assistance, and with no preconceptions as to story went to Arizona in 1897 to get a play. It was an important turning-point in my career.

XIX

SOME EXPERIENCES IN ARIZONA

In preceding chapters, in trying to tell how I came to go at the business of writing plays, to tell how my attention was led in that direction and how information, experience, and material for the work were gathered, I have tried to use discrimination. This is probably not apparent, but as I mentally review what I have considered the high lights of this irregular report I am conscious of much that has been omitted.

For example, there were the facts and happenings connected with making a play which was called "New Blood," and was produced by Mr. Joseph Brooks late in the summer of 1894. If this publication were political in its character I might slam ahead and call a lot of people a lot of names, because, fair-minded and unprejudiced as I have tried to be, I fear that I am a good deal partisan. I have frankly told that as a young man I was a Master Workman in the Knights of Labor. I deeply sympathized with the working classes of the country, to which I thought I belonged, and their problems became my own as far as study and investigation went, and also as far as I could express myself and be tolerated as a member of one of the principal political parties. I made speeches in all the presidential campaigns after I became of age, and occasionally talked in local campaigns in the congressional years.

It will be remembered that in the early 90's two absorbing considerations in the country were the trusts and the money question. The Populists and—strongly influenced by them—the Democrats were urging the free and unlimited coinage of silver; the Republicans were also urging the coinage of silver, but after an international agreement. The most outspoken of their party at that time, Senator Henry Cabot Lodge, was for the unlimited coinage of silver and a discriminating tariff that should force England from her gold standard into bimetallism. Senator William V. Allen, of Nebraska, a man who had much of the physical appearance, the habit of thought, and the oratorical power of our present Senator Borah, characterized this advice by Senator Lodge as "simply a piece of Yankee ingenuity." Mr. Allen's party, the Populist, was at one with the Democratic Party in its fight against the trusts, and the Republican Party was not far behind in a wish to regulate those combinations.

With the trusts as a sustaining theme, I had written a play in which a manufacturing company was divided against itself. A son, impersonated by Mr. Wilton Lackaye, in sympathy with the new spirit of regulation, was at war in the board of directors with his father, played by Mr. E. M. Holland, who adhered to the older ideas of a man managing his own business in his own way. When the play was ready Mr. Brooks engaged one of the best companies that could be got together at that time. Besides the two excellent actors named, the cast included also Maurice Barrymore, C. W. Couldock, J. H. Stoddart, George Nash, Jack Barnes, Ffolliet Paget, and Anne O'Neill, a prominent ingénue of that time who soon afterward married and left the stage.

Shortly before we got ready for our production some of the forces that I had been endeavoring to estimate and depict came into collision. The most outstanding figure on the labor side was Mr. Eugene Debs, now, in 1922, in the public eye because of his attitude during the World War and his consequent incarceration at Atlanta and his subsequent pardon from that place by President Harding. In 1894 Mr. Debs had asked that a difference of opinion between the Pullman Company and the men working in the Pullman car shops at the town of Pullman, near Chicago, should be submitted to arbitration. Mr. George M. Pullman, the president, who had been a great benefactor, in that he had built a model city for his employees, was deeply hurt at what he considered their ingratitude, and declined to discuss arbitration. Writing in a magazine of his attitude at that time, and the various patents the Government had granted him, Doctor Albert Shaw said:

Mr. Pullman should certainly feel very good-natured, indeed, toward a nation that has afforded him such unparalleled opportunities and has rewarded his talent and energy with such colossal tributes of wealth. . . . To very many people it seemed clear that he ought not to have allowed his local quarrel to go on unsettled and unappeased until it had assumed continental proportions.

The same impartial writer condemned Mr. Debs for extending the strike to the American railroad unions and through them obstructing trains that carried Mr. Pullman's cars. When Mr. Debs did this he also stopped trains on which there were the United States mails, with the result that President Cleveland stepped into the situation, and when our "New Blood" company approached Chicago toward the end of July the train on which it was ran through a district with miles of burning freight-cars on either side and arrived in Chicago to find that city under martial rule, with field artillery strung along the lake front and commanding the approaching streets. The people who came at night to see our Chicago performance were obliged to show tickets to soldiers at intersecting corners and establish the peaceable character of their errands.

Of course, in that *milieu*, with that subject and that excellent company, the management thought we had the greatest American play that could be written. Mr. Palmer came on to see it, and immediately offered Mr. Brooks time at his Broadway theatre. He even suggested strengthening the already strong cast by substituting Elita Proctor Otis and Katherine Grey for the ladies already named. Mr. Charles Richman was engaged in the place of Mr. Barnes. This desire for betterment went through every department of the production. At a little tête-à-tête between Barrymore and Lackaye in the piece, followed by a love scene between Barrymore and Miss Grey, the men in Chicago had lighted their cigarettes with a match, but for New York we had a fine double-decked copper outfit that stood on the table and burned alcohol.

On the first night in New York, at the most critical moment, this alcohol became superheated, overflowed its lamp, made a flare on the copper tray. People in the audience began to gather up their wraps; Reuben Fax, who was playing a butler, came on and backed off with this flaming exhibition, but too late to recover attention, and a most essential part of the exposition of the story was lost. Miss Otis had procured a new silk dress for the new engagement, very snugly fitting a week before the play. That interval of hope and maybe entertainment, however, contributed enough added outline to burst the new dress in a hurried adjustment, and a second act was held several minutes while the modiste put in a gore. The whole night took on a tone of unreality. In a dispute between Mr. Palmer and Mr. Brooks over stage hands, extra ones, though needed, were not engaged, and altogether it was one o'clock before our first performance ended. Our New York press was as bad as Chicago's had been favorable. Charley Frohman saw the play in the middle of the week and liked it. But in his characteristic way he touched at once upon what he thought made it fail.

A strike-leader who has been shown into his employer's breakfast-room, after stating his claim and the condition of his people, points to the table and says, "What you have left there on your plate," and so on.

Charley said: "That workman saying, 'Those bones are as much as one of our families gets for a day,' was speaking to a parquet full of people that leave bones. You can't say those things on the Atlantic seaboard, although you may in Chicago."

My own belief is that the play came when papers and magazines were so full of the stuff that the public looking for entertainment didn't want any more of it. But it had been written under conditions less hectic.

As a playwright I was depressed and needed encouragement. I thought I had been writing from my knowledge of the Middle West and from my experiences as a young man, and that those were all I had that was valuable to tell. I was forgetting that a man's education may constantly go forward, and if he is a writer or a painter or sculptor people would still be interested in seeing things through his temperament. An older man at that time, L. J. B. Lincoln, said encouraging things.

He was not a writer himself, but he had been a lecturer, and was more particularly a handler of literary men. He had a paper organization of audiences in Boston, New York, and Chicago to which he gave what he called uncut leaves, papers yet unpublished, that their respective authors read aloud.

Lincoln was walking with me up Fifth Avenue to the Grand Central Station, on his way to spend the night at our home in New Rochelle, and I said: "Linc, I think I'm written out."

He laughed the jolliest, most reassuring laugh that a man making that speech could ask to hear, and then told me of the number of men he had heard say the same thing at about the same period in experience. His observation was that this fear came to them in a fallow time, and frequently preceded the best of their work. Supporting his belief, he said much more in the same direction. The first play I wrote after this encouragement of Lincoln's was "Arizona." Among other plays written after that time, also, were "The Earl of Pawtucket," "The Other Girl," "Mrs. Leffingwell's Boots," "The Witching Hour," "As a Man Thinks," and "The Copperhead."

That night at New Rochelle, as Lincoln sat reading, I endeavored to make in the guest book a caricature of him; but as I look at it now it is less caricature than portrait. I have said Lincoln was not a writer, by which I mean writing was not a source of income to him; but he was skilful and entertaining when he tried it. A year or two later he had to furnish an introduction to some "Annals" of The Lambs, at that time the most powerful and most interesting theatrical club in America. Because the opening paragraph of his paper leads attractively to

its subject, and because it is a fairly condensed expression
upon masculine club life in general, and because it is a
good indication of Lincoln's style as well as a good example of impromptu performances, I wish to quote it.
He said:

The evolution of Bohemia as a factor in civilization may be written
from the annals of clubdom.   From the day when neolithic man
emerged from his cave and discovered that the grape-juice which
he had squeezed into a cocoanut shell the day before had become a
beverage whose ruddy glow tingled his heartstrings and made him
forget his troubles, he became convivial.   Becoming convivial, he
called his friends about him and established a club.   Since, an unbroken line of care-dispelling, self-forgetting, self-despising good
fellows; Arcadians, Corinthians, Bohemians.   So the Anglo-Saxon,
in his gradual absorption of the best things in civilization, has developed to its greatest value the essence of club life—the dining club.
Literature in English rings with that especial institution.   From the
imagination of Chaucer in his Canterbury Pilgrimage to the realities
of Ben Jonson's Apollo and the Mermaid Inn; from the Kit-Kat
Club, Will's Coffee-House, and the still extant Cheshire Cheese—
with its hallowed chair of Doctor Johnson—to the countless groups
which now meet in and out of Alsatia to engender the flow of wisdom
which a hospitable round-table can alone induce, there is one long
and brilliant procession of Bohemians of every rank and class, without whom language becomes tame, art pedantic, and life, as Mr. Man-
talini so succinctly put it, "one demnition grind."

Having been thus respectful to Luther Lincoln's
memory, and after stating further that he was one of
the most vital influences of an artistic and literary kind
that ever came into The Lambs, I hope I shall be for-
given for talking of him in lighter vein.   With all his
ability to encourage other men, there was a touch of
fatalistic despondency in him concerning himself.   Not
any of his male forbears of whom he had information

had lived beyond fifty years. Lincoln had a premonition that fifty would be his limit, and it was. This death-sentence feeling made him take the pleasures of life as they came. Like the preceding members of his family, he lost some ten years before his death the sight of one eye. To save the other it became necessary to remove this useless member, and it was replaced by an artificial eye. Both eyes were overhung with fairly heavy brows and were behind spectacles. Lincoln during the last hours of some all-night sessions sometimes closed the good eye and slept, while the artificial eye remained on duty, and looked steadily at the detaining monologist. In one of these slumbering moments he was leaning on the little bar of the old Thirty-sixth Street clubhouse, seemingly listening to a club bore considerably intoxicated. It was a warm night, and this talker was gradually fascinated by the unwinking attention of Lincoln's glass eye. When he saw this steady gaze still maintained, although a fly alighted upon the pupil of the eye and twiddled its hind legs, he felt that he was the victim of alcoholic hallucinations. The few to whom he confided his experience said nothing of the eye's being artificial. Lincoln died soon afterward, and the man never drank alcohol again.

When I started West to get "Arizona," Frederic Remington superintended the organization of my kit just as he would have arranged his own. It was very much on the camping-out order, with a shift to something that would be presentable on formal occasions. I carried, as I have said before, a letter from General Miles to the officers commanding the Western posts. I started at Lincoln's encouragement and counsel, with Frederic Remington's good wishes, and the color that I had absorbed from his talk and stories in the preceding eight or nine years, and added to this equipment a most useful admonition from Captain Jack Summerhayes, whom I met in St. Louis, where I stopped a day or two to see my people. Summerhayes was attending to some war preparations at Jefferson Barracks and happened in the city for that day only. Our meeting was accidental. His contribution was this:

That department letter you carry will command anything those men can give you; but they'll feel happier if their contributions seem voluntary and come only under the head of General Miles's permission. Also you will find that they are marooned out there, and that they will be mighty glad to see you; that about the only thing they have worth while to them is their rank, and at all times, especially in the presence of their junior officers, the more respect you pay to that, the more you do to preserve its traditions, the happier you will make those old fellows feel.

When, after several weeks in the territory, I came to say good-by to Colonel Edwin V. Sumner, who had given up to me the best room and private bath in his quarters, he said:

Thomas, although you've been a member of my family here, I never came into a room or went onto the porch where you were or left a group of which you were a member but that you stood up at my going and coming just as one of these lieutenants would, and I want to say to you it made me feel damned fine.

I don't think I would have done anything to hurt that brave officer, but I am sure I would not have been so punctiliously attentive to that little ceremony if it hadn't been for the friendly counsel of Jack Summerhayes.

On the way to Fort Grant one leaves the railroad at

Willcox, at that time a little one-street row of one-story shops and barrooms. The hotel proprietor told me as I came off the train for my first night in Arizona that an ambulance with four mules was there to carry over to the fort a captain who was expected on the train arriving at five in the morning. I saw the driver of this outfit that night. He promised to tell the captain of my presence, and in the morning I was standing around ready to be invited. But again, under the remembered advice of Summerhayes, I didn't spring my headquarters paper on the captain or try to address anybody except the commandants to whom the letter was directed; and as it meant very little to this captain to learn that a stranger wanted to go to the fort, his four mules and his ambulance ambled off without me. I went some hours later on a little two-horse depot wagon that made a daily trip, and was again fortunate in that fact, as the driver on that twenty-mile jog told me many useful things. I was directed from the colonel's quarters to the officers' club. There was no attendant. The single room contained four or five officers playing cards around the table. After a pause one of them casually looked up. I asked for Colonel Sumner. He nodded toward that officer. Sumner, with his cards, paid no attention.

I said, "Letter from Washington," and handed it to him; and then, exactly as I had seen messengers rehearsed in "Held by the Enemy" and "Shenandoah," I stepped back and stood still. The colonel opened his letter, glanced at it quickly, struck the table a blow.

"Gentlemen!"

All the poker-players stood promptly. I was welcomed and introduced to the group, with which I spent the great part of one of the most enjoyable sojourns of my

life. The poker game was immediately broken up and
adjourned, and a half-hour afterward I came from a
refreshing bath and in my store clothes to a fine midday
dinner in the colonel's home with his amiable wife and
wholesome and attractive daughter.

That was on March 17, 1897. I don't have to refer
to any records to recover the date, because from the
lunch we went to the parade-grounds, where a big tent
had been set up with a telegraph wire leading into it,
and the men of three troops of cavalry, and I think two
infantry companies, gathered to hear the report by rounds
of the championship prize-fight between Jim Corbett and
Bob Fitzsimmons, then beginning in Carson City,
Nevada. Among the officers I saw one or two faces that
struck me as familiar, and then one of the few civilians
there, limping a bit on a cane, I recognized as my Leavenworth attorney, Hon. Thomas P. Fenlon. He introduced
me to his son-in-law, Captain Nicholson, also at the post
and in whose quarters he was staying. Nicholson had
been one of the officers in Plowman's court-room that
busy afternoon eleven years before when they had ridden
over from Fort Leavenworth in full dress to protest the
foolish slander of the talented Helen M. Gouger.

I am working now between the need to economize
space and a wish to talk freely enough about my experience to fix whatever significance it may have to other
men trying to make plays. And when I say significance
I mean only that. I don't mean a rule or a way of doing.
Each man writing plays makes his own rules, and one
man at different times will have different ways. If I
seem occasionally minute it will not be because I regard
any act of mine in epic fashion, but only because I remember it as an articulating part of what subsequently

became machinery in a play. I had been writing plays too long to be entirely free from habit. I suppose that a man sent out to write a comic opera would at least begin by thinking in terms of a quartet. All those fine soldiers, every sturdy private, the smart officers, the forceful old colonel, each of them began to be in my mind a possible factor if not centre of romance.

The officers' quarters there in Fort Grant are doby, and face the parade-ground. To the western end of the row the first two or three are two-story buildings, substantial as any brick or brownstone residences of the city. They then tail off into bungalows, with fine shady porches, and all, because of their doby walls, with cool window and door recesses from eighteen inches to two feet deep. I don't remember how many ladies were in the fort; I should say half a dozen. The majority of these, of course, were married; and when we have checked off their husbands it left a fine circle of unattached officers, attentive, complimentary, respectful. I heard no breath of scandal or even of gossip that in any way involved this compact little community, but it was impossible to view them with an imagination bent by the theatre without beginning to play chess with their reputations. Nothing could be further from fact than any hint of discordance in the household of Colonel Win Sumner and his wife, almost his own age; but as I wanted to use him as a principal character, I had no compunction in mentally hooking him up with a much younger woman, somewhat regretful of the disparity in their years. Of course this discontent of the wife would be evident to more than one of the young officers, if not actually shared in or promoted by one or another. Besides domestic life at the quarters, there were a few wives down at the barracks, and one or two daughters of enlisted men. My difficulty on the first day or two was to keep an open mind and not have these characters form associations in my fancy that would by repetition of the concept begin to take on the authority of fact.

As I listened to Colonel Sumner talk at his dinner-table of cattlemen, Indians, and soldiers; as I heard Mrs. Sumner tell of Tony, the doby messenger that came down the valley with social notes, I felt that the field was too rich to make immediate commitments of selection.

Some dispenser of mental tonic has said that thoughts are things. I offer no opinion on that, but if they are they're curious things, and it is hard for one who trades in them to keep clear of superstition. I have seldom begun to work earnestly upon any line of reflection but what that line has been frequently twanged by cross-currents that the overcredulous would misread. I wrote earlier in these chapters of coincidences, naming two that were noteworthy in my own experience. Personally, I am willing to accept the explanation of somebody whose words, but not whose name, I remember, to the effect that a line of thought is like a magnetized wire, and that particles from all the waves and currents that cross it adhere when there is sufficient affinity. If that is true, a man thinking along certain lines would mistake the selection made by his attention for fateful response.

I wonder if this is an approach too clumsy to another one of these points. I was slowly dictating the stuff above about the military post and was thinking as I had been thinking for a day or two about Hooker's ranch, some ten or twelve miles away from it, and how I could be accurate about certain items, when Robert Bruce, of Clinton, Oneida County, New York, came to the door. Mr. Bruce has written historically of incidents in the Civil and Revolutionary wars. He and I had an exchange of letters about the first two or three installments of these reminiscences which at this writing have appeared in this publication, and he had promised to stop in and see me sometime when he was in the city. His call just now interrupting my dictation about the army post was prompted by that invitation, and was determined by the fact that he had two leaves of the *Erie Railroad Magazine* of December with an article in it about Mrs. Forrestine Hooker, author of "The Long Dim Trail" and other stories.

He brought it to me because near the finish of the article the writer said of Mrs. Hooker: "She married E. R. Hooker, son of Henry C. Hooker, the cattle king of Arizona, and lived at the Sierra Bonita ranch near Fort Grant and Willcox, where the famous play, 'Arizona,' was written around her as *Bonita* by Augustus Thomas."

Thanks to Mr. Bruce's call, I don't have to cudgel my brain to remember Mr. Hooker's first name, or the name of his beautiful daughter-in-law, who away out in the wilds played the piano with such delightful skill.

To distinguish him from his brother, Colonel Sam Sumner, of Fort Myer fame, my Colonel Sumner was called by his army friends Bull. This was an appellation affectionate and descriptive, but not critical. He told me of the several elements in the life of that section of Arizona, particularly of the wild station of San Carlos on the Gila River, where so many times a year a troop of cavalry on guard was relieved by one from the post in its monotonous duty of guarding that end of the Apache reservation and dealing out beef and flour to the poor Indians who came periodically to get their supplies from the government. He told me also of the ranchers who were his neighbors at intervals of ten and fifteen miles.

After a few days at the post I was taken over to Hooker's ranch. The administrative centre of this was also the residence of Mr. Hooker, his daughter-in-law and grandson. This doby hacienda was a quadrangle about one hundred feet square, with blank walls some eighteen feet high outside. Three sides of the inner court were made up of little rooms one-story high, with roofs sloping to the centre and rising to somewhat less than the height of the outer walls, whose superior margin served as parapet in case of attack. A fourth side of the quadrangle, besides having a room or two and a shed for vehicles, had a large reinforced double gate that could be thrown to and fastened with heavy bars and staples. In the centre of the court thus formed there was a well, so that the colony might have water to withstand a siege.

Henry C. Hooker was a quiet little man who had been some twenty-five or thirty years in that locality selling beef to "government and Apaches"; at times on the defensive, and at other times on friendly terms with his savage neighbors. He had known the old Apache chief, Cochise, the predecessor of Geronimo, and had a hundred interesting tales of his experiences with Indians, and cowboys, and soldiers. He was under the average height of the American, was slight and quiet, and while adopting him I took the liberty of replacing him in my mind with a more robust and typical frontiersman; but hundreds of the lines I finally gave to *Henry Canby*, the rancher in the play of "Arizona," were Hooker's own words, which I remembered, and as soon as I was alone set down because of their picturesque quality and their great simplicity and directness.

One speech that all the *Canbys*—some ten or fourteen that finally played it—used to like, and which Douglas Fairbanks, an aspiring youngster of the theatre long before he went into the movies, learned to recite, although there was never the remotest chance of his playing that part, was Hooker's description of his method in selecting a cowboy. Before I had any situation to justify it or any theme to which it was pertinent, I had this speech from that remarkable man. Think what a helpful nugget this is to be picked up by a writer looking for material:

"We take a man on here and ask no questions. We know when he throws his saddle on his horse whether he understands his business or not. He may be a minister backslidin', or a banker savin' his last lung, or a train-robber on his vacation—we don't care. A good many of our most useful men have made their mistakes. All we care about now is, will they stand the gaff? Will they set sixty hours in the saddle, holdin' a herd that's tryin' to stampede all the time?"

At Hooker's ranch I decided his daughter-in-law should be the heroine of my story. It would take me out of the too closely knitted life of the army post, and while giving a heroine who would appeal to a young cavalryman, as the girls on the ranch rode as well as the men did, it would be a truthful and breezy touch of character, especially as this self-reliant and athletic side was associated with the most feminine characteristics and accomplishments. Colonel Sumner thought I should see life at San Carlos. That had been my wish when planning the play, as I expected to get the element of stir and bustle for it in an Indian uprising. This had the disadvantage of harking back to several other American plays, and to something of the color of Jessie Brown and the relief of Lucknow. But there was nothing else in sight. To reach San Carlos from Fort Grant was a day's cavalry march up the valley to Dunlop's, and another day's ride over the mountains. The first half of this journey was made in an ambulance with mules drawing it, while a small detachment of cavalry, a telegraph construction outfit, two Indian guides, and five or six pack-mules with supplies were in the escort. Dunlop's was another doby house, with ornamental steel ceilings on the ground floor, and an upright piano.

We had an early start the second morning, with everybody in the saddle. Captain Myer, in charge of our detachment, lent me a handsome pacing stallion, gentle and a weight-carrier. The features of our second day's trip, none of which I used in the play and which therefore have little place in this recital except as they contribute to a sense of hardship and the stamina needed to meet it, were narrow trails on the hogback of the mountains, where the aneroid barometer showed five thousand feet, and where the path was so narrow that everything was intrusted to the animals, which carefully picked their way one foot in absolute line before the other, sometimes all four set for a short slide and often each stone gingerly tested to make sure of footing, climbing grades on which no horse could have carried any rider, and where no tenderfoot, no matter how stout of lung, could have climbed in that thin air unaided.

The procedure was to take with one hand a tight grip on the long tail of your horse, and let him pull you as you walked behind him and led the horse for the man that followed. When the height was reached where a modification of the grade made it possible to get again into the saddle, all the company, troopers and Indians alike, were glad to pause and recover breath before attempting to mount.

Across these ridges the wind, which is always blowing at that season, came at a pace of forty miles. Shoulder high on our left was a wall that occasionally grazed a stirrup; nearer, on the other side, a declivity dropping at an angle of eighty degrees for three thousand feet.

Myer called back: "Look out for your hat! Can't go down there for a hat!"

I said: "I wouldn't go down there for a suit of clothes!"

If I had to write of a man under sentence of death I believe I could do it with something resembling insight. Dickens had *Fagin*, the night before his execution, counting the nail-heads on his cell door. As our horses gingerly crept over that trail I dramatized the roll or two down the sidehill before a fellow's breath would be out of him, and found myself computing the protective value of a ten-thousand-dollar insurance policy in a Massachusetts company and another accident policy somewhere else, and just what provision a widow could make of that money and of a fairly new house after the mortgage was deducted.

There were long stretches through the little brooks between these mountains where the chaparral dragged at your bootlegs and the higher switches slapped you on the head so that you kept it tucked into the shoulders, with the campaign hat pulled down to fend them from drawing blood. From the perspiration gathered in one of these levels we went again to other heights so cold that last week in March that we turned up the collars of our leather jackets lined with sheepskin; yet we rode through bright air so clear that the sun burned our cheeks more swiftly than August in the Mississippi Valley.

At noon we stopped a half hour for dinner and to rest the horses. It was astonishing to see an Indian put a coffee-pot on two or three little stones the size of a hen's egg, slip under it a bunch of burning grass not larger than a shaving brush, feed it with a few splinters, and boil two quarts of coffee quicker than I have ever seen it heated upon a stove.

The Gila River is filled with quicksand. Here and there is a ford. As we approached the river a trooper rode from the fort a mile away, took his station on the opposite bank to guide our string, which made the ford in Indian fashion.

Captain Myer called back: "Lift your feet out of the water! Hold up your horse's head or he'll lie down and roll! Follow your leader closely!"

At that hour of sundown, after a day in the saddle, I could do everything commanded except hold up my feet; they dragged inertly alongside the stallion and the river flowed into them over the boot-tops. When we pulled up at the little bungalows which were our destination two troopers helped me get my right leg over the back of the saddle and kept me from falling when it reached the ground.

A kindly fat old doctor who was there looked me over and without the formality of an introduction said: "Put this man in a hot bath." As he did so I put him into my play.

While in the tub a striker brought me a telegram from Colonel Sumner:

"How's the patient?"

I dictated the answer: "Not so beautiful as he was, but knows more."

When I came down the four steps of the little shack to go to the mess-room the next morning I took each degree slowly and hung onto the banisters like a man half paralyzed. There is nothing like a good case of horse rheumatism to put a tenderfoot out of commission.

A week at San Carlos was interesting. One had the Apache at first hand; but as all that color was revised from the play before production, space for it here would only emphasize the fact that there are a good many chips and much rejected material in every workshop. But such discarded stuff is still valuable to have in the lumber-room. I sha'n't talk of deceptive distances or tell any stories of men starting to walk a seeming three miles and learning that their visible objective is fifteen miles away.

Besides, one isn't always credited. On the trip home, an hour or two out of El Paso, is the station Alamogordo.

A shrewd New Englander asked: "What are those mount'ins to the northeast there?"

"Those are the Sierra Blanca—White Mountains."

A real Pinkerton, penetrating, unwavering look; a self-possessed stroke of the chin whiskers and then cold rebuke:

"Young man, the White Mount'ins air in New Hampshire."

In the territories on the way back and at home I was busy on the play, with an Indian uprising as my principal machinery. And in its first draft the play was so finished.

Early in the morning of February 16, 1898, James

Waterbury, the agent of the Western Union Company at New Rochelle, telephoned me that the *Maine* had been blown up and sunk in the harbor of Havana. Knowing the interest the report would have for my neighbor, Frederic Remington, I immediately called him on the telephone and repeated the information. His only thanks or comment was to shout "Ring off!" In the process of doing so I could hear him calling the private telephone number of his publishers in New York. In his mind his own campaign was already actively under way.

One incident of that campaign illustrates the primitive man in Remington. He and Richard Harding Davis were engaged to go into Cuba by the back way and send material to an evening newspaper. The two men were to cross in the night from Key West to Cuba on a mackerel-shaped speed boat of sheet-iron and shallow draft. Three times the boat put out from Key West and three times turned back, unable to stand the weather. The last time even the crew lost hope of regaining port. Davis and Remington were lying in the scuppers and clinging to the shallow rail to keep from being washed overboard. The Chinaman cook, between lurches, was lashing together a door and some boxes to serve as a raft. Davis suggested to Remington the advisability of trying something of the kind for themselves.

"Lie still!" Remington commanded. "You and I don't know how to do that. Let him make his raft. If we capsize I'll throttle him and take it from him."

Some months later, on learning of the incident, I tried to discuss the moral phase of it with him.

But he brushed my hypocrisy aside with the remark: "Why, Davis alone was worth a dozen sea cooks! I don't have to talk of myself."

It wasn't a difficult task to take out all the Indian stuff in my manuscript and to make the motive the getting together of a troop of cowboys. My impulse was prophetic of the Rough Riders. I wrote Denton's cowboy troop and the khaki jacket into the play at once, and changed such few speeches of the script as this introduction made necessary. On July 8, President McKinley nominated Colonel Leonard Wood to be brigadier-general, and Lieutentant-Colonel Theodore Roosevelt to be colonel of the First Volunteer Cavalry.

A few years ago I wrote some prefaces to precede certain printed plays of mine. If it wasn't for fear that watchful editors would strike out the statement I would quote the Boston *Transcript* to the effect that when Thomas is dead these prefaces will be put together in limp leather and printed as little classics. Perhaps if I don't tell the names of the plays or their publisher this statement will get by. In one of them I said:

"This play was salvage; that is to say, it was a marketing of odds and ends and remnants utterly useless for any other purpose." And elsewhere in these remembrances I've said that all is fish that comes to a playwright's pond.

Late in the winter of 1896, when the other guests had gone home after dinner, Mr. Joseph D. Redding, of the Bohemian Club, San Francisco, was at the piano in our living-room at New Rochelle; listening to him were Mr. Will Gillette, my wife, and I. Redding was running over the keys and talking through the music in that entertaining way which as musician and talker he has in such eminent degree.

Over one haunting melody he said: "Here's something

I heard a little girl singing alone, hidden from the rain in a doby doorway in Santa Barbara."

There was a moment's silence when he finished the melody, and my wife said: "A little girl that could sing like that wouldn't be alone."

Gillette, in his metallic tenor, added, "Besides, it never rains in Santa Barbara."

Each of these lines was worth a smile to our firelight party; and just as I am telling the story to you I told it at a banquet-table at the Santa Barbara Club in 1901. I hoped only for good-natured reception and was at utter loss to understand why men slapped each other on the back and roared with glee and rocked on their unsteady chairs. The toastmaster felt I was entitled to an explanation. A real-estate man present explained the laugh by telling that Gillette some years before had bought a considerable country estate at Montecito, a suburb of Santa Barbara. He had bought it on blue-prints and photographs shown by the agent. One of these photographs showed a bounding, purling brook, snapped immediately after one of the infrequent rainstorms of that section. On the other three hundred and sixty-four days in the year this watercourse was dry.

That kind of thing amuses real-estate men.

On that winter evening, however, Gillette told us nothing of this dusty brook, but asked Redding to repeat his rainy music.

Those were the firelight times before the introduction of auction bridge and when people of sensibility sometimes sat about and played or listened to little interpretations of that Redding kind. I have more than once solved some knotty problem in play-building by a mood invited by such musical half-hours. That night as Redding repeated his melody I slowly hammered out these verses:

"Her smile is of pearl and of coral,
　Her eyes hold the dusk and the dew,
Her sigh has the breath of the laurel,
　Her heart but the poisonous rue.

The heavenly star far above her,
　The breeze of the infinite sea,
Who know all her perfidy, love her,
　Then why call it madness in me?"

And so on.

As much as the character of the music, the fact that Redding's romantic waif was or was not standing in an adobe doorway made the subject doby to me. So that when Colonel Sumner's daughter, Nan, told me that Tony, the *vaquero*, who brought the letters from her friends and who had such white teeth, played the mandolin and sang, and I saw him, I began weaving him into my story, and I gave him that song of Redding's. Later Vincent Serrano's mother put the words into Spanish. I never thought of Tony without humming its melody, and when the play was done, it being a melodrama and having the powerful old-fashioned advantage of the right to use identifying musical themes, "Adios Amor," as the song was called when published, accompanied Tony through the play. By having it accompany also Lena, the unhappy German girl with whom he was in love, it knitted these two together more firmly in the minds of the audience than any dialogue could do. Nan Sumner called my attention also to Tony's naïve indifference to English profanity. He had learned good-bad all together, and was unable to make and untroubled by any distinction, so that when I got him into the play I was able to have him finish his lover's declaration after the song with "and damn to hell my soul, I love you!"

XX

GAMBOLS AND TRAVELS

In its revised shape I submitted my completed manuscript to Charles Frohman. Although his influence had procured the railroad transportation that I had used in getting to Arizona, and he had been looking forward to the completion of the play, something in the script or in my reading of it, because he listened to the four acts as I read them, decided him against this production. With the war on, managers were timid and my melodrama seemed unlikely of early production. I amused myself with the conduct of The Lambs' first all-star gambol.

There are few social clubs to whose functions one can with propriety ask attention. But The Lambs, because of its theatrical membership and prominence, is among that few. For many years an occasional night had been taken in the club when members free from professional calls got together in an entertainment the backbone of which was some burlesque by some skilled man upon some current success. Programmes from several of these intimate performances had occasionally been given to the public of New York. In 1898 it was decided to make a much more pretentious appeal by players, all of whom should be stars. Contracts for the exclusive services at one dollar per week for the last week in May were drawn between the club on one side and on the other Nat Goodwin, De Wolf Hopper, Stuart Robson, William Crane,

Willie Collier, Jefferson D'Angelis, Chauncey Olcott, Digby Bell, Francis Carlyle, Wilton Lackaye, Harry Woodruff, Charles Klein, Eugene Cowles, Joseph Holland, Harry Conor, Fritz Williams, Burr McIntosh, Joseph Grismer, Jesse Williams, Victor Herbert, Ignatio Martinetti, Victor Harris, and some forty other men of almost equal prominence; a half dozen playwrights and as many musicians; also Victor Herbert's band and orchestra of fifty pieces.

The company, all told, included over one hundred men. It was computed that their joint salaries, according to what they were then getting upon the road, would for that week have amounted to one hundred and twenty-five thousand dollars. Theatres were leased for one night only in New York, Brooklyn, Washington, Philadelphia, Boston, Springfield, Pittsburgh, and Chicago. Advance work for publicity was done in all these cities. Contracts existed for a special train of four sleepers, three dining-cars, and two baggage-cars. Rehearsals were well under way when war was declared. Matters of equal importance from the amusement point of view were crowded from the papers by the war news. It would have been possible to cancel the tour and contracts and pay all claims incurred for some fifteen thousand dollars, and such a course was advised by Joseph Brooks, the manager at the head of the business group. As general amusement director of this gambol, which was to lift the debt from a new clubhouse recently built, the necessity of additional indebtedness if we gave up the trip decided me to go on with it. When Brooks quit I put the business management up to Kirke La Shelle, then handling the Bostonians. The club gave the week of gambols in the cities named and took in sixty-two thousand dollars.

This businesslike résumé of that venture is impressive, but the sentimental side of it will appeal to those acquainted with the players. I shall tell only of the first feature of the programme: an old-style-minstrel first part, pyramided on the stage of the Metropolitan Opera House, in which, with Herbert's band, there were one hundred men. The interlocutor, end men, and vocalists, all in the regulation evening dress, at the end of the opening chorus were on their feet. The great auditorium of the Metropolitan Opera House was crowded from parquet to dome with one of the most select audiences ever assembled within its walls. When we remember that we were only in the first month of our war with Spain we can form some conception of the enthusiasm as this audience rose when the medley finished with the "Star-Spangled Banner," and then the burst as every nigger singer at cue drew from the inside of his white vest, instead of a pocket handkerchief, an American flag of silk.

We had been under pressure to start promptly in order to make train connections for the next town, and I am not sure that anybody has ever explained just why the curtain was held. The facts are, however, that it was difficult for my wife to get to the Metropolitan at 8.15 owing to certain attention that our baby had to have at that time before it got to bed. She had promised to make haste, and I had promised to stand in the prompt entrance and if possible to hold the curtain until I saw her take her seat in the front row of the dress circle. Men on the stage were fretting, and the audience—there was twenty-seven thousand dollars in the house—was getting impatient, but the baby delayed them only four minutes.

In June of that year, 1898, I made my first crossing

of the Atlantic Ocean. With us on that boat were seven members of The Lambs Club—Chauncey Olcott, Walter Hale, Vincent Serrano, Rowland Buckstone, Joe Wheelock, Jr., Ruckstull, and one other. First-class fare was fifty dollars; the lowest quotation now is two hundred and fifty. The old *Victoria* was a cattle-boat with bilge-keels—that is, an additional keel on each side, somewhat below the water-line, to prevent her rolling. The cattle were where the steerage ordinarily is, and we never knew of them. The usual organizing person was among the passengers, bent upon getting up a concert for the benefit of disabled seamen. And the captain thought it would take the passengers' minds from the constant fear of Spanish gunboats—submarines were not yet in use. Our American actors couldn't recite, but they could play if they had a manuscript; so with their urging and advice and occasional assistance I wrote a comedy about twenty-five minutes long dealing entirely with the ship's company, which we called "Three Days Out." In it Chauncey Olcott played an old Irishwoman, Hale a romantic tenor, Buckstone an English financier, and young Wheelock, who looked like the bathroom steward, impersonated that official, borrowing and wearing his clothes for the performance; Serrano played a Spanish cattle-raiser, Ruckstull was a walking gentleman, I was an American business man. We went aft near the steering-gear to rehearse it in the open sunshine. Three days before we got into port we gave a performance which netted a handsome purse for the beneficiaries.

Charles Frohman was in London at that time laying his first plans for his extensive theatrical control that developed later. We had our card filled with all kinds of agreeable appointments, and I met then for the first time J. M. Barrie, Bernard Shaw, Alfred Sutro, Beerbohm Tree, George Alexander, Arthur Bourchier, and Max Beerbohm.

Our first night in Paris was the evening of July 14, the anniversary of the fall of the Bastille. Instead of the firecrackers and pinwheels of America, Paris expressed itself in street festivals and dances. In every *arrondissement*, or ward, there was a central gathering where music was furnished by a municipal band and where the neighborhood people danced on the clean asphalt of the street. It was into one of these circles only a few years before that Charley Evans and Bill (Old Hoss) Hoey walked, and catching the time of the music began an impromptu dance of the American model. To visualize this fully one must remember Hoey, with his full black beard and eccentric manner; and remember the natty, smooth-shaven Charley Evans of those days in his flat-brimmed straw hat; and then the pair of them surrounded by the gradually widening circle of astonished Paris tradesmen as those two American boys competed with each other in remembered and invented steps of vaudeville assortment. That would be a rare treat to-day for an American audience familiar with that character of dancing and gathered at Longacre Square. But at that time, for that simple pirouetting *bourgeoisie*, it was electrically eccentric.

I shall offer no tourist's impression of Paris, but there is a notable remembrance of Jean Jaurès, the great socialist, pleading for evolution, not revolution. He was assassinated a few years later, but Ruck and I went to hear him then. He talked upon the theme I have furtively referred to in earlier chapters, and which in the past hard winter of unemployment more than one publicist advanced. Jaurès was sure that the trouble with capital and labor was not one of class warfare, but that both classes in some fashion were troubled by the machine in industry; by competition between owners of competing machinery, but principally by competition of the human creature against the insensate Frankenstein creation. His remedy was an ownership by the state of all the mechanical facilities of production.

Some day we shall discriminately tax them according to wise conferences between all nations.

When we came to recross the Atlantic, in August, there was still some fear of the Spanish gunboats.

As our trouble with Spain subsided I carried the play, "Arizona," to Kirke La Shelle. There was no theatre available in New York; he arranged for the production of the play at Hamlin's Grand Opera House in Chicago the following summer, 1899. I have said earlier that Kirke La Shelle had the quality of the captain, and I am sure that had he lived he would have been one of the most dominant influences in the American theatre. Only to the theatrical reader will the following be significant, but the original cast of "Arizona" included Theodore Roberts, Edwin Holt, Mattie Earle, Mabel Burt, Robert Edeson, Olive May, Sam Edwards, Arthur Byron, Vincent Serrano, Franklin Garland, Walter Hale, Lionel Barrymore, and Menifee Johnstone; and the four or five other characters were by people of less repute but of equal earnestness and ability. Few authors doing a melodrama have had better co-operation than that.

There was an incident of the first night that seems to me worth telling. I had rehearsed the piece myself, and in that work been busy. Having need for a squad of soldiers to bring on two men under arrest, a few days before our opening, I spoke to a group of supers that had been called.

"Any of you had military experience?"

Two or three replied affirmatively. To the most likely of these I said: "Where?"

"In Cuba."

"Can you train four men in the manual and the drill?" He said, "Yes, sir."

"Pick your four and report when you have done it."

In a little while he was ready. At our dress rehearsal La Shelle and I sat apart in the parquet. Things had gone well. We were on the last act. Two sympathetic characters were to come on in the custody of the noncom and the squad. They did so, the seven of them marching to their proper places on the stage, with a smart "halt" and "carry arms."

I stopped the rehearsal and said to the young man, "Go back and make that entrance again."

While they were going out to do this La Shelle came across the parquet in the greatest earnestness.

"I thought that was splendidly done."

"So did I."

"Why did you send them back?"

"I want to see them do it again."

In a curtain speech the next night I told this incident, then reverted to a rehearsal of "In Mizzoura" some five or six years before in Chicago, when from a similar group of supers I had asked for a man who could heat and weld and put a tire on a wheel, and found exactly the proper helper for Burr McIntosh, the blacksmith. I ventured the belief that if I were to write a play about the stars and called upon a bunch of Chicago supers I could find among them a volunteer astronomer. I told the audience that this young man who had responded so promptly as a soldier and had drilled his squad so effectively would be on in the next act; he didn't know I was speaking of him, but if the audience thought as much of his performance as La Shelle and I had thought they would understand why I emphasized it. When the two prisoners and the squad came on a few minutes later they got the biggest round of the play. That young super was a lad named Sydney Ainsworth, who the following year was playing a responsible part in the play, and the next year with one of the road companies was playing the hero. He became a favorite leading man.

On August 18, in that summer of 1899, Kid McCoy was to meet Jack McCormack. McCoy had many admirers in our company, and, as I remember, the general odds were some four to one on him. The dressing-rooms, which were under the stage of the Grand Opera House at that time, were buzzing with interest in the approaching battle as our men were making up for the night. Harry Hamlin and I had tickets for the fight, but declined to take any of the attractive odds that were offered at the theatre.

The meeting was only three or four blocks away. As the two men faced each other in the first round Hamlin was searching his pockets for some matches. A sound from the ring and a startled response from the audience reclaimed his attention. While McCoy had been gaily guying with some of the press men at the ringside, McCormack had knocked him out with the first punch. Hamlin and I were soon back in the theatre. We seemed to have been only wandering from one dressing-room to another. Lionel Barrymore, Arthur Byron, Robert Edeson, and Walter Hale had not yet gone on. Theodore

Roberts, Edwin Holt, and Vincent Serrano came off in a minute or two from the first act, and we were able quickly to take all the bets offered on McCoy at the excessive odds. We disappeared. Later news came duly to the theatre and found a sad family. At Rector's, after the performance, Hamlin and I confessed to having seen the fight before the betting and disgorged our ill-gotten gains.

One notable engagement made that summer takes my mind back a few years further to a set of incidents that seem amusing. In writing these reminiscences I have hit only the high spots. To give even a paragraph to each of some sixty-four plays produced would be an itemized bill of grief, unpardonable in any recollections. A couple of years before my trip to Arizona I had done a play for Mr. Daniel Frohman which I read to his scenic artist and stage-manager and him, and which at that time was acceptable. Something prevented the production and I revamped it from a serious four-act play to a three-act comedy called "Don't Tell Her Husband." T. D. Frawley had a stock company at the Columbia Theatre, San Francisco, under the management of Gottlob and Friedlander. They wanted to produce the play under my direction and sent me in advance money for railroad fares, sleeper, and expenses across the continent.

At the railroad office I met Crane's manager, Joseph Brooks, who, learning my destination, linked his arm with mine and said: "Just starting for California with the Crane company. There's an empty section in our car and glad to have you." He declined to take my money, saying it would vitiate his railroad contract if he made any subsales, but he added: "The boys play poker and they will be glad to win that from you."

We were four days crossing the continent. The poker players in Mr. Crane's company were himself, Brooks, and my good friends Walter Hale and Vincent Serrano. Under a moral obligation to lose those one hundred and twenty-five dollars to them, I came in on every little pair only to call up that protecting fate that is said to hover over the weak-minded and the infantile. I landed at the old Baldwin Hotel with the hundred and twenty-five intact and some more contributed by the four gentlemen named. In the delightful grill of that old hotel, long since destroyed by fire, I saw Gottlob and Friedlander having dinner. Gottlob came over to my table. I told him the arrangement under which I had travelled and that had I lost the money I should have considered it a legitimate although circuitous application of the expense fund. Not having lost it, I returned it to him. It was worth one hundred and twenty-five dollars to see that new sensation in his business experience. He carried the money back to Friedlander. They held an excited consultation, regarded me curiously; later both joined me, and after many tentatives as to the kind of entertainment I would find most agreeable carried me off to a private box at a prize-fight that was occurring that evening.

In Mr. Frawley's company, which contained such excellent players as Frank Worthing, Frank Carlyle, Frawley himself, and Maxine Elliott, there was also the more experienced actress, Madge Carr Cook. Her little daughter was just beginning her stage experience, and as I remember took the part of a maid to carry on a card in our play. The girl's stage name was Eleanor Robson. She did so well with Frawley that a short time thereafter she was playing leads in Denver, and when Olive May had to leave the "Arizona" company during our summer in Chicago Eleanor Robson came to take her place. Not since the early days with Mar owe had I seen a young woman who had come on the stage with so many fine natural qualities, and before she opened in the part of *Bonita* I told La Shelle that she would be a star in a short while, and it would be wise to make an immediate arrangement with her. He agreed with me; but, deferring his negotiations until after the New York opening of the company, found that Eleanor Robson was then under a starring contract with Mr. George Tyler. New York will remember its artistic disappointment when after a few brilliant characterizations Eleanor Robson became Mrs. August Belmont and society and charitable enterprises gained what the stage lost.

My little play, "Don't Tell Her Husband," was taken by Stuart Robson, who changed the title to "The Meddler," and played it for two years. The increased friendship between Hale, Serrano, and myself at the poker table in the Crane car, together with our transatlantic trip, deepened my wish to have them in the "Arizona" company, where their grip upon the public was the result of their own merits.

There is a series of happenings in the relationship of those two friends that carries an interesting psychological study. After a time in the original company Hale quit the German-character part and played the heavy man opposite Serrano, now advanced to hero. Near the end of the third act it was Serrano's business to walk over to Hale, who stood well down left, and after looking him in the eye a minute slap him over the side of the face with a sombrero; a trick slap with the force of the blow falling more on Hale's shoulder than upon his face. In one of the early performances, however, a leather band around the sombrero had struck Hale's face and hurt him slightly, but enough to make him apprehensive thereafter; and one day on the street he fell unconscious. The doctor traced his difficulty to this fear of the blow. Hale left the engagement and returned to his earlier work as etcher and illustrator. He travelled with his talented wife, Louise Closser, for some time in Europe, came back to the theatre, and played several parts with distinction. After a total interval of some ten years he was playing in my piece, "As a Man Thinks," in which John Mason was the star and Vincent Serrano was the hero.

On our opening night in Hartford, near the end of the third act, Hale forgot his lines and couldn't take them from the prompter. He was all right at the next day's rehearsal. But again at night the same lapse occurred. He was a conscientious artist, and in great depression came to me and wanted to surrender his part. I asked him to try another performance and let me look at it from the front. For the third time his lines escaped him. When the play was over Hale was positive in his decision to quit. I said:

"Walter, I think the trouble is that it is Serrano who comes down left and confronts you. Your position on the stage and your personal relations in the story are just what they were in that old cowboy play; but if you will remember that Serrano doesn't wear a sombrero and is not going to strike you with one, and that you are playing *Mr. De Lota* in a parlor story of New York, the difficulty will disappear."

He played perfectly that night and was never troubled in that manner again.

Since these papers began to appear in serial form

many men have written me and more have spoken to me concerning the wonderful memory that I must have —"Or have you kept records of all that?"

I have not kept records and I have not more than the ordinary memory. But here are two sides of that interesting subject: In the previous chapter I have written of Mr. Robert Bruce bringing me some information that I needed about Henry C. Hooker, the Arizona ranchman. Until Mr. Bruce came in at that opportune moment I had never seen him.

Now on the other side: I wished to write about a cornet-player and his performance on a memorable night in 1901. It would be all right to refer to him impersonally, but my effort to get his name is a fair example of much of the work that has been incident to all that I have written. This cornetist was in a company supporting Mr. Peter Dailey in a musical play called "Champagne Charlie," which I wrote for him and which was produced late in August in that year. Last October, 1921, I tried to get Dailey's manager, Mr. Frank McKee. He was out of the city, address unknown. After two later attempts to locate him, the question of the cornetist came up again just now as I reached the end of this chapter.

I stopped dictation and for thirty minutes my secretary and I pursued the following process: Walter Jordan, a play agent and sometime friend of McKee, is called; he gives McKee's residence; information gives his telephone; we talk to McKee; he remembers the cornetist very well, but the enterprise was twenty years ago and he forgets his name. Peter Dailey is dead. The next important member of the company is that excellent comedian Eddie Garvey; Garvey would probably remember the musician. We try to locate Garvey. Miss Humbert, of the Packard Theatrical Agency, thinks Garvey is with Charlotte Greenwood's company on the road under the management of Oliver Morosco. Morosco's office is called in order to locate the company. They tell us that Garvey left the company two or three weeks ago; they haven't his address, but the engagement was made through an agent named Leslie Morosco.

Leslie Morosco, when called, knows Mr. Garvey's address and his telephone number, but is reluctant to give them to persons inquiring over the phone. Our identity is established, the nature of the business explained, and the *Saturday Evening Post* referred to; then Garvey's number is given; fortunately Garvey is at home; he remembers the name of the cornetist and the man himself very well. He says that the cornetist was William Disston, of Philadelphia, where his father was a skilled maker of cornets. William Disston and Garvey were together in many of the Charles Hoyt productions, notably "The Milk White Flag," and Disston's singular skill as a cornetist, almost equalling that of the famous Jules Levy, got him his engagement along with Garvey in the Peter Dailey company referred to in which he was featured on the programme and gave a cornet solo. Garvey remembers the night in question, although he doesn't remember the exact date. He and Disston left the theatre together. Disston was a convivial person, and the company being that week in Providence, Rhode Island, Disston and Garvey went to the rooms of the Musicians' Union, where there were some beer and songs and music until a late hour. They then started to go home, but in order to do so were obliged to pass the office of the Providence *Journal*. In front of this building about a thousand men were gathered, watching the bulletins in the windows. As the last one appeared Disston took his cornet from its case.

My own relation to that occasion was this: I was in bed in the stately old Narragansett Hotel. The night was warm. Two windows of the room were open. At about three o'clock in the morning I was wakened by the sound of the cornet. It came over the night air, carrying the strains of that impressive old hymn, "Nearer, My God, to Thee." It took a moment to recognize this, and then the expertness of the playing convinced me that the player was Disston. I got out of bed and leaned on the window-sill. As the cornet began a repetition of the hymn it was joined by a male chorus of some thousand voices, and there plainly came the words: "E'en though it be a cross that raiseth me." I knew then that President William McKinley, who had lain wounded for a week in Buffalo, was dead. I was surprised as I listened to the finish of the hymn to find that my cheeks were wet with tears. "Nearer, My God, to Thee" had been a favorite hymn with my grandmother. My mind went back to her and the death of President Lincoln—to the tears, the solemnity of that tragic time—and, in the middle distance, Garfield.

Walter Wellman, famous journalist, wrote of that night in Buffalo, where in the Milburn residence President McKinley died: "In his last period of consciousness . . . the surgeons bent down to hear his words. He chanted the first lines of his favorite hymn, 'Nearer, My God, to Thee.' A little later he spoke again; Doctor Mann wrote the words down at the bedside, and the last conscious utterance of William McKinley was:

"'Good-by, all; good-by. It is God's way. His will be done.'

"The President soon afterward lapsed into unconsciousness, and did not rally again. The end came at 2.15 A. M., Saturday, September 14."

Three Presidents of the United States had been killed by madmen. The reverberations of those three shots I heard.

TO COLORADO FOR NEW MATERIAL

I have written of a visit to and sojourn in Arizona in order to get material for the play of that name. I wrote earlier of going back to Missouri, where I was perfectly familiar with the country, in order to refresh my ideas of its local color. In my opinion it would be difficult to overstate the value of this plan of getting information at first hand. It was Fred Remington's way of keeping himself fresh on his own subjects both for writing and illustrating. Richard Harding Davis made it his practice, visiting nearly every country in the temperate zone in his search for his varied and attractive material. So when Charles Frohman, frankly regretting his failure to produce "Arizona," wanted something with similar color I was glad to go to Colorado to look for it.

The result of that trip is not very heartening to write about. I got a play that was heavy and overcumbered with material and dramatic machinery. It opened with a string of burros bringing ore down a mountain trail as I had seen them do it in New Mexico. It seemed a fine touch on paper and very excellent at rehearsals, but when the burros got temperamental on our first night and drew attention from the dialogue they weren't so valuable. The greatest fault with the play was its scattered interest. I fancy that some time or other every playwright fails because of the very things that he has considered his strength; that is, fails from an excessive use of such things. About 1902 that facile and versatile dramatist, Mr. Clyde Fitch, produced a play called "Her Own Way," in which Maxine Elliott was the heroine, but in which a little hairdresser girl who talked East Side slang made the most pronounced impression.

Nothing had been easier for Fitch than to write this character bit, and when he found it was so acceptable he said: "Well, if you like that kind of thing I'll give you twenty such characters," and immediately wrote a play in which he did. This was a piece called "Glad of It," in which he multiplied his East Side hairdresser till she was a blemish.

I had been successful with "Alabama," with "In Mizzoura," and with "Arizona" in carrying forward a simultaneous interest in two or three different couples, being careful, of course, to have them contribute to what was the climax of each story. In "Colorado" I had practically five such interests, and though the material in the main was good, it failed to focus.

The gathering of this material, however, may have an interest. My intention had been to write a play about the Colorado mines. To get the material I had meant to go to work in one of them. I didn't believe that any practical miner would mistake me for an expert. I planned to get something in a clerical way on the surface of one of the properties or in the sheds. To do this I went, by the advice of my Rocky Mountain friend, John C. Montgomery, to the law offices of ex-Governor Charles Thomas and Harry Lee. Harry Lee, who was a man of about my own age, advised against my project. There had just been a strike in the mines, and there were still a number of secret-service men working under various guises.

"In the way you propose," Lee said, "you won't be

in any danger, but the men will promptly put you down as a private detective, and though they wouldn't molest you, you would never get near them, and the intimate stuff you are trying for would elude you."

There was an experienced, practical miner, tough man and strike leader, on their books by the name of Phil Flynn. He was a good deal of a free-lance, constantly moving about on new prospects. If they could locate Flynn and put me under his care I'd be in the way of getting the desired information. A long-distance telephone caught Flynn at Colorado City on his way to a copper district in Northern New Mexico. He waited over a train for my coming. I had had a rather romantic account given me of Flynn before joining him. According to the men in Lee's office he had been educated for the priesthood and had abandoned it. At any rate, he had a fashion of quoting Latin. To my mind, after a few minutes with him, he suggested neither the priest nor the scholar, but rather the railroad foreman. He already knew my business from his long-distance telephone talk, and as we went along on the railroad gathered my purpose in detail. It was decided that I was not to pose as a practical miner but as a mine-owner investing in properties. He gave me a few stock phrases that would partly carry out this impression, and when in doubt I was to be silent. We stopped at a junction called Trinidad, where the yard foreman knew Flynn. Flynn told him I was from Leadville. The foreman asked how things were up there. I could answer only in the general way that they were pretty good, but a main difficulty was the lack of cars. He knew this, and was trying to forward empties.

"Where did you get that car stuff?" Flynn said as

our own train moved on. I told him I had seen it in the morning paper.

"Well, you'll do, Tom."

In the evening we left our railroad at a town called Springer, from which we had a few miles' ride in a stage to the driver's home, where we passed the night. Next morning we started with a two-horse wagon for the foot of the Little Cimarron—pronounced Simmaroon. A prospector was camped there with a tent and a few cattle. Flynn made his acquaintance and left our wagon in his care. We went up the trail on horseback. At the end of the afternoon we had got as far as the animals could comfortably go. They were headed down the trail again and started with a spank. Flynn explained that there wasn't any way that they could get lost. They had to follow the little stream by which ran our trail. No matter how long it took them, they would bring up at the camper's outfit where the wagon was.

The kit I started with we had left at the stage-driver's home in the valley, and each carried only a blanket, besides such toilet articles as one could put in the pockets of his reefer. Leaving Colorado City, Flynn had asked me if I had a gun. I showed him a .38 hammerless which he thought would do. Before reaching the mining-camp he suggested shifting it to the right-hand pocket of my reefer instead of the hip, where I had it. He didn't think there would be any trouble, but though my pose was buying certain copper mines, he was really going back to recover these claims, which he had learned had been jumped by the employees of the big mining company operating in that district. I learned this with a creepy feeling in certain peripheral nerves, but have reason to think it was not betrayed.

The camp which was our destination consisted of a bunk-house and a cook-house, some fifty feet apart, both log cabins. The bunk-house had accommodations, such as they were, for eight men. Its interior was divided by a little gangway, say three feet wide, into two parts, each about nine by six. Each part contained two rough sapling bunks, one above the other, each bunk a little larger than the ordinary double bed, and all with bedding of pine boughs. On these boughs the miners at night lay rolled up in their army blankets, two to a bunk.

In the cook-house, besides a stove, a shelf for dishes and utensils, there was a wooden table about ten feet long, flanked on each side by a rough wooden bench. In one corner of this room were two single bunks, one over the other, for the cook and his helper. There was no accommodation in sight for Flynn and me, and when the miners came in from their work, which they did about half an hour after our arrival, there was no welcome. One of the party was a romantic-looking boy in his early twenties, with corduroy suit and camping boots, as picturesque a figure as one now sees in the movies. There was one other American, a third miner apparently of Latin origin, and five Irishmen. The boy in corduroys was good-natured and genial. He seemed to be operating for himself. The other men worked for the company that owned the buildings, the adjacent territory, and the few burros that carried the ore down the trail. We were at a considerable elevation.

The place grew suddenly cold at nightfall, although the days were warm. After supper the men smoked plug tobacco and played cards. The cook let his fire go out in order to get rid of them. When they got too cold they went to bed in the bunk-house. The cook said that

Flynn and I couldn't stay in the cook-house. Flynn told him he was wrong about that; his friend Thomas would sleep on the table; himself he was going to stretch out on one of the benches and some boxes that he put alongside.

Without removing boots or any garments, with a folded gunny-sack for a pillow, and covered by the blanket, I slept four nights on the kitchen-table. The foreman of the outfit would have had authority to oust us, but he made no attempt to exert it. The first morning, after a solemn breakfast, during which nobody but the boy in corduroy spoke to us, Flynn and I went a mile down the trail to borrow a couple of picks. The company had plenty in their blacksmith shop, but refused to lend them. The blacksmith, when alone, seemed a little more communicative and more willing to be friendly with Flynn.

When, after getting our picks and an hour's walk, we got to the ground where Flynn had located we found that his identifying stakes and signs had been replaced by newer claimants. These evidences Flynn promptly destroyed, and set up again stakes with his own name on them. This done, we put in the rest of our time digging what in mining parlance was called an assessment. This is the removal of enough cubic material to meet the requirement of the mining laws, and we were just within the expiration of the time-limit to do it.

We were in a singular social atmosphere and set of circumstances. The cooks turned us out the same rough meals that they provided the company miners, without any discussion as to the propriety of doing so. The miners ignored us during the meals, although Phil swore roundly at the unidentified thieves who had tried to steal his claims. The cook and his helper were rather poor stuff, and even if they had been friendly, which they were not, Flynn and I and the boy in corduroys, who diplomatically affected an ignorance, all together would have been in the minority against the remaining members of the group.

Alone each day on the claims, Flynn said he didn't think any of the men had nerve enough to begin shooting, and in his opinion the claim-jumping had been inspired by the company, and the men were not to get much out of it, anyway; so that his fears, if he had any, were considerably less than my own, which were numerous. On the fourth morning after our arrival we started on foot down the trail, and to my eyes the landscape grew more beautiful with every rod we covered. We found our horses and wagon with the camping outfit in the little valley, where we arrived in the afternoon. Late that night we were again in the stage-driver's highly civilized quarters, which when quitting I had thought so rude.

On the way north for Cripple Creek we stopped off at the little town, at that time the central office of the Maxwell Land Grant, where Flynn had to make certification of his assessment work, and where much to my astonishment he filed one of his claims as the Little Luke, naming it after my boy and turning over to me the certificate of ownership. The adjoining property belonging to the big copper company was paying heavily, and Phil hoped there might be a fortune in this claim. To hold it required an occasional return to the property and some work with the pick in that unfriendly altitude of the foe and the stranger. So, though I still have the certificate, the claim of the Little Luke is like the grave of Sir John Moore.

At Cripple Creek I met interesting characters and learned much about Flynn. There had been a fire a couple of years before—while Flynn was absent—that swept the side hills and left men, women, and children without shelter. Flynn returned when the conflagration was over, and to his astonishment his little cabin was the only one left in that district.

He looked over the surrounding misery a moment and quietly went over to his own cabin and set it on fire. When he rejoined the sufferers he said, "Now I'm with you."

As we went through the little mining city on that first night of our visit we gradually accumulated a crowd of admirers. I was in a fair way to make a mistake about Flynn's popularity until I discovered that the interest was in me. I got Flynn in a corner and made him confess. Some one had asked the name of his companion. As a great secret he had whispered, "Jim Jeffries." Some two years before Jeffries had won the championship from Bob Fitzsimmons, had later won from Sharkey, and some months preceding the time of which I write had knocked out James J. Corbett. On the sidewalks and in the barrooms, much to Flynn's amusement, men jostled us a little unpleasantly. I feared that as enthusiasm mounted some local celebrity would take a wallop at me in the belief that he was measuring his capacity against the world champion. Under a pretense of important letters I got back to our hotel.

The stuff I got from Cripple Creek was principally character studies. By the time we reached Leadville, Flynn was thoroughly enjoying the fiction in which we were mutually interested. In that city I was introduced to a man anxious to get rid of a gold mine. It became necessary to inspect it, and I wanted the information that such an inspection would give. To reach its most significant level we had to make a descent of eight hundred feet in the shaft. Our vehicle was what was called a bucket. This was a vessel made of boiler iron, about four feet high, with a diameter of two feet at its rim, used for lifting ore. It was held by a strong iron bale suspended by a steel cable. The rim of this bucket stopped at the ground level. We three men, the mine foreman, Flynn, and myself, took hold of the steel cable and stepped on the rim, distributing our weight so that the thing rode level. Upon a signal to the engineer the bucket began to descend. The shaft through which we were going was about four feet square. From one hundred feet down its opening, as one looked up, seemed about the size of a window-pane. When we stopped at eight hundred feet it was a pinhole in a sheet of black paper. Our illumination was the three candles that we carried, each set in a miner's candlestick, which was somewhat like an ornamental skewer or steel dagger holding a candle at right angles, and devised to scrape dirt out of crevices or a candle-holder to stick point first into a wall. The alley through which we travelled was about as wide as a private hallway in a cheap flat, and not high enough to permit of standing erect.

One trouble with this particular gold mine was that some two hundred feet along this drift the roof had caved in. The owners had dug through this heap a kind of rat hole big enough to permit the passage of a man's body, if he got flat on his stomach and pulled himself along like a lizard. The foreman went first; urged by Flynn, I followed, second. There was no retreat except confession, and the dark shaft from which we had just escaped. After a cold crawl of twelve or fifteen feet we emerged into the unobstructed gallery again. There was no guaranty that the material through which we crawled wouldn't shift once more and imprison us, or even catch us in transit. But it didn't, and after a terrifying hour we were again on the surface in God's free air. I didn't buy the gold mine; the best I could do was to take the matter under advisement. But I was so overloaded with sensations that when I came to write my play I had my villain and his guilty partner eight hundred feet under ground, in a cage on a cable controlled by the hero, who was on the surface with the damning evidence in his hands.

When we got back to Denver, Flynn refused to leave me until I had been given safely into the hands of our friend, Harry Lee. As he said good-by for the time being he turned to Lee:

"What I like about your friend Tom here is we took this two weeks' trip together, and we were in some tough places. But he never said once, 'When are we going to get out of here?' or 'How long does this last?' He's all right."

I confessed to Lee that I'd often thought those questions, but had refrained from asking them because they would in nowise hasten our departure or terminate our difficulties; and, furthermore, I didn't want Phil Flynn to think I was a quitter, which in my heart I was.

Flynn was much interested in stories of the theatre, and also the things about Fred Remington, and a year later showed up unexpectedly, but not without welcome, at New Rochelle.

Remington thought him a veritable nugget, and spent

all the time with him he could in Flynn's two or three days in the East.

The twenty years that have gone by have probably retired Phil from very active service, but there are hundreds in Colorado, Arizona, and New Mexico who remember him and I hope still meet him.

Ex-Governor Charles Thomas' law partner, Harry Lee, now dead, was one of the most gifted men of the Middle West. I will quote two examples of his wit if I can set the stage for them without too much delay: A dinner to me in the Denver Club at which were toastmaster and speeches and one orator, who, I had been led to believe, was the most eloquent in the State. When this speaker began to talk he made three separate starts at his subject. His friends regretted the indulgence that left him a little scattered, and as for the third time he said, "Frémont came through here in '48," Harry Lee remarked, "The record's been lowered since then." The orator joined in the laugh, and under its cover gave way to the next speaker. On one of Lee's visits to New York a club tête-à-tête with Lackaye was interrupted by an English actor, who like the oratorical friend at Denver was not in full possession of his faculties. Each attempt to score off Lackaye proved more of a cue than a hit. His continued failure and the triumph of Lackaye growing a little monotonous, Lee interposed:

"I don't know what the game laws are in New York, Mr. Lackaye, but in Colorado it's considered very unsportsmanlike to shoot mackerel in a barrel."

"Mackerel in a barrel" is now a Lambs Club stencil.

Human nature is so constituted that the wish to escape from boredom is one of its strongest motives. Nearly every playwright is driven into new kinds of endeavor

by his wish for change. Bronson Howard, after his comedies of "Saratoga" and "Green Room Fun," wrote
"The Banker's Daughter," "Young Mrs. Winthrop,"
and after another comedy, "The Henrietta," returned to
serious work in "Shenandoah" and "Aristocracy." Gillette wrote his comedies, "The Professor," "The Legal
Wreck," then his serious play, "Held by the Enemy,"
and, after a string of comedies which included "Mr. Wil-
kinson's Widows," "Too Much Johnson," and "Because
She Loved Him So," returned to serious work in "Secret
Service" and "Sherlock Holmes." Henry Arthur Jones
had even a wider range through outright melodrama and
farce, ranging from "The Silver King" to "Whitewashing
of Julia." Clyde Fitch, after his lighter social portraiture,
wrote his big play, "The City." One will not be accused
of claiming a professional kinship to these masters if like
them he confesses the human side which craves variety.
My own attempts ranged all the way from melodrama to
musical comedies and broad farce. After the experience
with "Colorado," the reaction was naturally to the
lighter moods.

Before "Colorado" was produced, and while it was in
rehearsals, I went one night to the Empire Theatre to
see H. V. Esmond's comedy, "The Wilderness." That
excellent company of Charles Frohman's contained such
actors, since stars, as Margaret Anglin, William Courtenay, Charles Richman, Mrs. Whiffen, Margaret Dale,
and in a quite minor rôle, Lawrence D'Orsay. My wife
and I were watching the play from a box, and when D'Orsay left the stage I noticed a movement in the parquet
like a receding wave as the audience settled back in their
seats. They had moved forward in their attention in
less concerted action; but as they heard D'Orsay ap-

proaching for his second scene their interest was immediate and the forward inclination was in unison. I called my wife's attention to the fact, and when D'Orsay came on for the third time we both noticed the peculiar response. I felt that the player so welcome in such negligible material as his slight rôle offered was of stellar quality.

I knew D'Orsay as an actor who had attracted attention in Captain Marshall's play, "The Royal Family," and as an interesting personal figure about the clubs. To describe him in a line, one would have to use the phrase so often applied to him by his critics: "The Ouida type of heavy guardsman." His expression is the dominant one of distinguished, opaque, English toleration, alternated with bland astonishment, not unmixed with good nature, but always self-confident, self-sufficient, and aristocratic. I began thinking about him as the central figure for a comedy that I had agreed to write for Mr. Frohman.

On the American stage, to get the greatest value from such a man as a kind of comic-paper Englishman of breeding, it was imperative to surround him with Americans and give him an American background. In doing this I naturally saw the Americans amused with his speech and manner as I had seen them amused by him in private life; but as I thought more intimately of him I remembered that his funniest moments were his attempts to be ultra-American. This phase seemed only incidentally valuable until, through dwelling on it, the idea came to me to put him in a situation where he would be seriously obliged to assume it altogether, and with the inception of that idea I had the bent and the impelling factor of my story. The construction would be along the line of establishing an Englishman who would have to pretend to be an American, and his experiences after he began to do so.

If I were permitted to say to a dozen English and American playwrights of to-day—Pinero, Jones, Gillette, Pollock, Al Thomas, Forbes, Winchell Smith, Davis, Maugham, and so on, "What made an ultra-Englishman in America pretend to be an American? Answer promptly," they would reply in chorus, "A woman." That is the dramatist's formula, and it was mine. And the dramatists would be agreed on the next step: Find the woman.

I felt that it would be piquant for the woman to be a grass-widow who had resumed her maiden name. Under the proverb this would make her twice shy, while at the same time it would remove her from the ingénue class, then being badly overworked. After considerable study, which must not be minimized by any ready relation of it, I hit upon the idea of having my Englishman masquerading as an American unwittingly take for sufficient reason the name of the girl's divorced husband. This was a great find, as any one interested in playmaking will readily agree. I decided that my Englishman should have seen and been attracted by this young woman while she was travelling on the Continent, and that instead of coming to America in search of an heiress his trip should be one definitely in search of the woman.

I have more than once in these pages spoken of the value of material which seemed to have no significance at the time of its acquisition. Here's another example: I didn't go up in the Ferris wheel at the Chicago World's Fair in 1893 because I dramatized the wheel sticking when my car should reach the top of the turn. In 1899

I said so to Maurice Barrymore as we stood looking at the same wheel transported to and set up at Earl's Court, London.

"Well, since it's been here the thing has stuck twice," said Barry; "one time for twenty-four hours."

A policeman standing by took up the story and told us how a sailorman climbed to the cars with coffee and sandwiches for the imprisoned patrons.

"A lot of good stories," he added, smiling, "fellows with other fellows' wives, and all that sort of thing."

I expressed my yokel astonishment as to how the sailorman could have managed it up to the topmost cars. The bobby's tolerant answer set the story in my mind for all time:

"Well, you see, sir, 'is mother'd taught 'im to 'old on good and 'ard, and 'e did."

The idea of putting two romantic people together for twenty-four hours in the same car at the top of the Ferris wheel seemed to me excellent preparation for a comedy. I adopted it.

When my story was well in hand, newspaper training impelled me to familiarize myself with the proposed scenes of it, the three locations in the Waldorf-Astoria Hotel. I stated my project to the business manager of the hotel, and met a chilling and discouraging reception. The house could lend itself to no enterprise of that kind. So two days later I drove to the hotel in a cab with my wife, and with a trunk and valises. The room clerk had us shown several rooms and suites. I chose a suite I thought suited to the earl. The rate, without meals, was forty dollars a day. We stopped only one day, but the forty dollars put into my hands many valuable physical suggestions, as well as the truthful color which is so valuable in a well-known district. It also enabled me to make sketches for the scenic artist and get suggestions helpful in the general construction of the story.

After I had begun to write the play Mr. Frohman had gone to London. I cabled him, asking if I might have D'Orsay for the piece.

With characteristic brevity he answered "Yes."

My comedy, "The Earl of Pawtucket," was done by the time Mr. Frohman came back, but the cable for D'Orsay had meant to him only the engagement of a minor character. He was warm in his approval of the play, but declined to risk D'Orsay as the star. I could see no other exponent. Frohman generously released D'Orsay. Two hours after he had done so I had completed an arrangement with Kirke La Shelle, who took the play solely upon my description of it, and because he had to move promptly in order to get time at the Madison Square Theatre, where Elizabeth Tyree was starring under her own management in a play not very successful. Miss Tyree was exactly the type of girl that we wanted for the heroine, and she had the additional attraction of being the owner of this lease for the Madison Square Theatre. While I was still in La Shelle's office, La Shelle arranged for Miss Tyree to hear the play, and before she went to the theatre that night I had read it to her, she had accepted it, and after giving the following day to the selection of the company we started on the second morning to rehearse the piece, with only eleven days between us and the Monday on which we proposed to open. Among the company assembled on the stage of the Madison Square Theatre for rehearsal was an actor of experience and ability, Mr. Ernest Elton, engaged for the part of the valet. He and D'Orsay had been together in an

English company some fifteen years before in the provinces, and met now for the first time since.

"Oh," said Elton to D'Orsay, "are you in this piece?"

D'Orsay said, "I hope to be."

Elton gradually realized he had been speaking to the star. The reported episode amused C. F.

We had one of our best first nights, and next morning a fine press; but our performance had been with insufficient preparation. Being familiar with the script from both writing and rehearsing it, I had at the first performance undertaken the office of prompter, and, in order that I might not be more audible than the players, stood in the first entrance with a small megaphone through which I whispered when they seemed to hesitate.

In the second intermission a prominent critic said, "I like everything about the play except the wretch with the megaphone."

But feeling that much more depended upon maintenance of our tempo than absence of the occasional note from the megaphone, I stuck to the method. Our stage-manager's time-card registered our last curtain at an hour that was not improved upon during the long run of the piece. D'Orsay starred in the play under La Shelle's management for three years, and at the end of that time returned to Mr. Frohman to star in another play.

Altogether I read or proposed many plays to Charles Frohman. Some were accepted, many were refused, both in script and in projected story. Charley one day said to me: "It's always a great pleasure to refuse a play of yours, because it seems to get the thing off your mind, and then we have an interesting conversation."

For my own part, as I look back, I can add that the

pleasure was not altogether one-sided, because Charley never refused a play or a story without proposing some project for another one.

When he turned back the script of "Pawtucket" and released D'Orsay from his company in order that I might do the play elsewhere he said: "As soon as this is off your mind start in and write me a comedy for John Drew, and if you can I'd like you to put a part in it for Lionel."

Drew had recently had great success in a play called "The Mummy and the Humming-Bird," in which his nephew, Lionel Barrymore, had the part of an Italian who had no English words and ventured on few Italian phrases, but trusted to convey most of his meaning by eloquent pantomime.

CHAPTER XXII

IN PARIS

I think Lionel Barrymore's fundamental ambition in life was not so much to be player as to be artist. Everything in black and white or on canvas or in stone interests him intensely, and for two or three years he left the stage to devote himself to the study of color in Paris. In the theatre his happiness is delineating character, and he goes at each new subject with the technical interest of an artist interested in surfaces and in the force behind them. He made his first big impression in New York by playing an old Boer general in a melodrama done at the Academy of Music. The part was a prophecy of his gallery of old-men portraits made notable in "The Copperhead" and again in "The Claw." For his Italian with John Drew he had taken lessons from a master in order to be right in the few phrases he had to ejaculate, and he had gone into the Italian colony to study the manners of its people. It may be that C. F.'s commission to put in a part also for Lionel centred my attention more than the obvious commission to get a story for Drew. At that time, to see Kid McCoy, champion middleweight fighter of the world, and Lionel Barrymore together no acquaintance of either would mistake one for the other. But the mistake could easily be made if either was seen alone half a block away. I began to think of a prize-fighter. In order to get a thoroughly contrasting part, I chose a minister of the gospel. I was indebted to the current newspapers for that idea, as there was some young clergyman at the time in the public eye through his advocacy of athletics.

There was no haste for the play. My friend Ruckstull was settled in a little town called St.-Leu, some fifteen miles out of Paris, working on his heroic equestrian statue of Wade Hampton. Letters from him carried the alluring post-cards of the city beautiful. I was a little track-sore with New York, and mentally a little weary with the vociferous self-approval of the National Administration. My boy and baby girl were beginning to lisp French, perhaps wrongly, from their uncertain *bonne*. My wife wanted to pursue her musical studies. I thought it would be fine to have an occasional half day in some Parisian *atelier*. "Arizona" was doing well. D'Orsay was making money. Letters of credit seemed possible! Paris!

There are too many guide-books of Paris, too many accurate pictures of its beauties, too many interesting and romantic descriptions of it from Dumas to Du Maurier, for an American playwright fatuously to attempt further to encumber the field. But for a man momentarily escaping from America, and especially from New York, there are some attractions that have not been enumerated.

An editor of a Western paper, recently writing of a local improvement society and of the conditions of individual premises, says of one citizen: "There is no hypocrisy about Brown. He is not one of those men who beautify their front yards and leave the back yards filled with ash-cans, rusty tin, and disorder. No hypocrisy. Brown's front yard is just as dirty as the back one."

New York has that kind of candor. When a visitor

debarks from a steamship and comes through our water-front streets, whether from Hoboken or the North River side of Manhattan, he has a ride through a front yard that prepares him for all the dump-heaps of the rear, broken pavements, dirty gutters, tumbled tenements, ragged hoardings; and then through our necessitated but oppressive canyons, where the sky-scrapers shut out the sun for all but a few minutes of the day. And if he happens to be a home-coming American from Paris he groans inwardly with a despair that he knows no effort of his own lifetime can lift. Having made one such round trip, I looked on Paris for a second time with a knowledge of these American features and a wish to find the elements that made the great contrast.

One principal item is sky-line. The building laws of Paris fix the limit of houses definitely at six stories, or twenty metres, sixty-five feet. The mansard roof is an intelligent effort to observe the letter of this law and yet steal a few additional vertical feet under the allowance of roof. As property is valuable, the legal limit is uniformly reached; but monotony is avoided because the race of architects turned out by the Beaux-Arts, where we send our Americans to learn the rudiments of their profession, has found a variety in the unity that makes for restful beauty. Again, the poverty of Paris in its water-supply seems to result in another blessing. The water in some of the mains is not potable, as they say, *pas de la source*, and the Parisian is as lavish with it in the streets and fountains as he is economical of its use in his bathtubs.

Every morning, in every block, a street-cleaner turns a little rivulet through the gutter, dams it into a little lake with a bunch of burlap, and with his long and homely

broom of osiers sweeps it over the wooden pavement
levels, washing back the débris to the run and gradually
extending rivulet and lake until he has accomplished his
block. The morning gutter and the sky-line call attention newly to each new day.

And then this third item: Intelligent Paris recognizes
and admits the eye as an organ. It is not to be more
lawlessly assailed than is the ear. No man for commercial purposes shall without restriction assault the passers'
attention with his blatant demand. The twenty-four-
sheet stand, the barbaric three-sheet poster do not exist,
because the municipality puts a tax upon every sheet of
paper that solicits its attention. Advertising space is
relatively as valuable on the walls as it is in the newspapers, and so posters are artistic, of more than ephemeral
value, and are in the main confined to handsome little
kiosks set up at intervals for their accommodation.

When will America learn this value of public right?
When will all the unsightly boards that confine our railway journeys to hideous alleys of proclamatory and mandatory attacks be regulated by proper assessment under
state domain to things of tolerable sightliness and sources
of revenue to the poor public whom they afflict? When
will unoffending citizens be permitted to travel and look
from their car windows on refreshing landscapes without
being commanded to use Startum's Alarm Clock or
Sokum's Condensed Milk? Why must there always be
interposed between the ruminative individual and the
stenography of his Maker the commercial persuasion of
his fellow man, money mad?

To one writing for the theatre Paris is always rich in
suggestion. Little plays that have not the importance
to get into *L'Illustration*, or even into the printed

brochure, dramatic bits that never make their way to America, are at the small theatres on the boulevards and the back streets and in the Quartier and in Montmartre, more than half of them containing each some little suggestive, facile scene that educates and urges. When I had my Drew-Barrymore play finished I sent it over to C. F. by mail under the title of "The Pug and the Parson," and under that title it was announced. But before I could get over to rehearse it Mr. Frohman had received a couple of letters from Protestant ministers protesting against the association. He had a racial reluctance to risk their displeasure, and although I stoutly stood for the title, feeling that the word "parson" was not so sacrosanct that one might not use it, his wish of course prevailed. We called the play "The Other Girl."

C. F. felt that it wouldn't do to put Drew into the part of the preacher, however, because the character, although an equal part in the play's value and in the writing, could not from its very kind compete with the character of the pugilist. He believed that Barrymore, again associated with his uncle, Mr. Drew, would lead those who judged superficially to proclaim the younger man the better actor, when the facts would be that in this play, as in "The Mummy and the Humming-Bird" he had only the more showy part. It was therefore decided to keep Lionel as the pugilist and put some available leading man in the part that had been meant for Mr. Drew. Frank Worthing was engaged for this, and I have never seen a manager move with more enthusiasm to get an adequate company.

I am sorry to forget the name of the play in which a very beautiful girl of that time had made an impression. This girl was Drina De Wolfe, the wife of Elsie De

Wolfe's brother. There was some slight domestic-in-law difference that made these ladies not agreeable to each other, and the wish to see them both in the same cast piqued Frohman's sense of humor so much that he set about the seemingly impossible task of persuading the two ladies, with the result that the valuable co-operation of both actresses was obtained. Selina Fetter, who had been a favorite New York leading woman when she married Edwin Milton Royle, was induced to take a part somewhat more mature than those she had previously shown in. For a young reporter, Richard Bennett was engaged; and such excellent actors as Joseph Wheelock, Jr., Ralph Delmore, and Joseph Whiting, together with Jessie Busley and Maggie Fielding, then one of the greatest favorites of the vaudeville theatres, were also engaged. The Criterion Theatre, in which we were ultimately to play, was given to us for all our rehearsals. That one should mention this may puzzle the layman, but such conditions are not always provided. I think the rule is to the contrary; that the majority of plays are moved about in their rehearsals from one theatre to another, and occasionally into some hired hall. There is a great advantage in rehearsing in the playhouse in which you are to open, and getting always the proper tonal values and the physical relations that are to be undisturbed and unrevised.

As soon as Lionel knew he was cast for the pugilist he hunted up Kid McCoy and passed much of his time outside the theatre with the champion. This admiration was reciprocated, and when the play opened McCoy came often to see his counterfeit presentment. One difference between Barrymore and McCoy was that the Kid's hair was as curly as Lionel's was straight. For a period in the early run of the piece, and for all I know during all the while he was in it, Lionel had his hair artificially curled each evening in order properly to present this international favorite.

I have reason to believe that an ether jag indicated by Mr. Wheelock, who impersonated a character just released from the table where he had undergone an operation under the influence of ether, was the first time that phenomenon was presented in the theatre. The use of sulphuric ether as an anæsthetic dates from some time since the Civil War, and we are familiar with most of the plays produced since that time. In the rehearsals of this scene Wheelock more than once offered to surrender his part, believing that the demonstrations I was asking of him were exaggerated and unreal; but he had never taken ether, and I'd had two jumps at it, so with the help of Mr. Frohman he was finally persuaded.

In Paris, Alfred Sutro had brought to our delighted attention the novels of Leonard Merrick, who is related to Sutro. One of these stories is called "The Position of Peggy Harper." It relates an author's patient training of Miss Peggy, even to the saucy lifting of her chin and other apparently unconscious personal tricks; the great hit of the young lady in London in the author's play, and then the unanimous comment of the press upon those delightful characteristics, chin-tipping and the like, and the author's great good fortune in finding an exponent who possessed them and thereby saved his piece from failure. I fancy this is not an unusual experience with playwrights who have positive ideas and who direct their own plays.

As I have written in earlier pages, I was obliged to go back to Paris a day or two after we opened at the Criterion; but before I left Barrymore's success was so pronounced and his identification with the part seemed so permanent that Frohman asked me what I thought of featuring him in the play. Of course, with my admiration for the boy and my older friendship with his parents, as well as a sense of justice, I was delighted with it. "The Other Girl" was produced late in December, 1903. Ethel Barrymore was at that time playing at the Hudson Theatre in "Cousin Kate." I saw her the following summer at her Uncle John Drew's house at East Hampton. The first vivid experience she had to report to me was of a night in midwinter when leaving the Hudson Theatre to go home she had encountered on Broadway a billboard on which was a great stand starring Lionel Barrymore, her brother. Ethel said she was so pleased that tears sprang to her eyes. I was able to tell her then of her own first night in "Captain Jinks" at the Garrick, when her father and I leaned on the bulkhead of the filled theatre.

Then Barry's eyes were full of tears as he turned to me and said: "My God, isn't she sweet?" And she was.

In my first saunter through my recollections, and through the contemporary suggestions that were about me for the search of a subject for the Drew play, my attention—not for the first time—went back to the little "Constitutional Point" that I had written for Mr. Palmer. It was unsuited to my needs, but its ultimate usefulness was not to be overlooked. After leaving my engagement with Bishop, which had been the inspiration for the little piece, I had been more and more intrigued with the subject. The basis for my information was in the series of books written by Doctor Thomas Hudson, of which his "Law of Psychic Phenomena" was the first. I was thereby led to a considerable interest in the experiments and findings of Doctor Baird, the Englishman, and Charcot and Janet, the Frenchmen, and occasionally when a kindred subject was on the calendar during my stay in Paris I would go into the indicated *salle* of the Sorbonne and hear some lecture on psychology.

There was a double purpose in this. To one learning French the philosophic and scientific vocabularies are much more easily followed than the vernacular of the modern theatre or that of the street and shops. I became convinced of telepathy as a fact and as a force, but adopted only the sense of the responsibility that it implied, and never in any wise felt the slightest call for any experiment on what might be called the aggressive or therapeutic side of it.

While we were rehearsing "The Other Girl," Lionel spent many evenings with me in my temporary quarters at the hotel and elsewhere, and often his brother Jack, not yet thoroughly launched upon his career, was with us. There is in both the boys a deep hospitality for everything approaching mysticism, and the forceful side of telepathy had for them a profound attraction.

There was a little incident in which we three were engaged, so isolated as to have no value in any scientific aspect, but nevertheless amusing. In the old Café Boulevard, on Second Avenue near Tenth Street, there was to the rear a section of the floor, evidently the level of some acquired addition, reached by the ascent of three or four steps. We were on that little mezzanine. I was referring to somebody's statement and demonstration of the possibility of making a person in front of one in an audience conscious of the gaze of another at a distance behind him. The boys proposed the experiment. To make it difficult they selected a woman in the fore part of the restaurant parquet who sat with back squarely toward us. We agreed upon her by hat and furs, and the like, and then—conforming to instructions—instead of merely mentally commanding the lady to look around, we in our minds definitely dramatized her doing so and focused thought and attention on her. In the time in which one can perhaps count ten, with a gesture of great annoyance the lady faced squarely about and glared at us.

I have referred in earlier chapters to a patron of the theatre whose theories were so reassuring, Mr. Thomas B. Clarke, a connoisseur and art collector. Men who know Mr. Clarke, and know him intimately enough to call him Tom, will understand my taking any excuse, however risky, to have an hour in his company. For some reason during this winter, 1903, in New York he wanted me to meet his friend, Mr. Frederick Gebhard. As I remember, Mr. Gebhard had requested the meeting, which was to be at a very small dinner at his home then on the eastern side of Park Avenue at about Thirty-ninth Street. I went with a fairly keen interest, wondering somewhat fatuously if Mr. Gebhard knew anything of my St. Louis newspaper reports of his visits there. As I recalled them, they were rather complimentary than otherwise, except for a hideous woodcut issued as a portrait. But a man about town would hardly invite a person to a small dinner party in order to assault him for that offense after so many years had intervened. It was a fine little dinner, arranged by an excellent chef and accompanied by good wine.

I had last seen Mr. Gebhard in 1884, twenty years before, then wearing the title of the King of Dudes. He was now a middle-aged, reserved, and serious gentleman,

talking entertainingly and modestly on questions of art
and literature. He was gray at the temples, decidedly
modelled as to face, a little heavier as to figure, but athletic still. Over the mantel of his living-room was the
picture of a beautiful woman set in a large oval frame.
The men of the small party regarded it with admiration.

"Where did you get it?" Clarke asked.

"You've seen that before. That's Lulu."

"Not the Eastman Johnson?"

"Yes," Gebhard answered. "I had Jones go over it
for me, change the color of the hair and the eyes."

"But why?"

"Well, one doesn't go on living with a portrait of a
divorced wife. I'm so damn poor I can't afford another
picture for that space. I had the coloring changed, and
it makes a decoration."

I knew nothing of the divorced wife, have learned
nothing since, nor of the circumstances. But the attitude of the lonely man, the cynical philosophy that made
that use of the canvas and gave that frank explanation
impressed me. I was looking for the as-yet-undiscovered
idea for a play for John Drew. I had kept the contract
with Mr. Frohman when I had furnished him "The Other
Girl," but the Drew project to my delight was still before me. A *divorcé*, and such a definite *divorcé* as Mr.
Gebhard, for a hero, with the intriguing idea of the re-
painted portrait, made a good starting-point. The cause
of the divorce must of course be a woman. The outcome
of the play would be a return to the wife or a marriage
with the other woman. Of those alternatives I chose
the woman. My problem was to have her the more desirable of the two; to have her innocent of any trans-
gression and unconscious of any charge. The wife would

some other listeners at East Hampton of a dinner attempted some ten years before at our house in New Rochelle. At that earlier dinner ten guests were expected, making a total party of twelve. All but one were coming from New York City. There was a blizzard on the day set, and the only guest to arrive was a lady living in New Rochelle. She did not reach the house until nearly nine o'clock in the evening, and was then in the arms of her coachman. The coupé in which she had passed nearly an hour trying to cover a quarter of a mile was stalled in the snow-drift on our lawn.

When the lady was thawed out and revived, and as we faced the flowers and the salted almonds, this solitary guest on my right said to my wife on my left, "If you were to put this on the stage nobody would believe it."

There was a feature of our table that became an effective property in a first act. This was a hole some eighteen inches square, which, contrary to the expostulations of our local carpenter, I had cut in the centre of the table. In this opening was fitted a copper pan that caught the drift from a tiny fountain that could play over stones and ferns when we had visitors or felt sentimental ourselves. It was a perfect little fountain, regulated under the table by a key which no man ought to expect a woman to reach, and it worked satisfactorily nine times out of ten, or until a bit of dirt or some aquatic insect got into its pinhole nozzle. Then it spurted eccentrically and was a regular fool thing.

One night Francis Wilson had the attention of the company and was telling a good story when the fountain took one of these fits. The stream struck fair and square on the stiff bosom of his dress shirt and made a noise like rain on a roof. Company tablecloths are long, and

before I could get under and find the key a good deal
of water went Mr. Wilson's way, but it didn't interrupt
his story. He turned up his lapels like a sailorman on
the bridge and held his place. We abandoned the fountain soon after that, but the Francis Wilson episode always impressed persons humorously when we told it
to explain the patch on the table where the copper pan
had been, and one gentle visitor said: "Mr. Thomas,
you ought to put that in a play."

When I presented this material to Dumay he said that
no playwright could make more than one act of it, and
it was upon his banter that I started out to show him that
the material was sufficient, with its suggestion, to furnish
forth a three-act comedy.

There was at East Hampton an empty box stall in the
stable, with windows set so high that one couldn't look
out of them. I put in only a kitchen chair and a small
pine table from the village general store—not even a
calendar to distract attention. My play material to
start with was a suburban house, isolated by a storm on
the evening of a prepared dinner. Persons once there
couldn't easily leave, and only the sturdy and the heroic
could arrive. Question: What is the best use to make
of that set of conditions? Answer: The exploitation of
a person or persons who would like to get away and can't
do so. What person would be the most effective figure
under such constraint? A girl!

I took the proposed-and-interrupted dinner-party indicated, made it in honor of the girl, a guest in the house;
made the lady neighbor who was carried into the house
by the coachman the girl's unidentified rival in the affections of a young man who had been temporarily cast
off by the girl because of a scandal of which both he and

the married lady were innocent, but which was sufficiently distorted in its first presentation. Then I drove
the young man, an architect, into the house from a near-
by job to telephone, unaware of the girl's presence or of
the projected dinner until he arrives. With the people
living in the house and the father and mother of the
hostess and the jealous husband of the married lady I
had people enough for a story. I cannot repeat a play,
not even a plot, in these pages, but believe I have here-
with given enough to indicate the sprightliness of the subject and the sufficiency of the material.

When the comedy was done, after some six weeks of
rather intensive writing, we called it "Mrs. Leffingwell's
Boots." Frohman immediately accepted it and told me
he would wire me to Paris when time and a place in the
theatres were ripe for it. I came over the next midwinter,
when I found the radiant C. F. with another one of his
extraordinary casts. It was a way with Mr. Frohman
to see unrecognized ability in a young woman and quickly
give her opportunities to prove her worth to the public.
Though these opportunities could be devised, it wasn't
always possible to make the public accept the lady at
his estimate of her. My recollection is that when the
public had failed, however, C. F. was more nearly right
than the general jury.

Such a girl had come under his attention at that time
in the person of Fay Davis, a most intelligent actress,
with a method perhaps a little too delicate if anything.
It had more the quality of the miniature painter's attention to subtleties and to details than is effective in the
playhouse, which responds more readily to the broader
touches. Mr. Frohman had starred her in "Lady Rose's
Daughter," featured her in "The Whitewashing of Julia"

and in "The Rich Mrs. Repton." To my great profit and delight he found for her in the young girl I have referred to in this story of mine what he thought was a rôle worthy of her attention. And then, in order to give Miss Davis a perfect support and companionship, he assembled a cast that included these excellent players: Margaret Illington, then prominently in the public affection; Jessie Busley, one of the best of the comédiennes; Dorothy Hammond, a very pretty leading woman; and that excellent actress, Annie Adams, mother of Maude. Among the men he had two leading men then as now of equal rank—William Courtenay and Vincent Serrano; also the popular Jack Barnes, English actor; Ernest Lawford, who had been featured in some Frohman productions; that excellent American comedian, Louis Payne; and that almost last of the fine old American gentleman type, the late John G. Saville. The remaining members of the company in the minor rôles were more than adequate. C. F. turned this cast over to me, with the Savoy Theatre, where rehearsals would be uninterrupted. There was nobody to replace in the company, no revisions or corrections to be made in the text, and C. F. never came near us until the night of our dress rehearsal.

It will be interesting to record a typical Frohman dress rehearsal. He sometimes departed from his rule, but his custom was to have such a rehearsal with nobody in front but the author and himself. Even an assistant director or a man who had held a book and was supposed to have some interest in the setting was not allowed to come in front of the curtain. I remember such an intrusion by a perfectly justified stage-manager who came into a box of the Criterion Theatre when we were doing "The Other Girl."

C. F. said to him, "What are you doing there?"

"I want to look at the scene, Mr. Frohman."

"We'll tell you about that," and the functionary disappeared.

Our dress rehearsal for "Mrs. Leffingwell's Boots" was at the Savoy. C. F. and I were alone. The presentation proceeded exactly as a first night, with every formality observed.

When the first act was over he said to me, "These people aren't acting."

"They're not?"

"No, they're living!"

It was a pretty compliment to the company, and I tried to steal some of it for the author; but that was entirely a mental process. When our last curtain fell, C. F. had it taken up again; the company was called on the stage and in a few heartening and sincere phrases he told them how highly he estimated their work. There was no need at our first performance to reverse his opinion. I like to recur in my thoughts to that engagement and to that happy family of players, and I like to write about it. Those ideal conditions are what every player dreams of when he comes into the theatre and what every playwright has in mind when he sets down a line. Nothing is so health-giving and beneficial as this full, unimpeded expression and interpretation.

In "The Earl of Pawtucket," of which I have written above, D'Orsay's success was marked. When he had played it well into the third year and there was only what was called the small time open to him he grew anxious for another vehicle, and felt that he could make better monetary arrangements elsewhere than he then had with La Shelle. Mr. Frohman had revised his measure of D'Orsay and now regarded him as of stellar magnitude. I was commissioned to write him a successor to "Pawtucket." D'Orsay's ambition made him ask also for a more substantial purpose in the play. The first version of "The Embassy Ball" was, in consequence, a four-act play, mainly attempting comedy, but with a quite serious note at the end of its third act. Our first night was in New Haven. Mr. Frohman could not attend. He said he would base his opinion of the play entirely upon my telegraphic report of its reception, and not upon the notices or opinions he would get from others.

I wired him, "A dignified frost."

There is little value in going into the reasons for this result. One of them, however, has interest. The end of the third act was a well-defined conflict between a sinister interest in the play and D'Orsay, who had the heroic element. The climax of this conflict was dramatized by D'Orsay's tearing from some diplomatic record the leaf that was the vital issue. This he did under the rhetorical encouragement of the character played by that excellent comedian, Harry Harwood. D'Orsay complained that his support at the serious moment was not sufficient. There was some justice in his claim. Harwood contended that there wasn't material in his lines to evoke the applause that we expected. In my own opinion the fate of the piece was so well settled that whether Harwood was right or we were right could not affect the ultimate result. And Mr. Harwood's effectiveness along the lines of his own work as a comedian is too well known to require anybody's reinforcement.

At Hartford one night I tried on Harwood's wig, and he generously consented to my going on for his character in that performance. With the different treatment of the stump-speech material the act got the calls that it potentially held. The value of this was only my own assay of the stuff, because Harwood's association with the enterprise was worth much more than the material in question.

Frohman saw the piece in Philadelphia and was depressed. The lay reader should understand the interests at stake. To fail then was to throw an entire company out of employment in November; to give in a measure a black eye to the reputation of the star and to leave on the hands of the management an expensive production, including scenery and costumes and a fair stock of printing. Despite its feebleness as theatrical text the play had shown us that D'Orsay was more acceptable in his proper comedy work than he was as a pseudo-leading man.

As C. F. and I leaned over the bulkhead of the Chestnut Street Theatre I recalled my experiences in rewriting the Crane plays "For Money" and "The Governor of Kentucky," and lesser work on the unsigned scripts that C. F. himself had called me in to patch or carpenter. I thought I saw my way to make a three-act comedy of what we had. I told him so. My family was in Paris. I was a bit uneasy about them. I said if he would lay off the company for four weeks that I would jump over to Paris and back, and I thought we could salvage all the investment enumerated, with the exception of the four weeks' time held in the theatres. C. F. was delighted with the proposal. D'Orsay and I took the same steamer for the other side, he going ostensibly to see some member of his family supposed to be ill. I wrote on the boat and worked rapidly in Paris.

In three weeks after leaving New York, D'Orsay and

I again took a same steamer for America, where we were two in a total of five first-cabin passengers. On the boat I finished the revision. Two days after we landed we had script and parts typed and began rehearsals, with that delightful actor, Forrest Robinson, added to the cast and associated with Harwood. The three-act version of "The Embassy Ball," a purely farcical attempt, was successful. We played it two years.

Paris lacks the ocean, but with this exception it has as many suburban enticements as New York, and the Parisian is as accustomed to running away from the city for a little one or two day vacation as any metropolitan that we know. To change the ideas—*changer les idées*, as they say—is with them a frequent act of mental sanitation. We made a party of some twelve or fifteen Americans, children included, who were at the pretty hamlet of Montigny-sur-Loing in the middle of April in 1906 on one of these adopted *vacances*. The terrace of the Hôtel Vanne Rouge has its retaining wall of stone, washed by the slow waters of the River Loing that meanders by, held almost in lakelike retardation by the *vanne*, or watergate, that accumulates them for the near-by mill. This little terrace, some fifty by fifty feet of gravelled level, with its circular tables of sheet-iron and weatherproof chairs, sets like a stage to the low and theatrical façade of the toy hotel, where by a fair jump from the ground one can almost catch the sill of the second-story window.

On Wednesday the trippers had gone home and our American colony had the place to ourselves. A very obvious bridal couple came that evening; the young man with the French whiskers of the period, the bride in the attractive and now antiquated costume of the date, both oblivious to the strangers who were speaking English.

After a little rowboat trip in the twilight the couple disappeared. We were at *café au lait* on the terrace on Thursday morning. The children at the balustrade were feeding the swans when the small diamond-paned comic-opera windows of the upper room opened and there appeared the bridegroom in a suit of lavender pajamas whose newly laundered and utterly unruffled condition invited attention.

Doctor Tom Robbins at our table said: "See those immaculate pajamas on the new groom!"

All looked and some one remarked, "Yes, a new groom sleeps clean"; an amusing line, but not so tenacious as alone to fix the Thursday morning of that nineteenth day of April. The event that did that was the arrival of the morning paper relating the catastrophe in San Francisco, then called an earthquake, but by common consent since referred to as the fire.

One of our laughing party was Mrs. Chase, who had been a Miss Mizner, sister of Wilson and Addison Mizner, Californians. Mr. Chase was still in the States, and the reports of the devastation included territory in which the family had important financial and sentimental interests. Other Californians were in our party, with parents, brothers, and sisters in the stricken city. The blow made everything else forgotten; not only those directly and personally affected but all the Americans knew their vacation was over and their stations were at the lines of quickest communication.

It is rather fine to remember the promptness with which the Americans in Paris acted at that time. The American Chamber of Commerce assembled the next morning upon a call from its president printed in the Paris New York *Herald*. It was a crowded meeting, attended not only by the members but by many sojourners and transients. There was some little personal information, not much; the cables were blocked. Men of prominence and power addressed the company, and running true to form after the American manner the first definite action by the chamber was an appropriation and a volunteer subscription. Thousands of dollars were immediately pledged. The mayor of San Francisco was telegraphed. When, after a period of two or three days, the rather proud but fairly self-reliant reply was received that outside subscriptions were not needed, the American chamber met again and the money was diverted to a loan fund available to such Californians as found themselves in Paris with their communications cut or their sources of supply destroyed. These were principally students in the art schools, the Sorbonne, the Beaux-Arts, and the musical institutions. But how fine the spirit, how admirable that highly cultivated ethical capacity to respond! How thrilling its demonstration! It was, of course, a comparatively small reaction, but it was very like the stir that went over all America that sixth day in April, 1917, when the resolution of Congress decided that we were in the war.

CHAPTER XXIII

SOURCES OF INSPIRATION

One of the delightful conditions in the home life in Paris, at least from the view-point of an American, is the attitude of the domestic servants to the enterprise. Paris is divided into *arrondissements*, or, as we would call them, wards, each with its own mayor and police and domestic courts and administration. In somewhat similar division, each neighborhood has its little four corners of shops that supply the neighborhood. There are the café, the baker, the grocer, and the butcher. To these shops each morning the cook, after the breakfast hour, goes for her purchases of the day. The shopkeepers very frankly allow her 10 per cent on the day's order and pay it to her then in cash. There is no attempt to conceal this and there is no way to get around it. If the mistress of the house thinks to get the supplies at a lower price or get them at the same price and to receive the commission that is paid to the cook she finds herself going contrary to established custom and badly mistaken. The cook's commissions run on all supplies bought that pass through her department and are in any way affected by her art. All other supplies, such as wines, candies, cakes, and candles, bought outside, pay a percentage to the waitress.

The receipt of this commission of 10 per cent to each of these functionaries results in the production of a perennial amiability. In America, in a modest family, the announcement of a projected dinner-party is apt to create some resentment. It is never the basis of increased happiness, and too frequently repeated is likely to call forth a demand for an increase in wages or a maid's notice of intention to quit. Either of these reactions is more apt to be brought about in Paris by a failure to have parties or a practice of having even too few of them.

Another feature of this buying by the domestics is its real economy. The French *cuisinière* who needs a bit of onion to flavor a soup will buy one spring onion, and the greengrocer makes no objection to selling it. Or she may buy one button from a bulb of garlic, or get a sprig of parsley the size of a teaspoon. These intimate ingredients in America are bought by the bunch, or ten cents' worth in the minimum, a small portion of them used and the remainder permitted to get stale and be thrown out.

Perhaps it was an appreciation of these economies that induced us to bring with us from France, when we finally came back, our waitress, Cecile. Perhaps it was because the children had taken a liking to her matronly attentions. At any rate, we found ourselves installed with Cecile in the middle distance of our domestic field at East Hampton in our first summer after our return. The cook was an Irishwoman, between whose temperament and Cecile's there seemed to be no friction whatever. The up-stairs maid was a German girl whom we had brought down from New Rochelle. She spoke no French and her English was fragmentary. Cecile spoke and understood only French.

The collision between these representatives from the opposite sides of the distant Rhine occurred in our pantry on a busy day when there was a house-party and some additional guests from the East Hampton colony.

I never got all the merits of the discussion, but I remember vividly it ended by Lizzie hitting Cecile on the forehead almost between the eyes with a raw egg. Cecile understood the raw egg and declined to remove any of the evidence until she had showed herself in her consequent plight to my wife and me.

Our previous experience with the two girls was sufficient to tell us that this was the culmination, and after a brisk but earnest talk on the back porch Lizzie got her valise and the chauffeur took her to the 2.13 train. When Cecile learned that Lizzie had gone she came into the dining-room and demanded to know if madame had permitted *l'allemande* to depart *"sans que je sois soulagée"*— "without me being soothed."

This end of the hostilities, with no treaty as to reparations, wore on Cecile's mind and she soon left for France. I escorted her from East Hampton one hundred and one miles to New York, and then through the city to the steamer *Savoie*. On the way I interpreted for her at four or five shoe-stores, in each of which she indulged her hope to find a pair of shoes for herself with *la nuance de la coupe de ceux de madame*—the shade of the cut of those of madame. We might ultimately have found them but that the French steamship line had a way of refusing to hold a departing boat for anybody.

Disappointed but *gaie*, Cecile went up the gangplank, which trembled like the drawbridge under the famed flight of Marmion, and into an agitated group of sailors whose voluble though informal but competing welcome promised spirited and articulate entertainment for the homeward trip. Perhaps that East Hampton egg started Cecile upon discoveries relatively as important as those following the one Columbus discussed with Isabella.

Down at East Hampton for the summer, one of our first callers in the woods was Mr. John Drew, who motored over from his summer home near the dunes. The talk of the San Francisco earthquake reminded him of a letter he had recently received from his nephew, Jack Barrymore. Jack had been in San Francisco the night of those shocks and that fire. He wrote of his experiences briefly but dramatically. Uncle John had the letter. At the first shock Jack had risen from his bed at the Palace Hotel. Another violent lurch had thrown him against a door, which had given way and let him fall upon the rim of the bathtub, hurting his side. He soon found himself in the street with an ill-assorted collection of apparel. The next day he met the other members of the Willie Collier Company, with which at that time he was playing. He and the other men of the company were taken in charge by the military and forced to help clear the streets by piling bricks.

I was entirely taken up with the dramatic side of the description; but Uncle John, who has always persisted in a comic view of his avuncular possessions, smiled somewhat sardonically as he said: "Yes, it took a convulsion of Nature to get him into a bathtub and the United States Army to make him work."

The thought of John Barrymore as a supporting member of the company of Willie Collier, then, and his present stellar position in the public esteem is indicative of the rapid changes always at work and perhaps more evident in the theatre than elsewhere. Among the successes of that year was Fritzi Scheff in "Mlle. Modiste," the book by Henry Blossom and music by Victor Herbert. Fritzi Scheff had just married my good and gentle friend, John Fox, Jr., the author of "A Mountain Europa," "The

Kentuckians," "The Little Shepherd of Kingdom Come," and other books. At the Lyceum Theatre "The Lion and the Mouse" was in its second year. "The Music Master," with David Warfield, was playing at the Bijou. Both of these plays were written by Charles Klein, who sank with Charles Frohman on the *Lusitania*. Klein was notably a dramatizer of popular themes. His art was largely the newspaper transferred to the stage. "The Lion and the Mouse" and "The Gamblers" were each a theatrical view of big business, and "The Third Degree" was a presentation of the police methods of the time. A young writer claiming attention with his second play, "The Chorus Lady," in which Rose Stahl was appearing at the Garrick Theatre, was James Forbes, now in the front rank of his profession and having to his credit "The Famous Mrs. Fair," in many respects the best of all the post-war plays. Henry Miller and Margaret Anglin were having a gratifying success in William Vaughan Moody's play, "The Great Divide," at the Princess Theatre. Henry Arthur Jones' "Hypocrites" was at the Hudson. Eleanor Robson was at the Liberty Theatre in "Nurse Marjorie" by Israel Zangwill, who had had a respectful hearing with his "Children of the Ghetto," played a year or two earlier. John Drew was playing Pinero's sombre, rectangular, but well-made "His House in Order." Marie Cahill was starring in "Marrying Mary" at Daly's, with the tuneful score by Silvio Hein. Alice Hegan Rice's "Mrs. Wiggs of the Cabbage Patch," later to be accepted in London as the typical American picture, was at the New York Theatre. Among the lighter pieces were Hattie Williams' production of "The Little Cherub," with Ivan Caryll's music. Lillian Russell at the Savoy in "Barbara's Millions," and

Thomas W. Ross at Wallack's in George Cohan's "Popularity." These, with two or three other offerings, were the theatrical presentations of that year.

Writing of Klein and Blossom and Ivan Caryll, all of whom are gone, takes my mind to one of our most usual meeting-places, the anteroom of Charles Frohman. Other dramatists whom one might encounter there and who are now with the majority were Henry Guy Carleton, Harry P. Mawson, the gifted Clyde Fitch, Paul Potter, of whom I have written, and Haddon Chambers, among the most likable of all the English dramatists. To-day, in trying to get the name of Mr. Owen Hall, who had written the book of "The Little Cherub," for which Ivan Caryll furnished the music, I telephoned the Empire Theatre. Peter Mason, the colored boy there in charge of the manuscripts, would be the one most likely to know. I couldn't remember the Empire Theatre when I hadn't seen Peter there. Peter told me to-day that he has been in this playhouse twenty-five years. He came first as a water boy, working down-stairs. Mr. Alf Hayman had promoted him to the anteroom on the office floor, where Charles Frohman, seeing him, had taken him on his personal staff. Frohman always had a great affection for him. Everybody's sympathy for Peter was because he had come with only one lung from a hospital and continued to have occasional hemorrhages. Everybody around the theatre spoke of him with pity. It was only a question of days when Peter would be worn out. He might drop off at any minute. But those men who took such an apprehensive interest in him, stout Alf Hayman and his stouter brother, Al, have both gone; Tommy Shea, the energetic young Irishman, for so many years in the box-office, is dead; Sam Meyers, ruddy and

CARICATURES FROM MR. THOMAS'S SKETCH BOOK. 1891–93.

1. Sydney Rosenfeld.　2. General George Sheridan.　3. William Marion Reedy.　4. Cyril Scott.　5. Henry Guy Carleton.
No. 3 is by Frederic Remington.　Nos. 1, 2, 4, and 5 are by Augustus Thomas.

genial publicity man and fixture about the place, one of Peter's patrons and sympathizers, is dead; Frohman went down with the *Lusitania;* none of the old force survives. But the colored boy, Peter Mason, with his one lung, is still, in 1922, the factotum of the theatre.

Soon after our return from France I had an experience which was important to me and which may have significance for people engaged in writing for the theatre. At least it will have if I can tell it in a way that will convey my own attitude toward the question it contains. Mr. Belasco had, at the theatre that then bore his name and is now the Republic, a drama of the California mining days called "The Girl of the Golden West," in which Miss Blanche Bates was featured. The story of this play, if I may indicate it by simply touching its structural features, is of a Western sheriff somewhat older than a girl with whom he is in love. The girl is his superior in social quality. Her fancy is taken by a more modern and modish man, a newcomer in the locality, who turns out to be a criminal. It is the sheriff's duty to arrest him. The man takes refuge in the house of the girl. She hides him and when the sheriff comes denies any knowledge of him. The sheriff is about to leave when a bit of evidence attracts his attention to the hiding-place; the man is forced to come forth; the sheriff, out of consideration for the girl and contrary to his duty, permits him to escape.

This is an excellent play, full of color of the epoch that it presents. Some of my friends on the press had written to me that it was manifestly a reproduction of my play of "In Mizzoura," written some thirteen years before. The story of "In Mizzoura," again telling by high lights in its construction, is of a Western sheriff somewhat older

than a girl with whom he is in love. The girl is his superior in social quality. Her fancy is taken by a more modern and modish man, a newcomer in the locality, who turns out to be a criminal. It is the sheriff's duty to arrest him. The man takes refuge in the house of the girl. She hides him and when the sheriff comes denies any knowledge of him. The sheriff is about to leave when a bit of evidence attracts his attention to the hiding-place; the man is forced to come forth. The sheriff, out of consideration for the girl and contrary to his duty, permits him to escape.

These identical situations in that perfect sequence could easily have been cited and in a reasonable court made to have in my own case a proprietary claim. But there had been a similar experience, somewhat earlier and with an equal resemblance, which had taught me consideration. My play of "Arizona" dealt with a young army officer who, trying to shield a woman, placed himself liable to a charge of theft. He resigned from the army, went West, became a cowboy, later met his old enemy of the earlier days, and in a quarrel with him the enemy was shot. That the hero had not killed him was proved by the fatal bullet being of another caliber than that of the hero's gun, and he was acquitted. Mr. Edwin Milton Royle some time later wrote a play with those relationships and that sequence of events which he called "The Squaw Man." One agent and one manager told me that upon the reading of it they had declined to consider it, feeling that it too closely resembled "Arizona."

Now I happened to have seen Mr. Royle's play when, so to speak, it was in the cradle. He produced at the Lambs Club a little piece in which an Englishman living with a squaw wife in the West was called upon by a so-

licitor from London who came for the purpose of telling
him that he had inherited a title, and, although he cared
nothing for it himself, it properly belonged to his little
half-breed son, whose mother was the squaw wife. The
squaw wife, overhearing and understanding enough of
this to know that she was standing in the way of both
the husband and the little half-breed boy for whom title
and fortune were waiting in England, killed herself. It
was a tragic one-act play, and Mr. Royle was advised
by everybody to elaborate it into a four-act drama. He
was obliged thereupon to think of his hero leaving England for sufficient reason, which, nevertheless, should be
nothing against his character; and by the dramatist's
formula he had him leaving for the sake of a woman,
and had him leaving under a cloud. The simplest cloud
for an army officer to quit under was a charge of mis-
appropriation of funds, and in the Wild West relations
that followed for the purpose of the play he had the fight
and the exculpation of the hero by the swift and simple
evidence of a bullet not fitting his gun.

I had used that device some years before in "Arizona."
But I didn't invent it. It was a bit of material evidence
in more than one Western inquest, and the fact of fitting
the bullet to the gun of a man accused of killing was one
of the first steps in legal identification familiar to every
reporter. And Mr. Royle was forced into the construction of his drama by most natural and logical sequences.

When Mr. Belasco wanted to write Blanche Bates
into a mining-camp a sheriff was the most likely lover;
and the most logical rival, in order to establish conflict,
would be a man who was rival not only in the affections
of the girl but an opponent in the line of the sheriff's
duty; that would make him a criminal. And if the sheriff

once got after that criminal any dramatist, in order to hold his people of interest together, would probably think of the criminal taking refuge in the home of the girl. If somebody had come along and pointed out the resemblance of these situations to those in "In Mizzoura," it would, nevertheless, have been Mr. Belasco's duty to go ahead with his play in its new color and in the dialect of its epoch and write his story. I thought he had done this in such fine fashion that I regarded his play as a valuable exhibit of how the mind of a trained dramatist works when once given a strong and stimulating suggestion to start back from and build a sequence of events. I speak of these two examples because the theatre is filled with their like. So are the other arts. There are five notable pictures of the "Last Supper" by painters of the Renaissance, each valuable principally because it shows the temperament of the artist working with his material.

The courts are sometimes burdened with questions of this kind, and it takes a wise judge to see where the individual right ceases and the common right in an idea begins. I remember reading that some Chicago judge had decided upon apparently sufficient evidence that Francis Bacon had written the plays of William Shakespeare. A Chicago judge decided that a citizen of that place had given Edmond Rostand the idea for his romantic poetical play, "Cyrano de Bergerac," apparently oblivious of the fact that Savinien Cyrano de Bergerac, born in 1620 at the château of that name in Périgord, was a French writer and duellist, had the personal idiosyncrasies that were the identifying marks of orginality in the work of the Chicago author; had himself written plays and poems and had already suggested by his life

and writings "Micromegas," a philosophic romance by Voltaire, and "Gulliver's Travels" by Dean Swift.

A year or two later than the time of which I am writing I was called as an expert witness in a suit at Washington, where a newspaper man somewhat new to the theatre was suing a dramatist who had never seen the newspaper man's libretto, charging that the second libretto was taken from it. One resemblance was that both books had two elderly couples and two juvenile couples in love. The judge thought this not so important when it was pointed out to him that a majority of operas, especially comic operas, were made up of double quartets. It was a musical rather than a literary requirement.

At a risk of being tiresome on the subject, let me relate an instance of this year 1922. A few weeks ago at the request of their author I wrote an introduction to four little plays by Mr. Percy Knight that are to be printed in a single volume. One of those plays has for its subject the burial of the unknown soldier in London, and deals in poetic fashion with the meeting of a girl and an English veteran who come to the palings of the graveyard, both believing that they knew the man. The girl has brought some flowers for a dead sweetheart; the soldier is morally certain that the unknown was his pal.

This little scene had been played in one of the Lambs' gambols. At a more recent gambol Mr. Emmett Corrigan had a sketch which I did not see, but which was reported in committee as being a dialogue between a man and wife in America who have lost a son. The topic is the burial of the unknown soldier at Washington. For some reason the father feels that the unknown boy is theirs, and upon the breast of the mother whom he has en-

deavored to console he pins a star. A very experienced
and indignant dramatist was proposing that Mr. Corrigan
should be disciplined for this appropriation of an idea.
When asked to give an opinion upon the propriety of
such a procedure my answer was that the unknown soldier's official burial in France and in England and in
America was for the very purpose of honoring all unidentified and giving to everybody who had a loved one
among the missing the faint comfort that might lie in
the slight belief that the unknown was his or her missing
boy. Poems had been written about it, and thousands
of editorials and thousands of patriotic and memorial
speeches had been made on the theme. The wonder
was not that an English playwright and another American playwright should have chosen the subject but that
hundreds had not done so.

There are so many starting-points for writing plays
that if one were to name all of them it would be a real
draft on attention. A good play is a completed thing,
with a beginning, a middle, and an end, and should make
some disposition of the considerations it raises and presents. Along this trajectory, this line of travel which
would be rather improperly but most effectively dia-
gramed by a circle, one can take almost any of its three
hundred and sixty degrees as a starting-point.

I have written in these chapters of beginning a play
with only the actor, Mr. Nat Goodwin, in mind; getting
a character that would fit him, a set of circumstances in
which the character would be put, and a series of situations through which he would pass in that environment.
I have suggested somewhat of the same process in speaking of "Pawtucket" for D'Orsay. Earlier I wrote of
"The Burglar," made from Mrs. Burnett's story, in

which the burglar is confronted by the ingenuousness
of a child. By making that child his own daughter the
meeting itself became a situation, which is another way
of starting a play.

Sometimes one takes a theme, a question acceptable
in the public mind, and by making it articulate, and
selecting characters expressive of it and affected by it,
uses the theme as his starting-point. Often the dramatist takes a story ready-made but in narrative form,
as was "The Soldiers of Fortune," by Richard Harding
Davis, eliminates the descriptions, arranges its dramatic
situations in proper sequence and crescendo, supplies
what other situations are needed, puts the whole expression into dialogue, and thereby achieves his play.

There have been many pictures that have inspired
plays. In one of the Paris salons of the early 70's there
was a canvas showing a wrecked boudoir in a château
in which a band of vandal German officers were carous-
ing. Paul Potter took that as the inspiration for one of
his acts in "The Conquerors." When Maurice Barrymore dramatized somebody's novel of "Roaring Dick"
he made a stage setting and a situation from another
salon picture called "The Wolf in the Sheepfold," which
showed a bland and unsuspecting husband introducing
to his wife a lady-killing officer in uniform. The group
was on a portico shaded by a large Japanese umbrella.

I have an impression that some of Hogarth's "Rake's
Progress" got into plays. But I don't recall any complete series of pictures used as the skeleton for a full
evening's play with the exception of Charles Dana Gibson's "Education of Mr. Pipp." That was a set of two-
page cartoons satirizing the little accidental, limited, un-
assertive American nouveau millionaire and his large,

aggressive, dominant, and overriding wife and the off-spring of this counterbalancing mixture, two lovely daughters. The daughters were the first of the famous Gibson girls of the middle 90's, with the crowning puffed-and-pompadoured hair, long necks, the stately bearing, and the royally draped costumes. When Gibson had made one or two of these pictures their reception created a demand, and he was obliged to show his family of Pipps in various situations and with occasional new acquaint-ances. When he had exhausted the round of fashionable entertainments in America and the stories had still to go on he carried the Pipp family to England, where their money got them into the fringe of the nobility, and later took them to Paris, where they were most unmercifully fleeced and imposed upon.

Without setting up to be the supreme court on mat-ters artistic in America, I will venture the opinion that Charles Dana Gibson is our most gifted and accomplished illustrator. There is a generation of young men that have followed and learned from him, and many of these have each an individual touch quite as agreeable in its way as the technic of Gibson. Some of them have his vigor of line and precision of execution; some have his understanding of character and his capacity to interpret it. But I know of none who has all these qualities, nor in Gibson's degree. Nor do I think of one that has his wide and deep understanding of the human family.

In the old New Rochelle days there used to hang over Fred Remington's buffet in the dining-room of his home on Webster Avenue an original drawing of Gibson's on a card eighteen by twenty-four inches. This had served as the original for a reduction in an early number of *Life*. In it two men stand at a sideboard. The host is a white-haired, white-mustached, amiable, high-bred, cultured, æsthetical-appearing person, slightly less than at his best at his apparent age of sixty because of his concession to a convivial temperament. He is well nourished but not overfed, twinkling, tolerant, human. He still holds a decanter from which he has just filled his own glass, and is directing his attention to his guest, who holds a glass of port. The guest is a Protestant bishop in the black cloth and neckerchief of his kind, rotund, sleek, artificial, uncertain, dissembling, sanctimonious, gluttonous, apprehensive. One man is so manifestly the host radiating cheer and the other the occasional guest surreptitiously accepting a prohibited but habitual ration that it is a delight to look at the drawing and see these characteristics which the master draftsman has understood, deduced, set down, and communicated with the magic of a few strokes of the pen.

To Remington himself, endeavoring character portrayal with no such subtlety, and to a man writing for the theatre who would have needed a scene of fifteen minutes, to communicate all that Gibson put into his single sketch, the drawing was a never-diminishing delight. In Gibson's character sketches of the Pipp family, and the friends and satellites that they attracted, there were exponents of every fine and nearly every despicable emotion; not only the broader Hogarthian elemental passions but the very shades and nuances into which any psychological spectrum could dissolve them.

It seemed to me that to translate these visible expressions into words, not the descriptive and narrative array that would make a novel but the etched and vital kind that would put them into a play, would be agreeable employment. Nothing that I remember writing was

more fun to do. The three-act comedy followed closely
the vicissitudes of the Pipp family as set down by Gibson.
That experienced comedian, the late Digby Bell, gave a
faithful and understanding interpretation of Pipp, and
the other characters of Gibson were closely realized by
the men and women that manager Kirke La Shelle was
able to find in the profession. Of course, the strong character parts more nearly realized the pictures. Two such
goddesses as we needed to impersonate the Gibson girl
and that long, rangy, athletic type of young man that
Gibson popularized at that time were harder to find.
The young men existed plentifully enough in America,
but they were in the engineering camps and on the fron-
tiers and directing great enterprises and not learning
lines in the theatre. The Gibson girls were also otherwise employed, and not numerously in the theatre or
the agencies. We were fortunate, however, in Janet
Beecher, then an unknown ingénue, and Miss Marion
Draughn for the girls. We had an ideal Mrs. Pipp, a
sterling actress by the name of Mrs. Eugene Jepson.
Gibson's heroic young men were well realized by Robert
Warwick, then playing his first engagement in America
after a fine tutelage in France, and by Mr. Frederick
Courtenay, younger and taller than his talented brother,
William Courtenay, still prominently in the public eye.
The rest of the cast, though actors then and now less
prominent than those named, were adequate.

Mr. Nat Goodwin at that time was living with his
third wife, Maxine Elliott, in a house on Riverside Drive.
Miss Elliott, who had a sense of the artistic, had 'remodelled this little house by taking out the partition
which divided its narrow drawing-room from the hallway, throwing all into one apartment, with the staircase

frankly mounting, English fashion, to the next story, and a corresponding staircase under this descending from the parlor level to the street. This, adopted for Pipp, made a most amusing set, the only one of its kind I ever saw in the theatre.

I am tempted here to tell a little comicality of Nat's. We were alone in the parlor. I was admiring a pretty landscape on the wall, a canvas some fifteen by eighteen inches, then the property of the third Mrs. Goodwin, as it had formerly been the property of the second Mrs. Goodwin.

As I expressed my admiration Nat said with the little stutter which he protectively assumed when he wanted to advertise a comic utterance: "Yes, that p-p-picture cost me thirty-five hundred dollars."

"Really?" It looked good, but not worth all that.

Nat continued, "Yes. Th-th-thirty-five hundred dollars—two thousand the first time I bought it and fifteen hundred the second."

In the part of Mr. Pipp, Bell, with his excellent support, was a success. He played the piece that season and the better part of the two years that followed.

In four years I had written in fairly close succession the comedies, "The Earl of Pawtucket," "The Education of Mr. Pipp," "The Other Girl," "Mrs. Leffingwell's Boots," "The Embassy Ball," and "De Lancey." I felt a real inclination to try something more serious. Among my papers was the little one-act play, "A Constitutional Point," made in 1890 for Mr. Palmer. Shortly after that year, perhaps in '92 or '93, my neighbor at New Rochelle, the late Henry Loomis Nelson, showed me a letter from Mark Twain refusing to write a short story for *Harper's* because Mark Twain had found "that a short story was a novel in the cradle, which, if taken out and occasionally fondled, would grow into a full-sized book." Partly on that hint, my one-act play was occasionally taken from its cradle and caressed. Mr. Palmer had refused the play because there is a maxim in the theatre that no material is useful there until it has served as subject-matter for all other literary forms and been made familiar to the public through poetry, fiction, lectures, and reportorial and editorial comment.

XXIV

"THE WITCHING HOUR" AND OTHERS

During the years since 1890 there had been an increasing public interest in telepathy, and the public's information had grown. In my own mind my playlet had also grown and was now a four-act play. Before wasting time on its actual writing, however, I accepted a chance to have the one-act piece played to a private audience of some two hundred men in the Lambs Club; and as the little play contained what was most diaphanous and attenuated in the whole story, if such an audience, entirely lacking the feminine element, would accept the fable, the remainder of the venture would be up to the skill of the dramatist. In the club, with the late Edward Abeles playing the woman's part and Forrest Robinson playing the part of the old judge, the little piece made a decided impression.

I have said earlier, I think when talking of Mr. Paul Potter, that plays are constructed backward. Paul Potter was the first person to bring that to my attention. The playwright doesn't take his pen in hand and begin placidly to write dialogue which develops without his intention into something dramatic. He starts with a dramatic situation which has a possibility in the theatre of some strong effect and tries to find for that the immediate cause, and for that cause one still further back in origin, and it is in that fashion that his construction grows. Very often this effect, which is the starting-point in the development of a story, can be expressed in one act, and it is not uncommon for a playwright to try out his idea in tabloid shape. If it has sufficient fibre and power to make a big scene of the play he may then develop it. Denman Thompson's "Old Homestead" began in that shape. "Muldoon's Picnic" was once a one-act vaudeville skit. Mr. Royle's "The Squaw Man," as told earlier, was done at the Lambs as a sketch. So was John Willard's "The Cat and the Canary," one of the reigning successes of 1922. My own plays, "The Burglar," "Alabama," "The Harvest Moon," "As a Man Thinks," "Rio Grande," and "The Copperhead" were each at first one act.

The one-act play, "A Constitutional Point," had grown out of my experiences with Bishop, the thought-reader, of whom I have written in an earlier chapter. Bishop was so constituted that by throwing himself into a receptive condition, which he called autohypnotic, he was impressed by thoughts of other people. He didn't see these thoughts as words, but as pictures, unless the thought was about a word in a book, when his percept would, of course, be that particular typed word and the surrounding print on its page. This power had come to be called telepathy. Oliver Wendell Holmes had written concerning it in his "Autocrat of the Breakfast Table," except that he called it cerebricity. Somewhat later Mark Twain, writing of his personal experiences in association with its phenomena, had referred to it as mental telegraphy. Doctor Thomas Hudson, in 1893, published his "The Law of Psychic Phenomena," the first of a series of five books on telepathy and related subjects. In one of these, in making an argument for immortality, he raises the question whether telepathy

might not be a means of communication between a dis-
embodied entity, or spirit, as commonly called, and a
person still living. I think it was this hint that brought
to my mind "A Newport Legend," the poem by Bret
Harte, about an old house at Newport, haunted. A
young girl in the colonial days died of a broken heart
in this house. It seems that her sweetheart sailed away
and left her. Bret Harte tells of her coming back:

"And ever since then when the clock strikes two,
    She walks unbidden from room to room,
And the air is filled, that she passes through,
    With a subtle, sad perfume.

The delicate odor of mignonette,
    The ghost of a dead-and-gone bouquet,
Is all that tells of her story; yet
    Could she think of a sweeter way?"

The poet's way of suggesting the idea is so much more
acceptable than a scientific one that I used those two
verses, which an old judge reads to another, as my way
to introduce the subject, and just after the reading had
him say:

"Beautiful to have a perfume suggest her. I suppose
it appeals to me especially because I used to know a girl
who was foolishly fond of mignonette."

So that when the daughter of the judge's old sweetheart comes to talk about her mother and brings a forgotten letter of the judge's from among the time-stained
papers that the mother left it seems to him somewhat
more than coincidence; and when the daughter has gone,
after a pathetic appeal for her son, who is under sentence
of death, and the old judge, alone, gets from the old letter the remembered odor of mignonette, the Bret Harte

lines come back to him, and he fancies there has been an influence upon him from the other side of the grave.

This little act I decided to make the second and not the third act of a four-act play, because, moving as it had been to the audience when it was tried in its detached presentation, I felt there should be something more positively dramatic as a climax for a play. Casting about for that, I encountered the subject of hypnotism. Telepathy and hypnotism are not especially related, except that telepathic communication is clearer under hypnosis. While Hudson and others had been writing of telepathy and of the therapeutic value of suggestion to hypnotized patients, a religious and ethical opposition to the practice had found expression in some notable protests. One of these, written in a tone of warning and with a claim to esoteric knowledge, called an act of hypnotism a great psychological crime. It implied that the hypnotist, once in control of the thought of his subject, was never freed of that connecting bond and that both individuals passed into eternity held together by it. This was a little deep and somewhat terrorizing for my use in the play, but I thought I'd be on safe ground in suggesting that the force was not a very good one for the layman to play with. In thinking also of telepathic influence, the control of the thought as well as the will of another presented an equal responsibility. I therefore made these two ethical considerations the theme and overtone of what I was projecting. The result of that, not to bore a lay reader with technical considerations of a playwright, was to give me a rather fine old character in sympathy with my contentions and a vigorous and indifferent one opposed to him and to convince whom would be the business of the play. I therefore had theme, definite direction and some situations. Despite the fact that I had been thinking and reading and having experiences in these subjects for something like eighteen years since my trip with Bishop, I spent another year getting helpful information from professional hypnotists and clairvoyants. I speak of the time thus spent on this play in contrast to some of the hasty efforts like "Mrs. Leffingwell's Boots." ·Perhaps there is a commensurate difference in the calibers.

When the play was done I read it to Charles Frohman. Nobody could have less scientific information on the subjects than he had, and his reception of it would be a fair indication of what an average audience might do. The reading was under rather test conditions too. The night was oppressively warm. C. F. was in his apartment, then on the top floor of Sherry's old building, Forty-fourth Street and Fifth Avenue, now remodelled into business offices. He had on a cotton shirt and a pair of trousers. He sat cross-legged in a big leather chair. As I finished each act his only comment was, "Go on." At the conclusion of the play there was a wait that filled me with apprehension.

At length he said: "That's almost too beautiful to bear."

The language was so unlike C. F.—in fact, the idea was so unlike him—that I thought for a moment there was mockery about it. But he was in earnest.

He added: "When shall we do it?"

We discussed and decided upon the men and women we would like for the company, and I left in an elated mood. I saw him again the next day to talk production. His enthusiasm for the play had not subsided. A week later he sent for me. We met in his office in the Empire

Theatre Building. He was embarrassed and unhappy, as he had to tell me that he had changed his mind about the piece. He had given the script to his brother, Daniel Frohman, to read, and Daniel had told him that the author of the play was evidently crazy. It was as impossible for me to argue the point with C. F. as it would have been for one to lift himself by his boot-straps. A crazy man can't act as both his own alienist and attorney without being an unattractive client. I met Daniel Frohman a day later. In the friendliest way he answered:

"Yes, I did say that. But I meant, of course, only in the treatment of that subject. Forget it, Gus; go out West and give us one of your wholesome 'Arizonas.'"

I never blamed Daniel Frohman for this opinion or thought less of his general judgment. Except to one who has made a study of the subjects of telepathy or hypnotism, all that can be said about them sounds invented and unreal. That Charles Frohman accepted them I think grew out of hearing the play, and his judgment would have been the same as Daniel's if he had only read the text and not seen it partly dramatized, as every author unconsciously does dramatize his own work when reading it.

Frohman was a most delightful manager to talk terms to. His method was simply to ask, "What do you want?" In my own experience I never heard him say, "We can't give it." It was after many years that I suggested terms which included an interest in the profits, and as he conceded these he smilingly added, "I have been wondering why you didn't ask for a share a long time ago." Somebody had told him something of space rates and the money that prominent authors had got per word for their product from publishers. With his keen sense of values, he was, of course, amused by the story that at one time Tennyson had received a pound a word on his poems. This may or may not be a fact, but Frohman took it seriously.

"And what do you think," he asked, "was the first poem he wrote after he touched the five-dollar rate? Think of it, five dollars a word! Well, here it is:

> "'What does little birdie say,
>   Singing, singing all the day?
>   Singing, singing all the day,
> What does little birdie say?'"

Charley thought it was pretty shrewd of the laureate to go down the line with these little words one way; but to make a round trip, collecting five dollars every jump, was just too hilarious. This may not be an accurate quotation of the verse, but it was the C. F. version.

My experience with Charles Frohman as an auditor made me believe that Mr. Lee Shubert, who perhaps had no more book knowledge of the subject or actual experience with it than C. F., might find in it a layman's equal interest. This proved to be the case. Before I read him the play I was careful to tell him its history— Mr. Palmer's uneasiness about the subject, Mr. Frohman's enthusiasm for it, and then the change of mind. To tell all about a play when one takes it to a manager is a good practice. It may be a little hard on a rejected manuscript at first, but when the managers come to understand that you are withholding nothing from them your statements acquire a value that outweighs the slight disadvantage in the history of any manuscript. If I were presuming to advise younger dramatists about the conduct of their business I think this is one of the points

I would emphasize. The manager ultimately learns the history of the play. If it is a failure some other man tells him he had read it and thought it would fail, or if it is a success the other man boasts that he might have had it. Any attempt at secrecy gains for the author only the unenviable record of disingenuousness. Mr. Shubert had the same sympathetic reception for the play that C. F. had had, and acting upon his decision immediately turned over its production to me. I don't think he heard any of it again until it was up to its dress rehearsals.

In discussing the cast, Charles Frohman and I had agreed upon John Mason as the central character for "The Witching Hour," and it was not difficult to persuade Mr. Shubert to this when the play was carried to him. Mason at that time was under contract with Mr. Harrison Grey Fiske, who generously released him to us. To those who knew John Mason's work nothing need be said in description of his art. To those who know only his reputation and have never seen him play, one may say that he was one of the best actors that America ever produced. To begin with, he was a man of great intelligence, and in the field of mathematics he had a talent that amounted to genius. I never saw any work to justify that statement, but several men have told me of his ability mentally to calculate sums and fractions and other problems in arithmetic that the ordinary man could do only laboriously with pencil.

As an actor his power lay in his great self-possession and a wonderful sense of time, which showed in his reading. He had the ability to put into a pause all the meaning that was carried in its context and somewhat more. His voice was deep and resonant, modulated and trained. He had that other great-actor quality of being able to listen on the stage and give his attention to another speaker; and in his dramatic work—I speak of that in contradistinction to his performances in opera, for which he was well known—he never showed a consciousness of his audience. Add to these qualities a fine sense of value of gesture, a wise restraint and very sparing use of which made every motion significant, then a physical relaxation that robbed everything he did of any seeming pose, although to a person trained in the theatre it was evident he knew the value of every position, and you have some considerations on which to base an understanding of his equipment as actor, and perhaps of some of his effects. The part of *Jack Brookfield* in the play was that of a gambler whose education was above the stratum into which his business threw him socially. Mason's speech and carriage secured that impression. To seem less than socially superior would have been an assumption. The gambler was supposed to be a dominant figure in personal affairs, will-power. Mason conveyed that idea also.

I don't remember any consultation with Mr. Shubert about any players. They must have been sent to him on the question of their salaries, but otherwise the wishes of the author were unopposed. I think it was John Mason who suggested the engagement of Russ Whytal for the old justice in the play. I have an idea that Whytal is not so well known throughout the country as some other men of less ability and less real prominence. Mr. Whytal is himself a dramatic author. Some years ago his play, "For Fair Virginia," was a reigning success. I can't think of a man on either side of the Atlantic who would have filled more completely the part of *Justice Prentiss* than Mr. Whytal did with his fine, sympathetic understanding of what the character stood for.

For the heavy man, a district attorney, we were able

to get George Nash. I had known Nash ever since he had been in the profession, some eighteen or twenty years before that time. He had played for me in "New Blood," "On the Quiet," "Arizona," and other pieces, and has about as sure a knowledge of effect as any man on the stage.

William Sampson, who played the comedy part, an almost dissolute and altogether unmoral old professional gambler, gray-haired and white-mustached, comes very near being our best American character comedian. He is as much like the late James Lewis, of Daly's, in method as one man can be like another. With him, Whytal, and Nash supporting Mason, we had a quartet that would have carried any reasonable material to success.

I have written before once or twice in these pages of coincidences occurring during their writing. These have not been remarkable, but they have been arresting, and their accent has perhaps for a moment interrupted the monotony of our march.

This above paragraph about William Sampson I dictated at the end of a session in the afternoon of April 5, 1922, and then, as I try to do after a day's work, went for a walk. On the wall just inside the door of the Lambs Club, in the usual place for such communications, was pinned a usual subscription paper, with some fifty or sixty signatures to it under the caption, "Flowers for William Sampson." It was a shock to learn that he had passed away suddenly the night before. I can add to the paragraph only the record of my deep affection for him and my esteem as man and artist.

In our first cast of "The Witching Hour" we were assisted also by the sterling actress, Jennie Eustace, and a very magnetic young woman no longer in the theatre, named Adelaide Nowak. I think it rather incumbent upon me, after having so frankly recorded Daniel Frohman's opinion, to say that the play was the biggest dramatic success of that year. It went through the season in New York, while a second company was playing it in Chicago, and John Mason continued to play in it until nearly three years later, when he went into another play in which I had written him an equally prominent but altogether different character.

I have said earlier in these chapters that I hope at some other time to write an article on psychic phenomena as I have found them. In my wish to be thoroughly informed concerning the background against which in "The Witching Hour" I was outlining comparatively so little I got a fund of information that would have served for fifty plays. It is not strange then that the two next plays after "The Witching Hour" should have been on somewhat related subjects. The older readers will remember that in the earlier stages of the cult of Christian Science there was a considerable public interest in the subject of mental science, so called, and therapeutical and metaphysical values of suggestion.

My next play, "The Harvest Moon," was upon this theme. There is not enough novelty in the story or incident in the history of the play to make it worth a reader's attention. One item, however, has, I think, significance. That was the performance of Mr. George Nash, of whom I have already written as an excellent actor. There are a few men who take acting as an art, and when we find one of these we usually find a character actor. I have written of Lionel Barrymore's qualities in this department, his willingness to put in study on the type he is to portray. George Nash, somewhat

Lionel's senior, is the same kind of man. When George knew he was to play a French savant, a member of the Academy, a celebrated person from his own country, he went over to Paris, with which he was already familiar, to get an intimate contact with the type; to study deportment, carriage, gesture, expression, and accent. He came back with all that and a complete wardrobe for the play made by a French tailor; his shirts and collars, linen and neckties and footwear were authentic. One might think that this attention would hardly be repaid; that only the most external showing would affect an audience; and it may be the case. But there was another effect upon the man himself which bred an authority that mere assumption could not have secured. The play was only moderately successful, but that element of the public that approved it remained very loyal to Mr. Nash; and although twelve years have gone by, I get an occasional letter inquiring about him and the possible reproduction of the play. It is the enthusiasm of such men as this in the theatre that keeps alive the interest of men writing for it.

About this time there came over the taste of the public one of those changes imperceptible in its progress but definite in its results, concerning the form of the musical play. People began to lose interest to some extent in the formal, well-made comic opera and turned to what came to be known as the musical comedy. With this in mind, a manager came to me to help him get a story suitable to the personality and talents of De Wolf Hopper. He had a facile and rapid-working musician with most melodic faculty, Mr. Silvio Hein, who stood ready to furnish the music, and also one or two young men who wanted to write verses for such a piece. All that he needed was a comic story with some vivacity, and a central character that would carry Mr. Hopper; or, to put it more complimentarily and more truthfully to that artist, a character which Mr. Hopper could properly animate.

If the call had not been a hurry one I probably should have started to build something from the ground up; but with the feeling of haste in the enterprise my mind by association drifted to other occasions of theatrical need. I remembered the times we had put up "His Last Legs" as an emergency bill. One important fact in its favor as the groundwork for a musical play was that it was short; it required no trimming; it was almost in shape ready for added lyrics and music. It needed a little change that would allow for the introduction of a female chorus, but this was easily fixed by making its scenes those of a female seminary instead of a private house. To emphasize Mr. Hopper's importance to the eye we gave him a little horse-racing kind of a valet of devoted attachment. This wasn't particularly new. Mr. Hopper had in two or three of his earlier successes been so seconded by Alfred Klein, a talented brother of the dramatist, Charles Klein. I gave the manager a synopsis of the story; his verse-writer and his musician went to work; chorus was assembled for rehearsal; I took the book of "His Last Legs," and dictating from it made a free transcription with such changes as would accommodate the differences I have described. The company was ready to play in four weeks, which is somewhat less than the time usually taken by musical rehearsals for a book that has already been completed.

Feeling that the public would be slow to accept a musical play from me, the manager announced the au-

thorship of the book as the joint work of Henri and
Bernard. Henri was a supposititious person, guessed
without any particular mental strain as the name indi-
cates. Bernard was the English author of "His Last
Legs." Mr. Hein's name went on the programme properly as the composer. The play, called "The Matinée
Idol," was, as I have implied in earlier chapters, an immediate success. Critics were a little at sea over the
English and French *collaborateurs* on the book, but they
were agreed upon its value to Mr. Hopper and were glad
to see him once more on Broadway with something suited
to his talents.

When John Mason had about finished playing "The
Witching Hour," I was trying to get for him a story of
equal seriousness and value, and a character necessarily
mature, that he could play, and follow his performance
of Jack Brookfield. The doctor in "As a Man Thinks"
was to my mind such a part, and his relationship to his
patient in the last act I regarded as a key-note for his
character, although the least dramatic of the things he
might do. I therefore tried it out, as I have said one
sometimes does, in a little one-act play. We gave this
at the Lambs. Mr. Eugene Presbrey played the sick
man, and I played the doctor myself. I felt that we had
a character that would stand development and that would
be acceptable. I knew a Jewish doctor who was giving
a great deal of his time to the care of crippled children,
and doing it with an unselfishness and a lack of advertising that made it admirable. I thought it would be
acceptable to the public to see a Jew put in that position
prominently instead of having him ridiculed as he generally was in the theatre. I share none of the hostility
that many do to the dominant management in the Ameri-

can theatre because it is Jewish. I felt then, and have said more than once in public since, that the Jews were in control of the American theatre because they deserved to be. The theatre as a business is one that does not lend itself readily to union hours for the persons in control. Its problems are constant from the moment one comes on duty to the time that the curtain drops and often later. There is something in the Anglo-Saxon temperament disposed to neglect these duties. The Jew will stick as close to the work as the work requires, just as he sticks to his work in the sweatshop, at the sewing-machine, or long hours in the second-hand clothing business. Starting out to do something, he persists. For that reason among others the theatre falls readily into his control.

Having made my doctor a Hebrew, I began to think in terms of Hebrew philosophy. I moved naturally to the double standard of morality discussed in the play; the fact that in modern society for a breach of the conjugal contract woman is more severely punished than is man. While with us the punishment is in the pillory of public opinion, in the old Jewish law the woman was stoned to death. The play tries to show that such punishment must persist so long as the family is the unit of our social structure. A woman knows or may know the father of her children. A father can be sure of his paternal relationship only in the degree of his faith in his wife. We can maintain a social structure, no matter how unworthy husbands and fathers may be; but as soon as mothers fail chaos has arrived. If womanhood becomes corrupt the only life-preserver that can keep even the heads of humanity above the waters is a paternal state, a strong socialistic government, in which the individual and not the family is the unit, in which the illegitimate, or foundling, child is just as important as one born lawfully.

The dramatization of that idea so clumsily stated in this dictated paragraph made a second theme in the play. These two ideas, one associated with mental science and the other associated with the Jewish idea of woman's greater responsibility, led to the construction of the story which is now in the book "As a Man Thinks."

In this play Mason made an impression as profound as the one he had made in "The Witching Hour," and in a character almost diametrically opposed. This is not my own partial estimate alone. There was hardly a principal city in the United States in which some Jewish rabbi did not speak upon his performance in the part. Few authors are so fortunate in their supporting casts as I was in this company that was associated with Mr. Mason in that play. Walter Hale and Vincent Serrano, about both of whom I have written fairly intimately in earlier chapters, had parts that suited them. William Sampson, referred to only a few paragraphs above, played the comedy old man with fine discretion and excellent effect; and that convincing player of American business men, Mr. John Flood, had such a rôle.

Some writer for the papers spoke of the flowerlike Chrystal Herne. I have no quarrel with that description of the lady, but what impressed me about her work as *Mrs. Clayton* was the expression of mental alertness, the constantly emotional and thinking personality. The play was printed as a book. When an author inscribes a book it isn't always easy to find the most proper phrase, but in the copy that was given to this actress I had no difficulty in writing, "To Chrystal Herne, who *was* Mrs.

Clayton." If in writing the part I had a conception that differed from her performance it was not sufficiently definite to hold its place against her lifelike and convincing assumption of the rôle. In the more mature part it would be impossible to get a better actress than Amelia Gardner. So, as I have said, taking the cast altogether, it was such another organization as I had had only three or four times in some thirty years. The other casts associated in my mind were the ones that played "Alabama" and "Arizona"; "Mrs. Leffingwell's Boots" and "The Other Girl."

XXV

INFLUENCES: BOOKS AND MEN

This report carries me to March 13, 1911. I am tempted to write of subsequent events, but will wait. Early in these chapters I referred to the remarks of the *Autocrat of the Breakfast Table*, as he decided to offer the brown seed capsules, as he called them, the early simple memories from which sprouted such "flowers as his garden grew." In rather haphazard manner I have tumbled my planting and some of its resultant vegetation into the notice of patient and hopeful readers, and now as I near the end of the hearing I fancy them saying, "Well?" and "What of it?" In one of Wilde's plays he has a speaker respond to the cue—experience. "Experience is the name Tuppy gives to his mistakes." As I remember, it was one of the best laughs in the scene. But experience is the name we all give to our mistakes.

What, as a matter of fact, is so significant as our mistakes? Certainly our successes are not so instructive. As I quickly review my own experience, more largely mistakes than I have felt at liberty to burden others with, and attempt the difficult feat of a summary, I find myself fronting the task with attention directed in such home-made method as mere habit has formed.

What is it that a patient friend would like me to report—a friend, let us say, like the poet stranger who has read some early chapters of this stuff and is moved to write to me this month of April, 1922, from beside his kerosene lamp in the town of Lost Cabin, Wyoming? Perhaps he would ask: "What have been the most potent influences you have known? Or to what opinions and beliefs have these influences and their consequent effects led you or inclined you?" That's what I'd like to ask any man whose book I've read. Perhaps that is what we all are practically asking every book.

Among the influences important to me have been a few men, more fine reputations, and still more fine books, some fine women, some music, both rather simple and both quite old-fashioned. The books, after the nursery jumble was past, were, in order of discovery, the Bible, Shakespeare, some other poets already named, Washington Irving, Holmes, Hawthorne, Ingersoll, Plutarch, Emerson, Doctor Thomas Jay Hudson, William James, Thomas Jefferson, Hugo, Voltaire, Montaigne. I think the Bible, Shakespeare, Holmes, and Emerson influenced my vocabulary as far as it was permeable under the callous of the railroad yard.

I didn't select the reading by any superior resolve or instinct. The New Testament I learned by rote to recite in Sunday-school for tickets exchangeable for prizes. I have a recollection of reciting on one Sunday one hundred and forty-four verses, beginning with, "In those days came John the Baptist," and so on. This was not a religious exercise with us boys. It was a business proposition. I have since gone to the New Testament with various motives; once to study out and as far as possible deduce from the speech and story the personal appearance of the Man of Nazareth when there was a project to produce a passion play. The Old Testament I read for its entertaining stories, skipping, boy-fashion, the begats.

Shakespeare, in his acting plays—that is to say, those in the regular and possible repertoires—I read and studied as a matter of professional requirement. My reading of Holmes was prompted by John Colby's liking for him. Plutarch was an assignment on the *Missouri Republican*. One day in 1887 I brought in the "Life of Lycurgus," revamped and adapted to the space of two columns and a half of dialogue between two boys, one of whom had read the story and was telling it to the other. This voluntary selection so pleased Frank O'Neill, the editor, that I was assigned to do one or two of the lives every week. I think there are fifty altogether. I rewrote and illustrated forty of them. One may learn much in reading a history such as Plutarch's "Life of Cæsar," but he learns it much more thoroughly when he is required to condense and rewrite it.

Emerson's essays were first called vividly to my attention by a little actress named Dudley who was in our Dickson's Sketch Club. She seemed to get a good deal of poise and self-possession from them. The essays fascinated me, and my first purchase of books, when I had a house of my own, was the Concord edition of Emerson's complete works in twelve volumes. In the year 1909 the same publishers issued a ten-volume edition of Emerson's "Journals." These were edited from his entries in his private journals from the year 1820, when he was seventeen years of age, until 1881, when he was in his seventy-eighth year. No writing could be more revealing than these almost daily notes and comments upon his observations, and his thoughts about the things he saw and the books he read. They let a reader into the very springs or fountainheads of Emerson's utterances throughout his life, and permit a study of the form and color that he gave the same ideas clothed in the dialect of his day.

For Voltaire I had the unreasoning abhorrence that is drilled into the consciousness of nearly all children raised under a church influence. Much as I admired Ingersoll, his unstinted eulogy of Voltaire did not remove this prejudice. In France I was astonished to see the life-sized seated figure of Voltaire by Houdon in the foyer of the Théâtre Français, and was again impressed by the standing statue by Caillé on the Quai Malaquais in front of the building of L'Institut de France. I began to believe there must be something admirable in the man, when at the most prominent points on both sides of the Seine a nation so honored him in its capital. Under the arcade of the Théâtre Odéon, in one of the rows of bookstalls there, I saw a large octavo edition of Voltaire, bound in leather, printed in 1829, on fine linen paper, no longer employed, so far as I know, in the manufacture of books. The edition consisted of fifty-four uniform volumes. The price was one franc each—a total of ten dollars and eighty cents in American money. I bought them as a possibly foolish adventure in property book backs. The dramas, being principally in verse, had little interest for me; but the numerous essays and letters were the most delightful reading.

To my astonishment, I found that the religious views of these great men, from Plutarch to Emerson, were not far enough apart to have the difference a matter of discussion. They all thought alike and expressed themselves in similar terms. Then one day I read in Emerson's latest notes, written in his sixty-sixth year, this single detached line: "When I find in people narrow religion I find narrow reading." My own reading is regrettably narrow, but it has been sufficient to make me wish not to disturb anybody's religious views or shake his creed. There is enough good in any one of the creeds to help its possessor through his life if he will permit it to guide him in his own conduct. But there is enough tyranny in any one of them to make its possessor intolerable when he attempts by force to impose his belief upon another.

In 1890 Funk and Wagnalls, encouraged by eighteen hundred gentlemen connected with the enterprise under the designation of patrons, printed what was called the "Jeffersonian Cyclopedia." This volume, as large as a law-book, contains over a thousand pages, with alphabetically arranged utterances of Mr. Jefferson, ranging from a line or two to paragraphs of half a column, and numerically listed to the number of nine thousand two hundred and twenty-eight quotations. In an appendix to these there is a document drawn by Mr. Jefferson in the year 1786 for the Assembly of Virginia, entitled, "A Bill for Establishing Religious Freedom." In the body of this bill, which is before me, is this sentence: "Our civil rights have no dependence on our religious opinions any more than our opinions of physics and chemistry."

This valuable book was a gift to me. The distinguished donor was Mr. William Jennings Bryan, and I am having a little difficulty in reconciling my idea of Mr. Bryan's admiration for the book and his recent earnest endeavor —which failed only by a vote of forty-two to forty-one —to persuade the Kentucky Legislature to forbid the discussion of the theory of evolution in the public schools because it didn't square with his deductions upon geology as set forth in the Book of Genesis. One glides so easily in these days from a discussion of religious beliefs into the consideration of questions political that I am impelled to take in lazy fashion this chance for digression and move on to a statement of my political views.

As a page-boy in Congress I was made aware of the two theories of government in America: the one advanced and advocated by Alexander Hamilton, whose genius nobody seems to dispute, and which as a matter of simple reference may be called the system of centralization; the other—the Jefferson idea—or the system of local self-government. All through my life, between those page-boy days and now, I have heard discussions of these two theories and occasionally had glimpses of the application of one or the other theory in practice. In my own mind I have finally come to something like an adjustment between them for America. I am not sure that my conclusions are right, but they have that consoling quality that sometimes comes with a decision—namely, peace. There has also been economy of time and attention through having some beliefs that were not dissolving views. One important contribution to this state of mind was made late in the year 1891, when I found at a book-stall a small octavo volume by John Fiske entitled "Civil Government in the United States." I read it carefully, and at times I studied it. In a bibliographical note on page 274, in a list of books valuable to the student of government, Mr. Fiske wrote the following:

A book of great merit, which ought to be reprinted as it is now not easy to obtain, is Toulmin Smith's "Local Self-Government and Centralization," London, 1851. Its point of view is sufficiently indicated by the following admirable pair of maxims (p. 12):

"Local self-government is that system of government under which the greatest number of minds, knowing the most, and having the fullest opportunities of knowing it, about the special matter in hand, and having the greatest interest in its well-working, have the management of it, or control over it.

"Centralization is that system of government under which the smallest number of minds, and those knowing the least, and having the fewest opportunities of knowing it, about the special matter in hand, and having the smallest interest in its well-working, have the management of it, or control over it."

An immense amount of wretched misgovernment would be avoided if all legislators and all voters would engrave these wholesome definitions upon their minds.

Later in a campaign, I quoted these two maxims at a meeting at which Mr. William Jennings Bryan was and I was "also." Mr. Bryan asked where I said I had got them, and then asked to have them typewritten for him. He subsequently used them, giving proper credit to their author. He told me they were the best definitions that he had ever heard for the purpose of showing the difference in the two systems of government. Certain benevolent considerations have recently made Mr. Bryan swerve a little from his complete reliance on local self-government, but I am going to hang onto my admiration for the system. I have thought there might be found a workable interplay of the two systems in our government—in all internal affairs; that is to say, in everything that affects our own well-being as a great commonwealth, the system of local self-government adopted and adhered to; in all questions that deal with our relations as a government to the governments of other countries, the system of centralization.

Something of the kind seems to have been in the minds of the founders when they wrote in Section II, Article II, of the Constitution: "The President shall be commander in chief of the Army and Navy of the United States and of the militia of the several States when called into the actual service of the United States."

This seems to apprehend national emergencies and something like centralization in meeting them. Also, all of those powers granted to Congress in Section VIII, Article I, under the heads of taxes, duties, imposts, coinage of money, weights and measures, punishment of counterfeiting, piracies and felonies on the high seas, and offenses against the laws of nations are on the centralization system. In the field of local self-government seem to lie those rights listed in the first ten amendments which Mr. Jefferson advised adopting before all the States ratified the Constitution, so that there should be no doubt about what powers were surrendered by the local governments to the central one, and what powers were by the central one definitely acquired. This may be saying "an undisputed thing in such a solemn way," but it has been a comforting possession. It has made me a Jeffersonian American. It has even enabled me to keep from meddling in family matters that seem to fall into similar but self-governing departments, such as those assumed by married children. And finally it has helped me to preserve a schoolboy respect for both those eminent and admirable characters, Alexander Hamilton and Thomas Jefferson, who were looking at the same shield from different sides.

Another department of life that I have thought a good deal about has been that of labor. As a lad I was with the working people; people with callous not only on their hands but well up the forearm where a brake-wheel caught it. I think every man should be capable of sustaining himself by the labor of his hands. I was quite a middle-aged person, much pampered and self-indulged, when I saw James M. Barrie's play, "The Admirable Crichton," in which a submerged butler of the English social caste becomes the principally capable person and commander as soon as the family is stranded on a South Sea island. In France I saw a much finer democracy than our own, as far as I could judge without being a part of it; a finer intercourse between the different social stations; the politeness of a stone-mason on the top of a bus asking a duke for a match with which to light a cigarette, and the fraternal compliance without mockery or condescension. And after a while I came to learn that that relationship had been acquired by men of those classes working in fine equality in their military training.

When the war was on and our American young men were enlisted and drafted I saw so many clerks and professional youngsters improved by the rough manual work that the army made them do that I became an advocate of universal military training, for the sole reason that it would give the government the power to call young men out of the mines, let us say, and send them elsewhere on other duties and to replace them by a lot of young fellows that are now selling neckties and watching stock tickers, who could be sent down into the mines as part of their training. One or two months of this transposing in their formative years, nineteen to twenty-one, would give them sympathetic understanding of the men who are performing the basic material and manual tasks. It might answer some other problems. Eight or ten years of such successive assignments would see the country equipped with a body of citizens not in those industries but yet partially educated in mining, railroading, and the like, which would be a great stabilizer.

A few lines above I said that I was with the working people. Maybe it will be well to confess that I am a little partisan about it. I know that is so because I sel-

dom read of a strike anywhere without the perhaps un-
fair hope that the strikers will be successful; this quite
outside of the merits of the dispute. When this partisanship appears I trace it as confirming a remembered proverb about training a child in the way he should go. In
a rather poverty-stricken boyhood I grew committed to
the side of the workers. I favor organized labor; but
recently in our Society of American Dramatists, which
after all is a kind of labor-union itself or at least a guild,
when the proposition came up to join the American Federation of Labor, I was opposed to it; and because of
my opposition I felt hopeful. I remember reading somewhere that an expert hatter had said there were only
two professional classes whose heads didn't change in
size between the years of adolescence and old age. These
two professions were clergymen and actors. Having
been an actor for a while, and having felt a good deal
like a clergyman in other whiles, I thought maybe I fell
within these restrictions; but if, despite my sympathy
for organized labor, I was opposed to going into its federation the chances were that I somehow had escaped
the hatter's arrested development.

I was aware of a new idea, although I found that it
leaned upon my old preconceptions concerning machinery.
Only to feed a machine seems to me a dreary thing; for
example, to do what I am told men in certain automobile
manufactories do—put apparently the same nut upon
apparently the same bolt hour after hour and day after
day as the piecework on an endless belt passes for a moment in front of them. That in its monotony must be
as near hell as any work can be. I think all men so working or similarly engaged, men whose work is not measured
in man-power, should be not only in unions but in a fed-

eration of unions to prevent too much speeding up of the endless belt. But that doesn't seem to be true of, let us say, a bricklayer, because his work is measured by the human unit, and after all he has some self-expression. There is a kind of artisanship in laying his courses to the plumb line and in finishing the surface seams. There is a measurable degree of self-expression in bricklaying; also, in other handicrafts.

I am not persuaded that everybody who gets any wage for anything should be in a federation against everybody who pays any wage. It seems to me, in my untrained approach of the question, that such a division comes pretty near to being class warfare. And if this republic is what Mr. Jefferson and I hoped it would be it shouldn't harbor or inspire or cultivate class warfare. And whether I am right about the bricklayers or not, I thought that the dramatists and perhaps college professors and artists of all kinds, and any other men who deal more or less in ideas, and are not simply feeding raw material to machines, and who because they deal in ideas may some day be called upon to arbitrate, or at least mediate in these industrial collisions, should stay outside of the federation. In the long run it might be better for the federation to have them do so. I feel that these are pretty big-league questions, and maybe far beyond my station in life; but they are products of experiences that have made me feel and perhaps made me think.

Aside from these gems on religion and politics and labor, I have some impressions about art and literature, and especially about standards in each of those departments, which people must be anxious to learn; but as they are good subjects for special essays, I will reserve them. Men and women who now begin to feel deserted and alone as

they draw to the end of these chapters should read over
again the last four or five pages containing my opinions
and beliefs.   Men who write their recollections often
forget to include these; and really a principal object of
life is to furnish a person with opinions and beliefs—I
think.

APPENDIX

LIST OF PLAYS

The following is a list of Thomas's plays, all with the dates of their production. Those marked with a single asterisk (*) are one-act plays. Those with dagger (†) were collaborations or dramatizations of books.

Alone	1875 . . .	Moberly, Mo.
The Big Rise	1882 . . .	St. Louis, Mo.
*† Editha's Burglar	1883 . . .	St. Louis, Mo.
* A New Year's Call	1883 . . .	St. Louis, Mo.
* A Man of the World	1883 . . .	St. Louis, Mo.
* Leaf from the Woods	1883 . . .	St. Louis, Mo.
* A Studio Picture	1883 . . .	St. Louis, Mo.
Combustion	1884 . . .	St. Louis, Mo.
The Burglar	1889 . . .	Boston, Mass.
A Night's Frolic	1890 . . .	New York City.
* A Woman of the World	1890 . . .	New York City.
* After Thoughts	1890 . . .	New York City.
Reckless Temple	1890 . . .	New York City.
Alabama	1891 . . .	New York City.
† For Money	1892 . . .	New York City.
Surrender	1893 . . .	Boston, Mass.
† Colonel Carter of Cartersville . .	1893 . . .	New York City.
In Mizzoura	1893 . . .	Chicago, Ill.
* A Proper Impropriety	1893 . . .	New York City.
* The Music Box	1894 . . .	New York City.
The Capitol	1894 . . .	New York City.
New Blood	1894 . . .	Chicago, Ill.
* The Man Upstairs	1895 . . .	New York City.
Colonel George of Mt. Vernon . .	1895 . . .	New York City.
* That Overcoat	1896 . . .	New York City.
† The Jucklins	1896 . . .	New York City.

† Chimmie Fadden	1897	. . New York City.
The Meddler	1898	. . New York City.
*† Holly Tree Inn	1898	. . New York City.
The Hoosier Doctor	1898	. . Washington, D. C.
† The Bonnie Briar Bush	1898	. . New York City.
Arizona	1898	. . Chicago, Ill.
On the Quiet	1900	. . New York City.
Oliver Goldsmith	1900	. . New York City.
Champagne Charley	1901	. . New York City.
Colorado	1901	. . New York City.
† Soldiers of Fortune	1902	. . New York City.
The Earl of Pawtucket	1903	. . New York City.
The Other Girl	1903	. . New York City.
† The Education of Mr. Pipp	1905	. . New York City.
Mrs. Leffingwell's Boots	1905	. . New York City.
De Lancey	1905	. . New York City.
The Embassy Ball	1905	. . New York City.
The Ranger	1907	. . New York City.
The Member from Ozark	1907	. . Detroit, Mich.
The Witching Hour	1907	. . New York City.
The Harvest Moon	1909	. . New York City.
The Matinée Idol	1909	. . New York City.
As a Man Thinks	1911	. . New York City.
The Model	1912	. . New York City.
Mere Man	1912	. . New York City.
† At Bay	1913	. . New York City.
† Three of Hearts	1913	. . New York City.
Indian Summer	1913	. . New York City.
† The Battle Cry	1914	. . New York City.
The Nightingale	1914	. . New York City.
Rio Grande	1916	. . Chicago, Ill.
The Copperhead	1917	. . New York City.
Palmy Days	1920	. . New York City.
* Tent of Pompey	1920	. . New York City.
Nemesis	1921	. . New York City.

INDEX